Political Science

An Introduction

THIRD EDITION

Michael G. Roskin
Lycoming College

Robert L. Cord
Northeastern University

James A. Medeiros

Walter S. Jones
Long Island University

PRENTICE HALL, Englewood Cliffs, New Jersey 07632

Library of Congress Cataloging-in-Publication Data

POLITICAL SCIENCE.

    Bibliography.
    Includes index.
    1. Political science. I. Roskin, Michael G., (date).
JA71.P623 1988   320   87-18744
ISBN 0-13-685082-0

Editorial/production supervision and
  interior design: Marianne Peters
Cover design: Diane Saxe
Manufacturing buyer: Margaret Rizzi

 © 1988 by Prentice Hall
A Division of Simon & Schuster
Englewood Cliffs, New Jersey 07632

Printed in the United States of America

10 9 8 7 6 5 4 3 2

ISBN 0-13-685082-0 01

Prentice-Hall International (UK) Limited, *London*
Prentice-Hall of Australia Pty. Limited, *Sydney*
Prentice-Hall Canada Inc., *Toronto*
Prentice-Hall Hispanoamericana, S.A., *Mexico*
Prentice-Hall of India Private Limited, *New Delhi*
Prentice-Hall of Japan, Inc., *Tokyo*
Simon & Schuster Asia Pte. Ltd., *Singapore*
Editora Prentice-Hall do Brasil, Ltda., *Rio de Janeiro*

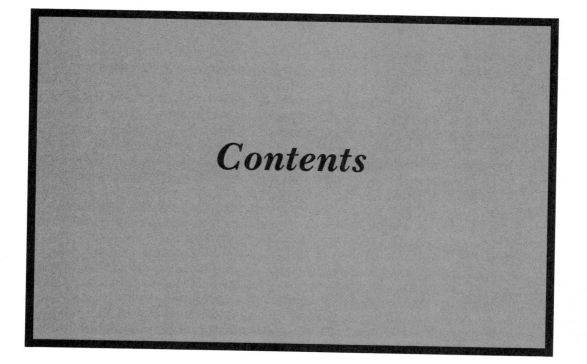

Contents

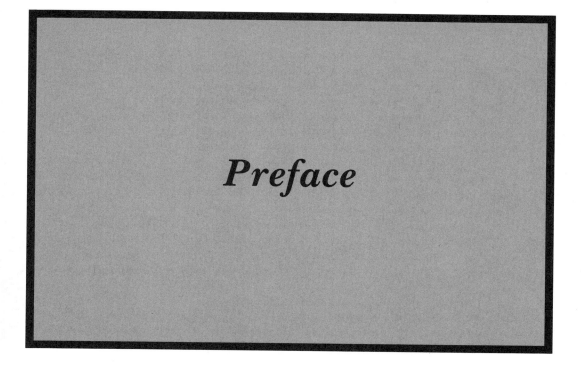

Preface

It is indeed gratifying to see a book one has worked on go to a third edition; it means you're doing something right. It also means the editors at Prentice Hall recognized that the original approach in the first edition was sound and should not be greatly altered. We therefore continue with an eclectic approach that avoids selling any single theory, conceptual framework, or paradigm as the key to political science. Attempts to impose a methodological grand design are both unwarranted by the nature of the discipline and unconducive to the broadening of a student's intellectual horizon. Instructors with a wide variety of viewpoints should have no trouble using this text. Above all, we still think politics is an exciting thing and try to communicate this to young people approaching the discipline for the first time.

Doing the third edition was both welcome and frustrating. It gave me an opportunity to pull some loose ends together and make the structure (I hope) a little more coherent. In particular I looked forward to redoing Chapter 1, changing it from an introduction to systems theory and political culture to a more general exploration in which all theories are viewed as tentative. I then took the political culture part of old Chapter 1 and merged it along with much new material into the old Chapter 7, giving us a new chapter devoted entirely to questions of political culture. Public opinion, being logically distinct from political culture, now gets its own chapter, Chapter 8, that includes much new material on current American opinion.

I also shortened and combined old Chapters 12 (on representation and electoral systems) and 16 (on unitary and federal systems) into new Chapter 13, The Basic Structures of Government, which also gave me a chance to make a few remarks on political institutions in general. While not wishing to shortchange electoral systems and federalism—actually, I like both topics—I felt I had to save our limited number of pages for other areas. If any of you believe this shortening and combining of topics is for the worse, please let me know.

The most difficult problem, though, was in trying to separate legislatures and executives, old Chapter 13 and new Chapter 14. I told myself when I was doing the second edition that I would split these two topics in the third edition, and indeed I began that way. But the more I tried to pull the legislative apart from the executive, the tighter the rascals stuck together. The United States, with its relatively clear separation of powers, facilitates talking about legislatures and executives separately. The parliamentary systems of most of the world, however, do not. Discussing parliaments without fully explaining the role of prime ministers and cabinets makes no sense. Legislatures do not stand alone but define themselves in relation to executives. I might be willing to make another try at separating these topics in a fourth edition; your input on this matter—or indeed on anything else relating to the book—would be highly valued. You may contact me directly at Lycoming College, Williamsport, PA 17701.

I would like to acknowledge those who reviewed this text and provided me with helpful comments and suggestions: Philip Abbott, Wayne State University; Douglas A. Brown, Arizona Western College; and Larry Elowitz, Georgia College.

Michael G. Roskin

chapter 1

A Science of Politics?

Antigovernment rioters pour through the streets of the capital of a Third World country, chanting slogans against the current president. They have had enough of grinding proverty while the friends and relatives of the president live in luxury. Even the privileged business community, aware that the government is hugely corrupt, has come out in favor of the president's resignation. The president, fearing for his life and wealth, orders the army to fire on the rioters. Instead, the army joins the rioters, and the president flees with suitcases of cash, jewels, and art treasures. Although he had himself celebrated as the father and savior of his country, it turned out that few supported him.

On another continent, members of a radical underground group meet in a small apartment to plan a terrorist bombing. They are frustrated and impatient with what they perceive as the deprivation of their national rights. Everyone else has a country, so why shouldn't they? The government they hate refuses to grant them any recognition; it even defines them as enemies of the state. Peaceful political protest is met with truncheons and arrests, so the militants decide to make their case more forcefully. They pack a car full of explosives and park it near a government building; a timer sets it off, killing passers-by. The terrorists think they have made an important point and are proud of their work.

Meanwhile, an American president is backpedaling on a question of policy. He was elected with a simple slogan that seemed to put him strongly on one side of a current issue. Once in office, however, he realizes how complicated the issue really is and how difficult it is to work his will on the Congress, the bureaucracy, and the interest groups. So the president tones down his policy, expresses his willingness to compromise, and tries to make himself look like a moderate on the issue. Critics say he is becoming indecisive and wishy-washy. Ironically, that was exactly what the president had said about his predecessor, the man he had defeated. Being president, he reflects silently, is a lot harder than he had thought.

What do a popular revolution in one country, a terrorist bombing in another, and an American president's change in policy have in common? All are examples of politics. They involve groups of people with conflicting interests competing for governmental power. The rioters, fed up with a corrupt and inept government, hope to replace it with a better one. The terrorists, seeing no point in trying to reason with a government that represses their aims, turn to violence in the hope of overthrowing that government. The American president, buffeted by conflicting pressures on all sides, is undergoing some painful rethinking before making a midcourse correction in his policy.

Political science is the study of these struggles and competitions for governmental power. In particular, it focuses on two interrelated questions: (1) Why and how do leaders make the decisions they do? (2) Why do citizens obey most of these decisions but sometimes disobey others? Let us consider the second question first.

THE THREE FACES OF LEGITIMACY

The preceding three examples, which could be culled from almost any month's news accounts, illustrate some of the enduring and basic problems of politics. They underlie the great question posed by political philosophers for centuries:

SI AND NO—Italians had to decide in a 1974 referendum whether to retain their divorce law.

Michael Roskin

Why do people obey, or why do they *not* obey the decisions of their leaders? (Actually, a *political philosopher* is more likely to ask why people *should* or *should not* obey these decisions. A *political scientist,* on the other hand, is more likely to ask why they *do* or *do not* obey.) The rioters, the terrorists, and the American president are all facing these questions in different ways. The three examples illustrate the related concepts of *legitimacy, sovereignty,* and *authority.*

Legitimacy

The rioters in the first example obviously no longer obey the corrupt regime. It has lost its *legitimacy.* Legitimacy is one of the most important concepts in political science. Originally it meant that the rightful king or queen was on the throne by reason of "legitimate" birth. Since the Middle Ages, the term legitimacy has broadened to mean not only the "legal right to govern" but also the *"psychological* right to govern." Legitimacy now refers to an attitude in people's minds that the government's rule is rightful. Therefore, even if we do not particularly like our government, we generally obey it. Most of us don't look forward to paying income tax, but most of us do it, and do it honestly, because we feel the government has a legitimate right to tax us.

Trouble begins for any government when that feeling of legitimacy erodes. People feel less obliged to pay their taxes and obey the law. Disobeying the law is no longer considered dirty or dishonest because the government itself is perceived as dirty and dishonest. Eventually, massive civil disobedience can break out. As the former Shah of Iran, ex-President Marcos of the Philippines, and ex-President "Baby Doc" Duvalier of Haiti discovered, once their regimes' legitimacy had disappeared, no amount of coercion could get people to obey. Indeed, attempts to apply force to control the disobedient crowds only made matters worse.

Legitimacy rests on consent, "the Consent of the Governed," as the Declaration of Independence puts it. Without consent, governments must rely on coercion. Accordingly, one way to determine the legitimacy of a given government is to see how many police are employed by the state. Where there are relatively few police, as in Sweden and Norway, it is a sign that legitimacy is high. Where there are many police, as in Franco's Spain or Jaruzelski's Poland, it is a sign that legitimacy is low. In these last two countries, the presence of special riot police (the *Policía Armada* in Spain and the ZOMO in Poland) indicates that the regime often turns to coercion.

How does a government get legitimacy? First, by existing a long time. Long-established governments are generally well respected by their citizens. The fact that the Constitution is two centuries old confers a great deal of legitimacy on the U.S. government. New governments, on the other hand, have shaky legitimacy; many of its citizens are not quite sure whether or not to respect them.

Second, a government can also gain legitimacy by governing well. Ensuring economic growth and high employment, providing protection from foreign invasion or domestic disturbance, and dispensing equal justice to all help governments to develop legitimacy. The government of West Germany, founded in 1949 after defeat in World War II, had little legitimacy at first, but level-headed political leadership with sound economic policies, providing rapid growth and jobs for all, gradually earned the Bonn government a good deal of legitimacy. On the other hand, the German Weimar Republic that followed World War I experienced a series of economic and political catastrophes that severely undermined its legitimacy and paved the way for Hitler's rise to power.

Third, the structure of government can also contribute to its legitimacy. If people feel they are fairly represented and have a say in the selection of their officials, they are more likely to obey. This is the most elemental reason for legislatures elected directly by the people. It's not that elected legislatures necessarily do a good job—often they are a shambles—but the people *feel* they are represented. Legislatures filled by appointment or by rigged elections do not contribute much to legitimacy.

Finally, governments try to shore up their legitimacy by the manipulation of national symbols. The national flag, historic monuments, patriotic parades, and ringing speeches are aimed at convincing people the government is legitimate and should be obeyed. When the other elements of legitimacy have fallen away, however, the manipulation of national symbols may appear as a hollow joke. A gigantic statue of ex-dictator Marcos of the Philippines became an object of ridicule and a symbol of what was wrong with his regime. Symbols by themselves don't create legitimacy.

Sovereignty

In our second example, the terrorist bombers dispute not only the regime's legitimacy but the legitimacy of the country itself. They want to destroy the *sovereignty* of the country they hate and replace it with another sovereign state. Legitimacy concerns the right of a given government to rule; sovereignty concerns the right of a given country to exist. For the terrorists, no change in regime will make them happy; they want not a new government but a new country.

Sovereignty, another word from the Middle Ages (from the Old French "to rule over"), originally meant the power of a monarch to rule over his or her kingdom. Later the term broadened to mean national control over the country's territory, boss of one's own turf. Nations are very jealous of their sovereignty, and governments take great care to safeguard it. They maintain armies to deter foreign invasion; they control their borders with passports and visas. And they hunt down terrorists who would destroy their sovereignty.

Disputes over sovereignty are among the nastiest the world faces. The violence associated with them ripples out to many other countries. Most Palestinians would like Israel to disappear and be replaced with a new sovereign entity, Palestine. Some Palestinian moderates would settle for a "rump state" (meaning the leftover pieces of a country) on the West Bank and Gaza Strip. Palestinian terrorists, however, are willing to murder anyone they think opposes them, including American tourists and fellow Arabs. The Israelis, of course, are not about to give up their sovereignty, so they fight back tenaciously.

In Northern Ireland, too, there is a question of sovereignty. Among the Catholic minority, the Irish Republican Army has turned to murder and bombings to pry Ulster away from British rule or sovereignty. The IRA wishes to unite Northern Ireland with the Republic of Ireland in the south. Among the Protestant majority, equally determined Loyalists vow they will never let that happen. The result: a low-level civil war in which some 2500 people have been killed.

On the northern border of Spain, Basque separatists assassinate police and government officials in a vain effort to establish an independent Basque country. No government in Madrid will ever let this happen.

Obviously, sovereignty and legitimacy are connected. A king or queen might establish sovereignty by the sword, but the heirs to the throne will lose sovereignty unless they can make their rule appear legitimate. With a decline of legitimacy may also come a decline of sovereignty. Lebanon illustrates how a question of regime legitimacy can turn into a question of national sovereignty. Lebanon was ruled for decades by Christians, even though they were a minority. In the eyes of many Lebanese Moslems, the Lebanese government in Beirut lacked legitimacy because it listened mostly to Christian demands and tended to ignore Moslems. In 1975, civil strife broke out as a dozen or more politico-religious militias battled to assume a leading role. Syria occupied eastern Lebanon in 1976, and Israel occupied southern Lebanon in 1982. Essentially

Lebanon had lost its sovereignty. It could neither control its own territory nor repel foreign invaders. Countries with weak legitimacy may lose sovereignty and be easy pickings for expansionist neighbors. On the other hand, the more diplomatic recognition a country can obtain from other nations, the more sovereignty and legitimacy it can maintain.

Authority

In our third example the American president, leader of a country with a high degree of legitimacy and sovereignty, is not automatically able to make his *authority* felt. *Authority* is the ability of a given leader to win obedience. Legitimacy is respect for a government; sovereignty is respect for a country; and authority is respect for an individual leader. Some political scientists distinguish authority from influence, manipulation, persuasion, and force.[1] Only authority (unlike influence, manipulation, persuasion, and force) relies on the obligation of the people to obey their leader by virtue of the legitimate power of his office. A private obeys a captain; a motorist obeys a state trooper; and a student obeys a professor. But not all people obey authority. Some privates are insubordinate, some motorists are speeders, and some students neglect the assigned reading. Still, most people obey what they perceive as legitimate authority most of the time.

Some authority comes with the office, but it must also be cultivated. Like legitimacy, authority is a psychological connection among people. An American president gets an awful lot of authority just because he is the president. Gerald Ford was respected and obeyed even though he was not elected either as president or vice-president. (Minority Leader of the House of Representatives, he became vice-president when Spiro T. Agnew resigned and president when Richard Nixon resigned.) But his elected predecessor, Richard Nixon, had some problems. Implicated in the Watergate scandal of 1972 Nixon suffered an "erosion of executive authority" so acute that he could not effectively govern, even if he were to be acquitted in possible impeachment proceedings before the Senate.[2] So he resigned in 1974 just before a House panel could vote on his impeachment. A president cannot rule by decree but must obtain the willing consent of Congress, the courts, the civil service, and important interest groups. When Nixon lost this consent, he was finished. His rule appeared increasingly without rightfulness.

How much obedience to authority derives from fear of punishment? Privates can be shot, motorists jailed, and students flunked. But this begs the question: what gives authorities the control over others so they will carry out orders to punish? The captain needs a command structure, the state trooper

[1]David Easton, "The Perception of Authority and Political Change," in *Authority*, ed. by Carl J. Friedrich (Cambridge, Mass.: Harvard University Press, 1958), pp. 178–81.

[2]The words are from the memoirs of a close witness to the process, National Security Adviser and Secretary of State Henry A. Kissinger, *Years of Upheaval* (Boston: Little, Brown, 1982), II, p. 123.

needs a criminal justice structure, and the college professor needs a disciplinary structure that will go along with orders or requests to punish. Without these structures to back them up, authority figures have little power. If a captain gets mad at a private and orders him taken out and shot, chances are he would not be obeyed. The guards would say, "Sir, that's an illegal order and you have no authority to give it." If, on the other hand, the private is convicted by court martial of desertion in the face of the enemy, he may indeed be taken out and shot by the same guards, who are now obeying duly constituted authority.

Just occupying an office may not be sufficient to command authority. The authority figure must also cultivate respect. A cowardly captain, a crooked policeman, or an indecisive professor may obtain only grudging compliance. Effective authority requires firm, fair, and wise leadership. Any taint of corruption undermines authority.

Notice that legitimacy, sovereignty, and authority are all related.[3] Where you find one, you find the others. Where one erodes, so usually do the others. What would have happened if Richard Nixon had tried to stay in office by blocking investigations of the Watergate scandal? Then the entire U.S. government might have started to appear illegitimate. His authority problem could have turned into a legitimacy problem. In 1958, Lebanese President Camille Chamoun, a Christian, tried to alter the constitution of his country to stay in power an additional term. As a result, a Moslem insurrection broke out and the legitimacy of Lebanon's government was severely damaged. Later, as we considered previously, the problem grew so severe as to wreck Lebanon's sovereignty. A collapse of authority led to a collapse of legitimacy which led to a collapse of sovereignty. President Nixon did his country a real service by resigning early.

If you think about it a minute, legitimacy, sovereignty, and authority are variations on the first term, legitimacy. If a government's rule is legitimate, it has legitimacy. If a country's existence is legitimate, it has sovereignty. If a leader's rule is legitimate, he or she has authority. All three terms can be grouped under the heading *political power*.

POLITICAL POWER

Some people don't like the concept of political power. It smacks of coercion, inequality, occasionally of brutality. Sometimes you hear speakers denounce "power politics." Implicit in this statement is the notion of governance without power, of a happy band of brothers and sisters regulating themselves on the basis of love and sharing. Communities formed on such a basis do not last; or if

---

[3]The Great German sociologist Max Weber connected authority closely with legitimacy. In fact, he distinguished between three types of political authority based on the type of legitimacy that supports them: (1) the traditional, where legitimacy is inherited, as in kingdoms; (2) the rational, where legitimacy derives from effective government; and (3) the charismatic, where legitimacy comes from a leader. See Max Weber, *The Theory of Social and Economic Organization* (New York: Free Press, 1947), pp. 324–26.

they do last, they transform themselves into conventional structures of leaders and the led buttressed by obedience patterns that look suspiciously like nasty old power. Power—defined as one person getting another to do something—seems to be built into the human condition. But why? Why do some people hold political power over others? No one has come up with a definitive explanation of political power. Biological, psychological, cultural, rational, and irrational explanations have all been put forward to answer these questions.

Biological

Aristotle said it first and perhaps best: "Man is by nature a political animal."[4] He meant that humans live naturally in herds, like dolphins or deer. They biologically need each other for sustenance and survival. It is also natural that they array themselves into ranks of leaders and led, like all herd animals. Taking a cue from Aristotle, a modern biological explanation would say that forming a political system and obeying its leaders is innate human behavior, passed on to future generations with one's genes.[5] The advantage of this theory is its simplicity.

But it raises a number of questions. If we grant that humankind is naturally political, how do we explain the instances when political groups fall apart and people disobey authority? Perhaps we could improve the theory by modifying it: Humans are imperfectly political (or social) animals. Most of the time people form groups and obey authority, but sometimes, under certain circumstances, people don't. This begs the question of which circumstances promote or do not promote the formation of political groups.

Psychological

Psychological explanations of politics and obedience are closely allied with biological theories. Both posit innate needs in the formation of political groups. The psychologists have refined their views with empirical research. One is the famous Milgram study in which unwitting subjects were instructed by a professor to administer progressively larger electric shocks to a victim.[6] The "victim," strapped in a chair, was actually an actor who only pretended to suffer. Most of the subjects were willing to administer potentially lethal doses of electricity simply because the professor—an authority figure in a white lab smock—told them to do so. Most of the subjects didn't like hurting the victim, but they rationalized that they were just following orders and that any harm

[4]Aristotle's words were *zoon politikon*, which can be translated as either "political animal" or "social animal," for the Greeks did not distinguish between polity and society. They lived in city-states in which the social system was the same as the political system. Richard McKeon, ed., *The Basic Works of Aristotle* (New York: Random House, 1941), p. 1129.

[5]For a modern exposition of the biological view, see Edward O. Wilson, *Sociobiology: The New Synthesis* (Cambridge, Mass.: Harvard University Press, 1975).

[6]Stanley Milgram, *Obedience to Authority: An Experimental View* (New York: Harper & Row, 1974).

done to the victim was really the professor's responsibility. They surrendered their independence of thought and action because an authority figure told them to. The Milgram study has been replicated and confirmed in other settings.

Psychological studies also show that most people are naturally conformist. Most members of a group see things a certain way. Psychologist Irving Janis found many of the great mistakes of U.S. foreign and defense policy were made in a climate of "groupthink," a situation where a leadership group tells itself that all is well and that the present policy is working.[7] Groups tend to ignore nonconformist troublemakers who tell them, for instance, that the Japanese will attack Pearl Harbor in 1941 or that the Bay of Pigs landing of Cuban exiles in 1961 will fail. "We know what we're doing," the group seems to say, "Don't bother us with doubts."

Obedience to authority and groupthink suggests that humans have deep-seated needs—possibly innate—to fit into groups and go along with their norms. Perhaps this is what makes human society possible. But it also makes possible horrors such as the Nazi Holocaust and fiascoes such as the Iran arms deal. One of the fascinating questions is why some individuals can disobey authority and go against group conformity to decry acts which are obviously illegal, immoral, or just plain stupid.

Cultural

How much of human behavior is learned as opposed to biologically inherited? Social scientists have debated this for decades without coming to a definitive answer. In the middle part of the twentieth century, however, the *cultural theorists*—those who believe behavior is learned—have dominated the debate. Anthropologists especially, in exploring foreign and primitive societies, concluded that all differences in behavior were learned. If some societies are cooperative and peaceful, it is because their children have been raised that way. Political communities are formed and hold together on the basis of cultural values transmitted by parents, schools, churches, and the mass media.[8] Political science has developed an interesting subfield called *political culture,* and researchers in this field often found that a country's political culture was formed by many long-term factors: child-rearing, land tenure, economic development, religion, and so forth.[9]

---

[7]Irving L. Janis, *Victims of Groupthink: A Psychological Study of Foreign-Policy Decisions and Fiascoes* (Boston: Houghton Mifflin, 1972).

[8]The classic political culture study is by Gabriel A. Almond and Sidney Verba, *The Civic Culture: Political Attitudes and Democracy in Five Nations* (Princeton, N.J.: Princeton University Press, 1965).

[9]For a model study of political culture, one that tries to explain the poverty of southern Italy, see Edward Banfield, *The Moral Basis of a Backward Society* (New York: Free Press, 1958). Banfield later applied this "culture of poverty" approach to explain America's urban poverty in Edward Banfield, *The Unheavenly City Revisited* (Boston: Little Brown, 1974).

The cultural school maintains that trouble comes when the political system gets out of touch with the cultural system, as when the Shah of Iran attempted to modernize an Islamic society that did not like Western values and lifestyles. The Iranians threw the Shah out and celebrated the return of a medieval-style religious leader, the Ayatollah Khomeini, who was much more in touch with their values. Cultural theories can also be applied to U.S. politics. Ronald Reagan won the presidency twice by articulating the values of religion, family, and self-reliance which are so deeply ingrained into American culture.

The cultural approach to political life contains an optimistic streak. If all human behavior is learned, bad behavior can be unlearned and society improved. Educating young people to be tolerant, cooperative, and just will gradually change a society's culture for the better.

While most thinkers agree that culture contributes a lot to political behavior, the theory has some difficulties. First, where does culture come from? Is it a product of the class structure, as the Marxists claim? Or is it a result of the psychological interactions between parents and children, as the Freudian psychologists argue? Or is it the current repository of the country's past, as many historians think? Second, if all behavior is cultural, various political systems should be as different from each other as their cultures. But, especially in the realm of politics, we see similar political attitudes and patterns in lands with very different cultures.

Rational

Another school of thought approaches politics as largely the application of human rationality; that is, people know what they want most of the time, and they have good reasons for doing what they do. Classic political theorists, such as Hobbes and Locke, held that humans form "civil society" because their powers of reason tell them that it is much better than anarchy. In the "state of nature" you can trust no one; anyone might take your life or your property. Accordingly, to safeguard both life and property, people form governments to protect themselves. If those governments become abusive, then the people have the right to dissolve them and start anew—this Lockean notion greatly influenced the U.S. Founding Fathers.

The biological, psychological, and cultural schools described above all downplay human reason. People are either born or conditioned to do certain things, and individuals seldom think rationally. But how can we then explain those cases when people break away from group conformity and argue independently? How can we explain people changing their minds? "Well, I was for Jones until he came out with his terrible economic policy, so now I'm voting for Smith." People make judgments like that all the time, based at least in part on their ability to reason.[10]

---

[10]At least one political scientist has adopted the view that politics is rational human behavior. See Steven J. Brams, *Rational Politics: Decisions, Games, and Strategy* (Washington, D.C.: Congressional Quarterly Press, 1985).

Further, a political system based on the presumption of human reason stands a lot better chance of governing justly and humanely. If leaders believe that people obey out of biological inheritance or cultural conditioning, they will think they can get away with all manner of corruption and misrule. If, on the other hand, they believe people are rational, rulers will respect the public's ability to discern wrongdoing. Accordingly, even if people are not completely rational, it is good that rulers fear the possible rationality of the public and their ability to protest misrule.

Irrational

Late in the nineteenth century a group of thinkers founded a new school of thought, called irrationalism, to explain political behavior. Taking the psychological view that people are basically irrational, dominated by primitive fears and stereotypes, the irrationalists argued that people are best led by using myths, symbols, and dramatic spectacles. The crowd is like a wild beast that can be whipped up by a charismatic leader to do his bidding. The irrationalists say that what people regard as rational is really just myth; all you have to do is keep feeding them myths and you will control them.

The first practitioner of this school was Mussolini, founder of Facism in Italy. He was followed by Hitler in Germany and Perón in Argentina. According to some, Stalin also used the techniques of the irrationalists in developing his hold on the Soviet people. He had himself turned into a "god" that most Russians willingly worshiped. Both Hitler's friends and enemies portrayed him as a genius at understanding and manipulating the innermost fears and feelings of the Germans.[11]

There may be a good deal of truth to the irrational view of human political behavior, but it has catastrophic consequences. The leaders who use irrationalist techniques start believing their own propaganda and eventually lead their nations to devastating war, economic ruin, or permanent slavery. Some critics detect traces of irrationalism in U.S. television ads, both political and commercial, that attempt to manipulate gut feelings.

Power as a Composite

We can see elements of truth in all the above explanations of political power. At different times in different situations, any one of them seems to explain power. The drafters of both the U.S. Declaration of Independence and Constitution were deeply imbued with the rationalism of their age. Following the philosophers then popular, they framed their arguments as if human political activity were as logical as Newtonian physics. One contemporary historian

---

[11]A German psychiatrist offers an explanation of Hitler's hold on the German people. See Erich Fromm, *Escape from Freedom* (New York: Holt, Rinehart and Winston, 1941).

referred to the Constitution as "the crown jewel of the enlightenment," the culmination of an age of reason.[12]

But how truly rational were they? By the late eighteenth century the thirteen American colonies had grown culturally separate from Britain. People thought of themselves as Americans rather than as English colonists. They increasingly read American newspapers and communicated among themselves rather than with Britain.[13] Perhaps the separation was more cultural than rational.

Nor can we forget the psychological and irrational factors. Samuel Adams was a gifted firebrand, Thomas Jefferson a powerful writer, and George Washington a charismatic general. Did Tom Paine's pamphlet *Common Sense* press rational or psychological buttons in his readers? It's hard to tell. And that is the point of this example. The American break with Britain and the founding of a new order is a complex mixture of all these factors. The same complex mixture of factors goes for any political system you can mention. To be sure, at times one factor seems more important than the others, but we cannot exactly determine the weight to give any one factor. And notice how the various factors blend one into the other. The biological factors lead to the psychological, which in turn lead to the cultural, the rational, and the irrational. A seamless web, difficult to untangle, is formed.

One common mistake about political power is to view it as a finite, measurable quantity. Power is a connection between people, the ability of one person to get another to do his or her bidding. Political power does not come in jars or megawatts. Revolutionaries in some lands speak of "seizing power," as if power were kept in the national treasury and they could sneak in and grab it at night. Afghan Communists "seized power" in 1978, but they were a small minority of the Afghan population. Most Afghanis hated them and refused to cooperate with them. The Communist Kabul regime exists only with massive Soviet help in the midst of a bloody civil war. Some revolutionaries think that they automatically get legitimacy and authority when they "seize power"; they do not. Power is earned, not seized.

IS POLITICS A SCIENCE?

But if we cannot pinpoint which of the preceding factors contribute what weight to politics, how can politics possibly be called a science? Part of the problem here is the definition of "science." The original meaning of "science," from the French, is simply "knowledge." Later, the natural sciences, such as physics and chemistry, that rely on precise measurement and mathematical calculation took over the term. Now most people think of science as precise and factual,

[12]Henry Steele Commager, *The Empire of Reason: How Europe Imagined and America Realized the Enlightenment* (Garden City, N.Y.: Doubleday, 1977).
[13]Richard L. Merritt, "Nation-Building in America: The Colonial Years," in *Nation-Building*, eds. Karl W. Deutsch and William J. Foltz (New York: Atherton Books, 1963).

supported by experiments and data. Some political scientists (as we will consider later) have in fact attempted to become like natural scientists; they collect quantified data and manipulate it statistically to validate hypotheses. (This process is known as "numbers crunching.") The quantifiers have made some good contributions, but usually they focus on small questions of detail rather than on large questions of meaning. This is because they generally have to stick to areas that can be quantified—public opinion, election returns, and congressional voting. (And sometimes these data are open to different interpretations.)

But large areas of politics are not quantifiable. This moves us back to one of the questions we asked near the beginning of the chapter: How and why do leaders make the decisions they do? Many decisions are made in secret, even in democracies. We don't know exactly how decisions are made in the White House in Washington, or in the Elysée Palace in Paris, much less in the Kremlin in Moscow. When a member of Congress votes on an issue, can we be certain why he or she voted that way? Constituents' desires, the good of the nation, or the campaign contributions of interest groups could have influenced the vote. What did the Supreme Court have in mind when it ruled that laying off schoolteachers based on race is unconstitutional but hiring them based on race is not?[14] Try putting that into a computer in a quantifiable way. A lot of politics—especially dealing with how and why decisions are made—is just too complex to be quantified.

Does that mean that politics can never be like a natural science? Part of it can be—the areas where we can get valid numbers—but much of it cannot be. Still, we can accumulate unquantified data. We can find persistent patterns in the way governments attempt to shore up their legitimacy, the way candidates strive for election, and in the way alliances form and fall apart. After a while, one notices that nothing is happening for the first time, that there are precedents for just about every type of political activity. Gradually, one begins to generalize. When the generalizations become firmer, we may call them theories. In a few cases, the theories become so firmly established that we may even call them "laws." In this way, the study of politics accumulates knowledge—and "knowledge" is the original meaning of "science." Some universities have departments of "politics" or departments of "government" in order to get away from the nagging question: Is politics a science? The answer to that question is up to you.

The Struggle to See Clearly

In one way, political science does resemble a natural science: Its researchers, if they are professional, attempt to study things as they are, not as they wish them to be. This is more difficult in the study of politics than in the study of stars and molecules, although even in these areas scientists sometimes have strongly partisan views. Political scientists are deeply immersed in politics,

---

[14]*Wygant v. Jackson Board of Education* (1986)

and most of them have viewpoints on current issues. It is very easy to let these views contaminate the analysis of politics. Indeed, precisely because a given question interests us enough to study it indicates that we bring a certain passion with us. Can you imagine setting to work on a study of a topic you cared absolutely nothing about? Behind each choice of topic is usually a little fire of interest in the mind of the researcher. Accordingly, our subject comes to us contaminated from its very birth. A little bias is therefore to be expected. There is a certain point, however, at which too much bias renders the study useless; it becomes a partisan outcry rather than a scholarly search for the truth. How can you tell when this happens? It's difficult, but the traditional hallmarks of scholarship give us some guidance. A scholarly work should be *reasoned, balanced,* and supported with *evidence.*

Reasoned.   You must spell out your reasoning, and it should make sense. If your perspective is colored by an underlying assumption, such as one of those discussed previously, you should say so. People should be told where you are coming from. You might say, "For the purpose of this study, we assume people are rational." Or, "This is a study of the psychology of voters in a small town." It is understood that your basic assumptions influence what you study and how you study it, but you can minimize the bias by honestly stating your assumptions. Early in the twentieth century the German sociologist Max Weber, who contributed so much to all the social sciences, held that any of your findings that come out in support of your own political views must be discarded as biased.[15] But a lot of research would never be undertaken if the researcher did not have some ax to grind. Nevertheless, Weber's point is well taken: beware of structuring the study so it comes out to support a given view. The axiom of computer specialists applies to political science: "Garbage in, garbage out."

Balanced.   You can also minimize bias by acknowledging that there are other ways of looking at your topic. In all fairness, you should mention the various approaches to your topic and what they have found. Instructors are impressed that you are familiar with the literature in the given area. They are even more impressed when you can then criticize the various studies and explain why you think they are incomplete or faulty: "The Jones study of voters found them largely apathetic, but this was an election of local officials so apathy might be expected." By putting several approaches and studies side-by-side and stating what you think of them and why, you present a much more objective and convincing case. Do not totally commit yourself to a particular viewpoint or theory but admit that your view is one among several.

Evidence.   All scholarly studies require evidence, ranging from the quantified evidence of the natural sciences to the qualitative evidence of the

[15]Max Weber, "Science as a Vocation," in *From Max Weber: Essays in Sociology,* eds. Hans H. Gerth and C. Wright Mills (New York: Oxford University Press, 1946).

humanities. Political science utilizes both types of evidence. Ideally, any statement open to interpretation or controversy should be supported with some evidence. Common knowledge does not have to be supported; you need not cite the U.S. Constitution to "prove" the president is inaugurated the January after the election. But if you say presidents have gained more and more power over the decades, you need to have some evidence. At a minimum, you would cite leading scholars who have amassed evidence to demonstrate this point. The evidence you use should be open to inspection and scrutiny. You cannot say, "I have classified information that proves this point, but it cannot be revealed." This is one of the problems faced by the political analysts employed by the U.S. State and Defense Departments. Anyone reading a study must be able to review your evidence and judge if it is valid.

What Good Is Political Science?

Some students think political science is political opinion; they write exams or turn in papers that ignore all or some of the preceding points. Yes, we all have political views, but if we let them dominate our study we get invalid results. A professional political scientist pushes his or her personal views well to one side while engaged in study and research. A first-rate thinker is able to come up with results that actually refute his or her previously held opinion. When that happens, we have real intellectual growth, an exciting experience that should be your aim. Something else comes with such an experience: you start concluding you shouldn't have been so partisan in the first place. You may start backing away from the strong views you had earlier. You start taking political views, even your own, with a grain of salt. Accordingly, political science is not necessarily training to become a practicing politician. Political science is training in the calm, dispassionate analysis of politics, while the practice of politics often requires fixed, popular, and simplified opinions.

Political science can contribute to good government, mainly by warning those in office that all is not well, "speaking truth to power," as the Quakers say. Sometimes this advice is useful to working politicians. Public opinion polls, for example, showed a slow erosion of governmental legitimacy in the United States from the mid-1960s to the early 1980s.[16] The precise cause could be debated: Was it Vietnam, Watergate, or inflation? Or some combination of all three? Candidates for office, knowing public opinion, could tailor their campaigns and policies to try to counteract this potentially dangerous decline. Ronald Reagan, with his sunny disposition and upbeat views, utilized this discontent to his advantage.

For decades, American political scientists warned about the weaknesses of U.S. political parties, saying they were too decentralized and uncontrolled. Political parties in the U.S. cannot even define what they stand for or who can be regarded as a member. In the 1986 Illinois Democratic primary, two extremists,

---

[16]Arthur Miller, "Is Confidence Rebounding?" *Public Opinion,* June and July 1983, pp. 16–20.

Lyndon LaRouche supporters, calling themselves Democrats, won the party's nomination to high state office. Many people voted for them in total ignorance. The Democratic nominee for governor resigned from the party ticket rather than run with the LaRouche supporters, thereby wrecking the Democrats' chances for victory in the election. As far back as 1950, the American Political Science Association had warned that weak parties bring negative consequences.[17]

In foreign affairs, political scientists warned for years of the weak basis of the Shah's regime in Iran.[18] Unfortunately, such warnings went unheeded. Washington's policy was to support the Shah; only two months before the end of his reign did the U.S. Embassy in Tehran start reporting accurately how unstable things had become.[19] This is an example of the contamination of political analysis by politics. The U.S. government would have had a more effective policy if it had listened to the political scientists and ignored its own embassy.

CHANGING POLITICAL SCIENCE

The discipline of political science does not stand still. Especially in the United States, it has passed through at least three distinct styles or approaches: the traditional, behavioral, and postbehavioral. It is impossible to say which is best, and all exist today, albeit sometimes uneasily with each other. To call the first "traditional" is a bit unfair—it was so named by the behavioralists—for it encompasses a wide range of approaches ranging from the philosophical and ethical to the institutional and power-oriented.

Most of the Greek, medieval, and Renaissance political thinkers took a normative approach to the study of government and politics. They sought to discover the "ought" or "should" and were often rather casual about the "is," the real-world situation. Informed by religious, legal, or philosophical values, they tried to ascertain which system of government would bring man closest to the good life, often as defined by the prevailing wisdom of that time. Although sometimes dismissed by behavioral thinkers as hopelessly speculative, the ideas of Aristotle, Hobbes, Locke, Rousseau, and many others still provide us with tremendous insights, which, ironically, are sometimes confirmed by the latest "scientific" research.

With Machiavelli emerged another approach, the focus on power. Although often deprecated by American political thinkers, who sometimes shied away from "power" as an inherently dirty thing, the approach took root in Europe and contributed to the elite analyses of Mosca, Pareto, and Michels.

[17]Committee on Political Parties, American Political Science Association, "Toward a More Responsible Two-Party System," *American Political Science Review* 44 (September 1950 supplement).

[18]Marvin Zonis, *The Political Elite of Iran* (Princeton, N.J.: Princeton University Press, 1971); James Bill, *The Politics of Iran* (Columbus, Ohio: Charles E. Merrill, 1972); Richard Cottam, *Nationalism in Iran* (Pittsburgh, Penn.: University of Pittsburgh Press, 1979).

[19]Barry Rubin, *Paved with Good Intentions: The American Experience and Iran* (New York: Penguin, 1981), chaps. 7 and 8.

Americans became acquainted with the power approach through the writings of the refugee German scholar of international relations Hans J. Morgenthau, who emphasized that "all politics is a struggle for power."[20]

American thinkers meanwhile focused heavily on institutions, the formal structures of government. In this they were showing the influence of law on the development of political science in the United States. Woodrow Wilson, for example, was a lawyer (albeit unsuccessful) before he became a political scientist; Wilson, too, concentrated on perfecting the institutions of government. Constitutions were a favorite subject for political scientists of this period, for they often assumed that the structure of the government on paper was pretty much how it worked in practice.

The rise of the Soviet, Italian, and German dictatorships and the horrors of World War II shook many political scientists in their belief in institutions. The constitution of Germany's ill-fated Weimar Republic (1919–33) on paper looked fine; it had been drafted by experts. How it worked in practice was something else, for Germans of that time did not have the necessary experience with or commitment to democracy. Likewise, the Stalin constitution of 1936 made the Soviet Union look like a perfect democracy, but obviously it didn't work that way.

Growing out of this was an effort to discover how politics really worked, not how it was supposed to work. Postwar American political scientists here followed in the tradition of the early nineteenth-century French philosopher Auguste Comte, who developed the doctrine of *positivism,* the application of natural science methods to the study of society. Comtean positivism was an optimistic philosophy, holding that as we accumulate valid data by means of scientific observation—without speculation or intuition—we will perfect a science of society and with it improve society. Psychologists were perhaps the most deeply imbued with this approach (and still are); many took the name "behavioralists" for their concentration on actual human behavior as opposed to thoughts or feelings.

Behaviorally inclined political scientists in the 1950s began to borrow the psychologists' approach and accumulated statistics from elections, public opinion surveys, votes in legislatures, and anything else they could hang a number on. Behavioralists made some remarkable contributions to political science, shooting down some long-held but unexamined assumptions and giving political theory an empirical basis from which to work. Behavioral studies were especially good in examining the "social bases" of politics, the attitudes and values of average citizens, which go a long way in making the system work the way it does.[21]

[20]Hans J. Morgenthau and Kenneth W. Thompson, *Politics Among Nations: The Struggle for Power and Peace,* 6th ed. (New York: Knopf, 1985), p. 31.

[21]An excellent behavioral capstone to the 1950s is Seymour Martin Lipset, *Political Man: The Social Bases of Politics* (New York: Doubleday, 1960). Lipset brought out an expanded and updated edition two decades later (Baltimore, Md.: Johns Hopkins University Press, 1981).

The Postbehavioral Synthesis

During the 1960s, the behavioral school established itself and won over much of the field. In the late 1960s, however, behavioralism came under heavy attack, and not just by rear-guard traditionalists. Many younger political scientists, some of them influenced by the radicalism of the anti-Vietnam war movement, complained that the behavioral approach was static, conservative, loaded with its practitioners' values, and irrelevant to the urgent tasks at hand. Far from being "scientific" and "value-free," behavioralists often defined the current situation in the United States as the norm and anything different as deviant. Easton's political system, discussed subsequently, is actually an idealized model of U.S. politics. Almond and Verba found that Americans embody all the good, "participant" virtues of the civic culture. By examining only what exists at a given moment, behavioralists neglect the possibility of change; their studies may be time-bound. Behavioralists have an unstated preference for the status quo; they like to examine settled, established systems, for that is where their methodological tools work best. They have a hard time grasping social upheaval and revolution, for their systems theories teach them all systems maintain balance or "equilibrium" and aren't supposed to break down.

Perhaps the most damaging criticism, though, was that the behavioralists focused on relatively minor topics and steered clear of the big questions of politics. Behavioralists can tell us, for example, what percentage of Detroit blue-collar Catholics vote Democratic, but they can't tell us much about what this means in terms of the quality of Detroit's governance or the kinds of decisions elected officials will make. There is no necessary connection between how citizens vote and what comes out of government. In short, the critics charged, behavioral studies were often irrelevant.

By 1969, even David Easton had to admit there was something to the criticism of what had earlier been called the "behavioral revolution." He called the new movement the "postbehavioral revolution." The postbehavioral approach can be seen, to a certain extent, as a synthesis of traditional and behavioral approaches.[22] Postbehavioralists recognize that facts and values are tied together; they are willing to use both the qualitative data of the traditionalists and the quantitative data of the behavioralists. They are willing to look at history and institutions as well as current public opinion. It would be premature to say the postbehavioralists have won, for if you inquire around your political science department you are apt to find traditional, behavioral, and postbehavioral viewpoints among the professors—or even within the same professor.

---

[22]For a useful comparison of the three approaches, see Ronald H. Chilcote, *Theories of Comparative Politics: The Search for a Paradigm* (Boulder, Colo.: Westview Press, 1981), pp. 56–58.

THE IMPORTANCE OF THEORY

Why bother with theories at all, wonder many students new to political science. Why not just accumulate a lot of facts, and let the facts structure themselves into a coherent whole? But just gathering facts without a guiding principle leads only to large collections of meaningless facts. To be sure, theories can grow too abstract and depart from the real world, but without at least some theoretical perspective, we don't even know what questions to ask. Even if you say you have no theories, you probably have some unspoken ones. Just in the kind of questions you ask and which questions you ask first are the beginning of theories.

Take, for example, the structure of this book. We have adopted the view—which has been widespread in political science for decades—that the proper beginning of political analysis is the society. That is, we tacitly assume that politics grows out of society. You start with people's attitudes and opinions and see how they influence government. The subtitle of one widely read and highly influential book by a leading sociologist was *The Social Bases of Politics*.[23] The implied message: You start with society and see how that influences politics.

But doesn't that stack the deck? If you assume that society is the basis of political analysis and that attitudes and opinions are the important facts, you will gather a great deal of material on attitudes and opinions and relatively little material on the history, structure, and policies of government. Everything else will appear secondary to citizen attitudes and opinions. And indeed, political science went through a period in which political science was essentially sociology, and many political scientists did survey research. This was part of the behavioral tide (discussed previously) that surged into political science; survey research was seen as the only way to be "scientific," because through such research public opinion data was quantified.

Textbooks tended to offer a "percolation up" model of politics. The first major bloc of most studies was concerned with the society: how political views were distributed, how interest groups were formed, who supported political parties, and how people voted. That was the basis, the bottom part of the pyramid. The second major bloc was usually the institutions of government. They were assumed to be a reflection of the underlying social base. Legislatures and executives reacted to public opinion, interest groups, and political parties. The study of politics looked like Figure 1-1.

But just using the term "social base" assumes that society is the underlying element in the study of politics. Could it not be the other way around? To use a coffee-making metaphor, instead of "percolating up," could politics "drip down"? If there were a book entitled *The Political Basis of Society*, such a book would posit society as largely the result of political decisions made over the decades. In that case, our model would look like Figure 1-2.

How can you prove which model is more nearly correct? It is possible (and very likely) that the flow is going both ways simultaneously and that both

[23]Lipset, *Political Man*.

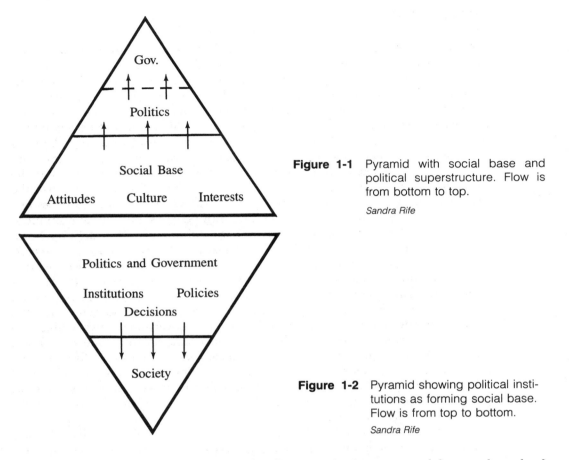

Figure 1-1 Pyramid with social base and political superstructure. Flow is from bottom to top.

Sandra Rife

Figure 1-2 Pyramid showing political institutions as forming social base. Flow is from top to bottom.

Sandra Rife

models are nearly correct. Why then emphasize one model over the other? There is no good reason; it is simply the current fashion in political study. Perhaps the societal based studies began as a reaction against the emphasis on institutions that dominated political science before World War II.

As has been noted, political science doesn't stand still. By the 1970s a certain reaction against the dominant behavioralism had begun. Political scientists began to voice discontent with the "social bases" approach, arguing that politics is not simply a reflection of people's attitudes, and that, in many cases, attitudes are the *result* of governmental policy. One text by a leading political scientist deliberately discussed institutions primarily and attitudes secondarily—and only in regard to political participation. He thereby indicated that the political culture approach was no longer so interesting.[24] Another political scientist, who had earlier been committed to the political culture approach, came to the conclusion that the modern democratic state is not simply the reflection of

[24]Joseph LaPalombara, *Politics Within Nations* (Englewood Cliffs, N.J.: Prentice-Hall, 1974).

its society but, in fact, is quite autonomous from society and often guides society.[25] The trouble with this newer approach is that it stacks the deck in favor of institutions, perhaps a needed corrective to the emphasis on attitudes.

In this text we are going to continue putting attitudes before institutions, simply because we have to begin somewhere. We are suggesting, however, that the "social bases" of politics are, in some measure, a reflection of political structures and decisions. Political attitudes are not simply givens; they are in large degree human reactions to the political structures one confronts through life. But how are political institutions created? By people who carry with them certain attitudes in forming political structures.

Notice how a seemingly minor matter—the order in which topics are presented—is itself a theoretical problem. Much as you might try to ignore theoretical questions, you can't escape them entirely. A book that puts attitudes first is at least suggesting, if not stating outright, a theory that attitudes are basic. A book that puts institutions first is suggesting a theory that they are basic. The ordering of topics has been a subtle bias in political science for a long time. It is time for us to make it a topic for open discussion and debate.

SIMPLIFYING REALITY

A model is a simplified picture of reality that social scientists develop to order data, to theorize, and to predict. We have already considered some of the models currently used in political science, and we will encounter others. By its very nature, a model must simplify reality. A model that is as complex as the real world would be of no help in understanding the real world, but in simplifying reality models run the risk of oversimplifying. The real problem is the finite capacity of the human mind. We cannot factor in all the information available at once; we must select which points are important and ignore the rest. But when we do this, we may drain the blood out of the study of politics and overlook many key points. Accordingly, as we encounter models of politics—and perhaps as we devise our own—pause a moment to ask if the model departs too much from reality. If it does, discard or alter the model. If there is conflict between the theoretical model and reality, always let reality be your guide.

Political Systems

Let us consider a prominent example, the "political system" model, that has both contributed to our understanding of politics by simplifying reality and

[25]Eric A. Nordlinger, *On the Autonomy of the Democratic State* (Cambridge, Mass.: Harvard University Press, 1981). Norlinger's earlier work was a study of English political attitudes. See Eric A. Nordlinger, *The Working-Class Tories* (Berkeley, Cal.: University of California Press, 1967).

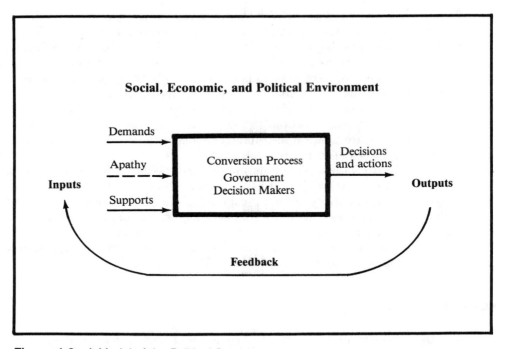

Figure 1-3   A Model of the Political System

Adapted from David Easton, A Systems Analysis of Political Life *(Chicago: University of Chicago Press, 1965), diagram 2, p. 32. Drawing by Sandra Rife.*

has, in some cases, departed from reality.[26] The idea of looking at complex entities as systems originated in biology. Living entities are complex and highly integrated. The heart, lungs, blood, digestive tract, and brain perform their functions in such a way as to keep the animal alive. Take away one organ and the animal dies. Damage one organ and the other components of the system alter their working in an effort to compensate and keep the animal alive. The crux of systems thinking is this: You can't change just one component. A change in one component will also change all the others.

In the "political system" model, the politics of a given country, many argued, worked the same way as a biological system. According to the Easton model (fig. 1-3), citizen's demands, "inputs," are felt by the government decision makers who process them into authoritative decisions and actions, "outputs." These outputs make an impact on the social, economic, and political environ-

[26]The leading thinker on political systems has been David Easton, *A Systems Analysis of Political Life* (New York: John Wiley, 1965). Gabriel Almond has accepted and refined a systems view of politics in Gabriel A. Almond and James S. Coleman, *Politics of Developing Areas* (Princeton, N.J.: Princeton University Press, 1960), Chap. 1; and Gabriel A. Almond and G. Bingham Powell, Jr., *Comparative Politics: System, Process, and Policy,* 2nd ed. (Boston: Little, Brown, 1978).

ment that the citizens may or may not like. The citizens express their demands anew—this is the crucial "feedback" link of the system which may modify the earlier decision. Precisely what goes on in the "conversion process", was left opaque, a "black box."

In some cases, the "political system" approach describes reality well. Crime in the United States increasingly alarmed citizens. A presidential candidate, Ronald Reagan, vowed to fight crime by appointing federal judges and Supreme Court justices who were more concerned with protecting citizens than with protecting the rights of criminals. As president, Ronald Reagan made such appointments and in a few years a tough-minded Supreme Court limited the rights of persons accused of crimes. Most Americans approved of these developments, and the feedback was positive. In another example, during the Vietnam war, feedback on the military draft was very negative. The Nixon administration defused much youthful anger by ending the draft in 1971 and going to an all-volunteer army. In yet another example, the socialist economics of French President François Mitterrand produced inflation and unemployment. The French people, especially the business community, complained loudly and Mitterrand altered his policy away from socialism and back to capitalism. This change in policy was further reinforced when Mitterrand's conservative opponents won the French legislative elections in 1986. The feedback loop was alive and well in France.

The Trouble with Systems

But in other cases, the systems model falls flat.[27] Would Hitler's Germany or Stalin's Russia really fit the systems model? How much attention do dictatorships pay to citizen demands? To be sure, there is always some citizen input and feedback. Hitler's generals tried to assassinate him—a type of feedback. Workers in communist systems make an impact on government policy by not working hard. They expect more consumer goods and by not exerting themselves they communicate this to the regime. Sooner or later the regime is forced to respond. In the USSR such a response has come from the Gorbachev regime. All over the Soviet bloc, workers chuckle: "They pretend to pay us and we pretend to work."

How could the systems model explain the Vietnam war? Did the citizens of the United States demand that the administration send half a million troops to fight there? No, precisely the opposite: Lyndon Johnson ran for election in 1964 on an antiwar platform and won resoundingly. We could utilize the system model to show how citizen discontent with the war contributed to Johnson's declining popularity and his decision not to seek reelection in 1968. The feedback loop did go into effect and work, but only long after the decision to send troops to Vietnam had been made. By the same token, how could the systems model explain the Watergate scandal? Did U.S. citizens demand that members of President Nixon's staff order

[27]For criticism of the political systems approach, see Chilcote, *Theories of Comparative Politics,* Chap. 5.

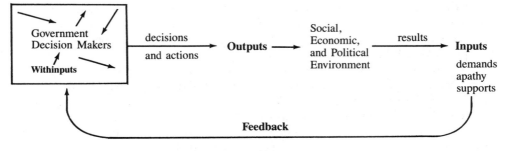

Figure 1-4   A Modified Model of the Political System
Sandra Rife

the Democratic headquarters bugged? No, but once details started leaking out in 1973 about the coverup, the feedback loop went into effect putting pressure on the House of Representatives to form an impeachment panel.

Plainly, there are some problems with the systems model, and they seem to be in the "black box" of the conversion process. A lot of things are happening in the mechanism of government that are not initiated by and have little to do with the wishes of citizens. Johnson was responding to the demands of a few generals and close advisers to send U.S. troops to Vietnam.[28] He was not happy about this because it was a betrayal of his election promise. But by early 1965, he could no longer ignore the demands of his advisers which weighed more heavily in his thinking than the public's wishes.

Let us modify the systems model to better reflect reality. By diagraming it as in Figure 1-4, we logically change nothing. We have the same feedback loop: outputs turning into inputs. But by putting the "conversion process" of government first, we suggest that it—rather than the citizenry—originates most decisions. The public reacts only later.

Next we add something that Easton himself later suggested. Inside the "black box", a lot more is happening than simply the processing of outside demands. Pressures from the various parts of government—government talking mostly to itself and short-circuiting the feedback loop—are what Easton called "withinputs."[29] These two alterations, of course, make our model more complicated, but this also reflects the complicated nature of reality.

We still do not have the perfect model to explain and predict political actions. We never will. Do the citizens decide and the leaders react? Or do the leaders decide and the people react? With the systems model, we have an example of how we must continually remake our ideas on politics to fit an ever-changing reality. Politics is slippery; it isn't easily confined to our mental constructs. By acknowledging this, we open our minds to the richness, complexity, and drama of political life.

[28]For a condensed account of decision making on the Vietnam war that utilizes numerous Defense department documents see Neil Sheehan and others, *The Pentagon Papers* (New York: Bantam Books, 1971).

[29]David Easton, *A Framework for Political Analysis* (Englewood Cliffs, N.J.: Prentice-Hall, 1965), p. 114.

SUGGESTED READINGS

ALMOND, GABRIEL A., AND SIDNEY VERBA. *The Civic Culture*. Princeton, N.J.: Princeton University Press, 1963. A major study of the political culture in five nations.

ARISTOTLE, *Politics*, trans. Ernest Barker. New York: Oxford University Press, 1962. Still a valuable work for beginning students of politics.

DAHL, ROBERT A. *Modern Political Analysis*, 4th ed. Englewood Cliffs, N.J.: Prentice-Hall, 1984. An excellent introduction by a noted Yale scholar to the several theories and approaches to the discipline.

EASTON, DAVID. *The Political System: An Inquiry into the State of Political Science*. 2d ed. New York: Knopf, 1971. An important contemporary statement of the view of politics as process and system.

FINIFTER, ADA W., ED. *Political Science: The State of the Discipline*. Washington, D.C.: American Political Science Association, 1983. Top U.S. political scientists explain the current evolutions of their specialties.

KAVANAH, DENNIS. *Political Science and Political Behaviour*. Winchester, Mass.: Allen & Unwin, 1983. A critical but still supportive review of the contributions of behavioralism to political science.

LAPALOMBARA, JOSEPH. *Politics Within Nations*. Englewood Cliffs, N.J.: Prentice-Hall, 1974. A sophisticated overview of comparative politics focusing on midrange empirical theory instead of systems.

LASSWELL, HAROLD. *Politics Who Gets What, When, How*. New York: McGraw-Hill, 1936. A classic statement, albeit heavy on unsupportable psychoanalytic insight, of the way politics works.

MORGENTHAU, HANS J. *Scientific Man vs. Power Politics*. Chicago: University of Chicago Press, 1946. Defines the limit of scientific approaches in the face of power realities.

NORDLINGER, ERIC A. *On the Autonomy of the Democratic State*. Cambridge, Mass.: Harvard University Press, 1981. An important argument that the modern state does not simply respond to popular demands but enjoys considerable autonomy.

RICCI, DAVID. *The Tragedy of Political Science: Politics, Scholarship, and Democracy*. New Haven, Conn.: Yale University Press, 1984. An interesting argument that political science, in trying to be scientific, has contributed neither to science nor to civic education.

SEIDELMAN, RAYMOND, AND EDWARD J. HARPHAM. *Disenchanted Realists: Political Science and the American Crisis, 1884–1984*. Albany, N.Y.: State University of New York Press, 1985. The authors argue that political science talks too much to itself, not enough to the polity.

SOMIT, ALBERT, AND JOSEPH TANNENHAUS. *The Development of American Political Science: From Burgess to Behavioralism*. Enlarged ed. New York: Irvington, 1982. A history of political science.

STORING, HERBERT J., ED. *Essays on the Scientific Study of Politics*. New York: Holt, Rinehart and Winston, 1962. A blistering critique of the behavioral revolution. The essay by Leo Strauss gives the student an idea of the traditional-versus-behavioral debate.

WEISBERG, HERBERT F., ED. *Political Science: The Science of Politics*. New York: Agathon Press, 1986. A dozen articles by top political scientists explore the meaning of science and whether our discipline can be scientific.

chapter 2

Nations
and
Governments

During most of man's history, any organized human society was considered a nation. A nation was a people with its own history, culture, and language; it did not always have a formal government or a clearly defined homeland. Many nations were actually tribes, such as the Cherokees of Oklahoma. But in the seventeenth century, the definition of a nation changed, as the ideal of the "nation-state" became the world's most powerful political force.[1] With the emergence of the modern concept of nationalism—a heightened sense of cultural, historical, and territorial identity—peoples saw themselves as having the right to govern themselves in their own nation-states. Today, we define a nation, or nation-state, as any sizable population with a distinct cultural identity that rules itself within formal territorial boundaries by means of an autonomous national government.

The dramatic rise of the modern nation has changed the face of the globe in a few centuries. Citizens transferred their loyalties from monarchs, churches, or feudal lords to the nation.[2] The twentieth century has continued to produce radical changes in the political structure of the world, as the development of modern communication and transportation has helped to make nationalism an even more powerful political force. Vast empires, such as those of Austria-Hungary and Great Britain, fell apart as subjected peoples around the world asked for the right to govern themselves. As a result, many new states were created, especially in the Americas, Asia, and Africa.[3] There are today at least 160 separate nations, and the emergence of new nations continues, although not at the same rapid pace.

WHAT IS A NATION?

The many nations of the world community represent a spectrum of stages of social, economic, and cultural development. Some, like the United States and Japan, are technological societies with high standards of living. Others, like Zaire and India, are struggling to overcome poverty. But despite their differences, all nations share a set of common characteristics that marks them as nation-states.

---

[1] The most correct label for an autonomously governed territory is "nation-state," but for purposes of simplicity, we will use the term "nation" throughout this text. The standard history of the rise of the modern nation is Hans Kohn, *Nationalism: Its Meaning and History* (New York: Crowell-Collier and Macmillan, 1955). Also useful are Karl Deutsch, *Nationalism and Social Communication: An Inquiry into the Foundations of Nationality* (New York: John Wiley, 1953); Louis Snyder, *The Meaning of Nationalism* (New Brunswick, N.J.: Rutgers University Press, 1954); and Seymour Martin Lipset, *The First New Nation: The United States in Historical and Comparative Perspective* (Garden City, N.Y.: Doubleday, 1967).

[2] Kohn, *Nationalism: Its Meaning and History*, p. 9.

[3] For treatments of non-Western nationalism and newly independent states, see Rupert Emerson, *From Empire to Nation: The Rise to Self-Assertion of Asian and African Peoples* (Cambridge, Mass.: Harvard University Press, 1960); David E. Apter, *The Politics of Modernization* (Chicago: University of Chicago Press, 1965); Fred R. von der Mehden, *Politics of the Developing Nations* (Englewood Cliffs, N.J.: Prentice-Hall, 1964); Gabriel A. Almond and James S. Coleman, *Politics of the Developing Areas* (Princeton, N.J.: Princeton University Press, 1960); and John H. Kautsky, *Political Change in Underdeveloped Countries* (New York: John Wiley, 1962).

INDEPENDENCE is the demand of these black Zimbabweans, from both the former British colonial masters of Rhodesia and the white-minority regime that followed from 1965 to 1980.

United Nations/Contact

Territory and Independence

Every nation occupies and independently controls a specific geographical area with the acknowledgment (if not approval) of most of the world community. For example, the world concedes that Wales is part of Great Britain and that the Ukraine is part of the Soviet Union even though Wales and the Ukraine have distinctive languages and cultures. Occasionally, one nation will refuse to grant diplomatic status to another for political or ideological reasons. For almost twenty-five years, the United States denied the People's Republic of China recognition as the true and lawful regime of mainland China. But the People's Republic of China was accepted as a sovereign state by the majority of the world community.

The territorial claims of nations sometimes lead to boundary disputes when two states feel that they should rightfully control a certain area. The United States and Mexico went to war over Texas in 1846, and India and Pakistan clashed over Kashmir and Bangla Desh. Such controversies are often not resolved until a war brings the victorious nation recognition of its claim.

A Cohesive Population: Nationalism

Nationalism is a mainstay of nationhood. In times of change, upheaval, and turmoil, a sense of national community serves as a unifying force, enabling a people to maintain a feeling of cohesiveness which makes the task of government easier. Nationalism helps to justify the authority of the state, as a people who share a sense of national community are less likely to view their government as a foreign political

NATIONALISM: What American's heart is not stirred by the collective remembrance of the 1776 signing of the Declaration of Independence? Such feelings are a powerful national cement.

New York Public Library

organization superimposed on them. Nationalism thus helps legitimate the state's use of force against its own people and other nations.[4]

A crucial element of nationalism is an emotional identification with a specific geographical area.[5] Every people attaches a special psychological meaning to its homeland. English colonists tried to bring a bit of the homeland with them to America when they gave settlements such names as Georgia, Virginia, and New York. Today, Russians speak of "Mother Russia," and the Japanese see Mount Fuji as a symbol of their nation.

But a territorial attachment is not enough to build a united national feeling. Nationalism also depends on the existence of a common history and culture.[6] The sharing of a historic past seems to bind people together, as it has the citizens of the Republic of Ireland, who remember centuries of struggling against England. Similarly, a common cultural heritage, such as a shared religion, a national literature, or an artistic or musical tradition, can promote a sense of national identity. Italy's Roman Catholicism and Renaissance heritage of art and architecture, and Russia's literary tradition, with such writers as Tolstoy and Dostoevsky, all contribute to the sense of national identity felt by Italians and Russians. Indeed, the absence of shared traditions is a part of the instability

[4]Kohn, *Nationalism: Its Meaning and History,* p. 11.
[5]Our discussion follows those of Kohn, *Nationalism;* and Snyder, *The Meaning of Nationalism.*
[6]See Lipset, *The First New Nation,* pp. 26–30.

of many new Asian and African states. These countries have had to depend on reinforcement from the mass media, "indoctrination" in schools, and the charisma of new national heroes (often military men) to develop a national spirit and sense of community in what often approximates a historical and cultural vacuum.

Like a common history or cultural heritage, national language is also an element of nationalism. Language is the carrier of a nation's history, culture, traditions, and social customs, and it is the sharpest way to distinguish ethnic groups. Some nations, like India and Switzerland, survive with two or more languages. But often the existence of many tongues will fragment a society, whereas a national language will unify it. The division of Canada into French-speaking and English-speaking populations has been a particularly disruptive force in that nation's history. Ironically, in some new states of Asia and Africa, which include many tribes, the closest thing to a national language is the English or French that was imposed on these nations while they were British or French colonies.

What holds a state together when it lacks a common tradition and contains people from many ethnic groups, each with its own distinct customs, religion, and history? The United States seems to lack many criteria of nation-hood: it has no national religion, and its culture is a "melting pot" of many foreign traditions. Dennis W. Brogan, a British observer, found that American nationalism is sustained primarily by a symbolic force: the country's ideals, as embodied in the Constitution and the Bill of Rights, act as a strong unifying force.[7] Indeed, the Mormon church teaches that the Constitution is a divinely inspired document drafted by the hand of God.

Autonomy and Legitimacy

A large part of nationalism is a historical and cultural heritage, but another part of nationalism is desire for autonomy. Nations are independent, governing their own affairs without outside interference. Puerto Rico is not a nation, nor is Guam: both are non-self-governing territories of the United States. Bangla Desh was not a nation until it won independence in 1971, even though it had for years retained a territorial identity, a sense of community, and a cultural heritage distinct from that of West Pakistan.

As we considered in Chapter 1, a bulwark of national independence is legitimacy, which can be defined as the ability of the government system to sustain the faith and trust of the people.[8] The citizens of a nation will feel that their government is legitimate if they have a general sense that it is rightful and that their well-being will be served by continuing the existing method of running the country. If the people see their government as illegitimate and not serving

---

[7]See Dennis W. Brogan, *Politics in America* (New York: Harper & Row, 1954); also see Karl Deutsch, *Politics and Government,* 3rd ed. (Boston: Houghton Mifflin, 1980), chap. 6.

[8]See Seymour Martin Lipset, *Political Man: The Social Bases of Politics* (Garden City, N.Y.: Doubleday, 1963), p. 63. Chapter 3 is especially useful in analyzing legitimacy.

their needs, they may attempt to overthrow it, as the American colonists did in the late eighteenth century.[9]

Political Organization

When the Americans ended British colonial rule in 1783, they created a new nation, and one of the first steps they took was to draw up the blueprint for a new political organization, or government. Every society has certain institutions that are responsible for making rules or policies and for allocating resources. Government converts the needs of the nation—including territorial independence, economic well-being and political stability—into public policies and enforces these policies throughout the society. It may take many forms, from the chieftaincies of African tribes to the complex bureaucracies of Western nations. A stable society requires some organizing force, and governments are created to perform that function.

HOW NATIONS DEVELOP

Which came first, states or nations? A nation is a population with a certain sense of itself, a cohesiveness, a commonality of attitudes and ideals, and often (but not always) a common language. A state is a governmental structure, usually sovereign and powerful enough to enforce its writ. (Notice that here we use "state" in its original sense; the fifty U.S. states are not states in this sense of the word.) Many people would argue that nations must have developed before states. States, after all, are rather artificial creations; they come and go and change form through the centuries. Surely nations must be the underlying element: groups of people with kindred feelings must antedate governmental structures.

Historical research tends to refute this common-sense view. In almost every case, it was states—governmental structures—that created their nations around them.[10] The Zulus of South Africa, for example, are not a tribe but an artificially created nation, one put together from many clans and tribes less than two centuries ago by a powerful and brutal warrior, Shaka. Present-day people think of themselves as Zulus only because Shaka united them by conquest, forced them to speak his language, and made them great warriors.

France often comes to mind as a "natural" nation, a neat hexagon with a common history, language, and culture. But present-day France consists of

[9]Of course, many oppressive governments have remained in power for centuries. A large part of the success of the feudal system for centuries in medieval Western Europe, and of the Roman Empire, lay in the perspective of the era. What we may think of as oppressive in modern America was viewed as acceptable and legitimate in medieval and ancient cultures.

[10]For studies of the multifaceted process of building nations in Western Europe, see Charles Tilly, ed., *The Formation of National States in Western Europe* (Princeton, N.J.: Princeton University Press, 1975).

several regions with very different languages and histories that were united—mostly by the sword—over the course of centuries. The Paris kings inculcated a sense of Frenchness by means of education, language, and centralized administration. The French nation is an artificial creation developed by the French state for its own convenience.

For many countries, the process of creation is not yet complete. The Spanish state coincides imperfectly with the Spanish nation. The kings of Toledo and Madrid tried to copy the French methods of centralization, but these Castilians were never able to impose a uniform sense of Spanishness on Catalans, Basques, Galicians, Andalucians, Navarese and others. Regionalism bedevils Spanish politics to this day. In another example, India scarcely existed as a concept before the British conquered the Indian subcontinent and turned it into the Raj. The English language, the railroad, and the telegraph stitched India together. It too is plagued by breakaway ethnic movements such as the independence movement of the Sikhs of the Punjab.

The most artificial nation of all could well be the United States—put together through deliberate design by a group of men meeting in Philadelphia from thirteen different colonies. While assimilating tens of millions of immigrants with different languages and cultures, the United States developed a sense of nationhood over the years based largely on the ideals articulated in its founding documents. Nations do not fall from heaven; they are created by human craftsmanship of varying degrees of quality.

The Crises of Nation-Building

Some social scientists argue that the process of constructing nations—if the process is to be successful—requires that countries go through the same five stages in approximately the same sequence.[11] Each opportunity for further growth represents a "crisis" in the life of the nation which the state structure must resolve with greater or lesser success.

Identity. The "identity crisis" is the first hurdle in building a nation. People who previously identified with a tribe, region, or other subnational group must come to think of themselves as first and foremost citizens of the nation. This does not happen easily, quickly, or automatically. The U.S. Civil War was fought over this point. France and Britain still contain regional groups that don't think of themselves as French or British but rather as Breton and Corsican (in France) or Scottish, Welsh, and Irish (in Britain). The Swiss and Yugoslavs, except when travelling abroad, will identify themselves as members of a canton (Bern, Geneva, Basel) or "republic" (Serbia, Croatia, Bosnia). Some countries, especially in the Third World, have not yet solved their identity crisis. In Africa,

---

[11]The concept of crises in nation-building was developed by Leonard Binder and others, *Crises and Sequences in Political Development* (Princeton, N.J.: Princeton University Press, 1971). For historical case studies, see Raymond Grew, ed., *Crises of Political Development in Europe and the United States* (Princeton, N.J.: Princeton University Press, 1978).

people still think of themselves as members of a tribe rather than as Ugandans or Nigerians.

Legitimacy. Nor does legitimacy fall from heaven. As we considered in Chapter 1, a government must cultivate the respect and willing obedience of its citizens, the widespread feeling among the people that the regime's rule is rightful. Regimes with legitimacy problems are prone to overthrow (often by military coup, as in Latin America and Africa) or revolution (as in Iran and South Africa). Ultimately, as in the case of Lebanon, no legitimacy means no nation.

Penetration. Related to both identity and legitimacy, the "crisis of penetration" means that the nation must get substantially all the population, even in outlying or culturally distinct regions, to obey the government's writ. One quick check of penetration: do all areas pay taxes? If not, there is a penetration problem. Typically, the regime establishes its rule first in the capital, then slowly extends its rule out over the country, often encountering resistance which requires military strength to overcome. Lack of penetration means that a government can have a law on its books—against cocaine production in Bolivia, for example—but most of the country, including some of the leadership, disregards the law.

Participation. As people become more aware that they are being governed, they demand to have a say in their governance. This feeling typically starts with the educated, better-off, and prominent people. The knights and wealthy burghers in effect tell the king or queen, "If you want taxes and military service from us, we demand a say in policy." The monarch, usually desperate for taxes, sets up a representative body to gain their compliance, such as the Parliament in England or *Riksdag* in Sweden. At first only the elite of society are thus represented, but gradually, the desire for participation reaches all sectors of society—the common men and women—and they demand the right to vote. At a minimum, people need to *feel* they can participate in order for nationhood to evolve.

Regimes are often fearful of the consequences of expanding voting rights. Women got the right to vote in the United States only with the Nineteenth Amendment in 1920; Swiss women only in 1971. The danger is that unrepresented people will oppose the government, and regime legitimacy will erode. Eventually, the regime usually decides that expanding participation is better than breeding revolution. Said one British Parliamentarian in the nineteenth century, "We count ballots rather than crack skulls." The white minority regime of South Africa, slow to realize this basic point, brought the country to revolution in the 1980s.

The best way to solve the participation crisis is through slow and incremental steps, as Britain succeeded in doing in the nineteenth century. A series of Reform Acts in Britain expanded the electoral franchise one step at a time, gradually giving more people the right to vote. This allowed both institutions and people time to adjust. Voting was meaningful and participation genuine. When suffrage is suddenly thrust on an unprepared people, however, the result is seldom democracy. On paper, Spain got universal male suffrage in 1874, well ahead of Britain, but in practice election results were controlled by local bosses and the interior ministry. Voting in much of the Third World—where largely uneducated people got the franchise all at once—is often problematic, as local strongmen or tribal leaders tell people how to vote.

Distribution. In a sense, the "crisis of distribution" is never permanently resolved. It concerns the classic question of "who gets what?"[12] Once the broad masses of citizens are participating in elections, it usually occurs to them that the economic rewards of the nation are unfairly apportioned. They desire to change the distribution of the nation's income in their favor. Much of the working class throws its vote to the party that promises higher wages, increased educational opportunities, and more welfare benefits. This is how the Labor parties of Britain and Norway and the Social Democratic parties of Germany and Sweden grew until they won power and established extensive welfare states funded by taxes that fall more heavily on the rich. To a lesser degree, the American working class gave much of its vote to the Democrats under Franklin D. Roosevelt and Lyndon Johnson in order to carry out a similar redistribution of national income.

The distribution question is never settled, however, because the poorer sectors of society always want more welfare, whereas the wealthy, represented by the more conservative parties, argue that the welfare state has gotten out of hand, that taxes are too high and benefits too generous. When conservatives win elections—as Margaret Thatcher did in Britain in 1979 and Ronald Reagan did in the United States in 1980—they try to cut welfare programs. This raises a hue and cry from voters who sympathize with the lower classes, and they try to resume the growth of the welfare state through the next election. In advanced, industrialized democracies most elections are, to some degree, centered around the distribution of wealth.

Happy is the nation that has throughout its history been able to deal with these crises one at a time and with sufficient pauses in between each crisis. This allows a country's institutions—its parties, parliament, executive departments, and so on—to become stronger each time they surmount a new crisis. But what if all five crises hit at the same time? This has been the situation in the Third World. Newly independent countries, many of them with serious identity and legitimacy problems, are expected to implement complex laws, to give all citizens the right to vote, and to provide rising and equitable living standards. It's too much for their weak institutions to bear all at once, and they collapse into revolution or military rule. The first item to go is usually participation, hence the

---

[12]Formulated by the great American political scientist Harold Lasswell, *Politics: Who Gets What, When, How* (New York: Meridian Books, 1958).

many Third World dictatorships.[13] Unfortunately, the Third World does not have the luxury of spreading out its crises in this world of rapid change.

The Role of War

One of the unfortunate aspects of nation-building is the role of warfare in the growth of states. We must recognize that most European nations were established and consolidated by conquest. Heresies, rebellions, and breakaway movements were put down with great bloodshed. In many Third World lands, this is still happening.

For any ruler, state survival is the top priority. Monarchs and presidents alike will do whatever they must to avoid foreign conquest or internal dismemberment. They become ruthless when either threatens them. In the interest of survival they build their military power to counter any combination of threats, and this means that they must also enlarge and modernize their political systems.[14]

First, they must constantly increase taxes to provide for armies and equipment. Peter the Great of Russia ordered his officials "to collect money, as much as possible, for money is the artery of war." The French monarchs instituted the mercantilist economic system with its protected industries in order to raise revenues for defense. As mentioned previously, it was to raise money that kings and queens began sharing power with parliaments. The power to tax is the preeminent power of legislatures. James I and Charles I precipitated the English Civil War when they tried to bypass parliament by decreeing their own taxes to pay for their wars in Europe. After winning the Civil War the Parliamentarians beheaded Charles I in 1649 and laid the groundwork for establishing the eventual predominance of the House of Commons.

The need for a larger and better military establishment forced monarchs to greatly improve the organization and administration of their kingdoms. They needed to raise both taxes and manpower. When a knight on horseback was the top fighting machine, the loose feudal system of government was all that was necessary to mobilize the kingdom's knights in time of war. In the fifteenth century, after Swiss pikemen showed how they could unseat a charging knight from his mount, all of Europe had to raise much larger armies of pikemen. This was a blow to the feudal state and a boost to the absolutism of monarchs. Failure to modernize one's administration and army could lead to loss of power. The map of Europe became much simpler as small states succumbed to military conquest and were absorbed by larger states. War was the great engine of modernization and consolidation.

---

[13]For a pessimistic look at how difficult the problem is in the developing lands, see Samuel P. Huntington and Joan M. Nelson, *No Easy Choice: Political Participation in Developing Countries* (Cambridge, Mass.: Harvard University Press, 1976).

[14]See Richard Bean, "War and the Birth of the Nation State," *Journal of Economic History*, 33(1973):203–221.

When French revolutionaries in 1792 faced an invading army of professional soldiers, they mobilized the entire population, "the nation in arms," and beat the invaders. Harnessing this new nationalism and using the new idea of the military draft, Napoleon built the largest army in Europe and proceeded to conquer the entire continent. To resist Napoleon's legions, other European lands turned to nationalism and conscription as well.

By either the power or example of its arms, European nations spread their organization, technology, and nationalism into what we call the Third World. In Asia, Africa, and the Middle East, one country after another fell to the conquering Europeans and soon adopted their ways. Those who were not conquered, the Turks and the Japanese, modernized sufficiently to stave off the Europeans. Warfare gave countries little choice: modernize or die. More recently, in fighting the Europeans for their freedom, independence movements in Third World countries have accelerated modernization in those lands. You can't stay backwards and beat the French, Portuguese, or Soviets.

Reflecting for a moment on U.S. history, we may ask which contributed more to modernization: the modest welfare measures of Roosevelt's New Deal or the gigantic industrial and manpower mobilization of World War II? Indeed, many welfare measures flowed as a result of the war. The G.I. Bill educated millions of ex-soldiers who never would have gone to college without it. The National Defense Education Act of 1958, triggered by the launch of the Soviet Sputnik the year before, pumped millions of dollars into U.S. higher education. One of the largest federal "welfare" programs is the Veterans Administration, a program which even conservatives support.

We do not propose that war is a wonderful thing and should be promoted as an accelerator of modernization. War is ghastly but it has the side effect of speeding up modernization. Much as we may dislike war, we must recognize that it plays a major role in the foundation and growth of the powers of government.

GOVERNMENT: WHAT IT IS AND WHAT IT DOES

All but the most primitive societies have had well-defined governmental structures. Mankind seems to need a way of organizing and making rules for communities, and various theories have been offered to explain this tendency. Psychologist Erich Fromm argued that men fear social isolation and the responsibilities of independence, and form larger groups (whether national, religious, or ideological) in order to escape from the tensions and demands of individual freedom and autonomy.[15] On the other hand, political theorists such as John Locke have viewed governments as devices to protect the rights and property of the people. "The great and chief end," wrote Locke in *Two Treatises of Civil Government,* "of men uniting . . . under government, is the preservation

[15]Erich Fromm, *Escape from Freedom* (New York: Holt, Rinehart and Winston, 1941).

of their property [and so, their natural rights]."[16] To Locke, government represented an agreement between the rulers and the ruled, who would support those in power as long as the government served in their interests.

A society without a government might be like a baseball game without umpires. The players would argue forever about whether the pitch was a ball or a strike, or whether the runner was safe or out. Each contest would turn into a raucous brawl. Government performs the same tasks as the umpires: it sets down the basic ground rules that everyone must abide by.

In part, a government is able to enforce its rules (or laws) because it controls the supreme penalty of death and has a monopoly on the legal use of force. Yet, to stay in power, a government must enjoy the support of its people. One way of maintaining legitimacy is to successfully fulfill the goals of nationhood.

Common Goals of Government

The task of every government is to provide for the independence, stability, and economic and social well-being of all its citizens. These are the ultimate goals of every nation in the modern world.

Each nation must preserve itself as a state and ensure its national survival, so that the world community recognizes that nation's autonomy and the integrity of its boundaries, in a word, its sovereignty. Recognition by other nations depends in part on a country's stability. A politically stable nation has an established system providing for the orderly transfer of power from one party or leader to another. It preserves domestic peace by maintaining law and order and by protecting property. A government can also enlist popular support by promoting an acceptable standard of living for all of its citizens; people who are receiving what they believe to be their due are more likely to see the regime as legitimate. Promoting the general welfare can include attempts to eliminate poverty, maximization of educational opportunities for all areas of society, and technological advances.

How can government best advance the economic and social well-being of its citizens? There is a wide disagreement, which generally can be divided into three basic governmental approaches to promoting the general welfare: the laissez-faire approach, the socialist society, and the welfare state. Under the philosophy of laissez-faire ("'let alone") of Adam Smith, government is an enemy of human liberty and therefore should not be allowed to intervene in the economy. Thomas Jefferson voiced his support of a laissez-faire approach in his statement, "That government is best which governs least." Proponents of the laissez-faire approach believe that people will prosper or fail on the basis of their own intelligence, ambition, and hard work, and that government has no right to intervene in this natural order.

---

[16]John Locke, *Two Treatises of Civil Government* (London: J. M. Dent & Sons, 1924), p. 180.

In a socialist society, almost the opposite is true. Government, rather than private individuals, owns the means of economic production and distribution, such as factories, mines, and transportation and communications networks. Government runs these industries in the interests of the society as a whole—something which private interests are not likely to do in a laissez-faire system.

Finally, the welfare-state approach is an attempt to preserve part of the laissez-faire philosophy while answering some of the socialist critiques of capitalism. The government establishes basic rules for the economic order and can act to eliminate industrial abuses. To protect the needy and underprivileged, it runs programs such as Social Security, aid to dependent children, and workmen's compensation. At the same time, the economy remains in private hands, and private funds finance most industrial development. The welfare state is not without fault, though, and many have argued that its drain on the nation's finances retards economic growth.

Classifying Governments

We could arrange all of the world's governments into a typology according to whether they follow the laissez-faire model, the socialist model, or the welfare-state model. Of course, any model represents only an ideal situation, and not its application in the real world. Despite the fact that they represent an unreachable situation, models are very useful to social scientists in classifying and comparing different political systems, and they aid in the understanding of a nation's political culture and development. But categorizing according to the economic strategies of governments is only one of many schemes for understanding governments. The earliest and most famous system of classification was developed by the Greek philosopher Aristotle in the fourth century B.C.

Aristotle's Six Types of Government. Aristotle distinguished among three benevolent kinds of government—where the ruling authority acts only according to legal guidelines, ruling in the interests of the entire society—and three corrupt types—where government acts only in its own selfish interests (fig. 2-1).

A monarchy is a benevolent dictatorship. Governmental power is vested in a man or woman of preeminent virtue and wisdom. The ideal monarch rules in behalf of all and will not benefit any one person or group at the expense of another. But monarchy can degenerate into tyranny, under which the monarch exercises all power for the benefit of himself or herself and his or her allies and ignores the good of the people.

Aristocracy can be thought of as a collective monarchy, ruled by the most virtuous, intelligent, and morally enlightened in the state. But this benevolent rule by an elite class can decay into oligarchy. Instead of governing in the best interests of the society, the oligarchs only wish to defend their privileged positions.

Aristotle saw a polity (or constitutional democracy) as the most practical form of government because of the limitations of man. All citizens have a voice in the selection of leaders and the framing of the law, but at the same time,

Table 2-1 Aristotle's System for Classifying Governments

WHO GOVERNS	LEGITIMATE FORMS RULE IN THE INTEREST OF ALL	CORRUPT FORMS RULE IN THE INTEREST OF THE RULERS
One person	Monarchy	Tyranny
A few people	Aristocracy	Oligarchy
The majority	Polity	Democracy

formal constitutional procedures protect minority rights. In Aristotle's classification, democracy (the rule of the many) was a corruption of the polity and the worst form of government. Deluded into thinking that one man is as good as another, the masses in a democracy blindly follow the lead of corrupt and selfish demagogues and plunder the property of the hard-working and the capable.

The Autonomy of Subsystems. Aristotle's classification system was used by scholars for nearly twenty-five centuries, but it is no longer satisfactory. Modern political scientists have had to create new models in order to understand a rapidly changing world. One recent approach identified the extent of *subsystem autonomy* as a key feature that distinguishes one type of government from another.[17]

Every modern society contains many institutions and organizations that can be thought of as subsystems of society. Religious denominations, colleges, labor unions, industrial corporations, civic associations, political parties, and the mass media are all subsystems of a modern industrial society such as the United States or Great Britain. We can classify governments according to how much autonomy they allow these subsystems. In other words, are churches, unions, and colleges free to run their own internal affairs without interference from government?

Totalitarian governments, such as Nazi Germany, permit little or no subsystem autonomy. As Carl J. Friedrich and Zbigniew Brzezinski pointed out, such societies have official and dogmatic ideologies to which all social institutions must adhere.[18] Thus, in the late 1930s, German churches had to reflect Nazi racial theories by trying to prove that Jesus Christ was a blond-haired, blue-eyed Aryan instead of a dark-haired, dark-eyed Jew.

Democratic or constitutional governments, on the other hand, give a relatively high degree of independence to subsystems. While there are limits established for the conduct of any private association, a constitutional state will allow as much autonomy as is consistent with the general well-being of the society. Thus, labor unions can strike without fear of government reprisal in the United States, except when the nation's security is affected. No subsystem has

[17]Robert A. Dahl, *Modern Political Analysis*, 4th ed. (Englewood Cliffs, N.J.: Prentice-Hall, 1984), pp. 40–41. See also Gabriel A. Almond and G. Bingham Powell, Jr., *Comparative Policies: System, Process, and Policy*, 2d ed. (Boston: Little, Brown, 1978), pp. 72–76.

[18]Carl J. Friedrich and Zbigniew Brzezinski, *Totalitarian Dictatorship and Autocracy* (Cambridge, Mass.: Harvard University Press, 1965), p. 9.

absolute freedom, but most are allowed to run their own affairs unless they threaten the public interest.

Centralization of Political Power within the State. Governments differ not only in the degree of initiative they allow all subsystems but also in the way political power is distributed among its different levels. Nations can be classified as unitary states, federal states, or confederations, depending on the way they distribute government authority.

Great Britain, France, Italy, Israel, and the vast majority of the world's 160-odd nations are unitary states. A single national or central government exercises supreme power over all areas of society and can override the decisions of local governments. Thus, the ministries in London or Paris can order Lincolnshire or Bordeaux to impose laws or programs in their localities. Such actions are unlikely in the world's twenty or so federal states. In federal nations such as the United States, West Germany, Australia, and Canada, power is divided between the national governments and the state or provincial governments. Usually, national governments control foreign affairs, military defense, and currency, whereas local authorities handle education, welfare, and policing.

MODERN GOVERNMENT: MAKING PUBLIC POLICY

All modern governments are involved in the complex business of making public policy. Public policies, the authoritative actions (not proposals or debates) of government officials and agencies, are created in order to meet perceived national needs. Policies include legislation, judicial edicts, executive decrees, and administrative decisions. Policies are implemented through programs, which are specific measures aimed at influencing the direction of government activity and public life. Government adopts policies and programs consistent with the broad goals of the nation.[19] Since resources are always limited, a priority of values must be established. For example, is it more important for the United States to send a man to the moon or to rebuild the ghettos of our cities? Should we use public funds to clean up polluted rivers or to put additional police officers on our streets? Decision makers must face this kind of choice in formulating public policy.

The determination of national priorities involves complex decision making which is a crucial part of the political process. In societies such as the United States, many groups lobby for policies that suit their own economic or ideological interests. The automobile industry works for increased spending for highways, and "right-to-life" groups pressure legislators into a strong stand against legalized abortions. Ultimately, the legislature and the executive must

---

[19]At least in theory; Theodore Lowi, however, argues that the policies and programs of government, in practice, more often than not have little to do with any long-term visions of national goals. Instead, they tend to be rather short-sighted, stop-gap measures. See Lowi's *The End of Liberalism: The Second Republic of the United States*, 2d ed. (New York: Norton, 1979).

decide in the name of the people which policies the nation will pursue. If they bankroll the space program rather than public housing, they have in effect made a statement of national priorities. In this sense, the creation of public policies usually involves a public choice among competing values and needs. During the Johnson administration, the president faced a choice between spending government funds on "guns" (for the Vietnam War) or "butter" (the Great Society social program). Costs of the war had escalated so rapidly that he could no longer finance both "guns" and "butter," as he had previously hoped; "guns" received priority.

When public policies involve a choice, they are often controversial and must be defended as being in the "public interest." In theory, the public interest is defined as the benefit of everyone as opposed to one specific group of people. But in practice, this term is impossible to define, and usually ends up being loosely invoked in public-policy debates by all sides in an attempt to gain support for rather one-sided interpretations of the "public interest."

Public Policies: Material and Symbolic

Modern governments adopt and pursue many kinds of public policies to protect what they define as the public interest. These policies can range from extensive preparations for national defense to efforts to end racial, ethnic, and sexual discrimination in public and private agencies. All policies, however, fall into two major categories: those that are material in nature and those that are symbolic.

Material public-policy decisions require the expenditure of public funds— a scarce national resource in every country. Government funds are finite. The national budget can be seen as a pie that must be divided among many hungry guests: there is only a limited amount to be distributed.

Once a national policy has been decided and a concrete legislative program has been enacted, machinery must be created to see that resources are properly distributed. For example, if Congress adopts a measure to defray hospital costs for the indigent, a government agency must determine who is eligible for such benefits. For a policy to be effective, adequate resources (both money and personnel) must be allocated to deal with the problem. If they are not, the program may disappoint the intended beneficiaries and accomplish little.

Unlike material policies, symbolic public policies usually do not involve the allocation of money or personnel and often are not a part of the legislative process. By symbolic or nonmaterial public policies is meant those acts of government that create sentimental attachments (patriotism, loyalty, deference, or national pride) or that confer social status on key segments of society. The proclamation of a new public holiday, such as for slain black civil-rights leader Martin Luther King, is a symbolic policy.

As Murray Edelman pointed out in *The Symbolic Uses of Politics,* symbolic policies can be more important than actual government performance and

ULTIMATE SYMBOL: President and Mrs. Reagan rededicate the
Statue of Liberty on July 4, 1986. The festivities, attended by millions
and televised nationwide, were calculated to make Americans feel
good about themselves, their country, and their government.

Pete Souza, The White House

results, for what people think often matters more than what the government
really does.[20] Because of this, all governments are careful to support and foster
outward symbols of national unity. Institutional symbols are created and
popularized to give people something they can identify with. Thus, when an
American thinks of the United States, he may get an image of the Statue of
Liberty, "Old Glory," or the Liberty Bell. Occasionally, such symbols can become
a source of controversy: in Canada a bitter debate over a proposal for a new
national flag contributed to the defeat of the Conservative party in 1963.

Moral symbols are often invoked by public officials to build a climate
supportive of the institutions in which they serve. Thus, in America, all
candidates for public office are careful to be photographed in church, regardless
of their true religious feelings. This is because religious worship has become a
powerful moral symbol linked with national pride and stability. Few high public
officials are seen smoking cigarettes in public or relaxing with a glass of scotch,

[20]Murray Edelman, *The Symbolic Uses of Politics* (Urbana, Ill.: University of Illinois Press, 1964), chap. 1, and Murray Edelman, *Politics as Symbolic Action* (Chicago: Markham, 1971).

and for many years it was taboo for any elected officer to obtain a divorce. (Conservative Ronald Reagan, ironically was the first divorced person to win the presidency). Symbolic issues can become politically explosive, as in the question of prayer in public schools.

The symbolic element is a strong part of political confrontations. At the height of the Vietnam war, some Catholic radicals, including priests and nuns, invaded draft board offices and poured blood over Selective Service records as a vivid protest against the violence of American bombings. Their expectation was not to paralyze the draft system, but rather to awaken the conscience of the nation. Similarly, in the 1980s, U.S. college students erected symbolic shanty-towns on their campuses to prod trustees into divesting stocks of companies doing business in South Africa. Often such protests have the aim of shocking the public into thinking about the moral issues raised; sometimes they backfire and lead to increased antagonism toward protesters.

SUMMARY

The modern concept of the nation-state has evolved over the last four centuries. Each nation consists of a people, headed by an organized political structure, which maintains autonomous control over a specific geographic territory. The nation preserves itself by promoting the faith and trust of the people in its system of government. Feelings of nationalism include a sense of national identity and pride, which stems from a feeling for the homeland or a common history, language, and culture. Government organizes society politically and preserves order within the modern nation-state.

Nations are rather artificial creations, inculcated by the state structures that precede them. For many countries, especially in the Third World, this process of nation-building is not complete. Nations typically go through five "crises" as they are built: an identity crisis as people develop national loyalties; a legitimacy crisis as governments strive to win obedience; a penetration crisis as governments extend their writ nationwide; a participation crisis as citizens demand a say in policy; and a continual distribution crisis as groups struggle over who gets what. The process of nation-building and political modernization is accelerated by war as states strengthen themselves against attack.

Government creates rules, known as laws, which all citizens must obey. It is the highest authority within a society, yet in order to maintain its legitimacy it must have the support of the people. The goals of independence, stability, and the economic and social well-being of the majority of the citizens are common ends of all governments, although these ends may be approached by means of a myriad of different methods. Because there are many different kinds of government, social scientists have devised numerous classification systems in order to better understand how man directs his society. The most famous method of classification was created by the Greek philosopher, Aristotle. Other schemes created since then include classifications according to the degree of autonomy given to subsystems or groups such as churches or political clubs, the degree of centralization of political power in government, and the degree of modernization of the social and political system.

The authoritative actions of modern governments are public policies and programs. Public policies may be either material or symbolic in nature. They can involve the collection and allocation of resources or of services, or the allocation of symbolic values. Government decision making involves a choice among competing priorities.

SUGGESTED READINGS

ALMOND, GABRIEL A., AND JAMES S. COLEMAN. *Politics of the Developing Areas.* Princeton, N.J.: Princeton University Press, 1960. A systematic, comparative treatment of the developing nations that uses the structural-functional approach. The first section provides an especially interesting discussion of the development of a structural-functional framework.

ARENDT, HANNAH. *On Revolution.* New York: Viking, 1963. A brilliant study of the bases of political authority.

BINDER, LEONARD, ET AL. *Crises and Sequences in Political Development.* Princeton, N.J.: Princeton University Press, 1971. Develops the concept of "crises" as stages that nations must surmount as they develop.

ELDER, CHARLES D., AND ROGER W COBB. *The Political Uses of Symbols.* New York: Longman, 1983. Excellent brief roundup of the symbolic analysis of politics.

GREW, RAYMOND, ED. *Crises of Political Development in Europe and the United States.* Princeton, N.J.: Princeton University Press, 1978. Historians use the development framework of political scientists to examine the growth of government in the West.

HUNTINGTON, SAMUEL P. *Political Order in Changing Societies.* New Haven, Conn.: Yale University Press, 1968. A magisterial overview of political instability in the Third World.

KOHN, HANS. *Nationalism: Its Meaning and History.* New York: Crowell-Collier and Macmillan, 1955. A thorough examination of the historical development of the modern nation-state.

LERNER, DANIEL. *The Passing of Traditional Societies: Modernizing the Middle East.* New York: Free Press, 1958. A classic study of change and its impact in modernizing nations.

LIPSET, SEYMOUR MARTIN. *Revolution and Counterrevolution: Change and Persistence in Social Structures,* rev. ed. Rutgers, N.J.: Transaction Books, 1987. A series of brilliant essays on how countries modernize, especially on the impact of values and religious beliefs.

chapter 3

The Individual
and
the Constitution

The problem of establishing and limiting power exists in every political system. Government and the people both must have certain powers and rights, but their activities must also be limited in order to keep them from encroaching on the rights of others. The choices involved in determining a fair balance between government powers and civil liberties, between the welfare of the majority and the rights of the minority, are not easy ones. For example, if air traffic controllers want higher wages, do they have the right to call a work stoppage and inconvenience thousands of people until the federal government offers them a satisfactory raise? If Congress votes "legislative vetoes" into bills as a way to supervise the executive branch, does the Supreme Court have the right to declare them unconstitutional? If religious parents believe that children should pray in public schools, does this conflict with the separation of church and state?

These questions raise problems of rights and political power, and some of these problems are admittedly more difficult than others. Most of us would probably agree that a Supreme Court decision is law even if Congress doesn't like it. We will probably disagree, though, on the right of air traffic controllers to strike. It can be argued that the controllers should not be denied the right to ask for higher wages simply because they perform a public service. Yet a case can also be made that no one, including underpaid air traffic controllers, has the right to deny the people such an important public service. The question of whether children have the right to pray in public school is also a difficult one. On the one hand, to deny them this right would be to deny them the right to practice their religion. But, on the other hand, if some children pray in school, should all? Which prayers would suit all religions? And what about children who do not wish to pray at all?

How does society determine how to limit political power and how to balance, in the most equitable fashion, the needs of the majority with the rights of individuals and minorities? Whereas decisions about who is right and who is wrong in specific cases such as those mentioned above must always be made by the decision makers in office at a particular time, it is evident that governments need some guidelines in determining where this balance should fall. These guidelines are provided by traditions, by statutes, and by national constitutions which lay down the basic ground rules for governing society.[1]

CONSTITUTIONS IN THE MODERN WORLD

In common usage, we think of a constitution as a written document which sets forth the fundamental rules by which a society is governed. Political scientists, though, define the word more broadly: a constitution is that set of rules and customs, either written or unwritten, legally established or extralegal, by which a government conducts its affairs.[2] By this definition, all nations have constitu-

[1]See Charles H. McIlwain, *Constitutionalism Ancient and Modern* (Ithaca, N.Y.: Cornell University Press, 1940); William G. Andrews, *Constitutions and Constitutionalism* (Princeton, N.J.: Van Nostrand, 1961); and Herbert J. Spiro, *Government by Constitution* (New York: Random House, 1959).

[2]See Francis D. Wormuth, *The Origins of Modern Constitutionalism* (New York: Harper & Brothers, 1949), p. 3.

tions, since each nation operates according to some set of rules. Britain has no written constitution, but custom, law, precedent, and tradition are so strong that the British government considers itself bound by practices which have developed over the centuries. Thus, Britain is governed by a constitution.[3]

In the modern world, nearly every nation has a written constitution which establishes the forms, institutions, and limits of government and sets guidelines for balancing minority and majority interests. The Constitution of the United States is very short: it is limited to seven articles, most of which have to do with establishing the powers of each branch of government, and twenty-six amendments. In contrast, most of the nations that have won independence since World War II have adopted constitutions of remarkable detail.[4] The postwar Japanese constitution, which was drafted by the U.S. military government after World War II, contains no less than forty separate articles outlining the rights and duties of the people alone. Among the individual rights enumerated in the Japanese constitution are the rights to productive employment, a decent standard of living, and social welfare benefits—a sharp contrast to the general values of "justice, domestic tranquility, common defense, general welfare, and liberty" outlined in the American preamble. Article 1 of the West German constitution (the Basic Law) also enumerates a long list of rights. These include not only fundamental rights, such as legal and political freedoms, but also a number of social and economic safeguards, including state supervision of the educational system and public control of the economy.

If an established nation such as Britain is able to get by with no written constitution per se, and if another, such as the United States, manages to function with a very general constitution, why has almost every recently established nation (with the exception of Israel) found it necessary to commit itself to not only a written constitution, but a very detailed constitution at that?

The Highest Law of the Land

Most modern nations adopt written constitutions for the same reason that the ancient Mesopotamian lawgiver Hammurabi codified the laws of Babylon: to establish a supreme law of the land. Constitutions state the fundamental laws of society and are not meant to be easily revised. They stand as a yardstick by which any activities of the government or the people are to be measured.[5] A legislature can pass a law one year and repeal it the next, but basic constitutional provisions cannot be amended so easily.[6] In Sweden, constitu-

---

[3]See the famous work of Walter Bagehot, *The English Constitution* (New York: Oxford University Press, 1936).

[4]The best compilation of world constitutions is Amos J. Peaslee, ed., *Constitutions of Nations,* 4th ed. (New York: International Publications Service, 1974).

[5]K. C. Wheare, *Modern Constitutions,* 2d ed. (New York: Oxford University Press, 1966), chap. 6.

[6]Britain is a notable exception. Parliamentary procedures can be changed by a simple legislative majority and the monarch's approval. The fact that they never have been changed without prolonged debate can be used to argue the point that truly constitutional rules need not be committed to writing. See Spiro, *Government by Constitution,* p. 390.

tional amendments must be passed by two successive legislatures, with a general election in between. In the United States, amending the Constitution is even more difficult. The most common procedure is to secure the approval of two-thirds of both the Senate and the House of Representatives, then obtain ratification by three-fourths of the state legislatures. The fact that our Constitution has been amended only sixteen times since the adoption of the Bill of Rights in 1791 illustrates how difficult the amendment procedure is. The Equal Rights Amendment failed to pass in 1983, for example, because fewer than three-fourths of the state legislatures had voted to ratify it.

The General Nature of Constitutional Law. Since constitutions, no matter how detailed, cannot provide specifically for every legal or administrative problem that may arise, they must be fairly general in nature. The United States Constitution says that "Congress shall make no law respecting an establishment of religion, or prohibiting the free exercise thereof" in Amendment I of the Bill of Rights. This is a very general statement. The way it will be interpreted in a specific case (such as the question of prayer in school, or perhaps a Satan cult that believes that animal sacrifice or illegal drugs are necessary for the practice of their religion) must depend on the decision makers in power at the time the case arises.

Constitutional law must be interpreted in order to be applied to specific incidents. Who is given the immense authority to decide what the general wording of a constitution means? In some thirty nations, including the United States, this responsibility belongs to the highest national court. The procedure by which the court rules on the constitutionality of a governmental act and declares null and void those acts it considers unconstitutional is known as judicial review.[7] The power of judicial review is a controversial one. Many critics have accused the United States Supreme Court (most notably when Earl Warren was chief justice from 1953 to 1969) of imposing a personal philosophy as the law of the land. To a large extent, the constitution is indeed what its interpreters say it is, but the possibility of too subjective an interpretation seems to be a necessary risk taken by any nation that has a constitution.[8]

The courts do not always interpret the constitution in a consistent fashion. In the United States, the Warren Court best exemplified the type of

[7]Actually, the United States Constitution does not specifically give the Supreme Court the authority to rule acts of Congress unconstitutional. The precedent was set in 1803, when the Supreme Court under Chief Justice John Marshall declared a section of the 1789 Judiciary Act to be unconstitutional in the case of *Marbury* v. *Madison.* Thomas Jefferson, Andrew Jackson, and Abraham Lincoln all expressed the view that the Supreme Court was not the sole or final arbiter of constitutionality. However, it has been commonly recognized as such since the Civil War. See David Deener, "Judicial Review in Modern Constitutional Systems," *American Political Science Review* 46 (December 1952): 1079–99; also see William H. Riker, *Democracy in the United States* (New York: Macmillan, 1965).

[8]Robert A. Dahl, "Decision Making in a Democracy: The Role of the Supreme Court as a National Policy Maker," *Journal of Public Law* 6 (1957): 279–95. For another discussion, see Martin Shapiro, ed., *The Supreme Court and Constitutional Rights* (Glenview, Ill: Scott Foresman, 1967).

judicial philosophy generally known as "loose constructionist" or "judicial activist." It broadly interpreted constitutional guarantees in favor of citizens' rights and nullified many laws and governmental practices which infringed even slightly on those safeguards. The opposite of loose constructionist is "strict constructionist" or "judicial quietist"—a generalization which describes a Supreme Court that sees its job not as legislating but as following the lead of Congress. Justices Oliver Wendell Holmes and Felix Frankfurter, who counselled the Court on judicial restraint, were regarded by many as "strict constructionists."

Likewise, West Germany's Federal Constitutional Court is no stranger to controversy. Modeled after the U.S. Supreme Court—except that it has sixteen justices—the German court is mandated to make sure all laws conform to the Basic Law. In 1975, the German court found that a law permitting abortions conflicted with the strong right-to-life provisions of the Basic Law—which had been put in to repudiate the horrors of the Nazi era—and declared abortion unconstitutional. In 1979, in one of its most important decisions, the Federal Constitutional Court found there was nothing unconstitutional about "worker codetermination"—that is, employees having nearly the same rights as owners and managers in determining the long-term future of businesses.

Few nations give their highest court the power to rule on the constitutionality of laws. In nations that do not have a clearly established procedure of judicial review, this responsibility is often given to the legislature. In Great Britain, Parliament itself makes the final determination of what is constitutional.

Constitutions and Constitutional Government.   The meaning of a constitution depends largely on the way in which it is interpreted. Indeed, two separate nations could conceivably adopt the same constitution (with a few variations in wording or language) but have entirely different forms of government and allow their citizens very different rights. What is written in the constitution does not necessarily occur in practice. The Constitution of the Soviet Union sets a framework for that nation's government—a federal system with a bicameral legislature, with executive and administrative powers given to the cabinetlike Council of Ministers—and accords to its citizens a long list of democratic rights.[9] Yet in actuality, the government is controlled by the Communist party, with little authority given to the states or to the legislature, and the rights of power are totally dependent on the interpretation of the leaders in power.

The governments of Canada, Great Britain, and the United States are constitutional governments; the government of the Soviet Union is not, although current party chief Mikhail Gorbachev may be trying to make it more constitutional. Constitutionalism refers to the degree to which the power of government is limited and individual rights are respected. In a constitutionally governed

[9]See Robert Sharlet, *The New Soviet Constitution of 1977: Analysis and Text* (Brunswick, Ohio: King's Court Communications, 1978).

nation (whether it has a written constitution or not), government is limited by internal institutions in such a way that the fundamental rights of citizens—such as freedom of speech, the right to practice one's religion, and freedom from arbitrary imprisonment—are safeguarded from violation by either government or hostile minorities. In contrast, an authoritarian government is not limited by the guidelines of the constitution. In an authoritarian government, the individual citizen and minority groups are assured no protection against arbitrary acts of government, in spite of what the constitution may say.

The Purpose of a Constitution

If many nations seem to pay no heed to what is written in their constitutions, why do some nations bother to write a constitution at all? Constitutions fulfill a variety of roles: they provide the symbolic function of putting in writing a statement of national ideals, they formalize the structure of government, and they attempt to justify the government's right to govern.

A Statement of National Ideals. According to the Preamble of the United States Constitution, our nation is dedicated to six goals: to form a more perfect union, to establish justice, to ensure domestic tranquility, to provide for the common defense, to promote the general welfare, and to secure the blessing of liberty. The Soviet Constitution proclaims the Soviet Union to be a "developed socialist society" dedicated to building a classless utopia. The Constitution of the Federal Republic of Germany, seeking to divest the nation of any traces of Nazi rule, states its determination to "serve the peace of the world" and expressly proclaims that no group of people can be denied the right to German citizenship—a reaction to Hitler's Nuremburg Laws, which stripped hundreds of thousands of citizens of their rights.

Preambles and lists of rights are symbolic statements: they indicate the values, ideas, and goals which seem to best express the spirit of the national political culture. But the value statements in preambles are by nature very general and have no legal force. How are they interpreted? What does the U.S. Constitution mean by a "more perfect union," for example? There is considerable disagreement over this question; in fact, debate over the meaning of this term led to the Civil War a century ago. What does the Constitution mean by "establishing justice"? What is justice, and is it the same for all citizens? If American blacks have been denied equal rights for two centuries, does this mean that it is just for them to be given an advantage now in admission to colleges, in hiring practices, or in securing low-rent housing? Or again, what does the Preamble mean by "promoting general welfare"? The question of what the general welfare is, and how it is to be balanced against the rights of the individual or of a minority group, are questions which are almost certain to produce different answers from everyone. Were children who wished to pray in school setting a precedent disruptive to the general welfare? Do laws allowing private citizens to purchase handguns like the "Saturday-night special," which are not accurate enough to have any legitimate use for hunting or target practice, harm the general welfare, even though the Bill of Rights specifically gives citizens the right to bear arms?

Although constitutions provide a statement of national ideals, the interpretation of these goals and values necessitates an active choice by the decision makers of government.

Formalizes the Structure of Government.

In addition to acting as a symbolic statement of national values, a constitution is also a blueprint. It is a written description of who does what in government, defining the authority and limiting the powers of each branch and providing for regularized channels through which conflict may be resolved. Articles I through III of the United States Constitution outline the duties of Congress, the president, and the judiciary. Congress may collect taxes and customs duties, but is prohibited from taxing exports. The president is named commander in chief of the armed forces, but he must have the "advice and consent" of the Senate in order to conclude treaties. In a system where there is a separation of powers, the constitution divides authority and responsibilities among the various branches of government; it also limits the power of each branch. No other constitution uses "checks and balances" like the American in an elaborate attempt to limit power; most, in fact, specify the unification of power.

A constitution also outlines the division of power between central and regional governments in a federal state. In a federal system of government, powers and responsibilities are divided between one national government and several regional or state governments. West Germany and Australia, like the United States, are federal states. Their constitutions give their central governments control over certain areas of responsibility, such as foreign policy, foreign commerce, and coinage. Thus, the *Land* of Bavaria in the Federal Republic of Germany may not sign a treaty with Austria; neither may the state of Texas mint its own currency. Whereas certain powers are delegated to the central government, the constitution leaves others to the states. In the United States Constitution, this division is a general one; any powers not accorded to the central government are reserved for the states and for the people. Thus, the states traditionally control education, police protection, health and welfare services, and local commerce. Of course, this division of power has become less clear-cut, especially in recent years, as the federal government has taken on a greater share of financing operations of education, health, welfare, housing, and scores of other services. But in spite of federal control of many of the purse strings, the states still retain predominant control of these powers.

Establishes the Legitimacy of Government.

A third role of a constitution is to give a government the stamp of legitimacy. Although this function is undeniably symbolic, its practical utility cannot be denied. Many nations in the world community will not even recognize a new state until it has adopted a written constitution; it is a sign of permanence and responsibility.

Most constitutions were written shortly after revolutionary upheavals, and their purpose was to help establish the new regime's right to rule. The Articles of Confederation and subsequently the United States Constitution symbolized American independence by replacing British authority with tangible evidence of a new government. The French constitution of 1791 (which never went into effect) tried to replace the divine right of Louis XVI with the sovereign right of the people. And the first Soviet constitution of 1918 established a "dictatorship of the people" to replace tsarist rule. Constitutions proclaim the values of a new regime while also establishing in writing a permanent outline for the organization of government. As a symbolic statement of intentions with a practical outline of structure, a constitution helps to set the stamp of legitimacy on a new regime. This is the primary reason why almost every nation, and especially new nations established since World War II, have adopted constitutions almost as soon as they have gained independence.

Of course, a written constitution is not absolutely necessary for a legitimate, stable regime. Neither Great Britain nor Israel has found it necessary to commit all their fundamental precepts and laws to writing in one document. Britain's constitution consists of many documents, such as the Magna Carta, the Petition of Rights, and the Bill of Rights; judicial decisions which have established precedents of common law; major acts of Parliament; and customs and traditions which have grown over the centuries. Israel's constitution is also an accumulated body of documents and precedents, some of which date back to biblical times.

Even in nations that have written constitutions, there are countless traditions, customs, and laws which are also a part of the constitutional order. For instance, no mention is made of political parties anywhere in the U.S. Constitution. Yet our party system is an established part of the American political process; indeed, a change in the party system would very likely change the entire American political structure.[10] Judicial precedents and government traditions, too, make up the fundamental laws of society. Thus, the body of constitutional law encompasses a wide variety of documents and traditions in all nations whether they have "written" or "unwritten" constitutions.

THE ADAPTABILITY OF THE CONSTITUTION

The United States Constitution

In 1789, when the American Constitution was adopted, the world was far different from what we know now. The United States was primarily agrarian, needing little in the way of technological services. The communications network was limited to little-read newspapers and pamphlets, and mostly to word of mouth. There were no skyscrapers, automobiles, pollution, or missile systems.

---

[10]See the discussion in Seymour Martin Lipset, *The First New Nation: The United States in Historical and Comparative Perspective* (Garden City, N.Y.: Doubleday, 1967), chap. 9.

SIGNING the U.S. Constitution in 1787 were such leading figures as Washington and Franklin. Their prestige helped win adoption for the short, flexible document two years later.

National Geographic Society Photographer/Courtesy U.S. Capitol Historical Society

How can a constitution which was written to fill the needs of such a primitive world be adapted to the highly industrialized, urbanized, crime-ridden society of modern America? A look at the way in which the Constitution has adapted in two major areas of change—the "right to bear arms" in a violent society and the growth of "big government" in the twentieth century—might give some insight into the flexibility of this document.

The Right to Bear Arms.   In 1789, the United States was a sparsely settled frontier nation where people often literally had to fight for their lives. Guns were necessary to the settlers' survival, and the Constitution reflected this. Amendment II of the Bill of Rights (adopted in 1791) guarantees the right of the citizens to "keep and bear arms."

In the 1980s, the United States is no longer sparsely settled: it is highly urbanized. Guns are no longer necessary to the average citizen's survival; instead, they add fuel to the fire in an already tense and violent society. In recent decades we have witnessed the assassinations of President John F. Kennedy, Dr. Martin Luther King, and Senator Robert F. Kennedy. President Ronald Reagan and former Alabama Governor George Wallace were seriously wounded by would-be assassins. Armed robbery and killings by firearms have reached alarming proportions. As a result, many concerned citizens argue that the age of the frontier has long since passed, and that it is time to drastically restrict the sale of lethal weapons. Yet opponents of gun-control legislation argue that the Constitution ensures the right of every citizen to purchase and own firearms. Sportsmen, shopkeepers who find themselves constant victims of armed robberies, and those who may feel their persons or property are in danger but cannot secure full-time protection from the police all argue that their constitutional right to pursue a hobby or to protect their very lives will be jeopardized by gun-control legislation.

The "right to bear arms" case illustrates that a two-century-old constitution—at least in its traditional interpretation—may not provide the right answer for all of the needs of modern society. If gun controls are necessary to limit violence in America (and there is by no means a consensus on the issue), can the Constitution be interpreted to allow such legislation to be passed? The Constitution is written in very general terms; it lends itself to the interpretations dictated by the times. Amendment II reads: "A well regulated Militia, being necessary to the security of a free State, the right of the people to keep and bear Arms, shall not be infringed." Does this mean that the citizens can own guns privately, or that they can own guns for the purpose of maintaining a militia or army? The traditional interpretation has been that individual persons can purchase and own firearms for private use. In the future, it may be necessary to reinterpret Amendment II to mean that the right to bear arms applies only to members of an organized militia.[11]

The Constitution has other clauses which make it flexible enough to keep up with changing times. The so-called elastic clause gives Congress the power to enact all legislation necessary and proper to carry out its enumerated powers. Under this clause, too, the Constitution might be interpreted to mean that Congress can impose restrictions on the people's right to bear arms. So the general nature of the eighteenth-century Constitution does allow it to adapt to an age of violence even where it gives citizens the right to bear arms. How has the Constitution adapted to the more general shift from the sharp division between federal and state powers envisioned by the founding fathers to the highly centralized "big government" of the late twentieth century?

The Shift in the Federal Balance of Power. The role of the central government has grown markedly in relation to the powers of the state governments since the era of the New Deal in the 1930s. This shift in balance stems partly from the changing needs caused by the Great Depression, which left around twelve million people out of work. They needed assistance in finding housing and in feeding their families, and the states could not afford to provide all of these services. In response, the federal government took on a broader

---

[11]See Earl R. Kruschke, *The Right to Keep and Bear Arms: A Continuing American Dilemma* (Springfield, Ill.: Charles C. Thomas, 1985).

range of education, welfare, health, and housing services than ever before, and this responsibility has grown since then. With the recent fiscal crises which have hit all areas of American society from the cities to the farms, and with the great increase in the need for highways, public transportation, and an endless list of other services, the role of the central government has continued to expand.

The writers of the American Constitution never envisioned that the federal government would some day take on the tasks of feeding welfare clients, licensing communications networks, financing chemical and atomic research, or building highways. They assumed that the basic balance of power between state and central government would remain relatively stable, and that this balance would be quite even (or weighted more heavily toward the states). How has the document they wrote been able to adapt to the centralized system of modern American federalism?

As it has been able to adapt to the growing undesirability of making the right to own firearms a basic right, so, too, the Constitution has been able to adapt to the increased role of the central government. Whereas the powers of the federal government have expanded into areas which the founding fathers couldn't possibly have foreseen, the writers of the Constitution did have the foresight to realize that the nation would experience many changes and would develop many needs which they couldn't specifically provide for in the document. So the Constitution was written in a deliberately flexible form, and the result is that it can still be interpreted to fit the needs of modern society and government. Feeding welfare clients, financing scientific research, and building highways can all be seen as promoting the general welfare (atomic and scientific research also help to provide for the common defense), and licensing communications networks falls under the powers granted to the Congress to lay and collect taxes and to regulate commerce.

The Adaptability of Constitutions: Can They Ensure Rights?

The case of the right to bear arms illustrates that a constitution written for one age may not always provide the best solutions for another age. If this is the case, and if constitutions must constantly be reinterpreted to keep up with the times, how can they ensure the rights of citizens?

Civil Liberties and Civil Rights.   In the 1930s, Joseph Stalin imprisoned nearly twenty million Soviet citizens in labor camps. Another ten to fifteen million were killed for resisting his agricultural collectivization program. At about the same time, Heinrich Himmler, at Adolf Hitler's behest, began organizing scientifically designed concentration camps which would systematically exterminate thousands of lives every hour of the day. And halfway around the world, the Japanese armies of Hideki Tojo were raping and pillaging their way through China.

In reaction to the outrages of World War II, the world community has taken steps to prevent any future tragedies of such great magnitude. In 1948, the General Assembly of the United Nations adopted the Universal Declaration on Human Rights to guarantee basic rights to all the citizens of the world. As a symbolic statement of world opinion (with no real power of sanction), the Universal Declaration establishes fundamental precepts and ideals which most nations are reluctant to violate. Of course, if a nation does choose to violate the "universal rights" named in the declaration, there is little anyone can do, short of war, to stop them. The Universal Declaration's value is symbolic.

The Universal Declaration, patterned on the French Declaration of the Rights of Man and Citizen, and on the American Declaration of Independence and the Bill of Rights, affirms the basic civil and human rights which are thought by most Western political thinkers to be fundamental. It declares that all people have certain rights which government may not arbitrarily take away.[12] These include the rights to life, free assembly, freedom of expression, freedom of movement, freedom of religion, and freedom to participate in the political process by voting or holding office. In addition to this list of civil and political rights, the Universal Declaration provides for many of the economic and cultural needs of citizens of every land. It specifies that the rights to work and to receive equal pay for equal work; the right to an education; the right to marry, raise a family, and provide that family with a decent standard of living; and the right to live according to one's culture are the heritage of every citizen. The Universal Declaration is not the only international list of fundamental rights and liberties: the Organization of American States and the Council of Europe have also published similar documents.

The overwhelming sentiment of the civilized world favors equal rights for all. Yet in spite of the lofty declarations that have been published, the fact is that rights and liberties are difficult to define, and all nations restrict civil liberties in some way. The problem of minority groups is almost universally applicable as a case in point.

Minority Groups and Civil Liberties. Of the more than 160 nations that make up the world community few are homogeneous. Most have citizens with a variety of racial, ethnic, religious, cultural, or linguistic backgrounds, and as a result, nearly every nation has at least one minority group whose civil or cultural liberties are compromised to some extent. French-Canadians living in Maine or Chicanos living in New Mexico are at a disadvantage unless they speak a language foreign to their culture; Indians and Pakistanis in Great Britain must conform to a way of life far different from what they are accustomed to. It is the minority group which must adjust itself to the ways of the majority.

The Universal Declaration states that minorities have the right to preserve their cultural uniqueness. But to make a statement such as this and to carry it through are two different things. Most difficult is defining exactly who or what a minority group is (Can black militants speak for black America? Can the

---

[12]For an exploration of human rights, see Jack Donnelly, *The Concept of Human Rights* (New York: St. Martin's, 1985).

radical Jewish Defense League speak for American Jews?) and what its rights should be in a state controlled by a dominant group with different interests. It may be easy to condemn South Africa, because its discrimination against blacks is open and blatant. But nations that grant all citizens a theoretical equality before the law may discriminate against minorities in other, more subtle ways. If South Tyrolian German-speakers are forced to use the Italian language, is their cultural heritage being stifled? Is the inclusion of Croatia in Yugoslavia an infringement of the cultural rights of Croatians, who are accustomed to a different dialect and different traditions than those of the dominant Serbs? Should Spanish Basques be permitted to set up their own school systems to teach their youngsters about their heritage? If so, should American blacks be permitted to do the same, with state funding? What of Spanish-speaking Puerto Ricans in New York, or Chicanos in the Southwest, or Italian-Americans? Assimilation of minority groups involves a compromise of traditions and culture and, therefore, sometimes one of equal rights. But it is also true that a state that does not assimilate its minorities stands little chance of remaining stable. Thus, despite the Universal Declaration's denunciation of discrimination against minorities, some discrimination is inevitable in every society.

In 1942, for example, some 120,000 Japanese-Americans on the West Coast were interned under the infamous executive order 9066. Robbed of their homes, businesses, and liberty without due process of law, they were sent to ramshackle, dusty camps surrounded by barbed wire and guard towers—in some ways similar to Nazi concentration camps. Not one case of disloyalty was ever demonstrated against a Japanese-American; they were victims of racism and wartime hysteria.[13] German- and Italian-Americans suffered no such suspicions or punishment. Even Secretary of War Henry L. Stimson, who signed the order, feared it "would make a tremendous hole in our Constitution." It did, but not until 1983 did a federal court overturn the legality of internment. The incident shows that even a well-established democracy can throw its civil liberties out the window in a moment of exaggerated and groundless panic. The 442d Regimental Combat Team, recruited from Japanese Americans, covered itself with glory and was the most decorated U.S. unit of World War II.

FREEDOM OF EXPRESSION IN THE UNITED STATES

"Congress shall make no law . . . abridging the freedom of speech, or of the press; or the right of the people peaceably to assemble, and to petition the government for a redress of grievances." So says Amendment I of the United States Bill of Rights. We think of freedom of expression as one of the hallmarks of any nation calling itself democratic. Citizens who think the president or prime minister is ruining a nation's economy have every right to say so to whomever they wish. And a surrealist antigovernment film should draw no interference or investigation from any agencies of government.

[13]Peter Irons, *Justice at War* (New York: Oxford University Press, 1983).

But while freedom of expression seems at first glance to be a straightforward guarantee, it is not that simple. Does freedom of speech give a charismatic young radical the right to incite masses of people to commit political murders? Does a newspaper have a right to publish information which might damage the security of the nation? Whereas we may all believe in the right of free expression, most of us would agree that this does not mean that anyone can say or write whatever he wants, whenever he wants, regardless of the consequences. In the example used by Justice Oliver Wendell Holmes, nobody should be permitted to yell "Fire!" in a crowded theater unless there really is a fire. Free speech does not necessarily include the right to spread dangerous or malicious falsehoods. Likewise, free speech does not include the right to call police to advise them that there is a bomb in the city hall when there is not.

According to Justice Holmes, freedom of expression must also be restricted in cases where statements or publications present a "clear and present danger" of bringing about "substantive evils" which Congress has a right to prevent. Under this reasoning, the Supreme Court in its 1925 *Gitlow* v. *New York* decisions upheld the conviction of a radical who had called for the violent overthrow of the government on the grounds that his words had represented a "bad tendency" which could "corrupt morals, incite crime, and disturb the public peace."

The questions of what presents a "clear and present danger" and what is a "substantive evil" are, of course, open to very subjective interpretation. Many people today would see no danger in publicly advocating the violent overthrow of government. And so the interpretation of the meaning of the constitutional guarantee of freedom of expression has varied considerably over the years since the Bill of Rights was adopted.[14]

A History of Freedom of Expression

Free Speech and Sedition.   Sedition is defined in the Common Law as any criticism of the government or government officials designed to produce discontent or rebellion among the populace. The charge of sedition has been used by the American government to suppress some forms of radical expression during several periods of our history since the adoption of the Bill of Rights.

Congress enacted the first Sedition Act in 1798, after the infamous XYZ affair. The law (which followed the Common Law definition) was aimed against the "Jacobins," as American defenders of the French Revolution were called, at a time when the United States was involved in an undeclared naval war with France. The Sedition Act was supposed to expire the day that President John Adams left office (a curious coincidence which indicates that its raison d'être may have also had something to do with the election contest). The act aroused controversy, but it lapsed without any test of constitutionality in the Supreme Court. The next Sedition Act went into effect during the Civil War, when

---

[14]For accounts of the Supreme Court and First Amendment rights, see Robert L. Cord, *Protest, Dissent and the Supreme Court* (Cambridge, Mass.: Winthrop Publishers, 1971).

President Lincoln acted under the war powers vested in his office to suppress northern opponents of the Union effort. The president's action was brought to the Supreme Court, which declined to judge on the legality of his actions. Whereas the action went untested, all "political prisoners" were pardoned at the end of the war. It was not until the twentieth century that another Sedition Act was passed in an attempt to tighten national security during World War I.

Twentieth-Century Sedition Acts. It was the Espionage Act of 1917 that gave rise to Justice Holmes's "clear and present danger" doctine. At a time when socialists and pacifists were urging people to protest U.S. involvement in World War I by refusing to serve in the army and to disrupt the war effort in other ways, this act prohibited any attempts to interfere with the military recruitment policies of the United States government. The Espionage Act resulted in several court cases in 1919. In one case, the Supreme Court upheld the law on the grounds that free speech could be restricted if it created a "clear and present danger" to national security. And so several hundred people, including Socialist party leader Eugene Debs, were imprisoned under the act, but most were pardoned as soon as the war ended.

More recent Sedition Acts have been directed primarily against Communists. The Smith Act of 1940, the most comprehensive Sedition Act ever passed by Congress, made it a crime to advocate the violent action of overthrow of government, to distribute literature urging such an overthrow, or to knowingly join any organization or group that advocated such actions. The Smith Act aroused much controversy, but was not put to a constitutional test until 1951, when the Supreme Court upheld the convictions of the leaders of the American Communist party even though they had not been charged with any overt acts of force against the government. "It is the existence of the conspiracy which constitutes the danger," ruled Chief Justice Vinson, "not the presence or absence of overt action." Since then, there have been other court rulings on the constitutionality of the Smith Act, and they have fluctuated. In *Yates* v. *the United States* in 1957, the Warren Court reversed the conviction of the American Communist party leaders on the grounds that there was no overt action, only abstract advocacy of rebellion.[15] And four years later, in *Scales* v. *the United States,* the Court upheld the section of the Smith Act which makes membership in the Communist party illegal—but this ruling also specified that it is active membership, involving the direct intent to bring about the violent overthrow of government, which is criminal. The Court was careful to point out that membership per se was not made illegal by the Smith Act.

Probably the most stringent legislation ever enacted in our history to counter the threat of Communist subversion was passed during the McCarthy era following World War II. The McCarran Act of 1950 (the Internal Security

---

[15]For accounts of the Warren Court and the First Amendment, see Milton R. Konvitz, *Expanding Liberties* (New York: Viking Press, 1966); and Philip B. Kurland, *Politics, the Constitution and the Warren Court* (Chicago: University of Chicago Press, 1970).

MINORITY RIGHTS let gay activists like these organize and protest even though their views are at odds with those of the majority.

Charles Gatewood

Act) barred Communists from working for the federal government or in defense-related industries, established a Subversive Activities Control Board (SACB) to enforce the act, and required organizations declared by the SACB to be Communist-influenced to register with the Attorney General. The McCarran Act aroused a great deal of controversy. Its critics charged that the law not only encroached on the rights of free speech and free assembly, but also violated the self-incrimination clause of the Fifth Amendment. While the Internal Security Act in its entirety has never been declared unconstitutional, every action by the SACB demanding specific organizational or individual registration with the Attorney General's office has been declared unconstitutional. Finally, with the realization on all sides that the SACB was accomplishing nothing, it was abolished in 1973.

The history of legislative action against sedition in the United States indicates that the guarantees of the First Amendment have been interpreted to mean different things at different periods, varying according to both the general aura of national security and the president, Congress, and Supreme Court justices in power at the time. The Supreme Court recognizes the danger of subversion, and it acknowledges that government must have some powers to restrict the freedoms of expression and assembly for the preservation of society as a whole. But its interpretation of what is subversive has fluctuated. Whereas recent decisions have leaned toward free exercise of liberties wherever possible, many of the decisions of earlier periods have been more protective of the state's security. It is almost impossible to find a balance between the state's need to safeguard its own security and the exercise of free expression and free assembly. And so the courts have never been able to produce a definitive statement on the extent to which government may restrict freedom of speech.

Government by Constitution: Does it Guarantee Anything?

In the quick look we have taken at constitutions, two observations are striking. First, almost every nation in the world has adopted a written constitution. Second, in spite of the almost universal use of written constitutions, the documents must depend to a very great extent on the interpretation given them by whoever is in power. After the Soviet Union adopted its 1936 Constitution, which enumerated a long list of democratic rights for its citizens, Stalin proceeded to strip those rights from broad segments of the population. And even in the United States, it is strikingly apparent that the freedoms of speech and free assembly have meant very different things at different times in our history, depending on the president, Congress, the courts, the climate of American public attitude, and the general air of national security (or lack of it) which reign at the moment.

The primary purpose of constitutions is not to provide inflexible guarantees of human rights. Indeed, there is sound reasoning behind the argument that a citizen's wartime rights should be different from his or her peacetime liberties, for during periods of war the national security may be threatened and may require extra measures of protection. Nor is the primary purpose of constitutions to outline a structure for the organization of the government. The government of the Soviet Union could hardly be recognized from its description in that nation's constitution; and the federal system of the United States is a far cry from that envisioned by the writers of our constitution.

Whereas in some countries, such as the United States, the constitution is the supreme law of the land, in almost all societies, written constitutions are more appropriately viewed as expressions of intention and ideals; they are embodiments of the highest goals of a people. A developing nation often feels that it must impose restrictions on its citizens' right to publish criticisms of government, even though its constitution gives them the right of freedom of the press. The United States may have placed restrictions on free speech during World War I, but this action reflected the prevailing opinion that there was a need for tightened national security rather than an all-out abandonment of the ideal of free expression. Because the needs of a nation vary so sharply between periods of war and peace, and of depression and prosperity, the function of a constitution must be symbolically rather than literally binding. And as a symbolic statement, its utility seems unquestionably to be borne out by its popularity. It is an accepted (if not quite universal) document of a nation's legitimacy in the modern world.

SUGGESTED READINGS

BARBER, SOTIRIOS A. *On What the Constitution Means.* Baltimore, Md.: Johns Hopkins University Press, 1983. A modern eclectic view of what the framers of the U.S. Constitution intended.

BOLLINGER, LEE C. *The Tolerant Society: Freedom of Speech and Extremist Speech in America.* New York: Oxford University Press, 1986. Argues for judicial adoption of a "tolerance model" to protect free speech.

DWORKIN, RONALD M. *A Matter of Principle.* Cambridge, Mass.: Harvard University Press, 1985. A probing discussion of what the U.S. Constitution should and should not cover.

EDELMAN, MARTIN. *Democratic Theories and the Constitution.* Albany, N.Y.: State University of New York Press, 1984. An exploration of how theories of democracy color interpretations of the Constitution.

KAMMEN, MICHAEL. *A Machine that Would Go of Itself: The Constitution in American Culture.* New York: Knopf, 1986. A noted historian explores how Americans tend to worship their Constitution more than they understand or practice it.

KRAMER, DANIEL C. *Comparative Civil Rights and Liberties.* Lanham, Md.: University Press of America, 1982. Introduces an important comparative perspective to the study of civil rights.

KURLAND, PHILIP B., AND RALPH LERNER, EDS. *The Founders' Constitution.* Chicago: University of Chicago Press, 1987. Five volume collection by two top scholars covers everything.

MILLER, WILLIAM LEE. *The First Liberty: Religion and the American Republic.* New York: Knopf, 1986. A historical view and exhortation on religious freedom in America.

PEARSON, SIDNEY A., JR., ED. *The Constitutional Polity: Essays on the Founding Principles of American Politics.* Lanhan, Md.: University Press of America, 1983. Diverse and sometimes controversial views on the bases of U.S. democracy.

SMOLLA, RODNEY A. *Suing the Press.* New York: Oxford University Press, 1986. A libel law specialist argues the press is more powerful than ever and therefore more likely to be sued.

WOLL, PETER. *Constitutional Democracy: Policies and Politics,* 2d ed. Boston: Little, Brown, 1986. A readable textbook that emphasizes the constitutional bases of American politics.

chapter 4

Democracy
and Totalitarianism

In 1943, when the Soviet Union was one of the allies in the war against the Axis powers, George Orwell startled the public with his publication of *1984,* a thinly disguised portrayal of life in the Soviet Union in particular and in totalitarian societies in general. In this nightmare, the individuals have no rights, only obligations. The government may spy on them, arrest them, and interrogate at will; television cameras monitor the streets, scan public places, and peer into homes. The purpose of this unrelenting surveillance is to make sure that everyone is under the state's control—even in private thoughts. The media are controlled carefully, and the people are told only what the government wants them to know. Every citizen needs the state's permission to marry, to bear children, and to change jobs or places of residence. Citizens are creatures of the state.

Perhaps the most extreme opposite we can find in the annals of history is the traditional image of life in Athens during the fifth century B.C. Here, all adult male citizens had the right to attend the General Assembly that met ten times a year. Regardless of his wealth or social standing, each man's vote carried the same weight. The Assembly enacted all laws, elected the state's officers, and could compel the state's leaders to appear before it to justify their actions. Decisions of the Assembly were reached by a simple majority vote. In general, the individual had a role in the decision-making processes of state and was thereby accorded an important, if intangible, sense of dignity and human worth.

George Orwell's picture of totalitarianism and the Athenian ideal of democracy are at opposite ends of the spectrum of governmental power, and in between are many variations. (Actually, anarchism is the true opposite of totalitarianism, but since its essence is a rejection of government, it need not concern us here.) Table 4-1 shows the principal gradations from perfect democracy to perfect totalitarianism and lists some characteristics typical of each of the governmental systems. The table follows the custom in countries adhering to the Western political tradition (such as the United States) of classifying nations generally as either "democratic" or "nondemocratic"—the democratic nations having governments with limited powers and the nondemocratic nations having governments with more or less unlimited power over citizens.

As with all attempts at generalization, the effort to list general characteristics for governmental systems in Table 4-1 cannot be wholly successful. There is no "average" democratic state or "average" nondemocratic state. Even Athens' democracy fell far short of being a perfect democracy, for most of the population—women, resident aliens, and slaves—were excluded from participation in the political process, and effective control actually belonged to an elite. The various characteristics listed for each governmental system may vary in different nations. For example, the Soviet Union claims to offer a broad voting franchise to its adult citizens and reports that 99 percent of eligible voters turn out for elections. However, Soviet voters have little freedom of choice on the ballot, and therefore the franchise has limited value. Similarly, whereas the democracies claim to protect civil liberties carefully, some persons would argue that these liberties are accorded unevenly—in high degree to middle-class whites and grudgingly or not at all to impoverished nonwhites.

Table 4-1 The Spectrum of Governmental Power

PERFECT DEMOCRACY (POWER IN HANDS OF THE PEOPLE)	DEMOCRATIC GOVERNMENT		NONDEMOCRATIC GOVERNMENT		PERFECT TOTALITARIANISM (ALL POWER HELD BY GOVERNMENT)
	Democracy (USA, Great Britain, France)	Limited Democracy (Mexico, Egypt, Indonesia)	Authoritarianism (Syria, Pakistan, Chile)	Totalitarianism (Communist China, USSR, Fascist Italy, and Nazi Germany)	
Nonpartisan politics	Two-party or multi-party politics	Two-party or multi-party politics	Single-party or no-party politics	Single-party politics	Single-party politics
Full individual participation in government	Popular elections with progress toward universal franchise	Popular elections with limited franchise	Self-determined or party-determined leadership	Self-determined or party-determined leadership	Absence of voting franchise
Virtually unlimited individual liberties	Carefully protected individual liberties	Limited individual liberties	Narrow voting right if franchise exists	Voting franchise varies in scope, limited to approval of party candidates	Absence of individual liberties
Absolute social and economic equality	Vertical mobility with progress toward social and economic equality	Approximate freedom of the press	Irregular tolerance of individual liberties	Absence of constitutionalism	Governmental control of press
Free access to administrative office	Detailed constitutional restraints on government	Limited social and economic equality	Little or no constitutional restraint on government	Extremely narrow political liberties	Enforced economic and social stratification
Absolute freedom of the press	Freedom of the press	Limited constitutional restraint on government	Intermittent martial law	Social structure determined by state	Total economic control by government
	Broad access to public office	Relatively broad access to public office	Direct military influence on government	Substantial economic control by government	Thought control and obliteration of individual conscience
	Unrestricted formation of political groups	Formation of some political groups	Governmental determination of economic system and structure	Government control of mass media	
			Government control of press		

TOWN MEETINGS, such as this one in Stowe, Vermont, are among the last vestiges of direct democracy in the United States.
Standard Oil Co., N.J.

MODERN DEMOCRACY

Within the entire vocabulary of political science, there is probably no single word which has been given more meanings than *democracy*. At the present time, the word has a rather magical connotation and a somewhat tranquilizing effect. Any citizenry which is persuaded that its own governmental system is a democratic one is likely to accept the political power exercised by that system. Hence the Soviet Union claims it is democratic; the government of mainland China calls itself the "People's Republic"; and governments the world over advertise their democratic attributes. However, the word *democracy* (from the Greek *dēmokratía: dēmos* = people and *kratía* = government) was not always held in such esteem and carried an unfavorable meaning until the nineteenth century. The Athenian example of direct democracy was for many years interpreted to mean unrestrained mob rule, for a "true" democracy had to be a system in which all citizens who so desired met periodically to elect state officials and personally enact laws. This kind of government has been extremely rare throughout history (the few examples are Athens' General Assembly, the New England town meeting, and the Swiss *Landsgemeinde*), because the classic model of democracy is extremely difficult to execute. While it may have been possible to have everyone's direct participation in a small town where the citizens were well known to each other and matters to be voted on were comparatively simple, it is far different to attempt direct democracy in a nation such as the United States, which has over 240 million people and which must deal with extremely complex issues. A government that had to submit each issue requiring a decision to so many voters would be too unwieldy to function efficiently in a modern technological society. Therefore, representative democracy has evolved as the only workable alternative.

Representative Democracy

In the modern world, democracy is no longer the direct determination of all government policy by the people. Instead the people play a more general role. Democracy today is "a political system which supplies regular constitutional opportunities for changing the governing officials, and a social mechanism which permits the largest possible part of the population to influence major decisions by choosing among contenders for political office.[1] "Constitutional" means that the government is a limited one. Restrictions on the legal exercise of power apply not only to the people, who must usually wait for election time to change their leadership, but also to the government, which can wield its authority only in specific ways. Representative democracy has several essential ingredients.

Popular Support of Government. Popular support is the crucial test of modern democratic government, for in a democracy the policy makers' legitimacy usually depends on the support they receive in the form of a majority or a plurality of votes cast. The preservation of such support for the leaders by their followers is a key underpinning of democracy, for in a democratic state no one has an inherent right to occupy a position of political power: he must be constitutionally elected by fellow citizens. To prevent legitimacy from becoming identified with only certain individuals, democratic systems provide for elections either at regular intervals (as in the United States) or at certain maximum time spans (as in Britain). Most systems permit reelection. However, the twenty-second amendment to the Constitution, which limits each president to two full terms, is an exception.

The institutions of democratic government also hold lesser officials accountable for their actions and provide for their dismissal if their leadership is found to be wanting. Senators, representatives, local justices of the peace, prime ministers, and presidents who perform their roles to most voters' satisfaction will usually be returned to office; if they fail to do what the majority of the voters want, they are not likely to be reelected. Thus, reelection is the people's means both of expressing support and of controlling the general direction of governmental policy.[2]

---

[1]Seymour M. Lipset, *Political Man* (Garden City, N.Y.: Doubleday, 1960) p. 27. This definition parallels and is drawn from the definition of democracy given in Joseph Schumpeter, *Capitalism, Socialism, and Democracy,* 3rd ed. (New York: Harper & Row, 1950).

[2]The most important statement of this position, and of the logical consequences which follow from it, is in Anthony Downs, *An Economic Theory of Democracy* (New York: Harper & Row, 1957).

Political Competition. The people's right to reject unsatisfactory officials at the polls is bolstered when a choice of policies (usually represented by competing political parties) is offered on the ballot. In the United States, for example, the leadership of the Democratic party has stood, generally, for social programs to correct economic and social problems (for example, Social Security, unemployment insurance, Medicare, and job training programs) and has—until recently—deemphasized a balanced budget. The leaders of the Republican party, on the other hand, have been more inclined to let the forces of the marketplace determine economic direction, and have—at least until Ronald Reagan—stressed fiscal responsibility. Whereas the lines between the two parties are usually not very clear-cut, in most elections there are discernible differences in both philosophy and approach between the two parties which may aid in voter selection. But the party system is not the sole means (and often it is not the most important means) by which the people may choose alternatives. In addition, voters may always choose among individual candidates, regardless of party backing. One representative or prime minister may be personally identified with an issue such as peace, the economy, or clean government. For example, Ronald Reagan's reelection in 1984 drew people from both parties pleased at the decline of inflation, and in 1987 Britons from both major parties reelected Margaret Thatcher as prime minister because they were pleased with her policies of economic growth.

Popular Representation. In representative democracies, the voters elect representatives to act as legislators and, as such, to voice and protect their general interest. Each legislator usually acts for a given district or group of people. The question of just how he or she should act has concerned political theorists for centuries. Some theorists claim that a system is not democratic unless legislators treat election as a mandate to carry out constituents' wishes. In this case, the legislators inform constituents about the alternatives in forthcoming decisions, let them decide what course of action they prefer, and then vote in accordance with constituents' preferences. Other theorists disagree, on the grounds that the constituents don't always have an opinion on issues, and claim that a representative must act as a trustee, carrying out the wishes of constituents when feasible but acting for what he or she feels are the best interests of the community as a whole. Joseph Schumpeter puts the argument against the mandate theory as follows:

> Our chief problems about the classical (democratic) theory centered in the proposition that "the people" hold a definite and rational opinion about every individual question and that they give effect to this opinion—in a democracy—by choosing "representatives" who will see to it that the opinion is carried out.[3]

Of course, the people as a whole do not hold definite opinions on each subject. If they were asked to vote on every question of truck tonnage

---

[3]Schumpeter, *Capitalism, Socialism, and Democracy,* p. 269.

restrictions, parliamentary rules of order, or the staff organization of the Weather Bureau, few would bother voting. Representative democracy, therefore, does not mean that the representative must become a cipher for constituents; rather, it means that the people as a body must be able to control the *general* direction of government policy. For example, if the people have made the general policy decision that equal economic opportunity belongs to everyone, they will leave the administrative details of achieving this goal to their legislators. It is this partnership between the people and the lawmakers that is the essence of modern democracy. E. E. Schattschneider summarizes the case succinctly:

> The beginning of wisdom in democratic theory is to distinguish between the things that the people can do and the things the people cannot do. The worst possible disservice that can be done to the democratic cause is to attribute to the people a mystical, magical omnipotence which takes no cognizance of what very large numbers of people cannot do by the sheer weight of numbers. At this point the common definition of democracy has invited us to make fools of ourselves.[4]

Majority Rule. In any government decision involving important policy making, there is rarely complete agreement. Usually one group of citizens will favor an issue and another group will be against it. If the government is to be the instrument of the popular will, but there is disagreement on issues, then how shall the popular will be determined? The simple answer is that the majority shall rule: in any controversy, the policy that has the support of the greatest number of citizens will become the policy of government. This is the procedure that was used in the democracies of ancient Greece. However, our more modern and practical concept of democracy is "majority rule with minority rights."

A look at any political controversy reveals that, as a fact of political and social life, political minorities do exist. Their members can be seen picketing outside Parliament in London, or protesting in the streets of Paris, or making their presence known in most other major capitals. And the influence of these minorities on government is very important. It is safe to say that every view that is now widely held was once a minority view. Virtually everything that is now public policy—except for laws prohibiting crimes such as murder—became public policy as a result of social conflict between majority and minority groups. Furthermore, just as it is true that a minority view may grow to be almost universally accepted over a period of time, so, too, a majority decision may eventually prove to be unwise, unworkable, or unwanted. Just as minorities may be right, so, too, may majorities be wrong.

Modern liberal democratic tradition tends to place limits on the concept of majority rule. It should not, for example, be used to oppress minorities, and minority rights should only be overruled within certain accepted standards. If minorities are oppressed by it, the will of the majority then becomes the "tyranny of the majority," which is just as foreboding as executive tyranny. In repre-

[4]E. E. Schattschneider, *The Semisovereign People: A Realist's View of Democracy in America* (New York: Holt, Rinehart and Winston, 1960), p. 139.

sentative democracies, the burden is on the majority to persuade minorities rather than to coerce them, and the right of all citizens to dissent is protected. If the majority in power does *not* act in accordance with democratic practice, then citizens may refuse to accept as legitimate the decisions of the governing party, since, in their judgment, it is not governing legitimately.

Ideally, in a democracy there should be a high level of social integration so that society will be tolerant of the differences among its members and so that political conflict will be interest-oriented—that is, directed to issues and policies—rather than based on differences of color, race, religion, nationality, or sex. In large industrialized states and in nations now striving to modernize, where society is composed of groups having very different political interests, the prospects for democracy may depend in large measure on the ability of social organizations to resolve conflicts. If members of different groups do not have adequate contact with one another to realize the pettiness of their prejudices, their intolerances, and other differences and to thereby develop a sense of community, then the fundamental conflicts of society may be irreconcilable by democratic and peaceful methods. The result is likely to be a tyranny of more powerful groups over less powerful ones, even though democratic institutions may exist, and members of the dominant groups may feel quite sure that they are practicing democracy. The smugness of majorities finally angered American blacks, Roman Catholics in Northern Ireland, and Lebanese Shiites.

One more point deserves mention in our discussion of majority rule. In a democracy, the reins of power will occasionally alternate, both in terms of actual officeholders and in terms of prevailing ideals. The party that was in the majority then becomes a minority. A vivid illustration was the change in the presidency from Herbert Hoover to Franklin Roosevelt in 1933, from an almost complete laissez-faire ("hands off") economic approach toward government to the more controlled policies of the New Deal. The Republican party, which had been in the majority, had to assume a minority rule. In a democratic system it is assumed that such changes will be accepted by those who identify themselves with the current minority party and that their opposition will be respectful, civil, legal, and tolerant. The British aptly label their out-parties as "the Loyal Opposition," which remains ready to take the reins of government by lawful means but which meanwhile engages vigorously in the political process in anticipation of the next election. These political tolerances are crucial to the maintenance of a stable democracy and for peaceful successions of power.

Right of Dissent and Disobedience.   If government exists to serve the people, then the people must have the right to resist the commands of government if those commands no longer serve the public will. This right was invoked in 1776 by Thomas Jefferson in the Declaration of Independence, and Henry Thoreau made probably the most profound American defense of civil disobedience when he declared, "All men recognize the right of revolution; that is, the right to refuse allegiance to, and to resist, the government, when its

DISSENT: This antiwar protester harks back to one of the founding fathers to deliver a message outside the White House.
Michael Roskin

tyranny or its inefficiency are great and unendurable."[5] But the most celebrated advocate of civil disobedience was the Indian philosopher Mahatma Gandhi. Gandhi considered his method of resistance to be "civil" because it was legal; that is, whereas it was disobedience, it did not exceed the general legal structure of the state and did not breach moral codes by doing personal harm to others through violence.

Whereas for the most part Thoreau and Gandhi looked on civil disobedience as an individual act of conscience, others have sought to organize it and mobilize it. The most prominent American organizer was Reverend Martin Luther King, Jr., whose nonviolent resistance campaigns of the 1960s in the name of civil rights brought him into controversy. The many sit-ins and marches which he planned, directed, and often led kept him face to face with the law for nearly a decade, and he and other members of his Southern Christian Leadership Conference were often imprisoned. The long-range consequence of their actions, however, was a minor revolution in judicial decisions concerning peaceful protest.

Political Equality. In a democracy, at least in theory, everyone is equally able to participate in government and to compete freely for public office. Critics of democracy point out that the reality is often different. They say it takes a great deal of money—and often specific racial and religious ties—to be able to enter public life, and so large numbers of people are barred from seeking public

[5]Henry David Thoreau, *Civil Disobedience* (Brookline, Mass.: David R. Godine, 1971).

office. A less cynical observer will note, though, that our democratic system of government allows for a change in this situation. Opportunities to serve in public office, at least at the lower levels, are gradually broadening, and minority groups are becoming more adept at political organization.

But there is a second side to political equality, and that is responsibility. If, in a democratic political system, individuals have equal opportunity to express their talents and to achieve personal advancement, then each individual is also honor-bound to resist the temptation to exploit society to achieve such personal advancement. In other words, democracy demands individual self-restraint. For example, a person who holds public office should not use that office for individual profit or for preferential treatment of a small group. Although citizens in a democracy are cynically (and perhaps rightly) prepared to assume that politicians are in politics for their own benefit, or that many selected officials are "on the take," they are still appalled by revelations of corruption in government and approve public censure of officials who misuse public funds or use their office for private gain.

A case in point is the public's reaction to the involvement of White House aides and presidential advisers in the 1972 attempts to place electronic surveillance equipment inside the Democratic National Headquarters in the Watergate. Some commentators, however, pointed to the success of the grand jury investigation, the House panel's vote to impeach, and President Nixon's resignation in 1974 as examples of the effectiveness of the built-in checks and balances in our political system. When both individual self-restraint and some form of checks and balances are lacking, the government may have to impose restraints. A familiar example of government-imposed restraint is antitrust legislation. Monopolistic business practices may provide an opportunity for a few businesspersons to become wealthy. But a business having a monopoly on a product is able to exploit its advantage by charging its customers high prices. Since the businesspersons, anxious to make the largest profits they can, may not regulate their own practices adequately, the government may introduce legislation to regulate their activities.

Popular Consultation. Most government leaders realize that to govern effectively they must know what the people want and must be responsive to these needs and demands. Are citizens disturbed—and, if so, *how* disturbed—about foreign policy, taxes, unemployment, the cost of living? Intelligent leaders realize that they must not get too far ahead of—nor fall too far behind—public opinion. Therefore, a range of techniques has evolved to test opinion. Public opinion polls are taken on specific issues. The media, by thoughtful probing, can create a dialogue between the people and their leaders. At press conferences and news interviews with elected officials, reporters will ask those questions that they believe the people want answers to. Editorials and letters to the editor are also indicators of citizens' moods and feelings.

In recent years, several critics have noted that U.S. officials often rely heavily on the opinions of small segments of their constituencies because they are well organized and highly vocal. On the issue of gun control, for example, polls have consistently shown the public at large to be in favor of stronger regulation of firearms. But the National Rifle Association, a tightly knit and outspoken lobbying organization, has managed to block efforts to strengthen legislation in this area.

TOTALITARIAN GOVERNMENT

It is natural for Americans to think of their system of government as democratic and of governments of the Communist and Fascist states as totalitarian. But not all countries would agree with this judgment. Some nations which Americans regard as totalitarian consider themselves to be "people's democracies" and claim that *their* form of democracy, not ours, is the authentic democratic system. The Western democracies see democracy as a means of achieving the greatest freedom and happiness consistent with the general good; the Communist states see democracy as an abolition of class differences. For the Communists, a truly democratic society is one in which social classes have ceased to exist. To make this goal a reality, there must be a temporary dictatorship with the power to destroy all vestiges of bourgeois capitalist society. In practice, then, communism has stressed the role of the state in bringing society close to the ideal. In common with fascism, it holds that the individual cannot develop in isolation, but only within the framework of service to the state.

What is Totalitarianism?

The twentieth-century phenomenon of totalitarianism is far removed from the autocracies of the past. Whereas rulers such as Peter the Great and Louis XIV were powerful despots, the scope and extent of their power and authority were severely limited by the relatively primitive means of communication and transportation and by the weaponry of the time. Until the twentieth century, communications were so slow and often so difficult that it was impossible for the most autocratic ruler to control effectively or completely all of the territory in his domain. He could demand and receive outward submission to his rule and acknowledgment of his authority, but even Louis XIV—who perhaps came closest to the figure of a modern totalitarian dictator—did not try to control everything in France. Average citizens retained control of their private lives. In contrast, totalitarian states of the twentieth century attempt to remold and transform the people under their control and to regulate every aspect of human life and activity.

Totalitarianism, then, is a unique development dating only from the post-World War I period and made possible by modern technology. It is essentially a system of government in which one party holds all political, economic, military, and judicial power. This party attempts to restructure society, to determine the values of society, and to interfere in the personal lives of individual citizens in such a way as to control their preferences, to monitor their movements, and to restrain their freedoms. Where the autocratic ruler was largely indifferent to his subjects' wishes, the totalitarian state insists on mass participation in activities and makes a deliberate effort to generate enthusiasm for the success of the system. With modern electronic devices, the state is able to control communications and private activities and thereby regulate political life and thought; through electronic data control it is able to coordinate and centralize the utilization of resources and thereby regulate economic life.

Carl J. Friedrich and Zbigniew Brzezinski identified six basic features that are common to all totalitarian states.[6] Four of them would have been impossible to achieve in preindustrial societies and are central to the system.

An All-Encompassing Ideology. Totalitarian ideology is an official body of doctrine that applies to all areas of human life. It includes theories of history, economics, and future political and social development and provides the philosophical framework according to which decisions are made. The ideology portrays the world in terms of black and white, with very little gray in between. Thus, a citizen is judged to be either for the state or against it. And the ideology usually points toward a perfect society which mankind will attain at some distant point in the future (such as Marx's prediction that the classless society would lead to an eventual withering away of the state). All citizens must give tacit adherence to the official ideology, and they usually devote time to its study. Courses on Marxist-Leninist thought are required in the schools of all Communist states.

A Single Party. Only one party may exist legally, and that party is usually led by one man who is so strongly identified with the doctrine and with the destiny of the state that he establishes a cult of personality while dictator. Throughout its history, Fascist Italy was ruled by Mussolini; no one but Hitler ruled Nazi Germany; and Mao Zedong was the sole formal leader of the People's Republic of China from its inception. Stalin was the undisputed leader of the Soviet Union while he lived.

Entrance into the party is controlled (official membership is usually less than 10 percent of the population) and is considered an honor. Certain privileges accompany membership and, in return, the members give their dedication and support to the party. Hierarchically organized and oligarchically controlled, the party is either superior to or tied in with the formal institutions of government. The party leader wields considerable power in the government, and party functionaries hold important posts in the bureaucracy. The party's cadres are responsible for imposing at least outward conformity at all levels of society. Some are responsible for their streets or towns, some for their assembly lines at factories, and still others for their fellow students.

[6]Carl J. Friedrich and Zbigniew Brzezinski, *Totalitarian Dictatorship and Autocracy* (Cambridge, Mass.: Harvard University Press, 1965). Another important study in this area is Hannah Arendt's *The Origins of Totalitarianism* (New York: Harcourt Brace Jovanovich, 1951).

SOVIETS wait in line for hours to file past Lenin's embalmed body in
his tomb facing Red Square and St. Basil's Cathedral.
Michael Roskin

Organized Terror.   A secret-police apparatus, using both physical and
psychological methods, is an essential prop of totalitarian regimes used to ensure
mass allegiance to the party ideology. The Nazi Gestapo, the Soviet NKVD
under Stalin, and Mussolini's OVRA were immune from judicial restraints.
Constitutional guarantees either did not exist or were ignored in these societies,
thus making possible secret arrests, holding people in jail without bringing
charges, and torture. The secret-police system may be directed not only against
specific individuals, but against whole classes of people as well. Depending on the
particular society, these "enemies of the people" may be Jews, landlords,
capitalists, socialists, or clergymen. The threat of the "knock at the door" serves
two purposes: it terrorizes large segments of the population into acquiescence
and it convinces the more gullible citizens that a conspiracy against the security
of the state does, in fact, exist. The mass extermination of entire groups of
people under Hitler and Stalin demonstrates the state's enormous power and the
individual's corresponding helplessness. Systematic terror rarely enforces loyalty
to the regime, however, and the Soviets long ago abandoned the more extreme
tactics of Stalin's era. But the purges and mass executions have been replaced by
the political trial, which dramatizes the value of conformity and provides a
forum for publicizing political doctrine. The trials of dissident literary figures in
the Soviet Union, for example, emphasize the limits of freedom there to write
and to publish.

Monopoly of Communications.   The primary function of the mass media
in totalitarian states is to indoctrinate the people with the official ideology.
Enlightenment and entertainment are subordinated to the needs of the state.

Monopoly of Weapons. Governments of totalitarian nations have a complete monopoly on weapons, thus effectively discouraging armed resistance.

Controlled Economy. Rigid, centralized control is imposed on the economy of every totalitarian state. This control serves a twofold purpose. First, it helps make the state powerful, for all natural resources can be allocated to heavy industrialization, to the production of weapons, or to other requirements of the state. Second, a centralized economy serves as an instrument of political management. For example, people can be forcibly moved wherever they are needed to increase productivity in underpopulated areas, and incentive programs can be initiated to stimulate productivity. In all totalitarian states, the needs or wants of the consumer are secondary to those of the government. This is demonstrated by comparing the technological development of two differently controlled national economies: the Soviet Union was the first to send men to outer space, for example, but the United States has always had superior consumer products.

The Soviet Five-Year plans and the Chinese agrarian reforms are examples of major, all-encompassing economic efforts, and their results cannot be denied. For the first time in Chinese history, the specter of famine no longer exists. And even the totalitarian systems can bend when necessary: whereas Soviet agriculture is collectivized, farmers are permitted to grow vegetables on small private plots and these vegetable gardens are, ironically, one of the most productive sectors of Soviet agriculture. Controlled economies are also possible in democracies (such as Austria), but in these states the goals are determined by democratically elected governments. In times of crisis, however, Western democracies are also capable of executing major, centralized economic plans that subordinate individual desires to the general good. During World War II, for example, both Britain and the United States imposed systems of rationing to make sure that available supplies of food and other necessities would be distributed equitably.

Image and Reality of Total Control

Just as there is no perfect democracy, so also is there no perfect totalitarian dictatorship. Often outsiders are overly impressed by the image of total control projected by these states. Visitors to Fascist Italy were impressed by the seeming law, order, cleanliness, and purposefulness of what they thought was one-man rule. We know now that many Italians thought Mussolini was a bluff, that his organizations and economic plans were mostly for show, and that he wasn't even in firm command of the country. In 1943, as the British and Americans overran the southern part of Italy, Mussolini's own generals—who had been disobeying and lying to him for years—overthrew him in a coup. Then the king of Italy—yes, Italy was technically a kingdom until 1946—*fired* Mussolini as prime minister. Now what kind of total control is that?

Since Stalin's death, every Soviet party chief has denounced the bureaucracy, the deadening hand of routine, and the economic irregularities that impede Soviet growth. But neither Khrushchev, Brezhnev, nor Gorbachev fixed the problem. Much of Soviet economic life runs by means of under-the-table deals and influence that defy centralized planning. Soviet workers steal everything from radios to locomotives and often show up to work drunk or not at all. Where is the total control? The pages of *Pravda* and *Izvestia* thunder against these problems, but the government can't seem to do anything about them.

We should bear in mind that the model of totalitarianism presented earlier is just that—a model—and it will never precisely match reality. The model describes an *attempt* to impose total control, not the achievement of it. At times, even the attempt breaks down and we behold little more than a shambles. Here is how Poland stacked up against the six criteria in the 1980s:

> *Ideology:* Few Poles believed in communism; most were serious Catholics.
>
> *Single Party:* The Polish United Workers party (Communist) was a wreck; many members had quit in disgust. The party as a whole was so weak that the army had to take over.
>
> *Organized Terror:* The ZOMO riot police, recruited from the juvenile thug element, was barely able to restrain crowds of demonstrators. Terror had lost its punch.
>
> *Communications Monopoly:* The official media were widely ignored as Poles picked up their information from rumor, Solidarity leaflets, Sunday mass, and foreign broadcasts.
>
> *Weapons Monopoly:* True, the Polish police and army had a monopoly on weapons, but this is true everywhere in Europe, east or west.
>
> *Controlled Economy:* The Polish economy was largely out of control and in poor health. Foolish foreign borrowing had left Poland with a massive international debt. Shelves were bare in Polish shops. Production dropped, and the regime pleaded for greater economic efforts.

In sum, Poland was a mess. Far from total control, Poland at times looked like total chaos. The Polish example may be an extreme one, but it does underscore the difficulty of applying a model to reality. In addition, we must be aware that there is more than one type of totalitarianism.

Right-wing Totalitarianism.   Right-wing totalitarianism, as exemplified in Italian Fascism and German National Socialism, developed in industrialized nations that were plagued by economic depression, social upheaval, and political confusion and weakness, and in which democratic roots and traditions were shallow and weak. Germany in the late 1920s and early 1930s was in turmoil. The nation was saddled with an enormous reparations debt following World War I; unemployment was widespread; labor disputes were frequent and violent; and a runaway inflation had wiped out the savings of the lower-middle and middle classes—the shopkeepers, the petty bureaucrats, and the skilled workers. In his rise to power, Hitler promised to discipline the labor unions, to restore order, to renounce the humiliating Versailles Treaty, and to protect private property from the communist menace to the east. His program appealed to industrialists, militarists, and middle-class people, who typically constitute the backbone of a Fascist state's support.[7]

Right-wing totalitarianism does not seek to revolutionize society completely; rather it aims to strengthen the existing social order and to glorify the state. It attempts to get rid of those elements of society or those institutions that are believed to prevent the state from achieving greatness, as Hitler strove to annihilate the Jewish and gypsy populations. Economic policies are also directed toward the national glory; they usually direct economic development and production through cartels and national trade associations. These organizations normally permit private ownership.

Left-wing Totalitarianism. The more radical totalitarian ideologies, as exemplified by Soviet and Chinese communism, seek to revolutionize society—to overthrow existing social and political structures in order to form entirely new ones modeled on some futuristic utopia. As a first step, communist regimes try to provide citizens with basic economic needs by taking wealth from the "haves" and distributing it among the "have nots."[8] Communism, therefore, does not appeal to a frustrated middle class, but rather to poor people and idealistic intellectuals. Karl Marx proved to be a poor prophet when he predicted that communism would triumph first in an industrially advanced nation. The system does not flourish in the poorest and most backward countries, either, but rather in those developing societies in which only the first stages of modernization have taken place. The societies most receptive to communism are those that have a frustrated intelligentsia, an urban industrial working class (small as it may be), and a peasantry that has become sufficiently awakened to demand land distribution and a voice in politics.

In communist states, economic change comes as soon as the new leaders have consolidated their control. The change is fundamental and reaches every area of economic activity. Agriculture is collectivized and the factories, means of transportation and communication, and other industries are taken over by the state and run by a centrally directed bureaucracy. The system in practice today is not completely rigid, however, and some communist systems have liberalized and decentralized, although none has ended party supremacy. In the 1950s, Yugoslavia abandoned the Soviet model and introduced "worker self-management," sharply decentralizing the economy. China in the 1980s, for example, turned away from Mao's extreme socialism and permitted small-scale free enterprise with excellent results in food production and industrial growth.[9] In the absence of political democracy in these countries, however, liberalization can always be reversed on orders from the top.

---

[7]Arendt, *The Origins of Totalitarianism.*

[8]Friedrich and Brzezinski, *Totalitarian Dictatorship and Autocracy.*

[9]See James C. F. Wang, *Contemporary Chinese Politics*, 2d ed. (Englewood Cliffs, N. J.: Prentice-Hall, 1985).

AUTHORITARIANISM

The terms *authoritarianism* and *totalitarianism* are often confused, but the two words have different meanings. Authoritarianism is a system of government in which power is exercised by some particular element with minimum popular input. The element may be a family, in which case the authoritarian regime is an absolute monarchy. It may be a social class, as in a liberal monarchy ruled by a king with the assistance of the nobility or in an elitist democracy where power is shared by a few prominent individuals. Or the element may be a strong political party, whose principal concern is to forge domestic solidarity at a time of national need. This type of one-party system is typical of the developing nations of Africa, most of Asia, and much of Latin America. Typically, however, it is the army that brings authoritarian rule.

Authoritarian governments generally do not attempt to control every aspect of human activity. Economic, social, religious, cultural, and familial matters are usually left up to the individual. Shakespeare's King Henry V summed up the authoritarian philosophy when he said, "Every subject's duty is the king's; but every subject's soul is his own."

This is not to say that authoritarian regimes promote individual freedoms. Authoritarianism views society as a hierarchical organization with a specific chain of command under the leadership of one ruler or group. Command, obedience, and order are higher values than freedom, consent, and involvement. Therefore, the citizen is expected to obey laws and pay taxes that he has no voice in establishing. Whereas the institutions of democracy may exist in an authoritarian state, they have little real function. The national legislature, for example, is usually little more than a "rubber stamp" to approve the ruling element's proposals. The theory and practice of an authoritarian ruler were expressed by Louis XIV when he declared, "I am the state."

Spain under Franco (1939–75) was "traditional authoritarian" rather than totalitarian, as the *Caudillo* (Leader) sought political passivity and obedience rather than enthusiastic participation and mobilization. Franco and his supporters had no single ideology to promote, and the economy and press were pluralistic within limited bounds.[10] Jeane J. Kirkpatrick, a political scientist and President Reagan's former ambassador to the United Nations, argued that there is a clear difference between authoritarian and totalitarian regimes. The former (such as Argentina and Brazil) can eventually change, but once a totalitarian system (such as communism) takes over, a country will not change.[11] Both Argentina and Brazil did return to democracy in the 1980s.[12]

---

[10]Juan J. Linz, "An Authoritarian Regime: Spain," in E. Allardt and Y. Littunen, eds., *Cleavages, Ideologies and Party Systems* (Helsinki: Academic Bookstore, 1964).

[11]Jeane J. Kirkpatrick, *Dictatorships and Double Standards: Rationalism and Reason in Politics* (New York: Simon and Schuster, 1982).

[12]For an interesting collection of studies on how countries go from authoritarianism to democracy, see Guillermo O'Donnell, Philippe C. Schmitter, and Laurence Whitehead, eds. *Transitions from Authoritarian Rule: Prospects for Democracy* (Baltimore, Md.: Johns Hopkins University Press, 1986).

Authoritarianism and the Developing Nations

Perhaps the most significant political movement since the end of World War II has been the breaking up of former colonial empires into independent nations. For the most part, the ideological struggle for national independence in these states followed the general philosophical argument of the American Declaration of Independence and the French Declaration of the Rights of Man and Citizen. Yet, once national independence was won, democracy did not last long. A political culture in which self-rule and self-determination were never integral values may not adapt well to political democracy. Then, too, democracy in the Western tradition is characterized by an individualism that is in large part the result of a capitalist market system that stresses competition. The developing societies have preindustrial, traditional peasant economies in which family and tribal cooperation have traditionally been far more important than individual competition and self-enrichment. In many of these societies, in which the levels of education and income are low, the majority of the people are absorbed in the struggle to survive. The leadership often feels that political and economic survival and growth are dependent on strong leaders who can act according to what they perceive is really needed rather than according to what is immediately popular.

Rejecting both Western-style democracy and communist totalitarianism, most of the developing countries have opted for a third alternative—that of single-party dominance. Zimbabwe started with a two-party system in 1980 but found that the parties encouraged tribal animosities and guerrilla terror. The leader of the largest party, Robert Mugabe, cracked down harshly with soldiers of his dominant tribe and created a single-party system, arguing that this was the only way to build unity and that Zimbabwe would still have democracy within the party. With such arguments, many Third World countries have become authoritarian. They preserve a tenuous stability, but at the price of restricted political and press freedom and one-man rule.

SUGGESTED READINGS

ARENDT, HANNAH. *The Origins of Totalitarianism.* New York: Harcourt Brace Jovanovich, 1951. Profound insights into the psychology and theory of totalitarianism by the philosopher who helped coin the word.

BURNHEIM, JOHN. *Is Democracy Possible?* Berkeley, Cal.: University of California Press, 1986. Worries about democracy in an age of gigantic institutions and offers ideas to restructure democracy.

DAHL, ROBERT A. *A Preface to Democratic Theory.* Chicago: University of Chicago Press, 1956. Original, insightful essays on democratic theory, from Madisonian democracy to polyarchy.

———. *After the Revolution? Authority in a Good Society.* New Haven, Conn.: Yale University Press, 1970. During a time of social upheaval, Dahl offered some wise and calming suggestions on democratic authority.

DUNCAN, GRAEME, ed. *Democratic Theory and Practice.* New York: Cambridge University Press, 1983. Sixteen essays review the theories and deficiencies of democracy in several lands.

FRIEDRICH, CARL J., AND ZBIGNIEW BRZEZINSKI. *Totalitarian Dictatorship and Autocracy.* Cambridge, Mass.: Harvard University Press, 1965. A comprehensive and penetrating analysis of the nature of totalitarianism.

FRIEDRICH, CARL J., MICHAEL CURTIS, AND BENJAMIN R. BARBER. *Totalitarianism in Perspective: Three Views.* New York: Praeger, 1969. Barber sharply criticizes the concept of "totalitarianism" and questions its validity.

LIJPHART, AREND. *Democracies: Patterns of Majoritarian and Consensus Government in Twenty-One Countries.* New Haven, Conn.: Yale University Press, 1984. Superb survey of the varieties of democracy, emphasizing that it can function in many settings.

O'DONNELL, GUILLERMO, ET AL., EDS. *Transitions from Authoritarian Rule: Prospects for Democracy.* Baltimore, Md: Johns Hopkins University Press, 1986. Case studies of the growth of democracy recently in Latin America and southern Europe.

ORWELL, GEORGE. *1984.* New York: New American Library, 1971. A futuristic vision of a society in which all human activity is regulated.

PEELER, JOHN A. *Latin American Democracies: Colombia, Costa Rica, Venezuela.* Chapel Hill, N.C.: University of North Carolina Press, 1985. A path-breaking study of how democracy is difficult but possible in Latin America.

PERLMUTTER, AMOS. *Modern Authoritarianism: A Comparative Institutional Analysis.* New Haven, Conn.: Yale University Press, 1984. Excellent synthesis of the varieties of authoritarianism, emphasizing its marriage of ideologies to institutions.

POWELL, G. BINGHAM, JR. *Contemporary Democracies: Participation, Stability, and Violence.* Cambridge, Mass.: Harvard University Press, 1982. A methodologically sophisticated study of how democracies attempt to reduce violence by offering citizen participation.

SCHUMPETER, JOSEPH. *Capitalism, Socialism, Democracy.* 3rd ed. New York: Harper & Row, 1950. A comprehensive examination of these three systems and the nature of the political systems that mix parts of each.

chapter 5

Democracy in America: Pluralist and Elitist Views

Among the many nations that claim democracy as the basis for government, is there one in which the people actually make decisions? Do the people really rule in the German Democratic Republic (East Germany) or in the People's Republic of China? Do the citizens of the United States decide whether to build a road, subsidize farmers, or sell wheat to the Soviet Union?

In theory, the American people do make these decisions—indirectly, through elected representatives. Few people would maintain that in a country as large and complex as the United States a democracy should or could be run in the classical sense of mass participation in every political decision. This might have been possible in ancient Greece, but some theorists argue that classical democracy has never been possible—and never will be. Italian political scientist Gaetano Mosca, for example, argued that government always falls into the hands of a few.

> In all societies—from societies that are very undeveloped and have largely attained the dawnings of civilization, down to the most advanced and powerful societies— two classes of people appear—a class that rules and a class that is ruled. The first class, always the less numerous, performs all of the political functions, monopolizes power, and enjoys the advantages that power brings, whereas the second, the more numerous class, is directed and controlled by the first, in a manner that is now more or less legal, now more or less arbitrary and violent.[1]

Even those political scientists who question Mosca's generalization to "all societies" feel that participatory democracy is not possible in large modern societies. Government is too big and the issues too complex for every citizen to have a voice in decisions. In the words of Robert Dahl, "The key political, economic, and social decisions . . . are made by tiny minorities. . . . It is difficult— nay, impossible—to see how it could be otherwise in large political systems."[2]

Given the impracticality—even the impossibility—of classical, participatory democracy in modern societies, and given the variety of governments "by the few" which claim to be democratic, the problem is to find answers to two questions: How can we determine whether or not a government is democratic? And who actually governs in a democracy?

In Chapter 4, democracy was defined as a political system which provides opportunities for changing public officials and which allows the people to influence decision making through voting. In that chapter, a set of criteria was proposed for evaluating the democratic nature of a governmental system:

1. Officials must have popular support in the form of votes, and elected officials must be held accountable.
2. There must be choice in voting and competition in the political system.
3. Legislation must be made through representation.
4. There must be majority rule with tolerance for the minority voice.
5. There must be right of dissent and civil disobedience.
6. There must be equal opportunity to try for public office.
7. Officials must strive to know public opinion.

[1]Gaetano Mosca, *The Ruling Class* (New York: McGraw-Hill, 1939), p. 50.
[2]Robert A. Dahl, "Power, Pluralism, and Democracy: A Modest Proposal" (Paper delivered at the 1964 annual meeting of the American Political Science Association), p. 3.

Using these criteria as a basis for judgment, we can begin to determine whether or not a system of government is democratic, thereby answering the first question posed before. But what about the second question? Who actually governs in a democracy? Are the wishes and desires of the majority reflected in the decisions of elected officials? In the United States, do the people govern, or is this country, too, a government "by the few"? In an attempt to answer these questions, this chapter examines two theories of democracy—elitism and pluralism.

TWO THEORIES: ELITISM AND PLURALISM

Elitism

Because this country's political culture is predominantly democratic, the concept of elitism is offensive to many Americans. We associate the term with the feudal aristocracies of medieval Europe, the warlords of China and Japan, and the political and military dictatorships of modern times (Hitler's and Stalin's inner circles). But an elite is not necessarily hereditary, tyrannical, or self-seeking.

Broadly defined, an elite is a small group of people who rule in the sense of directly initiating (or vetoing) decisions about "who gets what, when, and how." For example, in a hospital doctors constitute an elite. They decide who gets what treatment, when, and how. No one is born a doctor; their elite status derives from expertise that is available to anyone who can complete medical training. Nor are doctors "tyrannical"; they do not deprive people of their freedom to move about or to eat certain foods out of caprice or out of desire for power.

A political elite may, like the medical profession, be open to anyone who seeks a position in government and is capable of filling that position, or it may be closed to all but those who were born to the "right" family or those with large sums of money or those of a certain religion. It may be responsive to the needs and desires of the many, or it may be aloof and self-seeking. A political elite may be temporary (lasting for a single administration or until a specific problem is solved) or long-lasting. It may hold a monopoly over power within a society, or it may share power with other, competing elites.

One prominent elite theorist was Robert Michels, a turn-of-the-century German Social Democrat, a believer in equality and democracy. Looking at his own party, though, Michels came to the conclusion that no matter what its democratic intent, the Social Democratic party was stratifying into clear classes of leaders and led and internally was not very democratic at all. Michels reasoned as follows: To accomplish its political goals, the Social Democrats had to be well-organized; they were doing political combat with powerful conservative forces. Organization means leaders. Once these leaders are in the party's top positions, they tend to see their role as permanent, to lock themselves into power. Most of the rank-and-file party members agree with this, obey the leaders, and do not attempt to replace them. The leadership then becomes an oligarchy, with rule by the few. Michels went so far as to call this tendency the

"Iron Law of Oligarchy": No matter how democratic they start out, human organizations become oligarchic.[3]

Michels, despairing of democracy, moved to Mussolini's Italy to embrace fascism. Should Michels have been so pessimistic about democracy? Later studies suggest that his "Iron Law of Oligarchy" is an exaggeration. In a detailed study of Norway's parties, Henry Valen and Daniel Katz found that the relationship of leaders and led was a two-way street, with party leaders paying attention to members' demands. "The political process within the party structure is of the character of rubber rather than of iron," they concluded.[4] Accordingly, a "Rubber Law of Oligarchy" might be a more accurate term.

Political scientists are divided over the question of what kind of elite or elites govern America. Some—for example, C. Wright Mills—take a "single elite" position.[5] According to this view, America is ruled by a single, relatively closed, upper-class elite that responds to public pressure only when its position is threatened. This group holds a power monopoly in America because it controls essential resources—including wealth, education, executive and legal experience, and "connections" (with political, military, business, and educational leaders). Membership in the ruling elite depends on socioeconomic status, not on elections or expertise. The elite is stable over time and through changing issues.

This elitist view holds that America's power elite does admit new members—partly to rejuvenate its own ranks, partly to prevent potential leaders from building counterelites. Once admitted, however, new members tend to become conservative. A common interest in preserving the system and their position in it holds the elite together. When members differ over specific issues they accommodate one another rather than disturb the existing power structure. The elite does take the "masses" into account, but only when it chooses to do so. Elections are largely symbolic; a candidate can seldom be elected to public office without elite support (specifically, money and "connections"). In short, the people must choose between two candidates who basically share a common orientation and background; thus, they have little chance of making a dramatic change in public policy. A number of advocates of elite theory argue that in the United States and other Western democracies the elite actually protects the basic democratic values of individual liberty, due process of law, limited government, and free enterprise. Research shows that members of the elite are more tolerant than the average person, who is typically ill-informed, intolerant, and antidemocratic.[6] The elitist position thus suggests that government by the elite, which

---

[3]Robert Michels, *Political Parties: A Sociological Study of the Oligarchic Tendency of Modern Democracy* (Glencoe, Ill.: Free Press, 1958).

[4]Henry Valen and Daniel Katz, *Political Parties in Norway: A Community Study* (Oslo, Norway: Universitetsforlaget, 1967), p. 98.

[5]C. Wright Mills, *The Power Elite* (New York: Oxford University Press, 1956).

[6]An important early study that uncovered the greater liberalism of elites is Samuel Stauffer, *Communism, Conformity, and Civil Liberties* (Garden City, N.Y.: Doubleday, 1955). A recent and more-detailed confirmation of this thesis is Herbert McClosky and Alida Brill, *Dimensions of Tolerance: What Americans Believe About Civil Liberties* (New York: Russell Sage, 1983).

PLURALISM OR ELITISM? Are U.S. party conventions such as this
one the meeting ground of many groups and interests or the behind-
the-scenes deals of a powerful few?

Stan Wakefield

seems inimical to the nature of democracy, is actually the means by which we
preserve the basic tenets of our system.

Pluralism

A second school of political scientists, the pluralists, contends that
America is governed not by a single elite, but by a number or plurality of
specialized, competing groups.[7] Membership in these influential groups varies
with the times and with the issues. Business lobbyists and union leaders, for
example, may unite to support high tariffs on foreign goods but oppose one
another on the issue of wage controls, with neither taking an active role in the
controversy over school busing. Competition among several groups prevents any
one person or group from gaining control of the political system. Pluralists
maintain that political decisions are the result of bargaining and competition
among groups. The government, according to this view, plays the role of
arbitrator, making sure that groups with differing interests adhere to the "rules
of the game."

Robert Dahl, among others, believes that this pluralist system is essentially democratic, in the sense that individuals and minorities *can* influence
decision makers through elections and interest groups. No public official can

[7]Note that pluralists do not believe America is a populist democracy, ruled by the people.
For this reason, pluralists are sometimes called "plural-elitists." See Robert Dahl, *A Preface
to Democratic Theory* (Chicago: University of Chicago Press, 1956).

afford to ignore his electorate. If a group of people with a stake in a particular decision organize and speak out, and if their viewpoint is considered legitimate by the majority of the electorate, their representatives will respond.[8] In the American political system, Dahl writes, "all active and legitimate groups in the population can make themselves heard at some crucial stage in the process of decision."[9] Thus, pluralists suggest that America is governed by a plurality of groups that check one another in open competition.

WHO RULES AMERICA?

Neither elitists nor pluralists accept the traditional image of America as a populist democracy governed by the common man. Both recognize that policy decisions are made by a small number of people who tend to be wealthier, better educated, and "better connected" than the average American. However, elitists and pluralists differ sharply over the question of elite solidarity and the meaning of public participation in elections and interest groups. Elitists hold that the "men at the top" work together and that elections and interest groups are largely symbolic; pluralists contend that those in power are highly competitive and that elections and interest groups give the common man access to the system.

The Elite View

America's Founding Fathers, according to elitists, were "bond holders, investors, merchants, real-estate owners, and planters"—not average citizens.[10] To these men, the primary function of government was to protect individuals from political tyranny (a king) and mass movements. They designed the Constitution to limit government and thus preserve economic individualism.

Between the Revolution and the Civil War, the government was dominated by three different elites. In 1800 Thomas Jefferson, a Virginia planter, unseated the mercantile aristocracy and its Federalist party; in 1828 Andrew Jackson, a Western *nouveau riche,* replaced the Jeffersonians. But basic policy changed only slightly when Jefferson and Jackson each took office. This peaceful transfer, say elitists, is evidence that the elite considered stability more important than political ideology.

Only once in American history did elite consensus break down—in the years leading up to the Civil War. Both northern and southern aristocrats saw

[8]Organization is a key point here. Pluralists do not argue that private individuals can influence decision makers, but that "active and legitimate" interest groups can.

[9]Robert A. Dahl, *A Preface to Democratic Theory,* p. 137. Dahl suggests that to be effective, a group must be *both* active and legitimate. Blacks prior to the 1960s had a legitimate claim to a role in politics, but they were not active; Communists have long been organized and active, but the majority of the electorate does not consider their viewpoint legitimate.

[10]See Charles Beard, *An Economic Interpretation of the Constitution* (New York: Free Press, 1935); and Forrest McDonald, *We the People: The Economic Origins of the Constitution* (Chicago: University of Chicago Press, 1958).

the West as the key to power. This rivalry, not ideological differences, led to war. When the South was defeated, control of the economy and, indirectly, of government passed to the rising class of industrial capitalists, who ruled unchecked for the next fifty to sixty years.

Pluralists often cite the New Deal as evidence that the people do influence the government. Elitists disagree. Roosevelt, himself, was a member of the upper class. He saw that the "rugged individualism" of the early capitalists had failed in the Great Depression and realized that the elite would have to become more public-minded if it was to maintain its position. The New Deal was based on a growing sense of *noblesse oblige,* and his new attitude led directly to America's involvement in international affairs as the guardian of democracy, and indirectly to the growth of the military.

Since World War II, the military has been industry's biggest consumer, and industry government's biggest supporter. "Corporate chieftains" and "professional warlords" rule America, according to C. Wright Mills.[11] President Eisenhower, on leaving office in 1961, warned of a "military-industrial complex" that exercised "unwarranted influence" on U.S. life. Elite theorists, many of whom have a leftist bent, see this as continuing.[12]

Of course, the past is always open to a degree of interpretation. How do elitists document the existence of a power elite in America today?

The Power Elite. A quick reading of *Who's Who in America,* elitists argue, shows that a relatively small group of men dominate executive positions in government, finance, industry, and education. These men move back and forth, working now in government, now in business. Elitists feel this overlap in personnel disproves the pluralist concept of independent, competing elites. Although formally separated, American business and American government are run by the same people.

The effect of personnel overlap is most obvious in the government's regulatory agencies, which often become covert lobbies for the interests they are supposed to regulate. Logically, the president appoints executives who have experience in the field. Most of these appointees consider their position in government temporary and are reluctant to make decisions that might jeopardize future jobs in the private sector. Because of budget limitations, regulatory agencies sometimes depend on private research for information. For example, a decision about whether to permit an oil company to drill offshore may depend on that company's study of the ocean floor. In addition, agency officials and industry lobbyists spend a good deal of time together. Familiarity—not necessarily corruption—may gradually cause them to think alike.

To these arguments, elitists add the fact that most government officials are wealthy, upper-class, and well educated—for several reasons. Only people

---

[11]C. Wright Mills' *The Power Elite* is the classic statement of this position.

[12]See, for example, the critical elite analysis of Michael Parenti, *Democracy for the Few,* 4th ed. (New York: St. Martin's, 1983).

POWER ELITE? Are American politicians, businesspeople, and military leaders so intertwined as to form a "power elite," as C. Wright Mills charged?

Karl H. Schumacher, The White House

who can afford to temporarily abandon their careers for a campaign or to take relatively low-paying government jobs are able to seek public office, appointed or elected. Moreover, a person who does not have executive experience and connections may fail as an administrator. C. Wright Mills wrote:

> To be celebrated, to be wealthy, to have power, requires access to major institutions, for the institutional positions men occupy determine in large part their chances to have and to hold valued experience.[13]

Elite theorists suggest that the executives of the country's biggest corporations have as much or more to say about "who gets what, when, and how" as do government officials. Despite antitrust laws, a handful of giant corporations dominates the economy. Like the government, they have the power to levy taxes (by raising prices), to affect the quality of life (with products and wages), and to change the environment (with chemical wastes, strip mining, smoke stacks). Corporations may influence legislators with campaign donations, with personal favors such as the loan of an airplane, and through their power to close a plant which a congressman's constituents depend on for jobs.

In recent years, regulation of corporations has been complicated by the growth of holding companies (whose only "product" is stock certificates) and

[13]Mills, *The Power Elite*, pp. 10–11.

institutional investors (banks, mutual funds, insurance companies) who have taken over the role once played by such men as Henry Ford. If the government suspects "foul play," it prosecutes General Motors or the Dreyfus Fund, not individuals; corporate officials are not held accountable for their decisions. In addition, a single man may be on the board of directors of several companies. Antitrust laws are, according to elitists, ineffective against these interlocking directorates.

Pluralists argue that the people—groups of people—*can* influence and regulate government and corporation policy. If a president or mayor appoints corrupt officials to regulatory agencies, the people can vote against him. They can refuse to buy unsafe automobiles or give time and money to citizen's lobbies. Elitists do not feel that public pressure—through elections or interest groups—influences those in power.

Elections.   For elections to be a truly effective democratic institution, say elite theorists Dye and Zeigler, they would have to meet four conditions:

1. Competing candidates would offer clear policy alternatives.
2. Voters would be concerned with policy questions.
3. Majority preference on these questions would be ascertained in election results.
4. Elected officials would be bound by the positions they assumed during the campaign.[14]

Only rarely, these authors conclude, do the two major parties offer voters a true choice of "policy alternatives"—partly because Republicans and Democrats agree on goals, if not on methods, and partly because both recognize that voters do not respond to ideological debate. Despite party loyalties, few Americans can identify their own political position (liberal, middle-of-the road, conservative), and few see clear differences between the two major parties. Apparently voters choose candidates on the basis of their personalities and presentation, not for their policies. In 1964, for example, Lyndon Johnson strongly opposed Barry Goldwater's "hawkish" stand on Vietnam. Polls indicated, however, that 52 percent of those who favored a stronger stand—even if it meant invading North Vietnam—voted not for Goldwater, but for Johnson.

Since so many eligible voters fail to exercise their franchise, no president in modern times has won the votes of a majority of the American people. In fact, in 1968 and 1980 a majority of eligible voters either stayed away from the polls or voted for a third-party candidate. In 1984, only 53 percent of the eligible population voted. Elections thus do not represent majority opinion.

But even if a majority of voters were to express their opinion on the issues at the polls, there is no guarantee that elected officials would abide by their

[14]Thomas R. Dye and L. Harmon Zeigler, *The Irony of Democracy: An Uncommon Introduction to American Politics,* 7th ed. (Monterey, Calif.: Brooks/Cole, 1986); this text forms the basis for this section.

campaign platforms. Once elected, President Johnson followed a policy in Vietnam that came close to Goldwater's platform. President Nixon took steps toward a wide-ranging détente with the USSR and reopened relations with the People's Republic of China even though he had campaigned domestically for years as a staunch anti-Communist. In 1932, Franklin D. Roosevelt campaigned as a fiscal conservative, but once in office he instituted the most liberal reforms of the century. In 1980, Ronald Reagan campaigned against federal budget deficits, but in office he produced the biggest budget deficits in U.S. history. What goes in (voting) and what comes out (policy) are not necessarily connected.

For these reasons, elitists consider elections a mere "symbolic exercise" designed to give the people the feeling that they participate. According to Murray Edelman, elections allow the people to express "quiet resentments and doubts about particular political acts [and] reaffirm belief in the fundamental rationality and democratic nature of the system."[15]

Interest Groups. According to elitist theorists, labor unions, professional associations, mass political movements, PTAs, and so on tend to become oligarchic. Few people have time to work actively in interest groups: control falls into the hands of the active few. As long as these leaders act within broad limits of propriety, the inactive majority accepts their authority as spokesmen. Gradually the leaders begin to personify the group; rank-and-file opinions are considered "unofficial." For example, in the early 1960s, AFL-CIO officials backed Johnson's civil rights legislation, although the rank and file generally preferred *not* to compete with black workers. Like government and corporation officials, interest group leaders develop a vested interest in maintaining the system and their position in it. In a sense, they join the elite.

The Pluralist View

The pluralist view of America is basically an extension of Madisonian democracy. Like other early American political thinkers, Madison believed that power corrupts—that public officials tend to become tyrannical if left unchecked. "Ambition must be made to counteract ambition," he wrote.[16] The constitutional system of separated legislative, executive, and judicial functions he and others designed was intended to check the power of individuals and the interests they represented.

Madison also believed that class conflict was inevitable and potentially disruptive: "Those who hold and those who are without property have ever formed distinct interests in society."[17] At any time, the unpropertied majority might rise up, threatening the propertied minority. In a rather sophisticated

---

[15]Murray Edelman, *The Symbolic Uses of Power* (Urbana, Ill.: University of Illinois Press, 1964), p. 17.
[16]*The Federalist*, No. 51.
[17]*The Federalist*, No. 10.

argument, Madison suggested that the way to protect minorities (such as the wealthy Founding Fathers) was to extend the vote to the entire population. The diversity of the American population, he reasoned, would prevent majority tyranny.

> Extend the sphere, and you take in a greater variety of parties and interests; you make it less probable that a majority of the whole will have a common motive to invade the rights of other citizens; or if such a common motive exists, it will be more difficult for all who feel it to discover their own strength, and to act in unison with each other.[18]

In *A Preface to Democratic Theory,* pluralist Robert Dahl maintains that America *does* operate on a checks-and-balances system, although not exactly the one Madison foresaw. The writers of the Constitution assumed that the House would become the instrument of the people—a hotbed of radical, populist thinking—and that the president would check Congress with his veto. In practice today, according to Dahl, these roles are reversed.

> It is the president who is the policy maker, the creator of legislation, and the self-appointed spokesman for the national majority, whereas the power of Congress is more and more that of a veto—a veto exercised, as often as not, on behalf of groups whose privileges are threatened by presidential policy.[19]

To carry out his policies, the president depends heavily on his party's organization. Madison did not foresee the role political parties would play in the American political system.

How do pluralists rebut the evidence that a power elite rules America? They reject, first, the notion of elite consensus.

Decentralized Power.   Pluralists feel that there is abundant evidence of disagreement and competition between powerful individuals and groups, both in government and in the private sector. Congress sometimes rejects presidential nominations for high office and legislative proposals. The government, under Congressional mandate, simultaneously subsidizes tobacco growing and warns against cigarette smoking. The federal government guaranteed loans to save Chrysler but did not put quotas or increase tariffs on Japanese cars. The gigantic U.S. oil industry is understandably pro-Arab, but Israel is the largest recipient of U.S. foreign aid. If government, industry, and military leaders were working together, as elitists suggest, these disagreements and inconsistencies would not occur.

What about personnel overlap? Pluralists argue that C. Wright Mills and other elitists overemphasize positions in government and business, confusing

---

[18]*Ibid.* The writers of the Constitution, for example, might have stipulated that only landowners could vote; small farmers might then have banded together to force their will on large landowners. (In fact, this happened in states that instituted property qualifications for the vote.) With everyone—that is, every white male—voting, clerks, merchants, shopkeepers, and so on would check the small farmers.

[19]Dahl, *A Preface to Democratic Theory,* p. 142.

potential and actual power. The fact that people are chairpersons or department secretaries or generals does not necessarily mean that they control their local school boards, interfere with plans for state highways, or influence foreign policy. They may not be interested in anything but their business; their company or agency may be organized in a way that limits their influence. For example, in most cases, members of a board of directors limit participation in a company to selecting managers. These managers, not the directors, form company policy. Pluralists feel that Mills and others have failed to demonstrate that people in high positions actually have much influence.

In addition, elitists are criticized for having failed to show evidence of a significant level of interaction among individuals in key positions. Does America's elite meet regularly to decide how to proceed on new issues? Does the automobile industry consult with the president of IBM before announcing that it will not be able to meet a deadline for antipollution devices? Pluralists see little proof of continuing accommodation and cooperation among members of the elite.

In a study of New Haven, Connecticut, Dahl found that the upper class tended to be aloof toward politics and community affairs. Decisions were the result of bargaining among interested groups. Some business leaders supported the mayor's efforts in urban renewal, primarily because they had a stake in the inner city. They did not become involved in education (most of their children attended private or suburban schools) or in local party politics. Power in American communities, Dahl concluded, is highly decentralized.[20]

Electoral Accountability. Pluralists categorically reject the idea that elections are merely a "symbolic exercise." All elected officials must go to the voters periodically, and this eventually influences both their policy decisions and their personal conduct in office. "Elected officials," wrote Dahl, "keep the real or imagined preferences of constituents constantly in mind in deciding what policies to adopt or reject."[21]

How do officials judge what their constituents want? They read their mail, the newspapers, and the polls.[22] They meet with businessmen who are bidding for a contract, backing a job training program or a new arts center, or contributing to their campaign fund. They also meet with senior citizens, black activists, and mothers demanding day-care centers—if these people are insistent. Their exposure to public opinion is thus biased in favor of those with a stake in a particular decision and those who express their views publicly. The so-called

[20]Robert A. Dahl, *Who Governs?* (New Haven, Conn.: Yale University Press, 1961). This study is discussed further in the next section.

[21]Ibid., p. 164.

[22]A study of the factors that influence a congressman's vote showed that it is the official's perception of his or her constituency's opinion rather than the constituency's actual attitude that influences his or her position. See Warren E. Miller and Donald E. Stokes, "Constituency Influence in Congress," *American Political Science Review* 57 (March 1963):45–56.

silent majority does not directly influence decisions, but active interest groups do. The people an elected official has either helped or offended are the people most likely to vote; he cannot afford to ignore them.

However, the silent majority does influence officials indirectly. If officials do not successfully reconcile competing or conflicting activists within their jurisdiction, they are likely to create new interest groups that oppose them. Elected officials must keep both the active and the potentially active constantly in mind in what political scientist Carl J. Friedrich called the "rule of anticipated reactions."[23] Even though the public is quiet for the moment, officials try to avoid decisions that will make people angry. In this way, even quiet people have an input.

Why are so many Americans apathetic? Nonvoting, according to pluralists, is primarily an expression of "passive consent," not just disillusionment with the political system. Although minority groups have been discouraged or prevented from voting, most nonvoters are simply more concerned about their homes, families, and jobs than about politics. It is only when these elements are threatened (for example, by unemployment), that the politically passive form interest groups and vote; otherwise they often leave decisions to the experts. Elections thus tend to be a combination of interested minority will and tacit majority consent. Voters and nonvoters influence political decision makers, even though they do not control them directly.

But do interested voters have a choice in elections? Pluralists reject the idea that the elite consensus within and between the two major parties goes so deep as to deny conflict over issues. Both parties are composed of people from different locales with different interests. The divisions within the Democratic party, which includes southern conservatives and northern liberals, are legendary. Because parties lack even internal consensus, party power is decentralized to state and local organizations. Party politics is a process of endless bargaining among interested minorities.

Interest Groups. Pluralists see interest groups as the key to American democracy. A single person may not be able to make his or her views heard, but organized groups can, in one of two ways. First, they can help candidates who are sympathetic to their cause by providing manpower, special skills, equipment, money, and publicity. A printers' union may donate handbills and posters; a PTA may invite a candidate to address its meeting; an ethnic group may raise money with a street fair. The degree of positive support a group can offer depends on its membership and resources and on whether it finds a sympathetic elected official. If it does not, the second way it can influence decision makers is by threatening the stability of their district. The ability to influence public opinion extends power to the powerless—to average citizens. In order to restore

---

[23]Carl J. Friedrich, *Constitutional Government and Politics* (New York: Harper, 1937), pp. 16–18.

INTEREST GROUPS, such as these Phila-delphia trade unionists voicing their demands during a 1982 visit by President Reagan, are a key element in the pluralist picture.

UPI/Bettmann Newsphotos

stability and public confidence, an official must respond to organized pressure, whatever its source.

Similarly, interest groups can influence corporate policy by pressuring elected officials to intervene on their behalf or by generating adverse publicity. Civil rights groups pressured the government to insist on integration in construction companies working on federal contracts; environmentalists, galvanized by the Three Mile Island accident, forced the nuclear power industry to adhere to stricter standards; women's rights organizations forced businesses to change their policies toward women.

Pluralists thus argue that organized minorities and social movements play an integral role in the American system. As Dahl wrote, "The making of governmental decisions is not a majestic march of great majorities united on certain matters of basic policy. It is the steady appeasement of relatively small groups."[24]

PLURAL ELITES: A SYNTHESIS

As the student may have judged, there are elements of truth in both the elite and the pluralist pictures of politics. A more accurate picture would combine the two views. A first step is to recognize that elites are plural; that is, rarely does a society have a single, fused elite, as C. Wright Mills proposed. In a complex, modern society, one can discern business elites, bureaucratic elites, military elites,

[24]Dahl, *A Preface to Democratic Theory.* p. 140.

agricultural elites, labor elites, and so on. They cooperate or conflict, depending on circumstances, much as pluralists have argued. But this interaction is not the whole group in question interacting with other whole groups; it is small, elite representatives of one group interacting with small, elite representatives of other groups.

The pure elitist views society as a single pyramid, with a tiny elite at the top. The pure pluralist views society as a collection of billiard balls colliding with each other and with government to produce policy. Both views are overdrawn. A synthesis that more accurately reflects reality might be a series of small pyramids, each capped by an elite, or a collection of small planets with a large mountain at each north pole also topped by an elite. There is interaction of many units, as the pluralists would have it, but there is also stratification of leaders and followers, as elitist thinkers would have it. (See fig. 5-1.)

Political scientists have tried to define this situation in various terms. Robert Dahl called it a "polyarchy," the rule of the leaders of several groups who have reached stable understandings with each other.[25] Arend Lijphart called it "consociational democracy," a means by which divided societies can prevent violence among groups.[26] The image of democracy offered by these authors goes beyond the one-man, one-vote definition of democracy. There may, of course, be universal suffrage, but in divided societies this can be a prescription for intergroup conflict and even civil war. What matters in such societies is that the elites of each important group have struck a bargain to play by the rules of a constitutional game and to restrain their followers from violence.

Lijphart's example of where this has worked successfully is the Netherlands, where there are serious differences among Catholics, Calvinists, and secular people. Why hasn't Holland fallen apart? Because the elites of these blocs have reached an "elite accommodation" or balance among each other. Such an accommodation is not automatically or necessarily the case. Elites must do two things: keep their people in line and reach bargains with the elites of other groups. When they do not, the results can be terrible to behold: consider Lebanon.

For centuries Lebanon has been deeply divided along religious lines among Maronite Christians, the Greek Orthodox, Greek Catholics, Sunni Moslems, Shiite Moslems, the Druse, and others. In 1943, leaders of the two largest groups, the Maronite Christians and the Sunni Moslems, reached an unwritten agreement known as the National Pact, requiring that the president of Lebanon be a Maronite, the prime minister a Sunni, the speaker of parliament a Shiite, the deputy prime minister Greek Orthodox, and the defense minister a Druse.[27] For some 30 years the National Pact, a model of "polyarchy" or

---

[25]Robert A. Dahl, *Polyarchy: Participation and Opposition* (New Haven, Conn.: Yale University Press, 1971).

[26]Arend Lijphart, *Democracy in Plural Societies: A Comparative Exploration* (New Haven, Conn.: Yale University Press, 1977).

[27]For an excellent discussion of Lebanon's problem, see Samir Khalaf, *Lebanon's Predicament* (New York: Columbia University Press, 1987).

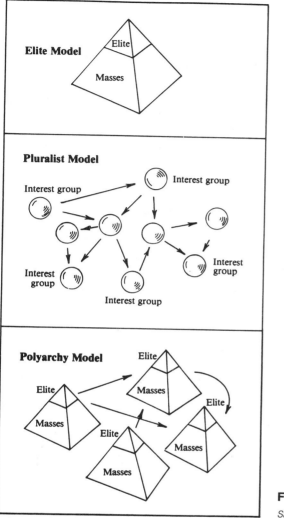

Figure 5-1

Sandra Rife

"consociation," worked well, and Lebanon became an island of stability and prosperity in the Middle East; but this lasted only as long as elites were able to keep their people in line and accommodate other elites.

The delicate balance began to tip when Moslems demanded a bigger say. Moslems had been assigned minority status using the out-of-date 1932 census; Christians deliberately avoided a newer census, but most observers agreed the Moslems had become a majority. In 1958 the Moslems sided with the pan-Arab aspirations of Egyptian President Nasser and serious fighting erupted, quelled in part by U.S. Marines. In 1975 Lebanon fell apart as the Moslems joined with radical Palestinians in full-scale civil war. Each religious group in Lebanon now has its private army and sometimes massacres civilians. Some wonder if Lebanon will ever be put back together again.

The Lebanese case is graphic. When there was accommodation among elites, the system worked. When elite consensus broke down, so did the system. During the period of the National Pact, members of the various groups did not slowly learn to love each other and temper their differences; the differences were too great. But they did live in peace for as long as their plural elites were able to strike a bargain. The elite bargain did not erase conflict, but it did serve to *manage* conflict.

To what extent are other countries examples of "conflict management" by elites? The United States can be seen in this fashion, with its interplay of business, labor, ethnic, regional, and other elites, each delivering enough to keep their people in line, each cooperating to varying degrees with other elites. When elite consensus broke down, the United States, too, experienced a bloody Civil War.

The "plural elites" model—or polyarchy or consociation—attempts to synthesize the partial views of the elitist and pluralist models. It explains some facets of political life, but not all. As with all models in political science, it must be taken as tentative and suggestive rather than as definitive.

Conclusion

If we accept the definition of democracy given in Chapter 4 and the criteria for judging the democratic nature of a government, then it is possible to discover which nations among the many that claim to be democracies are actually governed democratically. The question to be answered, then, is who actually governs in a democracy? More specifically, for the purposes of this chapter, who makes decisions in the United States?

The elitist view holds that America is governed by a power monopoly whose members are similar in background, wealth, and interests. Although this group is self-serving, bowing to public opinion only when that opinion serves the interests of the elite, it maintains that its function is that of a trustee of democracy. Because they are better educated and more tolerant than the average citizen, elite control of decision making and politics is ultimately in the best interests of the people.

The pluralist maintains that the United States is governed by a plurality of competing groups. These groups can bargain, agree, disagree, and compete, thereby providing a system in which a variety of voices can be heard. Whereas elitists hold that their approach protects democratic values, pluralists contend that it suppresses the individual and denies him or her meaningful choice.

The elite theorist believes in the catharsis of symbolic election and in the eventual oligarchical nature of any interest group. The pluralist, on the other hand, maintains that people in key positions do interact, that elected officials can be held accountable by the public, and that interest groups can influence public policy.

Trying to synthesize the elitist and pluralist positions, some thinkers have come up with a "plural elite" model of politics in which the elites of various societal groups interact and strike bargains. This is neither the perfect democracy envisioned by some pluralists nor the perfect hierarchy envisioned by some elite theorists. The plural elite model, where successful, can contribute to conflict management in societies that might otherwise break down into violence. The plural elite model accepts the twin facts that societies are made up of groups and that political power is distributed very unequally. As such, it is a workable model for the United States.

SUGGESTED READINGS

BACHRACH, PETER. *The Theory of Democratic Elitism.* Boston: Little, Brown, 1967. A critique of pluralism and a discussion of the need for equal opportunity.

BENTLEY, ARTHUR F. *The Process of Government.* San Antonio, Texas: Principia Press, 1949. Originally published in 1908, Bentley's views on the importance of groups in politics, radical at the time, laid the groundwork for pluralist thinking.

CZUDNOWSKI, MOSHE M., ED. *Does Who Governs Matter? Elite Circulation in Contemporary Societies.* DeKalb, Ill.: Northern Illinois University Press, 1982. Elite changes in several contemporary societies.

DAHL, ROBERT A. *Polyarchy: Participation and Opposition.* New Haven, Conn.: Yale University Press, 1971. Dahl's theory of plural elites.

———. *Who Governs: Democracy and Power in an American City.* New Haven, Conn.: Yale University Press, 1961. A pluralist statement; Dahl concludes that power is fragmented and shifting. This work helped form basis for Dahl's *Polyarchy.*

DOMHOFF, G. WILLIAM. *Who Rules America Now?: A View for the '80s.* Englewood Cliffs, N.J.: Prentice-Hall, 1983. A more sophisticated and data-supported exploration of the U.S. elite than Mills's classic (below).

DYE, THOMAS R. *Who's Running America?: The Reagan Years,* 3rd ed. Englewood Cliffs, N.J.: Prentice-Hall, 1983. Latest edition of a readable and forceful elite argument.

EDELMAN, MURRAY. *The Symbolic Uses of Power.* Urbana, Ill.: University of Illinois Press, 1964. A study of the power, operation, and use and abuse of symbols in politics.

LIJPHART, AREND. *Democracy in Plural Societies: A Comparative Exploration.* New Haven, Conn.: Yale University Press, 1977. Develops the concept of "consociational democracy," akin to Dahl's "polyarchy."

MILLS, C. WRIGHT. *The Power Elite.* New York: Oxford University Press, 1956. A forceful, original, and persuasive, if not sophisticated, argument regarding the power elite in America.

MOSCA, GAETANO. *The Ruling Class.* New York: McGraw-Hill, 1939. An early statement that the few will rule.

PARENTI, MICHAEL. *Democracy for the Few,* 4th ed. New York: St. Martin's, 1983. A radical, Millsian view of U.S. government by a rich elite.

PREWITT, KENNETH, AND ALAN STONE. *The Ruling Elites: Elite Theory, Power, and American Democracy.* New York: Harper & Row, 1973. Good application of elite theory to U.S. politics.

PUTNAM, ROBERT D. *The Comparative Study of Political Elites.* Englewood Cliffs, N.J.: Prentice-Hall, 1976. Methodologically sophisticated synthesis of elite theory and data.

SULEIMAN, EZRA N. *Elites in French Society: The Politics of Survival.* Princeton, N.J.: Princeton University Press, 1978. Paris governments may come and go, but the French bureaucratic elite doesn't budge.

WELSH, WILLIAM A. *Leaders and Elites.* New York: Holt, Rinehart and Winston, 1979. Good introductory roundup.

chapter 6

Political Ideologies

Ronald Reagan's tenure in the White House reminded us that political ideology is still very much alive in the United States. The Reagan people were distinctly ideological, prescribing what they called conservatism to solve problems ranging from the economy and inner cities to energy and the environment. Probably few Reaganites knew it, but they were actually classic *liberals*, harkening back to Adam Smith's two-century-old admonition to get government out of the economy. Reagan's ideas on individual initiative, a deregulated economy, and the self-correcting power of the marketplace were pure Adam Smith.

The people that Reagan put on the defensive, the so-called liberals, also had a history of which they were probably unaware. Although they accepted the name of liberalism, associated with Adam Smith, they actually applied a greatly changed brand of liberalism dating from the late nineteenth century. The point here is that Americans, who usually like to think of themselves as pragmatic rather than ideological, are heirs to centuries of ideological thought and are indeed subscribing (if unwittingly) to one or another doctrine that was penned generations ago.

WHAT IS IDEOLOGY?

An ideology begins with the belief that things can be better than they are; it is basically a plan to improve society. As Anthony Downs put it, ideology is "a verbal image of the good society, and of the chief means of constructing such a society."[1] Followers of a given ideology argue that if their plan is followed, things will be much better than they are at present. Political ideologies, then, are not the same as political science; that is, they are not calm, rational attempts to understand political systems. They are, rather, commitments to *change* political systems. (The one exception here might be classical conservatism, which aimed at keeping the system from changing too much.) People caught up in political ideology are apt to make poor political scientists, for they often confuse the "should" or "ought" of ideology with the "is" of political science.

The eighteenth-century French philosopher, Antoine Destutt de Tracy, coined the term ideology to describe what he called the new "science of ideas." Most ideologies can be traced back to philosophers (Fig. 6-1). Classic liberalism, for example, can be traced back to the seventeenth-century English philosopher, John Locke, who emphasized individual rights, property, and reason. Communism can be traced back to the late-eighteenth-century German philosopher, G. W. F. Hegel, who emphasized that all facets of a society—art, music, architecture, statecraft, law, and so on—hang together as a package, the expression of an underlying cause.

However, philosophers' ideas are often simplified, popularized, and changed beyond recognition. Ideologists want plans for action, not abstract ideas. Marx, for example, "stood Hegel on his head" to make economics the great underlying cause for everything else in society. Lenin later stood Marx on *his* head to make his ideas apply to a backward country where Marx never

---

[1] Anthony Downs, *An Economic System of Democracy* (New York: Harper & Row, 1957), p. 96.

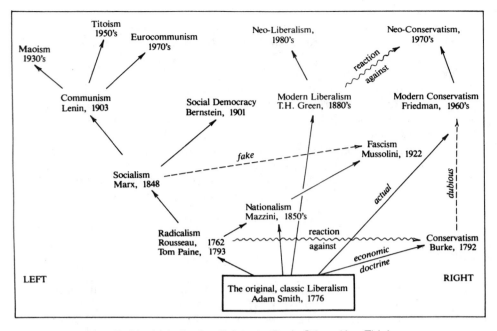

Figure 6-1 How Political Ideologies Relate to Each Other; Key Thinkers and Dates of Emergence

thought they should. Mao Zedong then applied Lenin's ideas to an even more backward country, where they didn't fit at all. Hegel and Marx must have been spinning in their graves. But ideologists are not concerned with fidelity to the original ideas; they want change.

As the ideas become more applied and less abstract, the ideology becomes an important cement, holding together movements, parties, or revolutionary groups. To fight well and endure sacrifices, people need ideological motivation. They need something to believe in. Americans have sometimes been unable to grasp this point. With their emphasis on moderation and pragmatism—"if it works, use it"—they fail to understand the energizing effect of ideology in the world today. "Our" Vietnamese, the South Vietnamese, were physically no different from the Vietcong and North Vietnamese. And they were better armed. But in the crunch, the Vietnamese who had a doctrine to believe in—a mixture of Marx, Lenin, and Mao with heavy doses of nationalism and anticolonialism—won against the Vietnamese who didn't have much to believe in. By the same token, Americans were amazed at the fall of the Shah and his replacement by fanatic politico-religious revolutionaries. We shouldn't have been so surprised; we should rather have looked more closely at whether the Shah had a plausible ideological package to sell his people. We tend to forget that more than two centuries ago Americans were quite ideological, too, and—imbued with a passion for freedom and self-rule, via the pens of John Locke and

Thomas Paine—beat a larger and better equipped army of Englishmen and Hessians who had no good reason to fight. Have we forgotten the power of ideas?

A large part of ideologies is their economic component. Most ideologies have quite a bit to say about economics, for it is economics that is to provide the basis for social improvement. This is as true of the conservatism of Ronald Reagan as it is of the communism of Mikhail Gorbachev: both place heavy emphasis on economics.

Ideologies can be classified—with some oversimplification—on a left-to-right spectrum. This dates back to the meeting of the French National Assembly in 1789. To allow delegates of similar views to caucus and to keep apart strong partisans who might fight with their fists as well as with words, members were seated as follows in a semicircular chamber: conservatives (who favored continuation of the monarchy) were on the speaker's right; radicals (who favored sweeping away the old system altogether in favor of a republic of freedom and equality) were seated to his left; and moderates (who wanted some change) were seated in the center. We have been calling their ideological descendents the left, the right, and the center ever since, even though the content of their views has changed quite a bit. The left now favors equality, welfare programs, and sometimes government takeover of the economy. The right stresses individual initiative and private economic activity. Centrists try to synthesize and moderate the views of both. People a little to one side or the other are said to be center-left or center-right. Sweden's political parties form a rather neat left-to-right spectrum: a small Communist party, a very large (and ruling) Social Democratic party, and medium-sized Center (formerly Farmers'), Liberal, and Conservative parties.

An ideology is a plan. How do ideologies work in practice? They never work precisely the way their advocates claim. Some are hideous failures. All ideologies contain a certain amount of wishful thinking that frequently collapses in the face of reality. Ideologies imagine a perfect world; reality is highly imperfect. The classic liberalism of Adam Smith did contribute to the nineteenth century's economic growth, but it also led to great inequalities of wealth and recurring depressions; it had to be modified into modern liberalism. Communism led to a series of more or less brutal tyrannies. The most livable Communist countries, Yugoslavia and Hungary, are where the doctrine has been watered down to the point where it nearly disappears. The millenial hopes of nationalist liberation movements have been repeatedly disappointed as soon as the revolutionaries have come to power. All ideologies, when measured against their actual performance, are to greater or lesser degrees defective. They should be taken with a grain of salt.

THE MAJOR IDEOLOGIES

Classic Liberalism

According to the late Frederick Watkins of Yale, 1776 could be called "the Year One of the Age of Ideology," and not just for the American Revolution. In that same year the Scottish economist, Adam Smith, published his *The Wealth*

COMPETITION: When the U.S. government forced the giant American Telephone and Telegraph Co. to break up, it was following Adam Smith's admonition to assure competition with a free market. Here consumers buy their own phones, one of the innovations that came with AT&T's breakup.

A.T. &T. Co. Photo Center

of Nations, thereby founding classic laissez-faire economics.[2] The true wealth of nations, Smith argued, is not in the amount of gold and silver they amass, but in the amount of goods and services their people produce. Smith was refuting an earlier notion called *mercantilism* that the bullion in a nation's treasury determined whether it was a rich country. Spain had followed this view in its looting of the New World but actually grew poorer. The French, too, since at least the time of Louis XIV in the previous century had followed mercantilist policies by means of government supervision of the economy with plans, grants of monopoly, subsidies, tariffs, and other restraints on trade.

Smith reasoned that that was not the way to produce maximum economic growth. Government interference always retards growth. If you give one firm a monopoly to manufacture something, you banish competition and with it efforts to produce new products at better prices: the economy stagnates. If you protect domestic industry by means of tariffs that effectively lock out foreign competition, you take away any incentive the domestic producer might have to make better or cheaper products. By getting the government out of the economy, by letting the economy alone (*laissez-faire* in French), you will actually have the best system.

But what about the chaos that will come with free competition unsupervised by government? Not to worry, said Smith; the market itself will regulate the economy. Efficient producers will prosper and the inefficient will go under. The public will get the best products for the lowest prices. Supply and demand determine prices better than any government official can. In the free marketplace, an "unseen hand" regulates and self-corrects the economy. If people want

---

[2]Isaac Kramnick and Frederick M. Watkins, *The Age of Ideology: Political Thought, 1750 to the Present,* 2d ed. (Englewood Cliffs, N.J.: Prentice-Hall, 1979), p. 8. Our discussion owes a great deal to this splendid little book.

more of a given item, manufacturers increase production, new manufacturers enter the field, foreign producers bring in their wares, or there is a combination of all three. The unseen hand—actually, the rational calculations of myriad individuals all pursuing their self-interest—guides the economic adjustments needed.

This ideology acquired the name "liberalism" from the Latin word for free, *liber:* society should be as free as possible from government interference. As aptly summarized by Thomas Jefferson, "That government is best that governs least." Americans took to classic liberalism like a duck takes to water. It seemed perfectly suited to the needs of a vigorous, freedom-loving population with plenty of room to expand. The noneconomic elements also suited Americans. Just as the government shouldn't supervise the economy, so also should it not supervise religion, the press, or free speech.

But, you say, what you're calling liberalism here is actually what everybody today calls conservatism. True. In the late nineteenth century liberalism changed and split into modern liberalism and what we now call conservatism, which we will discuss below. To keep our terminology straight, we should call the original ideas of Adam Smith "classic liberalism" to distinguish it from the modern variety.

Classic Conservatism

By the same token, we should call the ideas of Edmund Burke, published in the late eighteenth century, "classic conservatism," for his conservatism diverges in many ways from modern conservatism. Burke, who came from Ireland but was a member of Parliament representing Bristol, England, knew Adam Smith and agreed that a free market was best. Burke also opposed sending troops to crush the rebellious American colonists; after all, they were only trying to regain the ancient freedoms of Englishmen, said Burke. So far, Burke sounds like a liberal.

But what Burke strongly objected to was the way liberal ideas were being applied in France by revolutionists. There, liberalism turned into radicalism, influenced by philosopher Jean-Jacques Rousseau and, fresh from the U.S. revolution, Thomas Paine. As is often the case, an ideology devised in one place became warped when applied to different circumstances. To apply liberalism in America was easy; once the English and their Tory sympathizers cleared out, it fell into place without resistance. But in France, a large aristocratic class and a state-supported Roman Catholic Church had a lot to lose. The revolutionaries tried to solve the problem with the guillotine; they swept away all established institutions.

This, warned Burke, was a terrible mistake. Liberals place too much confidence in human reason. People are only partly rational; they also have wildly irrational passions. To contain them, society over the years has evolved traditions, institutions, and standards of morality, such as the monarchy and an established church. Sweep these aside, said Burke, and man's irrational impulses will lead to chaos, which in turn will end in tyranny far worse than what the revolutionaries overthrew. Burke, in his 1792 *Reflexions on the Revolution in France,* actually predicted that France would fall under the rule of a military dictator. In 1799, Napoleon took over.

Institutions and traditions which currently exist can't be all bad, Burke reasoned, for they are the products of hundreds of years of trial and error. People have become used to them. The best should be preserved or "conserved" (hence the name "conservatism"). Never mind if they aren't perfect; they work. This is not to say that things should never change. Of course they should change, wrote Burke, but only gradually, giving people time to adjust. Burke was no "stand-patter," a point some current conservatives fail to grasp. "A state without the means of some change is without the means of its conservation," wrote Burke.[3]

Burke was an important thinker for several reasons. He helped discover the *irrational* in human behavior. He saw that institutions are like living things; they grow and adapt over time. And most important, he saw that revolutions tend to end badly, for society cannot be instantly remade according to the dictates of human reason. Although Burke's ideas have been called an *anti-ideology*—for they aimed to shoot down the radicalism that was then engulfing France—they have considerable staying power. Burke's emphasis on religion, traditions, and morality strikes a responsive chord in many a modern conservative's heart. His doubts about applying reason to solve social problems were echoed by Jeane Kirkpatrick, President Reagan's U.N. ambassador and a political scientist. Mrs. Kirkpatrick found that leftists are always imagining that things can be much better than they are when in point of fact violent upheaval always makes things worse.[4] In these ways, classic conservatism is still alive in modern thought.

Modern Liberalism

Now, what happened to the original, classic liberalism of Adam Smith? By the late nineteenth century it had become apparent that the free market was not as self-regulating as Smith had thought. Competition was not perfect. Manufacturers tended to rig the market—a point which Smith himself had warned about. There was a drift to bigness and fewness: monopoly. The system seemed to produce a large underclass of the terribly poor. Class positions to a certain extent were inherited: children of better-off families got a good education and the right connections to speed them on their way. Worst of all, there were recurring economic depressions in which the poor and the working class suffered greatly. In short, the laissez-faire society had some negative aspects.

[3]Edmund Burke, cited in Michael Curtis, ed., *The Great Political Theories* (New York: Avon, 1962), Vol. 2, p. 49.
[4]Jeane J. Kirkpatrick, *Dictatorships and Double Standards: Rationalism and Reason in Politics* (New York: Simon and Schuster, 1982).

The Englishman Thomas Hill Green rethought liberalism in the 1880s. The goal of liberalism, reasoned Green, was a free society. But what happens when economic developments take away that very freedom? The classic liberals placed great store in contracts (agreements between consenting parties with no government supervision): If you don't like the deal, don't take it. But what if the bargaining power of the two parties is greatly unequal, as between a rich employer and a poor person desperate for a job? Does the latter really have a free choice in accepting or rejecting a job with very low wages? Classic liberalism said let it be, wages will find their own level. But what if the wage is below starvation level? Here Green said it was time for government to step in. In such a case it would not be a question of government infringing on freedoms but of government protecting them. Instead of the purely negative "freedom from," there had to be a certain amount of the positive "freedom to." Green called this *positive freedom*. Government was to step in to guarantee the freedom to live at an adequate level.

Classic liberalism had expelled government from the marketplace; modern liberalism brought it back in, this time to protect people from a sometimes unfair economic system. Modern liberals championed wage and hour laws, the right to form unions, unemployment and health insurance, and improved educational opportunity for all. To do this, they were willing to place heavier taxes on the rich than on the working class. This is the liberalism we speak of in the twentieth-century United States, the liberalism of Woodrow Wilson and Franklin D. Roosevelt. One strand of the old liberalism remains in the new, however, the emphasis on freedom of speech and press.

Modern Conservatism

What happened to the other branch of liberalism, the people who stayed true to Adam Smith's original doctrine of minimal government? They are very much around, only we call them conservatives. (In Europe, liberal parties are generally pretty conservative by American standards; that is, they favor free-market solutions. Such is the orientation of Italian, Swedish, and West German liberals.) American conservatives got a big boost from Milton Friedman, the Nobel Prize–winning economist. Friedman argued forcefully that the free market is still the best route, that the original doctrine of Adam Smith was right, that wherever government intervenes it messes things up.[5] Margaret Thatcher in Britain and Ronald Reagan in the United States attempted to apply this revival of classic liberalism in the 1980s. Results were mixed. Inflation came down, but unemployment went up, and budgets—long a conservative touchstone—went wildly into deficit. Both Britain and the United States experienced serious recessions in the early 1980s. Government regulations were rolled back, but, especially in the United States, this raised cries that the government was

---

[5]Milton Friedman and Rose Friedman, *Tyranny of the Status Quo* (New York: Harcourt, Brace, Jovanovich, 1984).

giving away natural resources and relaxing environmental standards so as to make rich people richer. As is the case with all ideologies, what's supposed to work in theory doesn't always work in practice.

Modern conservatism also borrows from Edmund Burke a concern for tradition, especially in religion. American conservatives have been eager to get prayer into public schools, to outlaw abortion, and to obtain tax relief for parents who send their children to church schools. Modern conservatives are also traditional as regards women's and homosexual rights: they oppose them. Modern conservatism is thus a blend of the economic ideas of Adam Smith and the traditionalist ideas of Edmund Burke.

Marxist Socialism

While liberalism (classic variety) dominated the nineteenth century, a strand of critical opinion arose in reaction to the obvious excesses of the capitalist system. Unlike T. H. Green (discussed earlier), some critics didn't believe that a few reforms would suffice; they wanted the overthrow of the capitalist system. They were the socialists, and their leading thinker was a German living in London, Karl Marx.

There had been earlier socialist theories, going as far back as the French Revolution, but they tended to be mostly sentimental, concerned with the plight of the poor, rather than rigorously thought out. Rigorous thought is what Marx attempted to provide in the middle of the last century. Trained in Hegelian ideas and with a doctorate in philosophy, Marx produced an exceedingly complex ideology consisting of at least three interrelated elements: a theory of economics, a theory of social class, and a theory of history.

Economics. In economics, Marx concentrated on the "surplus value"— what we would call profit. Workers produce things but get paid only a fraction of the value of what they produce. The capitalist owners skim off the rest, the surplus value. Not only is this unfair, argued Marx (who paid no attention to the fact that capitalists pay overhead, risk their money, and often work quite hard themselves), but it also leads to recurring economic depressions. The workers, paid only for a fraction of what they produce, cannot go out on the market and buy all the products. The capitalist system pumps out an abundance of goods onto the market, but the bulk of the population—what Marx called the *proletariat* (industrial working class)—can't afford to buy them. The result is repeated overproduction, which, when products can't be sold, leads to depressions. Eventually, argued Marx, there will be a depression so big it will doom the capitalist system.

Social Class. Another important element is social class. Every society divides into two classes: a small class of those who own the means of production and a large class of those who work for the small class. Society is run according to the dictates of the upper class, which sets up the laws, arts, and styles needed to maintain itself in power. Notice how many laws concern property rights, said Marx. That is not surprising, for the *bourgeoisie* (the capitalists) are obsessed with hanging on to their property, which, according to Marx, is nothing but skimmed-off surplus value anyway. If the country goes to war, said Marx, it is not because of the wishes of the common people, but because the ruling bourgeoisie needs a war for economic gain. The proletariat, in fact, has no country; proletarians are international, all suffering under the heel of the capitalists.

History.   Now, putting together his economic theory and his social-class theory, Marx had an explanation for historical change. When the underlying economic basis of society gets out of kilter with the structure the dominant class has established (its laws, institutions, ways of doing business, and so on), the system collapses. This, said Marx, is what happened in the French Revolution. The ruling class before the Revolution was the feudal nobility. Their system was from the middle ages, based on hereditary ownership of great estates worked by serfs, on laws stressing the inheritance of these estates and the titles that went with them, and on chivalry and honor. All were part and parcel of a feudal society. But the economic basis changed. Ownership of land and feudal values grew increasingly anachronistic with the rise of manufacturing. A new class came to the fore, the urban capitalists, or bourgeoisie. Their way of life and economy were quite different from those of the old feudal nobility. By the late eighteenth century, France had an economy based on manufacturing but was still dominated by feudal aristocrats with their minds in the past. The system was out of kilter: the economic basis had moved ahead but the social-class superstructure had stayed behind. In 1789, the superstructure came down with a crash, and the bourgeoisie took over with its new capitalist and liberal values of a free market, individual gain, and legal (but not material) equality.

The capitalists did a good job, Marx had to admit. They industrialized and modernized much of the globe. They put out new products and inventions that would have amazed people of the previous century. But they too are doomed, Marx wrote, because the faster they transform the economy, the more it becomes out of step with the capitalist superstructure, just as the previous feudal society was left behind by the economy. This leads us back to Marx's theory of surplus value and recurring economic depressions. Eventually, reasoned Marx, the economy will be so far disjointed from the bourgeois setup that it too will come crashing down. What will come next?

Here Marx put his books aside and became a prophet. The next stage, he predicted, will be socialism. The proletariat will overthrow the bourgeoisie and establish a just, productive society *without* class distinctions. At a certain stage (and here Marx got awfully vague), this socialist society will reach a level of perfection where there won't need to be police, money, or even government. Goods will be in such plenty that people will be able to just take what they need. There won't be private property, so there will be no need for police. Since government is simply an instrument of class domination, with the abolition of distinct classes there won't need to be government; it will "wither away." The name of this utopia is *communism,* the stage beyond socialism.

Marx himself was more of a theorist than an organizer, but during the late nineteenth century his ideas—or popularizations of them—caught on in the new socialist parties and labor movements of most of Europe, especially in that "mother of socialist parties," the German Social Democratic party (SPD), and in its daughter, the Russian Social Democratic Labor party. Marx was to socialism what Adam Smith was to liberalism: the original, the founder. But Marxian socialism also split, as we shall see. Marx might have trouble recognizing his offspring today.

Social Democracy

At the turn of the century the German Social Democrats, espousing a sort of Marxist theory, had become the biggest party in Germany. Marx hadn't thought much of conventional parties and labor unions; bourgeois governments would simply crush them, he believed. At most, they could be training grounds for more serious revolutionary action. But the German Social Democrats started having success. Their members got elected to the *Reichstag* and local offices; their unions started winning higher wages and better working conditions. Some began to think that the working class could accomplish its aims without revolution. Why use bullets when there are ballots?

Eduard Bernstein developed this viewpoint. In his *Evolutionary Socialism* (1901), he pointed out the very real gains the working class was making and concluded that Marx had been wrong about the necessity for collapse of the system and revolution. Reforms that won concrete benefits for the working class could also lead to socialism, he argued. In revising Marxism, Bernstein earned the name *revisionist,* originally a pejorative hurled at him by orthodox Marxists.

Although the SPD as a whole was not won over, by the time of the ill-fated Weimar Republic in Germany (1919–33), the Social Democrats had greatly toned down their militancy and worked together with Liberals and Catholics to try to save the faltering democracy. Persecuted by the Nazis, the Social Democrats revived after World War II. In 1959 they dropped Marxism altogether, as did virtually all social democratic parties. As social democrats in many countries moderated their positions, they found themselves getting elected more and more; voters no longer worried about them fomenting revolution. In 1979 the Spanish Socialists (PSOE) dropped "Marxist" from party descriptions, and in 1982 they won national elections by a landslide and took over the government. Everywhere the social democrats had succeeded in transforming themselves into center-left parties.

What then do social democrats stand for? They have for the most part abandoned their plans to nationalize industry. Sweden, for example, has only about 12 percent of its industry nationalized, and much of that was done a long time ago by conservatives to keep firms from going under and creating unemployment. Said the late Olof Palme, Sweden's Social Democratic prime minister:

SOCIALISTS give their traditional clenched-fist salute at a rally for Spain's 1977 elections, the first free elections in 41 years.

Michael Roskin

> If industry's primary purpose is to expand its production, to succeed in new markets, to provide good jobs for their employees, they need have no fears. Swedish industry has never expanded so rapidly as during these years of Social Democratic rule.[6]

Instead of nationalization of industry, social democrats have used *welfare* measures to improve living conditions: unemployment insurance, national medical plans, generous pensions, and subsidized food and housing. Social democracies have become welfare states; *welfarism* would be a more accurate term than socialism.

There's one catch—there's always at least one catch—and that is that welfare states are terribly expensive. To pay for these welfare measures, taxes climb. In Sweden, taxes consume a majority of the gross national product (Table 6-1). One of every two *kronas* a Swede earns goes to the government. This is exactly the kind of thing conservative economist Milton Friedman (mentioned earlier) warned about. With those kinds of taxes, soon you are not free to choose how you live. Social democrats and modern liberals have in some places grown close to one another, although they come from very different backgrounds. In Britain, moderate members of the Labor party split off in 1981 to form a new Social Democratic party. In the 1987 elections they joined together with the small Liberal party to run on a combined ticket and won 23 percent of the vote. In the United States, what is called liberalism is tinged with social democratic ideas on the welfare state. It might be fair to say that the left wing of the Democratic party resembles ideologically the moderate wings of European social democratic parties.

---

[6]See Michael Roskin, *Other Governments of Europe: Sweden, Spain, Italy, Yugoslavia, and East Germany* (Englewood Cliffs, N.J.: Prentice-Hall, 1977), chap. 2.

Table 6-1   Taxes as a Percentage of GNP, 1983

Sweden	50.5
Holland	47.3
France	44.6
Italy	40.6
Britain	37.8
West Germany	37.4
Canada	33.0
Switzerland	31.6
United States	29.0
Japan	27.7
Spain	27.2

Source: Organization for Economic Cooperation and Development

Communism

While the Social Democrats were undergoing their evolution into moderate reformists and welfarists, another, smaller wing of the original socialists stayed with Marx. These became the communists. The key figure in this transformation was a Russian intellectual, Vladimir I. Lenin. He made several changes in Marxism to make it fit the situation Russia was in early in this century. The resultant combination, Marxism-Leninism, is another name for communism.

Imperialism.   Marxism caught on early and deeply among Russian intellectuals in the last century. Many of them hated the tsarist system and found in Marxism a theory they could use to overthrow that system. Ironically, Marx meant his theory to apply in the most *advanced* capitalist countries, not in backward Russia, where capitalism was just beginning. But, as we noted before, ideologies often become warped when transplanted from their country of origin. Lenin, mostly in exile in Zurich, Switzerland, faced the problem of how to make Marxism fit backward Russia. To do this, he came up with a theory of economic imperialism, one borrowed from German communist Rosa Luxemburg and English economist J. A. Hobson. These thinkers had all wondered why the proletarian revolutions Marx had foreseen had not broken out in the advanced industrialized lands. They concluded that capitalism had succeeded in transforming itself, expanding overseas into colonies to exploit their raw materials, cheap labor, and new markets. Capitalism had won a temporary new lease on life by turning into imperialism. The domestic market couldn't absorb what the capitalist system was producing, so it found overseas markets. Making enormous profits from its colonies, the mother imperialist country could also pay off its working class a bit to render it reformist rather than revolutionary.

While imperialism was expanding, Lenin noted, it was growing unevenly. Some countries, such as Britain and Germany, were highly developed, but where capitalism was just starting, as in Spain and Russia, it was weak. The latter sort of countries were exploited as a whole by the international capitalist system. It was in them that revolutionary fever burned brightest; they were

LENIN LIVES: Moscow newlyweds place a wreath at Lenin's tomb, long a tradition in this officially atheistic country that tries to make Lenin's image live forever.

Michael Roskin

imperialism's "weakest link." Accordingly, a revolution could break out in a backward country, reasoned Lenin, and then spread into advanced countries. The imperialist countries were highly dependent on their empires; once cut off from exploiting them, the imperialists would fall.[7] Further, Lenin thought he had an explanation for World War I: it was the collision of imperialist powers in an effort to dominate the globe economically.

Lenin, in effect, shifted the Marxian focus from the situation *within* capitalist countries to the situation *among* countries. The focus went from Marx's proletariat rising up against the bourgeoisie to exploited nations rising up against imperialist powers. Marx would probably not have approved of such a shift.

Organization. But Lenin's real contribution lay in his attention to *organization*. With the tsarist secret police always on their trail, Lenin argued, the Russian socialist party could not be like other parties—large, open, and trying to win votes. Instead, it had to be small, secretive, composed of professional revolutionaries, and tightly organized under central command. In 1903 the Russian Social Democratic Labor party split over this issue. Lenin had enough of his supporters at their party's Brussels meeting to win the votes of 33 of the 51 delegates present. Lenin called his faction *bolshevik* (Russian for "majority"), whereas the losers, who advocated a more moderate line and a more open party,

[7]V. I. Lenin, *Imperialism: The Highest Stage of Capitalism* (New York: International Publishers, 1939).

took the name *menshevik* ("minority"). In 1918 the Bolsheviks changed the party name to Communist.

In the chaos of 1917, Lenin's attention to organization paid off. Russia was terribly weakened by the war. In March of 1917, a group of moderates had seized power from the tsar, but they were barely able to govern the country. In November the Bolsheviks, shrewdly manipulating councils (*soviets* in Russian) that had sprung up in the leading cities, seized control from the moderates. After consolidating power in a desperate civil war, Lenin called on all true socialists around the world to join in a new international movement under Moscow's direct control. It was called the Communist International, or Comintern. Almost all socialist parties in the world split; their left wings went into the Comintern and became Communist parties in 1920–21.

The resultant Social Democratic and Communist parties have been more or less natural enemies ever since. While the democratic socialist parties went on to cooperate with their countrymen, trying to promote welfare measures, the Communists denounced them as traitors and sellouts and followed Moscow's orders. Electorally, an interesting thing happened: where socialist parties are big, Communist parties are small, and vice-versa. They are sometimes bitter rivals.

How much Marxism-Leninism do the current rulers of the Soviet Union really believe? They constantly use Marxist rhetoric, but some observers suggest they are actually indifferent or even cynical about ideology and just use it as window dressing.[8] The Soviets do not define their society as communist—that is yet to come; it is what they are working on—but rather as "developed socialism." It is we in the West who call these countries "communist." In 1961, party chief Nikita Khrushchev was rash enough to promise "communism in our generation," indicating that utopia would be reached by 1980.[9] Needless to say, the party never made it, and no one in the Soviet Union is promising Marx's perfect society any time soon.

Maoism and Titoism.

In the 1930s Mao Zedong concluded that the Chinese Communist party (CCP) had to be based on poor peasants and guerrilla warfare. This was a break with Stalin's leadership, and after decades of fighting the CCP took over mainland China in 1949. Mao pursued a radical course that included a failed attempt at overnight industrialization (the Great Leap Forward in 1958), the destruction of bureaucratic authority (the Proletarian Cultural Revolution in 1966), and even border fighting with the Soviet Union in 1969. After Mao's death in 1976, calmer heads moved China away from Mao's extremism, which had severely damaged China's economic progress. Still, a few

[8]For the classic debate about ideology in the Kremlin, see R. N. Hunt, Samuel Sharp, Richard Lowenthal, and Leopold Labedz, "Ideology and Power—A Symposium," in Abraham Brumberg, ed., *Russia under Khrushchev: An Anthology* (New York: Praeger, 1962).

[9]See Jan F. Triska, ed., *Soviet Communism: Programs and Rules* (San Francisco: Chandler, 1962), pp. 68–129.

revolutionary groups hearken to Maoist extremism: Italy's Red Brigades, West Germany's Baader-Meinhoff gang, Japan's Red Army Faction, and Peru's Shining Path. Maoism might be defined as a form of ultra-radical communism.

Yugoslav party chief Josip Tito went the other way, developing a more moderate and liberal form of communism. Even though Tito's partisans fought the Germans in Stalin's name, Stalin felt he didn't fully control Tito, and in 1948 had Yugoslavia kicked out of the Communist camp. During the 1950s, the Yugoslav Communists radically reformed their system, basing it on decentralization, debureaucratization, and worker self-management. The Yugoslav economy operates mostly on a market basis but, argue the Yugoslavs, has not returned to capitalism because workers own and run their factories. This alternative path to socialism, which has made Yugoslavia freer than other Communist countries, intrigues many thinkers in East Europe and challenges the strongly centralized Soviet model. Ideologies, including communism, tend to evolve and split.

Nationalism

So far, the ideologies we have discussed have been fairly complicated, especially the Marxist strand. But the real winner among ideologies—and the one that's still dominant today—is extremely simple: it is nationalism, the exaggerated belief in the greatness and unity of one's country. Often there's little thought involved in nationalism, just "Hooray for my country!" But it has triumphed over all other ideologies and indeed has infected all the others, so that in the United States classic liberalism is combined with American nationalism, and in the Soviet Union, Marxism-Leninism is intertwined with Russian nationalism.

It was not always so. Indeed, the very idea of a nation is fairly new. Go back far enough in history and you will find people unable to imagine themselves as belonging to a "nation." Some scholars trace the beginning of nationalism back to the monarchs and princes who broke away from Rome in the sixteenth century. Henry VIII of England, Gustav Vasa of Sweden, and the Protestant princes of North Germany shattered the medieval image of a Europe united, at least nominally, under the pope. The wars of religion deepened the split and enabled ambitious monarchs to amass more power, centralizing authority in their kingdoms and bypassing the nobles. The movement was called *absolutism*. Absolute monarchs began to stress the unity and greatness of their kingdoms.

Still, nationalism didn't appear as a mass movement until the French Revolution. It let nationalism out of the bottle, and no one has been able to get it back in. The French Revolution, because it was based on the "people," heightened French feelings about themselves as a special, leading people destined to free the rest of Europe. When conservatives tried to invade France in 1792, the "nation in arms" stopped them at Valmy; enthusiastic volunteers beat professional soldiers. The stirring *Marseillaise*, France's national anthem, appeared that same year. With Napoleon, French nationalism first conquered and then infected the rest of Europe. While Napoleon's legions were ostensibly spreading the radical liberalism of the French Revolution, in actuality they were spreading nationalism. The conquered nations of Europe quickly grew to hate the arrogant French occupiers. Spaniards, Germans, and Russians soon became nationalistic themselves as they struggled to expel the French. True, French radicalism did wake up Europe, but it did so in a nationalistic way at least as much as in a liberal way. Nationalism in early-nineteenth-century Europe was like a contagious disease; as soon as one country caught it, it spread to all the others.

By the midnineteenth century, thinkers all over Europe—and especially in Germany and Italy—were defining the nation as the ultimate human value. In some cases, they actually began to worship the nation, seeing in it the source of all things good. Italian writer Giuseppe Mazzini espoused freedom not for individuals—that was mere liberalism—but for nations instead. To be personally free was nothing; one achieved true freedom by subordinating onself to the nation. Education, for example, had to inculcate a sense of nationalism that blotted out individualism, argued Mazzini.

Nationalism was especially relevant in Italy and Germany in the middle of the last century because they were not yet unified. Both countries achieved full unification only in 1871 after decades of struggle. They were relative latecomers to the world of nations, a point that may have lent some passion to their nationalist arguments. In Mazzinian theory, once all peoples are gathered into their respective nations—all Frenchmen living in France, all Italians living in Italy, and so on—then these nations will be happy and satisfied and all will live in peace. There were some flaws to this reasoning. The planet does not have neat boundary lines inscribed in its surface with, say, Germans on one side and French on the other. There are areas of mixed population. Which nation should claim them? If both do, there will be tension, possibly war. In 1871 the new German Reich took Alsace, with its partly German-speaking population, from France, and the French longed for revenge. (The Alsatians themselves could play it either way; when France won the area they were good Frenchmen, and when Germany won they were good Germans. Alsace has been French since the end of World War II.) Far from bringing peace, nationalism increased the amount of war in the world.

A deeper problem with nationalism, though, is that it is largely without content; that is, it has little to say about the great issues that face society: problems of unemployment, economic growth, and improvement of the human condition. Instead, nationalism suggests that if you keep cheering for your nation long and hard enough, other problems will sort themselves out. More than any of the previous ideologies, nationalism depends on emotional appeals. The feeling of belonging to a nation seems to cut to the psychological center of most of us. What other human organization would we fight and kill for? Nationalism usually involves an outside enemy: Israelis hate Arabs and vice-versa; Greeks hate Turks and vice-versa; Spain demands Britain give back Gibraltar (although the Gibraltarians emphatically want to stay with Britain);

Austria wants the South Tyrol back from Italy; the Republic of Ireland wants Ulster back from Britain; Argentina demands the Falkland Islands. . . . The emotions involved in these and similar problems are nationalism.

Regional Nationalism. In recent decades the world has seen the rise of another kind of nationalism: regional nationalism. In a sense, it is the antithesis of the old nationalism, for it aims at breaking up existing nations into what its proponents argue are the true nations. Militant Quebeckers want to separate from Canada, Basques want separation from Spain, Corsicans from France, Croats from Yugoslavia, and Scots from the rest of the United Kingdom. Would breaking up existing countries really solve any problems?

Fascism

The big problem with nationalism is that in at least two cases it grew into fascism—in Italy and Germany. Fascism may be defined as an extreme form of nationalism with a small element of fake socialism added. One quick test of whether a movement is Fascist is to note if its members wear uniforms. Before World War I, Italian journalist Benito Mussolini was a firebreathing socialist revolutionary. Military service changed him into an ardent nationalist. Italy was on the winning side in World War I but had suffered greatly and was full of discontented people after the war. Maximalist socialists seemed to be threatening revolution. In those chaotic times, Mussolini gathered around him a strange collection of people in black shirts who dreamed of getting rid of democracy and political parties and imposing stern central authority and discipline. These Fascists—a word taken from the ancient Roman symbol of authority, a bundle of sticks bound around an ax (the *fasces*)—most of all hated disorder and wanted strong leadership to end it.

In 1922 they got their chance. Amidst growing disorder, the king of Italy handed power to Mussolini. By 1924 Mussolini had turned Italy into a one-party state with himself as *Duce* (leader). Instead of nationalizing the economy the way the socialists might have, the Fascists supervised it by having their men in the right places. Italy looked impressive: there was little crime, much monumental construction, and stable prices, and, as they used to say, "The trains ran on time." Behind the scenes, however, Fascism was a mess, with hidden unemployment, poor economic performance, and corruption.

With the collapse of the world economy in 1929, however, Italian fascism looked impressive. Some thought fascism was the wave of the future. Adolf Hitler in Germany copied many of the trappings of fascism—the uniforms, the flare for spectacle, the hatred of democracy, the one-party state, the single dictator—but added a racist element. For Hitler, it wasn't just Germans as a nation that were rising up against the punitive and unfair Versailles Treaty and chaos of the Weimar Republic, it was Germans as a distinct and superior race. Hitler didn't invent German racism; that went back generations. Hitler adroitly utilized these widespread racist feelings. The racist line held that a special branch of the white race, the Aryans, were the bearers of all civilization. A subbranch, the Nordics, were even better. The Germans, naturally, were all supposed to be Nordics. (Actually, Germans like most Europeans, are of highly mixed stock, including Celts, Romans, several German tribes, Slavs, and even Jews). Hitler argued that the superior Nordics were being subjugated to sinister, non-German forces. Jews, communism, capitalism, even Roman Catholicism were all mixed up in a conspiracy to keep Germans down.

Like Mussolini, Hitler came to power legally; he was named chancellor (prime minister) in 1933 in a situation of turmoil and, like Mussolini, within two years had perfected a dictatorship. Although a free election was never held, probably a majority of Germans did support Hitler. With Nazis "coordinating" the economy, unemployment lessened, production increased, and a kind of prosperity appeared. Many working people felt they were getting a good deal with the jobs, vacations, and welfare the regime provided. After all, the Nazis' full name was the National Socialist German Workers party; it sounded like a type of socialism, and indeed it had a pseudosocialist element. Hitler's true aim, however, was war, and his economic policies were designed to build a powerful military machine.

At a minimum, Hitler wanted Germany to completely dominate Europe, and for a brief time he nearly achieved his goal. He especially wanted the Slavic lands of Eastern Europe as a colony for Germans—*Lebensraum* (living space), he called it. Jews and many Slavic peoples were simply exterminated. Nazi death camps killed some six million Jews and a similar number of Christians who were in the way. Was Hitler mad? It's hard to say. Many of his views were widely held among Germans. Hitler did not build and maintain the elaborate Nazi structure by himself; he had millions of enthusiastic helpers. Rather than insanity, Hitler and the Nazis demonstrate the danger of nationalism run amok.

The word "fascist" has been overused and misused. Some leftists hurl it at everything they don't like. Spanish dictator Francisco Franco, for example, was long considered a fascist, but on closer examination he was actually a "traditional authoritarian," for he tried to minimize mass political involvement rather than stir it up the way Mussolini and Hitler did.[10] Brazilian President Getulio Vargas decreed a fascist-sounding "New State" in 1937, but he was merely borrowing some fascist rhetoric at a time when the movement was having its heyday in Europe. The Ku Klux Klan in the United States is sometimes called fascist, and its members do indeed wear uniforms. The Klan's populist racism is similar to the Nazis', but with one important difference: the Klan strongly opposes the power of the national government, whereas the Nazis and Fascists worshipped it.

Is fascism totally dead? Although it will probably never reappear as a major movement, here and there neofascists raise their heads, for example, the

---

[10]See Juan Linz, "An Authoritarian Regime: Spain," in E. Allardt and Y. Littunen, eds., *Cleavages, Ideologies and Party Systems* (Helsinki: Akademic Bookstore, 1964).

National Democratic party in West Germany, the Italian Social Movement, and various fundamentalist-racist groups in western United States. It is one ideology the world can do without.

IDEOLOGY IN OUR DAY

Eurocommunism

Much like the democratic socialists earlier in the century, the Communist parties of West Europe found they had to adjust their style, tactics, and even ideology as they competed in free elections and worked in democratic parliaments. West European voters, witnessing both the growing prosperity of their own societies after World War II and the continuing repression in Soviet-dominated countries, could not swallow the old-style Communist lines of

SPANISH BARTENDER lets people know his political affiliation with a real hammer and sickle. The Spanish Communist party is considered "Eurocommunist."

Richard Barker

revolutionary takeover, nationalization of all industry, and obedience to Moscow. Accordingly, the Communist leaders of most West European countries were by the 1970s articulating a new democratic approach which took the name of Eurocommunism.

The leading exponent of this was the Italian Communist party (PCI) and its chief, Enrico Berlinguer. Winning as much as a third of the Italian vote but blocked from national power by the even-larger Christian Democrats, the PCI struggled to demonstrate that it would be level-headed and nonrevolutionary in office. Italian Communists greatly toned down the party line: No, we don't want revolution, just major change. No, we aren't authoritarian; we play strictly by the rules of the democratic game. No, we don't want to nationalize industry, just to make it more responsive to people's needs. No, we are not opposed to NATO and American bases; we need them to counterbalance Soviet military power. No, we are not against religion; we want to cooperate with Catholics, who, after all, share our basic ideals. Some suggested that the PCI was turning itself into a democratic socialist party.[11]

Other West European Communist parties picked up the Italian line. Santiago Carrillo of the Spanish Communist party (PCE) became a leading advocate of Eurocommunism.[12] He even seemed to delight at having the Kremlin snub him. In 1978 he had the word "Leninist" dropped from the party's description. Not all West European Communist parties went Eurocommunist, however. The Portuguese Communist party (PCP) stayed "Stalinist," and the French Communist party (PCF) was markedly more rigid and militant than its Italian and Spanish counterparts. For Moscow, Eurocommunism is as big a threat as Maoism or Titoism, for it, too, breaks Kremlin control over the world-wide Marxist-Leninist movement.

Neo-Conservatism

In the 1970s, a variation of modern conservatism emerged: neo-conservatism. Its basic ideas were the same as modern conservatism, but it came from an interesting group of people: disillusioned liberals and leftists. As neo-conservative writer Irving Kristol put it, "A neo-conservative is a liberal who's been mugged by reality." Many neo-conservatives claimed that they were actually staying true to the modern liberalism of the Franklin D. Roosevelt variety, whereas the Democratic party had moved too far to the left with unrealistic ideas on domestic reforms and a pacifist foreign policy.

Specifically, the neo-conservatives reacted against the perceived excesses of the Great Society legislation introduced by Lyndon Johnson in the mid-1960s. This ambitious program aimed to wipe out poverty and discrimination in America. It included food stamps, medical care for the elderly, regional

---

[11]See Eric Hobsbawm, *The Italian Road to Socialism: An Interview with Giorgio Napolitano of the Italian Communist Party* (Westport, Conn.: Lawrence Hill, 1977).

[12]Santiago Carrillo, *Eurocommunism and the State* (Westport, Conn.: Lawrence Hill, 1978).

development, urban renewal, prekindergarten education, voting and civil rights for blacks, and "affirmative action" to hire minorities. Some liberals said the Great Society was never given a chance because funds for it were siphoned away by the Vietnam war. But disillusioned liberals said it worked badly, that many of the programs achieved nothing. The cities grew worse, educational standards declined, medical aid became extremely costly, and a class of welfare-dependent poor emerged, people who had little incentive to work. Neo-conservatives spoke of negative "unforeseen consequences" of well-intentioned liberal programs. One point especially bothered neo-conservatives: affirmative action seemed to give blacks preferential treatment in hiring, sometimes ahead of better-qualified whites. This really hit home when affirmative-action quotas were applied to academic hiring; liberal, white, male professors sometimes had to taste their own medicine in getting turned down for teaching jobs that went to blacks, hispanics, and women.

Culturally, many neo-conservatives were former liberals who had become fed up with the rising tide of shoddy thinking, poor writing, slack work attitudes, and extreme relativism among the younger generation. The popular ideas of the 1960s and early 1970s—such as "It's all right if it feels good" and "Well, it just depends on your point of view" and "Who's to say what's right and wrong?"—drove many liberals to neo-conservatism. Ironically, some neo-conservatives were college professors who had earlier tried to broaden their students' views by stressing the relativity of all viewpoints. Some professors discovered, to their chagrin, that students were becoming vacuous rather than enlightened.

Does neo-conservatism have any staying power, or is it a short-term reaction against specific excesses? During the presidency of Ronald Reagan, many liberal programs were ended or underfunded in order to render them ineffective. President Reagan preached a tougher anti-Soviet line and greatly increased defense spending, another neo-conservative point. But what do you do when you get what you want? The neo-conservatives advanced generally negative arguments against the Great Society and related measures, but they had little positive to offer. In the end, they simply merged with modern conservatives.

Neo-Liberalism

While the neo-conservatives were having their heyday with Ronald Reagan, a loose group of opponents emerged, largely among the battered Democrats. These were called neo-liberals and were rather distinct from the modern liberals of Roosevelt and Johnson. The neo-liberals, mostly younger senators, had to admit that a lot of what neo-conservatives said was true: many Great Society programs were flops or too expensive for what they achieved. But that didn't mean, the neo-liberals argued, that the Reagan people were doing everything right. In some cases they had ended useful programs; in other cases they had sabotaged government agencies by staffing them with enemies of the agencies or not staffing them at all. And the Reagan White House seemed to turn its back on very real national problems in education, technology, the environment, and the economy, especially concerning unemployment. The Reagan administration, with its devotion to the free market, was letting America slip behind, they charged.

Feminism

Springing to new life in the 1960s with a handful of female writers, by the 1970s the women's movement had become an appreciable force in the United States and West Europe. As a political question, the status of women was not new; it had been debated for centuries. Whereas many thought the question had been settled—women had long since ceased to be treated as property, had won the right to vote and hold office, and had moved ahead in education—feminist writers treated these gains as mere beginnings. They pointed out that women were paid less than men for the same work, were passed over for promotion to leading positions, were subjected to psychological and physical abuse from men, were denied bank loans and insurance unless their husbands would cosign, and were, in general, second-class citizens.

The problem, at heart, was a psychological one, argued feminists. Women and men were forced into "sex roles" that had little to do with biology. Boys were conditioned to be tough, domineering, competitive, and "macho," whereas girls were taught to be meek, submissive, unsure of themselves, and "feminine." It didn't have to be this way, feminists believed. With proper child rearing, males could cultivate a gentler, less aggressive manner and females could learn to become assertive and self-confident. Biologically, there were no important differences in mental capacities; the differences that showed up were almost entirely learned behavior, taught by parents and schools of a "patriarchal" society that had long been dominated by men. Why was it taken for granted that boys would grow up to be doctors and girls to be nurses, boys to be lawyers and girls to be secretaries, boys to be builders and girls to be homemakers? Women could do as well as men in most jobs, and men could often become good "househusbands." Sex roles had been learned; they could be unlearned.

Feminists started "consciousness-raising" groups to awaken women around the country to their inferior status. Feminists used the term "male chauvinist pigs" in describing their male enemies. Feminism started having an impact. Many employers gave women a fairer chance, sometimes hiring them over men. Women moved up to higher management positions (although seldom to the corporate top). Working wives became the norm. Sometimes husbands even gave up their jobs to follow the wife's career moves. Commuting marriages became common. Husbands started homemaking and child rearing.

Politically, however, feminists did not achieve all they wished. The Equal Rights Amendment (ERA) to the Constitution failed to win ratification in a sufficient number of state legislatures. It would have guaranteed equality of treatment regardless of sex. Antifeminists, some of them conservative women, argued that ERA would take away women's privileges and protections under the law, would make women eligible for the draft, and would even lead to unisex lavatories. Despite this setback, women learned that there was one way they could count for a lot, politically—by voting. In the 1980 election, for the first time in U.S. history, a significant "gender gap" appeared between male and female voting: women were several percentage points more likely to vote Democratic than were men. While Republicans stressed macho themes of rugged individualism and increased defense spending, Democrats emphasized social welfare measures that helped children and working mothers. Many women were attracted to the peace and antinuclear movements, again to the detriment of the Republicans. In the 1980s, politicians of both major parties learned that women formed an important voting bloc.

Environmentalism

At about the same time that feminists were awakening, another movement began to ripple through the advanced industrialized countries: the ecology or environmental movement. Economic development had typically paid little heed to the damage it was inflicting on the environment. Any growth was good growth: "We'll never run out of nature." While the economy grew, mining produced acid runoff that poisoned streams. Industries and automobiles polluted the air. Chemical wastes made whole communities uninhabitable. And nuclear power raised questions of radioactive leaks and disposal of nuclear wastes.

To the credo of "growth" the ecologists responded with "limits": "We can't go on like this forever without producing an environmental catastrophe." Events such as those at Love Canal, Three Mile Island, and Times Beach seemed to prove the ecologists right. In the first case, Hooker Chemical had used an area in upstate New York as a dump, then turned it over to residential development without warnings of the toxic substances buried just beneath the surface. In the second, a Pennsylvania nuclear power plant, through human incompetence, came as close as anyone would ever want to "meltdown." In the last case, a Missouri area was liberally sprayed with deadly dioxin by a waste-disposal operator. These are just the warning signs, said the environmentalists; a real disaster could be much bigger. And a huge disaster did occur with the massive release of radioactivity from the Soviet nuclear station at Chernobyl in 1986. This event pushed many people into the ecologists' camp both in the United States and Europe.

The ecologists' demands were partly satisfied with the founding of the Environmental Protection Agency (EPA) in 1970. Industrial groups, however, found that EPA regulations restricted growth and ate into profits; under President Reagan, the EPA was rendered ineffective and became a scandal.

But government regulation was only part of the environmental credo. Many argued that consumption patterns and lifestyles in the advanced countries should change in order to conserve the Earth's resources, natural beauty, and clean air and water. Americans, only about six percent of the world's population,

ENVIRONMENTALISM: North Carolina protesters demand safe disposal of toxic wastes that appeared in their area. For good measure some would dump the governor as well.

UPI/Bettman Newsphotos

consume close to half the world's manufactured goods and a third of its energy. In addition to being out of balance with the poor nations of the world, this profligate lifestyle was seen to be unnecessary and unhealthy. Ecologists recommended shifting to public transportation and bicycles instead of cars; to whole-grain foods and vegetables instead of meat; and to decentralized, renewable energy sources, such as wind and solar energy, instead of fossil- or nuclear-fueled power plants. The ecology movement helped trigger the American interest in running, biking, camping, natural foods, and relocating to rural areas. Ecologists wanted man to live in balance with nature rather than to destroy it.

Whereas some environmentalists formed a political party, the Citizens party, and ran ecologist Barry Commoner for president in 1980, their main impact was within the two big parties, both of which came to realize they could not ignore the real dangers that an industrialized society poses for the environment. In Germany, the Greens, espousing a mixture of environmentalism, pacifism, and socialism, won seats in parliament in the 1980s.

The Power of Ideology

Are people motivated by their interests or by their beliefs? No clear-cut answer has been found; obviously both influence people. Marxists maintain that concrete economic interests dominate ideas. A capitalist will naturally favor parties, candidates, and ideas that support capitalism. A worker, by the same token, will favor parties, candidates, and ideas that support the working class. But things aren't that simple. Many wealthy people are very liberal, even leftist, out of sheer conviction. Poor people are often quite conservative. In the 1983

British elections, one out of four unemployed workers, many of whom had lost their jobs because of the Thatcher economic policy, still voted for the Conservatives and Margaret Thatcher! Although their immediate interests had been harmed, they felt that in the long run, Thatcher's policies would reinvigorate the British economy. They had become ideologically convinced that the Labor party and its socialism were wrong and that the Conservatives and their capitalism were right. A more graphic refutation of the Marxist thesis of interests determining viewpoints would be hard to find.[13]

Ideas are important in politics. They are not, to be sure, the only thing, but time and again, ideas have proved crucial in shaping political events. The founding fathers of the United States shaped the Constitution the way they did because they were convinced of the rightness of the ideas of Locke and Montesquieu. In the Third World, young revolutionaries are still fired by the ideas of Mao Zedong and Franz Fanon, an apostle of revolutionary violence against colonialism. No political analysis can be complete without an examination of the ideology and ideas of the relevant groups. As economist John Maynard Keynes put it half a century ago:

> Madmen in authority, who hear voices in the air, are distilling their frenzy from some academic scribbler of a few years back. I am sure that the power of vested interest is vastly exaggerated compared with the gradual encroachment of ideas.[14]

SUGGESTED READINGS

BARADAT, LEON P. *Political Ideologies: Their Origin and Impact*, 2d ed. Englewood Cliffs, N.J.: Prentice-Hall, 1984. An overview of the main current ideological groups.

BRACHER, KARL DIETRICH. *The Age of Ideologies: A History of Political Thought in the Twentieth Century*. New York: St. Martin's, 1984. A critical view of the growth of simplified ideological thinking, especially totalitarianism.

COMMONER, BARRY. *The Closing Circle: Confronting the Environmental Crisis*. New York: Beekman, 1973. Plea from a leading ecologist to prevent environmental damage.

DAHL, ROBERT A. *A Preface to Economic Democracy*. Berkeley, Cal.: University of California Press, 1985. A top political theorist argues that democracy must be extended into the workplace.

GREGOR, A. JAMES. *The Ideology of Fascism*. New York: Free Press, 1969. Survey of fascism by a lifelong student of the subject.

HAGOPIAN, MARK N. *Ideals and Ideologies of Modern Politics*. New York: Longman, 1985. A good introduction, stressing the difference between ideals and ideologies.

HUBERMAN, LEO, AND PAUL M. SWEEZY. *Introduction to Socialism*. New York: Monthly Review Press, 1968. The best short introduction available, by two American Marxists.

HUNT, R. N. CAREW. *The Theory and Practice of Communism*, 5th ed., revised. New York: Macmillan, 1959. Superb historical explanation and criticism of communism.

INGERSOLL, DAVID E., AND RICHARD K. MATTHEWS. *The Philosophic Roots of Modern Ideology, Liberalism, Com-*

[13]The Marxists say they have an answer for this: The people have been brainwashed by the capitalists' control of the mass media, education, churches, and other organizations. Pre–World War II Italian Communist Antonio Gramsci called this "cultural hegemony" and used it to explain why the working class was not as revolutionary as it was supposed to be.

[14]John Maynard Keynes, *The General Theory of Employment, Interest and Money* (New York: Harcourt, Brace 1936), p. 383.

munism, Fascism. Englewood Cliffs, N.J.: Prentice-Hall, 1986. An excellent exploration of the intellectual origins of modern ideologies.

KEOHANE, NANERL O., AND MICHELLE Z. ROSALDO, EDS. *Feminist Theory: A Critique of Ideology.* Chicago: University of Chicago Press, 1982. Review and criticism of feminist arguments.

KOHN, HANS. *Political Ideologies of the Twentieth Century,* 3rd ed., revised. New York: Harper & Row, 1966. Masterful study of the great ideological currents by a scholar who has lived through them personally.

KRISTOL, IRVING. *Two Cheers for Capitalism.* New York: Basic Books, 1978. A neo-conservative's conclusion that capitalist democracy is still best.

MADDOX, WILLIAM S., AND STUART A. LILIE. *Beyond Liberal and Conservative: Reassessing the Political Spectrum.* Washington, D.C.: Cato Institute, 1984. Argues that current political labels are simplistic and out of date.

MEYER, ALFRED G. *Communism,* 4th ed. New York: Random House, 1984. Traces evolution of communism from Marx to present variations.

OZINGA, JAMES R. *Communism: The Story of the Idea and Its Implementation.* Englewood Cliffs, N.J.: Prentice-Hall, 1987. An all-inclusive study taking the idea from Marx to present Third-World variations.

REICH, ROBERT B. *Tales of a New America.* New York: New York Times Books, 1987. A critical, neo-liberal view of the Reagan years.

STEINFELS, PETER. *The Neo-Conservatives.* New York: Simon and Schuster, 1979. A critical look at this successful new ideology.

chapter 7

Political Culture

Everyone agrees that the United States and Canada are quite similar in terms of culture. Americans and Canadians read many of the same books and magazines, watch many of the same television shows, and have similar lifestyles. But in terms of *political* culture, Americans and Canadians are somewhat different. Americans are more insistent about their individual rights and limits on governmental authority than Canadians. Canadians are more law-abiding and willing to let government assume a paternalistic role in guiding the economy and society.[1] Americans sometimes find Canadians a little too obedient; Canadians think Americans are too wild and lawless. The Royal Canadian Mounted Police (RCMP) taps phones and gathers evidence in ways that the Federal Bureau of Investigation wouldn't dare. U.S. civil liberties groups would be outraged at the powers of the RCMP, which are accepted as normal by Canadians.

The modern American and Canadian ideas of the proper role of government are, in some ways, divergent. But so are American conceptions of the twentieth century and the eighteenth century. If Thomas Jefferson suddenly found himself in the twentieth century, he would probably be aghast. Instead of a government limited to protecting our frontiers and our Bill of Rights, he would be confronted with a monstrous organization that collects our garbage, keeps tabs on our earnings, tells us to wear seatbelts, and makes us obtain licenses to sell liquor or own a dog.

The modern Canadian, the modern American, and the American of two hundred years ago have very different perceptions of what government is and should be. What are the forces that work to make their opinions and ideals so strikingly different?

THE ENVIRONMENT OF GOVERNMENT: POLITICAL CULTURE

Each society imparts its own characteristic set of norms and values to its people, and the people in turn have distinct sets of ideals about how the political system is supposed to work, about what the government may do to them and for them, and about their own claims on the system and their obligations to it. This set of beliefs, symbols, and values about the political system forms the political culture of a nation—and it varies considerably from one nation to another. Simply put, political culture is the psychology of the nation in regard to politics.

The politics of a nation is influenced by many aspects of society: its economy, its religion, its traditions. As Karl Marx pointed out long ago, the way people earn their livings has a lot to do with the type of government they have. Industrial societies require far more services—welfare, transportation, urban housing, sanitation facilities—than do agricultural nations, as a glance at the America of the Civil War era and the nation we know now will reveal. When a nation develops a complex industrial system, its culture and political needs change accordingly. Indeed, Marx argued that the economy of a nation was *the* determinant of its political system, and a basic tenet of communist ideology today

---

[1]For the reactions of one American scholar who settled in Canada, see Edgar Z. Friedenberg, *Deference to Authority: The Case of Canada* (Armonk, N.Y.: M. E. Sharpe, 1980).

is that the economy is the foundation for the social and political superstructures of every nation.

A people's religious beliefs also are reflected in politics. The controversy over abortion is a case in point. In contrast to the noble American ground rule of separation of church and state, the state is here involved in the sanctity of human life, an issue which can hardly be separated from religion and morality. In Roman Catholic Italy, religion is recognized as a concern of the state. The Republic of Ireland still does not permit divorce because of the church's opposition; in a nationwide referendum in 1986, three out of five Irish voters rejected divorce.

The social structure of a country is also reflected in the political system. The strict divisions of medieval society found their political expression in a hereditary government where kings, barons, and lords were born into leadership roles. Despite a traditional American commitment to democracy the world over, some political scientists argue that perhaps not all societies are able to sustain a democratic government for various reasons, including physical size, economic level, educational levels of the people, and traditions of class divisions and authoritarian forms of government.

What is Political Culture?[2]

As defined by political scientist Sidney Verba, political culture is "the system of empirical beliefs, expressive symbols, and values, which defines the situation in which political action takes place."[3] What are these beliefs, symbols, and values which determine how a people interprets the proper role of government and how that government itself is organized?

A people's perception of the role of government—the proper relationship between ruler and ruled—has a great deal of influence on the political system. In Japan, where the vestiges of a traditional feudal class system still pervade social structure and social relationships, it is often possible to tell who is whose social superior by watching the way acquaintances greet each other when they meet in the street: the person who bows lower is of inferior status.[4] The Japanese have also been traditionally submissive to the authority of those in office, preferring to leave fundamental policy decisions in the hands of their leaders. Americans, who are not influenced by a tradition of strict class divisions,

[2]For excellent discussions of political culture, see Gabriel A. Almond and Sidney Verba, *The Civic Culture: Political Attitudes and Democracy in Five Nations* (Boston: Little, Brown, 1965); Lucian W. Pye and Sidney Verba, eds., *Political Culture and Political Development* (Princeton, N.J.: Princeton University Press, 1965).

[3]Pye and Verba, *Political Culture and Political Development*, p. 513.

[4]When questioned in the year 1958, 60 percent of the Japanese people who were questioned preferred using status-connoting pronouns to neutral ones such as "I" or "you." When asked who should control policy making for national reconstruction, over one-third thought that the job should be in the hands of the preeminent politicians, *not* elected representatives. Warren Tsuneishi, *Japanese Political Style* (New York: Harper & Row, 1966), pp. 16ff.

take a far different view of the people's right to participate in government. Although Americans may not be particularly well informed about the issues of the day, they consider it their democratic birthright to have a say in the way the country is governed. Clearly, the way a people think of themselves, their leaders, and the relationship between the two has a vital bearing on the nature of a political system.

In America, even people who are hostile to the president will, in most cases, respect his office and his authority. But Latin Americans do not share the same tradition of respect for their heads of government. They have instead been historically more loyal to *caudillos* (charismatic military leaders), with less attachment to the executive office, and have been plagued with coup and countercoup. Nations that stress the importance of institutions are generally more stable than those that depend on charismatic figures for leadership.

Political Culture and Public Opinion. What is the difference between political culture and public opinion? Obviously, the two overlap, for both look at attitudes toward politics. Political culture aims to tap basic, general feelings toward politics and government. Public opinion, on the other hand, focuses on views about specific leaders and policies. Political culture looks for the underpinnings of legitimacy, the gut feelings that sustain a political system, whereas public opinion seeks responses to current questions.

The methodology of political culture and public opinion also overlap: random samples of the population are asked questions and the responses are correlated with subgroups in the population. The questions, however, will be different. A political culture survey might ask how much you trust government; a public opinion survey might ask how much you like the current administration. The political culture study is more likely to ask the same questions in several countries in order to gain a comparative perspective. Both may want to keep track of responses over time to see, in the case of political culture, if legitimacy is gaining or declining, or, in the case of public opinion, how a president's popularity compares with his predecessors.

Political culture studies are apt to go beyond surveys, however. They might use the methods of anthropology and psychology in the close observation of daily life and in the deep questioning of individuals about their feelings.[5] Public opinion studies rarely go beyond the clipboard with quantified data, while political culture studies can use history and literature to gain insights into a particular country. For instance, one noted scholar found the observations of nineteenth-century travelers provided evidence of continuity in American political and social attitudes.[6] Indeed, the brilliant comments of Alexis de Tocqueville, who traveled through the United States in the 1830s, still generally

[5]One political scientist who used anthropological and psychological techniques was Edward C. Banfield, *The Moral Basis of a Backward Society* (New York: Free Press, 1958).
[6]Seymour Martin Lipset, *The First New Nation: The United States in Historical and Comparative Perspective* (New York: Anchor Books, 1967), chap. 3.

apply a century and a half later.[7] Tocqueville can be fairly described as one of the founders of the political culture approach in political science.

It used to be widely assumed that political culture was nearly permanent or changed only slowly, whereas public opinion was fickle and changed quickly. Recent studies, however, have shown that political culture is rather changeable, too. Periods of stable, efficient government and economic growth solidify feelings of legitimacy; periods of indecisive, chaotic government and economic downturn are reflected in weakening legitimacy. Public opinion, if held long enough, eventually turns into political culture. In the 1960s public opinion on Vietnam showed declining support for the war. Over precisely this same time period, confidence in the U.S. government also declined. Public opinion on a given question was infecting the general political culture, making it more cynical about the political system.

To be sure, a country's political culture changes more slowly than its public opinions, and certain underlying elements of political culture tend to persist for generations, perhaps for centuries. One can easily recognize the America of de Tocqueville in the America of today; basic attitudes haven't changed that much. The French are still inclined to take to the streets of Paris to protest perceived injustice, just as their ancestors did. Italians continue their centuries-old cynicism towards anything governmental. While not as firm as bedrock, political culture is an underlying layer of attitudes that can support— or fail to support—the rest of the political system.

The Civic Culture

The pioneering study of cross-national differences in political beliefs, symbols, and values was made by Gabriel Almond and Sidney Verba.[8] Interviewing some five thousand people in five different nations in 1959 and 1960, the authors sought to measure national political attitudes by testing three important variables: what impact the people felt government had on their lives; what obligation they felt they had toward government; and what they expected from government. Almond and Verba discerned three general political cultures: participant, subject, and parochial.

Participant.   In a participant political culture people understand they are citizens and pay attention to politics. They are proud of their country's political system and are generally willing to discuss politics. They believe they can influence politics to some degree and claim they would organize a group to protest something unfair. Accordingly, they show a high degree of *political competence* (knowing how to accomplish something politically) and *political efficacy*

[7]Alexis de Tocqueville, *Democracy in America* (New York: Washington Square Press, 1964). The original was published in French during 1835–40.

[8]Almond and Verba, *The Civic Culture.* The nations which Almond and Verba studied were Great Britain, the United States, Germany, Italy, and Mexico.

(feeling that they have at least a little political power). They say they take pride in voting and believe people should participate in politics. They are active in their communities and often belong to one or more voluntary organizations. They are more likely to trust other people and to recall participating in family discussions as children. A participant political culture is clearly the ideal soil in which to sustain a democracy.

Subject.   A notch lower than the participant political culture is the subject political culture. People in the subject political culture still understand they are citizens and pay attention to politics, but they are involved in a more passive way. They follow political news but are not proud of their country's political system and feel little emotional commitment toward it. They feel uncomfortable in speaking about politics; it is not a good topic for conversation. They feel they can influence politics only to the extent of speaking with a local official. It does not ordinarily occur to them to organize a group. Their sense of political competence and efficacy are lower; some feel powerless. They say they vote, but they vote without enthusiasm. They are less likely to trust other people and to recall voicing their views as children. Democracy has more difficulty sinking roots in a culture where people are used to thinking of themselves as obedient subjects rather than as active participants.

Parochial.   At yet another notch lower is the parochial political culture where people may not even feel they are citizens of a nation. They identify with the immediate locality, hence the term "parochial" (of a parish). They take no pride in their country's political system and expect little of it. They pay no attention to politics, have little knowledge of politics, and seldom speak about political matters. They have neither the desire nor the ability to participate in politics. They have no sense of political competence or efficacy and feel powerless in the face of existing institutions. Attempting to grow a democracy in a parochial political culture is very difficult, requiring not only new institutions but a new sense of citizenship.

Now, as Almond and Verba warn, there is no country that has a purely participant, subject, or parochial political culture. All nations are mixtures in varying degrees of the three types. The United States, they found, was heavily participant with some subject and even a few residual parochial attitudes. One of the problems with U.S. political culture, they suggest, is the relatively weak subject component, causing Americans to be not particularly law-abiding. Britain was closer to a happy balance between participatory and subject political cultures: sufficiently participant to be a democracy and sufficiently subject to obey authority. In Germany, the subject culture dominated; people obeyed authority but didn't want to get involved in politics. The same applied to Italy, with a bigger dose of parochial attitudes. Both Germany and Italy at the time of Almond and Verba's studies illustrated the difficulty of starting a democracy in a relatively weak participant culture. Mexico was a strange mixture in which people's statements sounded participatory but in practice they behaved in a subject and parochial manner. Almond and Verba called Mexico an "aspiration-al" political culture—where hopes exceed reality.

If you think about it a minute, any country would have to be a mixture of political cultures. If a country were purely parochial—with no one interested in anything political—it would either fall apart or succumb to foreign conquest. This is what happened when European nations conquered much of Asia, Africa, and Latin America. Someone has got to participate in politics—at least the king and queen and their court. And someone has got to obey as good subjects—at least the knights and merchants. Without some participation you haven't got a country. The masses of people in the countryside can be parochial with only a few loyal subjects and political participants to guide them. That is the picture of ancient China: 80 percent of the population toiled as peasants, then a layer of gentry and merchants to run things, and a tiny layer of mandarins and court officials to supervise the empire.[9] Even traditional political systems were not completely parochial.

Today, it would be hard to find parochial political cultures. All corners of the globe have been penetrated by communications, and even very poor and backward people are generally aware of current events. The fathers of the Afghan *mujahedin* may have been tribal and parochial, but their sons know how to shoot and clean machine guns, and they know why they are fighting: for a political cause, to rid their country of Soviet domination. In not much more than one generation, parochial people have been transformed into participants. By the same token, the white regime of South Africa imagines that the country's blacks—almost three-quarters of the population—are still tribal and parochial with little interest (apart from a few troublemakers) in politics. On the contrary, many black South Africans are itching to participate in their nation's politics and when not allowed to do so they turn to violence. It was, indeed, the white South Africans themselves who, with modern industry, education, transportation, and communication, awakened the previously parochial Africans to the possibility of political participation. Modern times have phased out parochial political cultures.

On the other hand, would a purely participant political culture be possible or even desireable? Probably not. What would happen if everyone were eager to participate in politics. There would be the danger of political turmoil as too many citizens passionately pursue interest in political causes. When that happens, as during political revolutions, the intense participatory political culture burns itself out after a period of tumult. The sudden growth of feelings of participation accompany and contribute to the revolutionary upheavals of newly free countries. It is perhaps just as well that few people are truly political animals; most concern themselves with politics only intermittently and devote their chief attention to personal concerns, such as family, church, and job. It is in the mixture of all three attitudes that democracy finds stability: parochial concerns for family, church, and job give individuals meaning and perspective;

[9]For a brief description of traditional China by a top scholar see John King Fairbank, *The United States and China*, 4th ed. (Cambridge, Mass.: Harvard University Press, 1979), chap. 2.

subject attitudes give the political system obedience and support; and participant attitudes keep leaders attentive and responsive to the attitudes of people.

Participation in America

Even in America, relatively few persons actively participate in politics. How then can Almond and Verba offer the United States as their model of a "civic culture"? One of their key findings was that for democracy to work, participation need only be "intermittent and potential."[10] In effect, they offer a "sleeping dogs" theory of democratic political culture. Leaders in a democracy know that most of the time most people are not paying close attention to politics. But they also know that if aroused—because of scandal, high unemployment, inflation, or unpopular war—the public can vote them out of office at the next election. Accordingly, leaders usually work to keep the unaroused public quiet. Following the "rule of anticipated reactions," leaders in democracies constantly ask themselves how the public will react to any of their decisions.[11] They are quite happy to have the public *not* react at all; they wish to let sleeping dogs lie.

This theory helps explain an embarrassing fact about U.S. political life; namely, its low voter turnout, the lowest of all the industrialized democracies. Little more than half U.S. voters bother to cast a ballot in presidential elections, even fewer in state and local contests. In Western Europe, voter turnout is usually about three-quarters of the electorate and sometimes tops 90 percent. How, then, can the United States boast of its democracy? Theorists reply that a democratic political culture does not necessarily require heavy participation. Rather it requires an attitude that, if aroused, the people will participate—vote, contribute time and money, organize groups, and circulate petitions—and that elected officials know this. Democracy in this view is a psychological connection between leaders and led that restrains officials from foolishness. It is the attitudes of the people, and not their actual participation, that makes a democratic political culture viable.

Another of Almond and Verba's key findings was the response to the question of what citizens of five countries would do to influence local government over an unjust ordinance. Far more Americans said they would "try to enlist the aid of others".[12]

United States	59 percent
Britain	36 percent
West Germany	21 percent
Italy	9 percent
Mexico	28 percent

[10]Almond and Verba, *The Civic Culture*, p. 347.

[11]Carl J. Friedrich, *Constitutional Government and Politics*, (New York: Harper & Row, 1937), pp. 16–18.

[12]Almond and Verba, *The Civic Culture*, p. 148. As noted earlier, the Mexican responses tended to express ideal rather than actual behavior.

Table 7-1   Trust in Government, 1985

Percent who say they trust government

	ALMOST ALWAYS	MOST OF THE TIME	SOME OF THE TIME	ALMOST NEVER
United States	8	41	42	7
West Germany	6	35	37	18
France	6	27	41	19
Italy	8	25	37	27
Britain	5	25	43	25
Spain	6	23	37	20

(People who had no answer were not counted.)

Source: New York Times, 16 Feb. 1986. Copyright © 1986 by *The New York Times Company.* Reprinted by permission.

Americans seem to be natural "group formers" when faced with a political problem, and this could be an important foundation of U.S. democracy. In more "subject" countries, this group forming attitude was weaker.

Americans also trust their government more than people in other countries. A 1985 survey found that nearly half of the Americans polled said they trusted the U.S. government most of the time.[13] Four out of ten Germans gave this reply about their own government. In Italy, only a third gave the same response, while over a quarter said they almost never trusted the government. (See Table 7–1.)

CHANGING POLITICAL CULTURE

Table 7–1 provides some interesting—and perhaps scary—insights into the origins of political cultures. Political cultures are in large measure reactions to current or past governmental performance. Governments who lead their peoples into calamity reap a harvest of mistrust. In the earlier Civic Culture data, both Germany and Italy showed the scars of totalitarianism: people were suspicious and cautious about government and politics. The more recent data of Table 7–1 suggests that West Germans, by dint of good political institutions, moderate political parties and leaders, and sound economic policies, have overcome much of their previous mistrust of government. Notice, however, that 18 percent of Germans still almost never trusted their government. Italy, however, has not recovered as well as West Germany. Government performance in Italy, due in part to clumsy institutions, has been shaky. The low degree of trust in Spain is also not surprising. Spaniards fought a bloody civil war from 1936 to 1939 and then lived under the dictatorship of Franco until 1975. Spain has been a democracy only for a short time and is beset by many problems.

[13]E. J. Dionne Jr., "Government Trust: Less in West Europe Than U.S.," *New York Times,* 16 Feb. 1986, p. 20.

Table 7-2   Americans' Trust in Government, 1964–84

	1964	1966	1968	1970	1972	1974	1976	1978	1980	1982	1984
Trust government all or most of the time	76%	65%	61%	54%	53%	37%	33%	30%	25%	33%	54%
Government run by a few big interests	29	33	40	50	53	66	66	67	69	61	55

Source: American National Election Studies, 1964–1978, Center for Political Studies, Institute for Social Research, The University of Michigan. (1958–1978 data originally published in W. E. Miller, et al. *American National Election Studies Data Sourcebook, 1951–1978.* Cambridge: Harvard University Press 1980.)

Economic problems are among the most corrosive on a positive political culture. In Spain and Britain government policy has been to bring down inflation even if it brings high unemployment. The result: people lose their trust in government. The British data are especially shocking, for Britons long showed high levels of trust in government. In this 1985 study, a quarter said they trusted government almost never, nearly reaching the Italian level of mistrust. Britain's declining political culture—which has resulted in unrest and violence—parallels its declining economy. A political culture can get better, as in Germany, or worse, as in Britain.

A case in point is the major slump in positive American attitudes that started in the 1960s and continued through the 1970s. Standardized questions about trust in government have been asked every two years by the respected Survey Research Center at the University of Michigan. Two key questions were: "How much of the time do you think you can trust the government in Washington to do what is right?" and "Would you say the government is pretty much run by a few big interests looking out for themselves or that it is run for the benefit of all people?" The cynical responses climbed until they outnumbered the trusting responses (Table 7–2). These were the years of the Vietnam War, the Watergate scandal, and inflation—all of which showed Washington in its worst light. Only in 1982 did the trusting responses start to grow again, a trend that increased in 1984. The growth in cynicism had made America harder to govern in the 1970s; the growth in trust made the country easier to govern in the 1980s. No nation is blessed with automatic and permanent legitimacy.

The point is that political culture changes. True, it does not change as rapidly as public opinion, but political culture at any given moment is a combination of long-remembered and deeply held attitudes plus reactions to current situations. Since the original Almond and Verba Civic Culture study was done, British political culture has turned untrusting and cynical. West German political culture has become more trusting and participatory. And American political culture went through a decline in the 1960s and 1970s and a recovery in the 1980s. All these changes are responses to government performance.[14] Political cultures do not fall down from heaven; they are created by governmental actions and inactions.

Elite and Mass Cultures

The political culture of a country is not uniform and monolithic. One can usually find within the political culture differences between the mainstream culture and subcultures (discussed below) and differences between elite and mass attitudes. Elites—meaning those people with better education, higher income, and more influence—have rather different political attitudes than the masses. Elites are much more participatory; they are more interested in politics. They are more inclined to vote, to protest injustice, to form groups, and even to run for office. One finding of the Civic Culture study has been confirmed over and over again: the more education a person has, the more likely he or she is to participate in politics.

Delegates to the 1984 Democratic convention illustrate the differences between the elites and the masses. Nearly half the delegates had some postgraduate education (often law school). Nationwide, only 4 percent of self-identified Democrats had gone to graduate school. Of the convention delegates, 42 percent came from households with annual incomes of $50,000 or more. Nationwide, only 5 percent of Democrats were so favored.[15] In other words, the people representing the Democratic party at the convention were not a representative cross-section of the party rank-and-file. The Democrats pride themselves on being the party of the common people, but Democrats with more education and money still tend to take the leading positions. There is nothing necessarily wrong with this; better-educated and better-off people are simply more inclined to political participation. The same is true of the Republican party in the U.S., or, for that matter, the Japanese Liberal-Democratic party, or the Soviet Communist party.

Why should this be so? Here we return to the words mentioned earlier: political competence and efficacy. Better-educated people know how to participate in political activity. They have a greater sense of self-confidence writing letters, speaking at meetings, and organizing groups. They feel that what they do may have at least some small result politically. The uneducated and the poor lack the knowledge and confidence to do these kinds of things. Many of them feel powerless.[16] "What I do doesn't matter, so why bother?" they think. Those at the bottom of the social ladder thus become apathetic.

---

[14]The authors of the original Civic Culture study fully realize the changing nature of political culture and brought out a book that examines the changes in the five countries of the original study. See Gabriel A. Almond and Sidney Verba, eds., *The Civic Culture Revisited* (Boston: Little, Brown, 1980).

[15]Barry Sussman and Kenneth E. John, "The Delegates Are Not the Democratic Rank and File," *Washington Post National Weekly Edition*, 23 July 1984, p. 8.

[16]See Giuseppe Di Palma, *Apathy and Participation: Mass Politics in Western Societies* (New York: Free Press, 1970). Di Palma used data from the Civic Culture study to demonstrate that modern society actually creates greater levels of apathy.

The differences in participation in politics between elites and masses is one of the great ironies of democracy. In theory and in law, politics is open to all in a democracy. In practice, some participate much more than others. Because the better-educated and better-off people (more education usually leads to more income) participate in politics to a greater degree, they are in a much stronger position to look out for their interests. It is not surprising that the 1986 U.S. tax reform bill retained the deduction of mortgage interest payments even for vacation houses, for these items are important to the better-off people who can make their voices heard in the political system. Yet, at the same time the federal government was cutting various welfare benefits because poor people are not as effective at being heard. There is no quick fix for this imbalance. The right to vote is a mere starting point for political participation; it does not guarantee equal access to decision making. A mass political culture of apathy and indifference toward politics effectively negates the potential of a mass vote. An elite political culture of competence and efficacy amplifies their influence.

Political Subcultures

Just as there are differences between the elites and the masses, so also are there differences among ethnic, religious, and regional groups in a country. When the differentiating qualities are strong enough in a particular group, we say that the group forms a *subculture*. Defining this is a bit tricky, however. It would probably be a mistake to label every distinct group in society a subculture. Do the Norwegian-Americans of "Lake Wobegon", Minnesota form a subculture? Their attitudes differ a bit from the mainstream, but their political reactions and orientations are substantially the same as the majority of Americans. We would probably not call them a subculture. But how about black Americans? They are often poorer and less-educated than white Americans. The black vote is overwhelmingly Democratic even during a Republican landslide, such as the election of Ronald Reagan. Blacks would seem to qualify as a subculture. But, on the other hand, are black political attitudes, desires, and reactions really that different from the American mainstream? Do they want to depart from the American mainstream or join it? As an example of regional differentiation, does the U.S. South qualify as a political subculture? Perhaps it used to, but that may no longer be the case. Designating a given group a subculture is often arbitrary. You can pick out almost any group and call it a subculture.

Some subcultures, to be sure, are easy to identify. Groups with a different language and tendencies to break away from the rest of the population surely qualify. The French-speaking people of Quebec, Canada for a time threatened to withdraw from the federation and become a separate country. The Bengalis of East Pakistan, ethnically and linguistically distinct from the peoples of West Pakistan did, in fact, secede and found their own country in 1971. The Basques of northern Spain and the Roman Catholics of Northern Ireland are sufficiently different to probably constitute political subcultures. The

Scots and Welsh of Britain harbor the resentments of the "Celtic fringe" against the dominant English: they vote heavily Labour while the English vote heavily Conservative. They, too, probably constitute subcultures.

Where subcultures are very distinct, the political system itself may be threatened. Lebanon virtually ceased to exist because citizens were more loyal to their religious groups than to the nation of Lebanon. In India, some Sikhs sought independence for the Punjab, their home province, and resorted to arms. Prime Minister Indira Gandhi's Sikh bodyguards assassinated her in 1985 and, in effect, said their subculture was more important than India's. Recalling a term we used earlier, such countries as Lebanon and India are still undergoing a crisis of identification.

Should a nation attempt to integrate its subcultures into the mainstream? Such efforts are bound to be difficult, but if left undone, the subculture in later years may decide it really doesn't belong in that country. After the English defeated the French in Canada, they let the French Canadians keep their language and culture. It was a magnanimous gesture, but it meant that two centuries later Canada was saddled with an angry and defiant Quebec separatist movement. Similarly the Spaniards in Peru who conquered the Incas let the Indians retain their language and culture. But now the Spanish-speaking Peruvians of the cities know little of the Quechua-speaking Peruvians of the mountains. Thirty percent of Peruvians speak no Spanish. Any nonintegrated subculture poses at least a problem and at worst a threat to the national political system.

The United States has relied largely upon voluntary integration to create a mainstream culture in which most Americans feel at home. Immigrants found they had to learn English to get ahead in the New World. The achievement oriented consumer society tended to standardized tastes and career patterns. The melting pot worked, but not perfectly. Many Americans retain small subculture distinctions—often in the areas of religion and cuisine—but these may not be politically important. Italian-Americans did not rally behind Geraldine Ferraro, the first Italian-American to run for national office as the vice-presidential candidate on the Democratic ticket in 1984. Their failure to do so pointed out how well Italian-Americans had become integrated into the mainstream: they really didn't care that one of their own was at last on the ballot. Asian Americans also integrated rapidly into the U.S. mainstream. Japanese-Americans, only one-quarter of one percent of the total U.S. population, held five of the 535 elected seats on Capitol Hill, or nearly one percent of those seats.[17]

Not all American groups have been so fortunate. Blacks and Hispanics are not yet fully integrated into the American mainstream. They form, arguably, subcultures. Should these subcultures be better integrated into American

---

[17]Michael G. Roskin and Moon H. Jo, "Asian-American Political Participation" in *Political Participation of Asian Americans: Problems and Strategies,* ed. Yung-Hwan Jo (n.p.: Pacific/Asian American Mental Health Research Center, 1980), p. 120.

The Hispanic, white, and black soldiers in this Washington, D.C.
statue symbolize the comradeship of all U.S. armed forces during the
Vietnam War, the first fully integrated war effort in U.S. history.
Michael Roskin

society? This has been one of the great questions of post-World War II U.S.
politics. With the 1954 *Brown* v. *Board of Education of Topeka* decision, the
Supreme Court began a major federal government effort to integrate U.S.
schools. It encountered massive resistance. In some instances federal judges had
to take control of local school systems to enforce integration by busing.
Underlying the reasons for integration was discussed previously: an uninte-
grated group represents a problem, even a danger, for the society. The
pro-integrationist Kennedy and Johnson administrations argued that America,
in its struggle against communism, could not field a good army and offer an
example of freedom and justice to the rest of the world if a considerable fraction
of its population was oppressed and poor. Integration was portrayed as a matter
of national strength.

Should integration be forced in the area of language? Should blacks be
forced to abandon their dialect in favor of standard English, and should
Hispanics be forced to learn English? If they don't, they will be severely
handicapped their whole lives, especially in regard to employment prospects.
But many blacks and Hispanics, and some native Americans, cling to their
language as a statement of ethnic identity and pride. The U.S. Constitution does

not specify any national language; nor does it outlaw using languages other than English. In some areas of the United States, signs and official documents come in both English and Spanish. In 1986, California voters approved a measure making English the state's official language by a wide margin. People, of course, could continue to speak what they wished, but official documents, such as ballots and other legal matters, would be in English only. Other states passed similar laws, arguing that designating an official language would encourage new immigrants to learn English and hence speed their integration.

POLITICAL SOCIALIZATION

When we think of the socializing process, we remember how we "picked up" such behavior patterns as table manners, correct terms of address, and the "dos and don'ts" of personal hygiene. Such behavior is not formally taught; it is mostly absorbed by watching other people who know what they are doing and imitating their actions. Political socialization operates in much the same manner: we watch, listen, and imitate the political attitudes and values of family, friends, and others whom we respect. Political socialization is the induction into political culture and the developmental process through which we learn the accepted attitudes and values of our political culture and subcultures.

Learning to pledge allegiance to the flag, to stand up to sing the national anthem, and to acknowledge the authority of political figures, from presidents to police officers, are all part of the political learning process. And families, friends, schoolteachers, and even television are all important teachers. If Catholic children in Northern Ireland or poor children in the urban ghettoes of America are raised to see only the problems and ways of life of their isolated neighbors, with no perspective as to how their small group fits into the national whole, then their political views will most likely form subcultures apart from the mainstream. If the process of political socialization disintegrates so much that membership in a small group becomes more relevant than membership in a nation, then the entire political culture will likely break down. Political socialization—the learning of political attitudes and social preferences—is crucial to stable government.

In the broadest sense, political socialization is the way in which a society perpetuates its political culture. It is a continuous, lifelong process which is part of each individual's conditioning and education as a member of the culture he is born into. It is a phenomenon of all political systems, and it does not necessarily involve deliberate indoctrination by agencies of the government.

The Roles of Political Socialization

Political socialization performs several functions for both the individual and the political system as a whole.

Training the Individual.   Political socialization instills in each person the prevailing values of the political system. It enables him or her to relate to the system—to expect certain treatment from government and to know what it expects: obeying the laws, keeping involved in local affairs, and voting at election time.

Supporting the Political System.[18] Political socialization helps to maintain and legitimize the political system and the government in office. It maintains the system by conditioning and educating its members to obey its rules and to fulfill its roles. The system works as it does, and succeeds in governing to the extent that it does, because most people obey the laws and accept different roles—such as judge, policeman, party activist, candidate, and voter—which interact to keep the system going.

Political socialization also plays the important role of training people to recognize those who have the right to exercise official authority, and to accept this right. The mother who brings her son to school on his first day and tells him, "Do as the teacher says," is legitimizing the teacher's authority by training her child to respect the teacher. In a more complex sense, we are all socialized to such an extent that even though we may be adversely affected by a law we disagree with, enacted by legislators we voted against, and carried out by order of a president we dislike, we will nevertheless feel obliged to obey the law. Earlier in this century, thousands of Americans who would have otherwise freely taken an occasional nip refused to let liquor touch their lips solely because it was against the government's prohibition policy (although thousands also broke the law and indulged). To some extent, of course, we obey the law because we fear punishment, but in perhaps many more cases, this obedience is due to our training to accept government's authority over us.

As we discussed in Chapter 1, this sense of obedience is called "legitimacy." When legitimacy erodes, governments must use more coercion to enforce their writ. One quick test of legitimacy, therefore, is to see how many police are needed. In England, where legitimacy is high, there are relatively few police, but in Northern Ireland, which forms a subculture within the United Kingdom, legitimacy is low, especially among the Catholic minority, and many police, backed by British army units, are needed. In Poland in the early 1980s, governmental legitimacy virtually collapsed, and the country was ruled by the army and police.

The Agencies of Socialization

Everything the child encounters is a potential agent of political socialization, but what he or she encounters earliest—the family—is apt to outweigh all the others. Attempts at "overt socialization," by government and schools,

---

[18]One leading sociologist fears that civic education has severely weakened in the present-day United States and this poses dangers for U.S. democracy. See Morris Janowitz, *The Reconstruction of Patriotism: Education for Civic Consciousness* (Chicago: University of Chicago Press, 1983).

generally fail if their values are at odds with family orientations. Many Communist countries have this problem: the regime tries to inculcate certain values in a child, but the family conditions the child to ignore regime messages. Where family and governmental values are generally congruent, as in the United States, the two modes of socialization reinforce each other.

The Family. Psychologists tell us that long after we've left home, our parents continue to exert a profound influence on us, and this includes our political behavior. An obvious example of this influence is the fact that most people vote as their parents did. More basically, the family forms the psychological makeup of the individual, which in turn determines many of his or her political attitudes. It imparts a set of norms and values that become the individual's "map" of what to expect of himself and others in all areas of life, including its political aspects, and it transmits beliefs and attitudes that are specifically political, such as party loyalty and trust or cynicism about government.

The effect of the conditioning and training of the early years is the strongest. A study of the shaping of political attitudes found that the most decisive of these attitudes are shaped in the years from ages three to thirteen.[19] The family has almost exclusive control of the child's training in the first three of these years and continues to have the dominant influence during the school years as well. It is natural that the children's mothers and fathers are their important models, because they are the main source for the satisfaction of all their basic needs—such needs as food and warmth, physical protection, love, and identity. Parents are figures of great power and authority in the children's world, and from them they accept many norms, values, and attitudes unconsciously and uncritically.

The psychological set children acquire as a result of family relationships affects their political behavior in adult life in many different ways.[20] In general, people give back to the world as adults what they got from it as children. One extensive study found that American college students with authoritarian personalities had almost invariably been treated roughly as children.[21] But, on the other hand, parental overprotection may be just as harmful, causing children to fear leaving the shelter of the family. This sense of fear may later be expressed politically as distrust and dislike of public figures.

As adults, people differ widely in the degree to which they participate in political affairs. Underlying this difference in behavior is a strong difference in

[19]David Easton and Stephen Hess, "The Child's Political World," *Journal of Political Science* 6 (August 1961): 229–46.

[20]For example, political scientist Robert Lane found that tense father-son relationships can result in the grown son's inability to criticize any figure of political authority. See "Fathers and Sons: Foundations of Political Belief," *American Sociological Review* 24 (August 1959): 502–11.

[21]T. W. Adorno, Else Frenkel-Brunswick, D. J. Levinson, and R. N. Sanford, *The Authoritarian Personality* (New York: Harper & Row, 1950).

beliefs about the effectiveness of their political activity. Those who feel they can influence government policy are, naturally, much more likely to be active. But where does the difference in beliefs originate? The five-nation study by Almond and Verba found an important clue in the style of family decision making.[22] Adults interviewed in the study were asked whether they remembered having had a voice in family decisions when they were children, and whether they felt that their actions as adults could influence the government. The answers showed a clear relation between the remembered family participation and the adult sense of "political competence": those who took part in family decisions were, on the average, more inclined to feel that expression of their political beliefs could influence the government.

Most of the political socialization that takes place in the family is informal—and sometimes it is unconscious. Neither the parent nor the child is actively aware that future political behavior is being shaped when, for example, the father "lays down the law" and refuses to hear any argument, or when the mother thinks aloud that there's no use complaining about the unfair amount of work she has to do around the house without any help, because her husband won't pay any attention. And parental attitudes and actions about political matters—for instance, their level of interest in election campaigns, or their readiness to accept special favors when they have a slight legal problem (getting a traffic ticket "fixed")—probably are more important in shaping the child's future political behavior than any of the specific ideas about government and politics that the parents consciously try to impart. In contrast is the more deliberate type of socialization that occurs in the schools.

The School. When a new nation is created, be it by revolution, civil war, or peaceful independence from a colonial power, one of the most important steps that the government must take is to teach its citizens that they are a national community. Schools are among the most important agents of socialization in turning scattered groups of people into a nation, since they are able to reach large numbers of individuals simultaneously and teach them that they belong to a community—a job for which the family is ill equipped. The developing nations of Africa are currently trying to unify a number of tribes that speak different dialects and that often have histories of conflict with each other. The role of U.S. schools has been profound, as they have been called on to turn immigrants with different political values into one nation. The Communist nations have also relied heavily on the schools for systematic inculcation of new political loyalties and concepts. As we see in Poland, though, this effort is not always successful; the Polish family and Church overrode the attempts of schools to make Poles believing Communists.

In nations where the government is already well established, the content of the school's political socialization is generally more in harmony with what the family teaches. Yet there is no doubt that even here, primary schools have a

---

[22]Almond and Verba, *The Civic Culture*, pp. 274–79.

YOUNG PIONEERS gather before St. Basil's Cathedral on Red Square in Moscow. The nearly compulsory Soviet youth group inculcates intense patriotism.

Michael Roskin

strong effect: they are able to reinforce the students' identification with the community and the nation. In classrooms around the globe, children salute different flags and are taught to feel positive emotion toward their own national symbols. The advocates of broad public schooling have usually stressed its value for teaching the meaning of citizenship and inculcating convictions about one's obligations to the national community.

The amount of schooling a person receives affects political attitudes at a more sophisticated level than the programmed loyalty to the Stars and Stripes or the Union Jack. For example, people with several years of education have a stronger sense of responsibility to their community and feel more able to influence public policy than do less-educated citizens. As Table 7–3 shows, even though there may be differences between the political cultures of separate nations, there is a striking correlation between a person's formal education and his or her attitudes toward the political system. Persons with more schooling show a greater awareness of political questions, pay more attention to politics, are more likely to engage in political discussion, and are more inclined to participate in politics.

How much of this is the direct result of what a person learns in class about his rights and responsibilities, and how much is explained by the fact that

Table 7-3   Percentage Who Say the Ordinary Man Should Be Active in His Local Community, by Nation and Education

NATION	OVERALL	PRIMARY SCHOOLING	SOME SECONDARY	SOME UNIVERSITY
United States	51	35	56	66
United Kingdom	39	37	42	42
West Germany	22	21	32	38
Italy	10	7	17	22
Mexico	26	24	37	38

Source: Gabriel A. Almond and Sidney Verba, *The Civic Culture* (Princeton, N.J.: Princeton University Press, 1963), p. 176. Reprinted by permission of Princeton University Press.

longer schooling is associated with higher socioeconomic status? Though this poses an analytical riddle, there is general recognition that education is a force in its own right aside from economic considerations, and consequently, intense battles are often fought over what and how the schools should teach. Black leaders rebelled against the use of textbooks which ignored or slighted the accomplishments of black people, especially those that appeared to do so deliberately. They saw the formal teaching of racial identity to be a vital element of what was needed for black people to progress toward the effective exercise of their political and civil rights.

According to one study, civics and government courses may impart very specific ideas and may even lay the basis for significantly greater political participation and sophistication. This study analyzed the political attitudes of high school students in three communities of varied economic background, before and after taking a civics course. It found that after taking the course, students were somewhat more likely to believe political participation was worthwhile, were more likely to support the rights of citizens and minorities to voice demands and dissent, and were less likely to have chauvinistic feelings that their nation was the only right nation.[23]

Peer Groups.   Whereas school lessons are a powerful socializing force, there is also some evidence that they may not have a very lasting effect unless other influences are pushing the individual in the same direction. For example, working-class children in Jamaica who went to school with children of higher social classes tended to take on the political attitudes of those classes, but when they attended school with only working-class peers, their attitudes did not change.[24]

The relative strength of peer-group influence compared with that of school and family appears to be growing. As a result of rapid change and

[23]Edgar Litt, "Civic Education, Community Norms, and Political Indoctrination," *American Sociological Review* 28 (February 1963): 69–75.

[24]Kenneth P. Langton, *Political Socialization* (New York: Oxford University Press, 1969), pp. 126–31.

economic specialization in modern society, parents cannot give their children a lot of the knowledge, skills, and perceptions they need in the outside world. Children consequently spend more time in school and out with their peers and less with their families. The results are that both schools and peer groups are growing more influential than the family, and peer groups seem to have increasingly more to do with the individual's assimilation of what the school presents.

The Mass Media. The media of mass communications constitute a fourth important socializing force. These media are part and parcel of modern industrial civilization. They have no counterpart in primitive societies, nor in classic civilizations of the past, and this is no accident. Modern technology created them, but more to the point, modern society, and particularly its government, depends heavily on them to perform even simple functions. Mass communications constitute a revolution in the way people get information about the world beyond their own daily experience and the way they form their perceptions about it. In the United States, even three-year-olds can recognize the president on television and understand that he is a sort of "boss" of the nation. Senators and congressmen, who receive much less coverage, are treated with relative indifference, a view the children may hold the rest of their lives.

As with schools, though, the mass media may be unsuccessful if the messages they beam are at odds with what family and religion teach. Poland's mass media attempted to teach respect for the Communist regime, but most Poles weren't buying. Iran's mass media, all firmly controlled by the Shah, tried to inculcate loyalty to him, but believing Moslems took the word of their local *mullahs* in the mosques and hated the Shah. Mass media can't do everything.

The Government. Government itself is inevitably an agent of political socialization. Virtually everything it does takes into account its citizens' reactions, and many government activities are intended explicitly to explain or display the government to the public.

All the actions of governing affect the people and, consequently, their attitudes, and the information, education, and propaganda supplied by the government are never designed to weaken public support and loyalty. Great spectacles of state, such as the crowning of a British king or queen, have a strengthening effect; so do parades with flags flying and impressive displays of military power. But many other activities, of a less formal character and implemented through other agents of socialization, such as the media and the schools, have similar effects. Schools, hospitals, and many office buildings fly flags; and proclamations of kings, presidents, prime ministers, and other dignitaries are announced in tones of respectful awe to young schoolchildren of all nations.

The power of government to control political attitudes is limited, however, because virtually all messages and experiences eventually reach the individual through conversations with primary groups of kin or peers, who interpret the original messages in terms of their own interests and established attitudes. Where alienated groups exist in a society, it is usually the family and the community that have "socialized" their children to dislike the government, in spite of the government's efforts to the contrary.

SUGGESTED READINGS

ABRAMSON, PAUL R. *Political Attitudes in America: Formation and Change.* San Francisco: Freeman, 1983. Excellent roundup of recent material on declining political attitudes with a good introduction to survey methodology.

ALMOND, GABRIEL A., AND SIDNEY VERBA. *The Civic Culture: Political Attitudes and Democracy in Five Nations.* Boston: Little, Brown, 1965. Landmark comparative study of political culture; a bit dated but still valuable.

————, EDS. *The Civic Culture Revisited.* Boston: Little, Brown, 1980. Critical, supporting, and updating essays on the original civic culture study; emphasizes change.

BELLAH, ROBERT N., ET AL. *Habits of the Heart: Individualism and Commitment in American Life.* New York: Harper & Row, 1986. Argues that American individualism erodes any sense of community.

DEVINE, DONALD J. *The Political Culture of the United States.* Boston: Little, Brown, 1972. A major synthesis of data that demonstrate the depth and continuity of U.S. political culture.

DI PALMA, GIUSEPPE. *Apathy and Participation: Mass Politics in Western Societies.* New York: Free Press, 1970. Demonstrates that political apathy is structured into modern democracy.

EASTON, DAVID, AND JACK DENNIS. *Children in the Political System.* New York: McGraw-Hill, 1969. A large, comprehensive survey of children's political development.

GREENSTEIN, FRED I. *Children and Politics.* New Haven, Conn.: Yale University Press, 1965. A study of how and what elementary and junior high school students learn about politics.

HUNTINGTON, SAMUEL P. *American Politics: The Promise of Disharmony.* Cambridge, Mass.: Belknap, 1981. A sophisticated argument that U.S. political culture is so hostile to power that it undermines American institutions.

LANE, ROBERT E. *Political Thinking and Consciousness: The Private Life of the Political Mind.* Chicago: Markham, 1969. An examination of why and how people come to think about politics as they do, based on twenty-four in-depth analyses of individuals.

LANGTON, KENNETH P. *Political Socialization.* New York: Oxford University Press, 1969. Good summary of what is known about the political socialization process.

LIPSET, SEYMOUR M., AND WILLIAM SCHNEIDER. *The Confidence Gap: Business, Labor and Government in the Public Mind,* rev. ed. Baltimore, Md: Johns Hopkins University Press, 1987. Finds that a series of "bad news," both economic and noneconomic, has eroded Americans' confidence in their institutions.

MANHEIM, JAROL B. *The Politics Within: A Primer in Political Attitudes and Behavior,* 2d ed. New York: Longman, 1982. Brief, readable survey of political psychology.

PYE, LUCIAN W., AND SIDNEY VERBA, EDS. *Political Culture and Political Development.* Princeton, N.J.: Princeton University Press, 1965. Excellent articles by top scholars on political culture and its problems in the Third World.

VERBA, SIDNEY, AND GARY R. ORREN. *Equality in America: The View from the Top.* Cambridge, Mass.: Harvard University Press, 1985. Demonstrates that U.S. political culture, especially that of the elite, favors only equality of opportunity, not of result.

chapter 8

Public Opinion

Political culture and public opinion are closely linked. They are generally formed through the same influences, and they merge together in a way that makes it hard to judge where one leaves off and the other begins. There is a clear connection between the process that shaped the general attitude of Americans toward communism during the late forties and early fifties and the process that shaped American opinion about the right of China's claim to Taiwan in 1988. Yet they are not the same thing. Political culture focuses on more or less permanent values, attitudes, and ideas which people learn from their society and apply to political questions. Most Americans are indoctrinated with the idea that communism in all its forms is evil: this feeling is built into the permanent value structure of American political culture just as clearly as the conviction that democracy is the only just form of government. Public opinion, whereas it is based on long-term convictions and ideals, relates to people's reactions to specific policies and problems rather than long-term value systems.

Just as public opinion is not synonymous with political culture, it is not to be confused with individual opinion, either. A woman's opinion of her neighbor's religion would not be part of public opinion, but her feeling that adolescents should pray in public schools would. Public opinion refers to political and social issues, not private matters of taste.

Finally, public opinion does not necessarily imply a strong, clear, united conviction of the masses. To be sure, there are subjects on which the majority of people are thus united in their opinion, and when that is the case, public opinion has mighty force indeed. But most often, public opinion involves several small groups of people with each group's views in conflict with those of the other groups, plus a large number who are undecided, plus an even larger number with no interest or opinion at all on the matter. On most subjects, public opinion is an array of diverse ideas and attitudes concerning political and social issues that can change fairly quickly.

The Role of Public Opinion

As a primary input by the people into the political system, does public opinion direct public policy? *Should* it? Both these questions are controversial and difficult to unravel. In a democracy, the man on the street's offhand answer would probably be, "Maybe it doesn't, but it certainly should." But the practical difficulties of realizing control by public opinion are profound. How could pollsters possibly keep tally of what the people think about every issue that comes before legislators and executives? The public doesn't even have an opinion on most issues, and the willingness of its members to make up answers when they don't feel competent to rely on their own knowledge further complicates matters. In 1948 a poll asked respondents what they thought of the "Metallic Metals Act." Fifty-nine percent supported the act, provided that discretion be left to individual states. Sixteen percent thought the act should not be imposed on the American people, and only 30 percent admitted they had no opinion on the matter. In fact, no such act existed, nor had any such bill been proposed.

Aside from the problems of the public's ignorance of many issues of government policy is the problem of morality: do numbers make right? Most Americans are opposed to raising taxes on gasoline. Does that mean that government should bar this means of taxation at all costs? In spite of public opinion's inadequacies as a guide for policy making, however, one cannot deny that it plays an important role in governing. Even in totalitarian states, the government knows that public support is vital for a stable rule and keeps an ear open for murmurs of dissent.

The role of public opinion in the political system is difficult to define. In a democracy, elections provide a formal means of popular control of government. But they provide only a very crude expression of public opinion. An election can only register the verdict of the voters on an official's overall performance; rarely is one issue so important that an election rides on it alone. Of course, if opinion is running strong in one direction, few candidates or legislators will defy it, so in this sense public opinion does provide some control. Few election hopefuls would run on a platform which advocated heavy tax increases or a severe cut in Social Security benefits. But for the most part, candidates, especially in two-party systems such as the British and the American, manage to ride through elections with little commitment to issues.

In many cases, public opinion is created, not followed, by the executive. Why else would some of our government leaders spend as much time as they do addressing the nation in front of TV cameras? When Richard Nixon announced in late 1971 that he would be the first American president to visit the People's Republic of China, he revolutionized public opinion about China (it quickly grew more favorable). Spanish Prime Minister Felipe González, head of a party that opposed Spain joining NATO, changed his mind and supported Spain's joining NATO. Public opinion polls, however, showed that most Spaniards didn't want Spain in NATO. González urged support for NATO in a 1986 referendum, and Spaniards swung around to support him. Governments can create public opinion.

If elections provide only a foggy outlet for public opinion, and executives often lead rather than follow the will of the people, the more direct participation of interest groups, be they concerned citizens or lobbyists, often allows opinions to be expressed in crystal-clear terms. In democracies which provide freedom to express dissent in bold and dramatic form, strategies for bringing grievances to public attention can be very effective in exciting widespread sympathy. The brutality of sheriff's deputies in Selma, Alabama, to blacks who were protesting denial of their right to vote was witnessed by television viewers across the nation, and the public reaction was a decisive force in passing the Voting Rights Act of 1965.

The Role of Public Opinion in Nondemocratic States.

Any government is vulnerable to public opinion powerfully mobilized against it. Mahatma Gandhi, by a simple drama of nonviolent protest, used the weapon of public opinion to win independence for India. A gaunt, bespectacled old man in a loincloth, he threatened to starve himself to death if the British did not pull out of India. So powerful was the support he generated that the British decided they could not risk the consequences of ignoring him.

SPANISH PRIME MINISTER FELIPE GONZALEZ, pictured here in a poster, persuaded Spaniards to vote for joining NATO. At least one sign painter, however, disapproved, calling NATO (OTAN in Spanish) a "Yankee monopoly."

Richard Barker

Government by sheer violence and coercion cannot last for any length of time. Even Nazi Germany, with all its brutal apparatus for suppressing dissent, depended on the dream of Germany's world supremacy—not night raids by the Gestapo—to rouse patriotic fervor. The importance of public support to the Hitler regime is attested to by the fact that the government kept careful tabs on how the German public felt about its policies. Documents found after World War II showed that the top Nazi leaders created a monumental network to test the people's reaction to each new policy and propaganda piece, and to gather reliable data on the people's morale.[1] Ironically, the regime's enormous power of coercion so intimidated expression that officials were afraid to send in negative reports. The result was that the Nazi government received rose-colored accounts rather than an accurate feedback, so that "public opinion" was never really fathomed.

[1] Aryeh L. Unger, "The Public Opinion Reports of the Nazi Party," *Public Opinion Quarterly* 29 (Winter 1965):565–82.

The Structure of Public Opinion

Within broad limits, social scientists have been able to discover roughly who thinks what about politics. It is important to bear in mind, however, that no social category is ever 100 percent for or against something. Indeed, 60 or 70 percent is often considered quite high. What we look for are *differences* among social categories, the significance of which can be tested by the rules of statistics. We look for different shades of gray, not for black and white. Once we have found significant differences, we may be able to say something about *salience*, the degree to which categories and issues affect the public opinion of a country. In Scandinavia, for example, social class is highly salient in structuring party preferences: the working class is heavily Social Democratic and middle class is heavily for the more conservative parties. In Latin Europe, social class is weakly salient, with the working class scattering its votes among parties of the left, right, and center. In Latin Europe, religion and region are typically most salient.

Social Class.   Karl Marx described social class as having massive salience. Workers, once they were aware of their situation, would become socialists. More recently, and with qualifications, social scientists have found that social class still matters, even in the relatively classless United States. Over the decades, the American manual worker tends to vote Democratic; the better-off or professional person tends to vote Republican.[2] But these are only tendencies, and they are often muddied by other factors. Poor people are often very conservative, whereas affluent people are liberal or even radical. During hard times, when bread-and-butter issues such as jobs become salient, the American working class tends to rediscover the Democratic party. When these issues lose their salience, however, the working class often finds that noneconomic issues gain in salience. Then, questions of morality (abortion, prayer in schools) and foreign policy (increasing defense spending) may siphon off a large part of the working class to the Republicans.

Social class can also be hard to measure. There are two general ways of going at the question: objective and subjective. An objective determination of social class involves asking a person his or her approximate annual income or judging the quality of the neighborhood. (This last is called an "ecological" determination of class because it utilizes surroundings.) The subjective determination of class involves simply asking the respondent what his or her social class is. Often this diverges from objective social class. A majority of Americans are used to thinking of themselves as middle class, even if they aren't. Sometimes even very wealthy people, thinking of their modest origins, call themselves middle class. The way a person earns a living may matter more than the amount he or she makes. Typically, American farmers are conservative about politics, and miners and steelworkers are not. Different political attitudes grow up around different jobs.

[2]Seymour Martin Lipset, *Political Man: The Social Bases of Politics,* expanded ed. (Baltimore, Md.: John Hopkins University Press, 1981) Chapter 7.

Sometimes social class works in precisely the opposite way envisioned by Marx. The liberalism of some affluent U.S. suburbs stands Marx on his head.[3] Spanish researchers found an *inverse* relationship between social class and preferring the left; that is, better-off persons were more leftist than poorer Spaniards. In the Spanish study, it was education that was most salient: a university education tended to radicalize Spaniards.[4]

Class matters in structuring opinion, but it is seldom a be-all or end-all. Usually social class is important when combined with one or more other factors, such as region or religion. In Britain, class plus region structures much of the vote; in France, it is class plus region plus religiosity (practicing Catholic vs. nonpracticing); in West Germany, it is class plus region plus denomination (Catholic or Protestant). As Yale's Joseph LaPalombara put it, the key question might be, "Class plus what?"[5]

Education.   Educational level is related to social class; that is, children of better-off families usually get more education, and education in turn leads to better-paying positions. Unlike the Spanish case, where university study tended to radicalize, education in the United States seems to have a split impact: it makes people more liberal on noneconomic issues but often makes them more conservative on economic issues. There are abundant survey data that show that college-educated people are more tolerant, more supportive of civil rights, and more likely to be acquainted with a variety of viewpoints. But when it comes to economic issues, many of these same people are skeptical of efforts to redistribute income in the form of higher taxes on the upper brackets—which happen to be them—and welfare measures for the nonworking. There are, to be sure, some educated people who are consistently liberal on both economic and noneconomic questions, but in the United States the categories sometimes diverge.[6] The same is often true of the American working class: its members want a bigger share of the national income but are intolerant in the areas of race, lifestyle, and patriotism. When college youths, mostly from middle-class families, protested the Vietnam war, they sometimes ran into the snarls and fists of unionized construction workers, a graphic illustration of the split between economic and noneconomic liberalism.

There is one thing that education does for sure: It increases political participation. College graduates are far more likely to vote, work in campaigns, follow politics, and contact officials than are people with only an elementary

---

[3]Everett Carll Ladd, "Liberalism Upside Down: The Inversion of the New Deal Order," *Political Science Quarterly* 91 (Winter 1976–77):4.

[4]Juan J. Linz, "El Electorado Espanol, un Electorado Europeo," *Opinión* [Madrid], 8 Jan. 1977.

[5]Joseph LaPalombara, *Politics within Nations* (Englewood Cliffs, N.J.: Prentice-Hall, 1974), pp. 440–44.

[6]Seymour Martin Lipset has long emphasized the difference between economic and noneconomic issues in public opinion. See I. L. Horowitz and S. M. Lipset, *Dialogues on American Politics* (New York: Oxford University Press, 1978), pp. 3–6.

education. Those who have completed high school are in an intermediate position. Education, in fact, is the nearly universal gateway to elite status. The elite of most countries are university graduates. (The exceptions to this are the revolutionary elites in power shortly after their takeover. The successor generation, however, is usually college-educated.) Education seems to contribute in many ways to political participation and then to elite status. Obviously, it increases knowledge, but it also increases self-confidence, speaking and writing ability, and the expectation of individual advancement. Indeed, the mere fact that you are reading this book indicates that you will likely participate in politics more than others and have a better chance of attaining some kind of political influence.

Region.   Every country has a south, goes an old saw, and this is certainly true in politics. What is uncertain, however, is whether a country's south is more conservative or more leftist than its north. France, south of the Loire River, and Spain, south of the Tagus, have for generations tended to go left. The south of Italy, though, is a bastion of conservatism, as is Bavaria in Germany's south. In Great Britain, England is heavily conservative, whereas Scotland and Wales go for Labor. And of course the U.S. South was famous for decades as the "solid South" that went automatically for the Democrats—no longer the case.

A country's outlying regions usually harbor resentment against the capital, creating what are called "center-periphery tensions." Often an outlying region was conquered or forcibly assimilated into the nation and has never been completely happy about it. Regional memories can last for centuries. This is true of the south of France, the U.S. South, the south of Italy, Quebec, and Scotland. Often the region feels economically disadvantaged by the central area. The region may have a different ethnic makeup, as in Catalonia and the Basque country in Spain, Wallonia in Belgium, Quebec in Canada, Croatia in Yugoslavia, and several parts of India.

Once a region gets set in its politics, the pattern is highly durable. Region plays a big role in the politics of Britain, France, and West Germany and even to a certain extent in the United States. The "solid South" has eroded, but the "sunbelt" of southern and western states is generally conservative on both economic and noneconomic issues and jealous of states' rights. The "frostbelt" of northern and eastern states, where industry has declined, tend to be more liberal, especially on questions of economic relief from Washington. In the early 1980s, when President Reagan cut both taxes and welfare expenditures, conservative southern Democrats, dubbed "boll weevils," supported him while some liberal northern Republicans, nicknamed "gypsy moths," opposed him, providing a vivid illustration of the effects of region on U.S. politics.

Religion.   Religion is often the most explosive issue in politics and contributes a great deal to the structuring of opinion. In many cases, religion has a greater impact on political viewpoints than does social class. Religion can mean either denomination or religiosity. In West Germany, Catholics tend to go to the

RELIGIOUS RIGHT mixes conservative politics with fundamentalist
Christianity at this small-town Fourth of July celebration.

Michael Roskin

Christian Democratic Union, whereas Protestants tend to go to the Social
Democrats or Free Democrats, although the question of social class is also bound
up with this choice. In Germany, it's a question of denomination. In France,
where most citizens are at least nominal Catholics, it's a question of religiosity, as
many French are indifferent to religion. The more often a French person goes
to mass, the more likely he or she is to vote for a conservative party. Few
communist voters are practicing Catholics. In Italy, religion and government are
linked through the large Christian Democratic party. One of the biggest
divisions in Catholic countries is between clericalists and anticlericalists; the
former are for a church role in politics, the latter against. France, Italy, and
Spain have long been split over this issue, with the conservative parties more
favorable to the Catholic Church and the parties of the left hostile to church
influence.

Religion plays a considerable role in the United States, too, although
here it overlaps with ethnicity. Catholics, especially Polish Catholics, have been
the most loyal Democrats of all.[7] In the great immigrations of previous decades,

[7]Andrew M. Greeley, "How Conservative are American Catholics?" *Political Science
Quarterly* 92 (Summer 1977):2.

big-city Democratic machines stood ready to welcome and help immigrants from Catholic countries, and in turn these people and their descendants stayed mostly Democratic. For a long time it was believed that no Catholic could be elected president of the United States; John F. Kennedy in 1960 put that view to rest, and now being Catholic probably does no harm to a candidate. Some Catholics and fundamentalist Protestants now have a common cause in fighting abortion.

Of major importance to U.S. politics has been the rise of the "religious right" during the 1980s. Many mainstream denominations became more conservative, and rapidly growing fundamentalist groups became highly political.[8] Ministers such as Jerry Falwell mobilized their television flocks against pornography and abortion and for a strong national defense and the Republican party. Another TV evangelist, Reverend Pat Robertson, made a try for the 1988 Republican presidential nomination.

American candidates, especially for the presidency, have always had to be known as churchgoers, but since the rise of fundamentalism many also wish to be known as "born-again" Christians. In 1980, both Ronald Reagan and Jimmy Carter claimed to have been born again in Christ. Former Senator Eugene McCarthy, who tried for the Democratic nomination in 1968, reflected in 1980 that he was the last presidental contender who had only been born once. Americans like their leaders to at least appear religious.

Age. There are two ways of measuring age in terms of political opinions: straight chronologically and generationally. Conventional wisdom sees young people as radical, ready to change the system, with older people more moderate or even conservative. With few responsibilities in youth, young people can indulge their fantasies, but with the burdens of home, job, and children of their own, people become more conservative.

This "life cycle" theory doesn't always work, for sometimes whole generations are marked for life by the great events of their young adulthood. Survivors of World War I and II, the Great Depression, and the Vietnam war have carried nervous remembrances of these upheavals for decades, coloring their views on war, economics, and politics. Sociologist Karl Mannheim called this phenomenon "political generations."[9] The young Americans of the 1960s and early 1970s who fought in or protested the Vietnam war, although they later became settled and more moderate in their views, reacted sharply to President Reagan's plans to stop Marxist revolutionaries in Central America. To the Vietnam generation, Nicaragua looked a lot like Southeast Asia. Likewise, older people who had personally experienced the depression of the 1930s were more supportive of federal welfare measures than younger people who had been raised in postwar prosperity. Age is not necessarily a mellowing process.

---

[8]For an excellent roundup of political shifts in U.S. denominations see A. James Reichley, "Religion and the Future of American Politics," *Political Science Quarterly* 101 (Spring 1986):1.
[9]Karl Mannheim, *Essays on the Sociology of Knowledge,* 2d ed., ed. by Paul Kecskemeti (New York: Oxford University Press, 1952), p. 291.

"WE THE UNDERSIGNED . . ." proclaims this Washington petition against the U.S. invasion of Cambodia in 1970.

Michael Roskin

Sex. Even before the women's movement, sex made a difference in politics. Traditionally, and especially in Catholic areas, women were more conservative, more concerned with home, family, and morality. This still applies in Catholic Spain and Italy. But as a society modernizes, men's and women's views become closer. Women leave the home to work, become more aware of social and economic problems, and do not necessarily just take over their husbands' political views. In the United States, an interesting "gender gap" appeared in the 1980s as women became several percentage points more liberal and Democratic than men.[10] And this was precisely because women had found the federal government necessary to support the old virtues of home and family. Further, many women disliked the Reagan Administration's emphasis on war preparation. It may be that in the modern political world, women will be the natural liberals.

Ethnic Group. Ethnicity is related to region and religion but sometimes plays a distinct role of its own, especially in the multi-ethnic United States. America was long touted as a "melting pot" of immigrant groups, but research has revealed the staying power and lively consciousness of ethnic groups for many generations. Democratic presidential aspirant Walter Mondale was described as modest and reticent about himself because he was Norwegian, and Norwegians are socialized in their families to never toot their own horns.

American politics is often described in ethnic terms, with WASPs (white Anglo-Saxon Protestants) and other northern Europeans generally conservative

[10]Adam Clymer, "Polls Suggest Women Support Democrats in '86 Races," *New York Times,* 11 May 1986, p. 22.

and Republican, and people of southern and eastern European origin, blacks, hispanics, and Asian Americans more liberal and Democratic. This simplification sometimes does violence to the complexity of individuals and of politics, but some working politicians still find it a valuable guide. Ethnic politics changes over the decades. After the Civil War, most blacks were Republican, the party of Lincoln. With Franklin D. Roosevelt and the New Deal, most blacks became Democrats and stayed that way. In the last century, American Jews were mostly Republican, for the Republicans sharply criticized the anti-Semitic repression of tsarist Russia. The Jewish immigrants of the turn of the century, introduced to U.S. politics by Democratic machines such as New York's Tammany Hall, went Democratic. In the 1970s, many Jews, influenced by neo-conservatism (see Chapter 6), swung to the Republicans. Ethnic politics is not fixed in concrete.

Public Opinion Patterns

What do the people as a whole think about a particular issue? In general, they can be for, against, or undecided. But the factors of uncertainty and changeability are so prominent in many areas that we can't always be confident that the "patterns" tell us a dependable story.

Classic Opinion Curves.   The way that different people feel about a question is often summarized statistically in a curve which shows the distribution of the different opinions sampled along a range from one extreme position to the opposite extreme. A noncontroversial issue—a "home, mother, and apple pie" matter on which there are only a few doubters and dissenters—will show most opinions massed at one extreme, a much smaller number with qualified opinions, or virtually none, at the opposite extreme. For example, if a cross-section of America is asked whether more effective measures should be developed to prevent environmental pollution, the answers could be mapped out along a very stable, one-sided curve (fig. 8-1).

On most issues, however, there is less consensus and little certainty. Here, public opinion takes the form of a "bell-shaped" curve or "unimodal distribution," which shows a relatively few people totally committed to a position at one extreme or the other, with the vast majority in the moderate area in between. Asked whether the size of the armed forces is too small, too large, or about right, it is unlikely that the majority will answer with either of the extremes. Conflicting factors such as the wish to keep taxes low, fear of Soviet power, and personal attitudes toward military service in general will cause the "too smalls" to be about equal to the "too larges"; but most people will reply with "about right."

A third characteristic pattern aggregate public opinion can take is that of extreme division or "bimodal distribution." On a large enough scale, this kind of opinion difference can lead to civil war. For years, there has been an almost total divergence between the Protestants and Catholics of Northern Ireland on virtually every question touching majority and minority rights, relations with

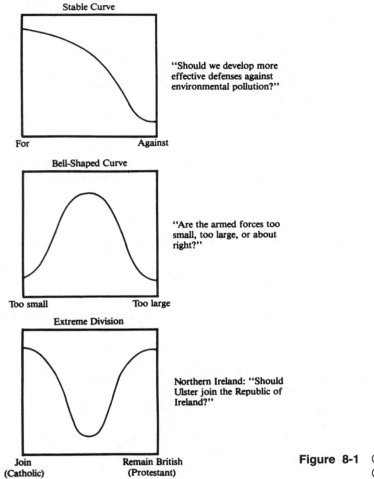

Figure 8-1 Classic Public Opinion Curves

Britain, and relations with Eire. The result has been violent civil conflict with almost no middle-of-the-roaders in Ulster.

Most often, though, opinion distribution does not fall into such well-defined patterns. The most important reason for this is that most people, most of the time, pay little attention to political and government issues. They have little sustained interest in issues that do not directly touch their lives, and therefore they acquire little information about these issues. Most public surveys, for example, will find that nearly half those questioned don't know who their congressman is.

Thus on most issues, only a small portion of the total public is attentive enough to news reports and editorials to hold a decisive opinion. And in many situations, a general public opinion curve will be a rather dim reflection of the opinion pattern within this "attentive public." With all of the uncertainties, personality quirks, and just plain ignorance involved in public opinion, how are surveys able to reflect an accurate picture of what the people are thinking?

PUBLIC OPINION POLLS

Any effort to gauge the attitude of the public by means of a representative sample is called a survey or poll. Published polls, particularly in election years, are prominent in today's political landscape. Almost daily we see statistics and percentages on what America thinks of crime, of civil defense, of abortion, of one candidate as opposed to another. The ubiquity of public opinion surveys serves as testament to their usefulness to policy makers and candidates alike. But debate has developed over some of their political side-effects. For example, do the polls give undue attention and influence to uncertain opinions? Do journalists create self-fulfilling prophecies by treating the polls as authoritative verdicts which people read about, then follow? Another area of controversy concerns the role of public opinion surveys. Should they be treated, as some propose, as a truly democratic method of deciding public policies? Even if one feels that all government action in a democracy should take its cue from the people's will, are public opinion polls reliable enough to determine policy? Who uses polls, what purpose do they serve, and can we trust them?

The History of Public Opinion Polls

In 1824, the *Harrisburg Pennsylvanian* sent its reporters to the streets to ask passers-by whether they intended to vote for John Quincy Adams or Andrew Jackson. The tally was printed on the theory that these "straws in the wind" indicated which way the political wind was blowing. Many other papers, using a variety of both careful and haphazard methods, conducted "straw polls" in various elections thereafter. But the popular magazine *Literary Digest* was the first to develop a survey of great prestige. In the early years of this century, it earned itself quite a batting average, accurately predicting the 1916, 1920, 1924, 1928, and 1932 presidential elections. The guiding principle of the *Literary Digest* technique was to use a huge sample, on the notion that the more people questioned, the more dependable the result. It conducted its survey by mail, drawing close to ten million addresses from lists of subscribers, car owners, and phone books. All went well until 1936, when 2.4 million people replied that they wanted Franklin D. Roosevelt out of office. The *Literary Digest* predicted the Republican candidate, Alfred M. Landon, as victor with 59.1 percent of the vote. Franklin Roosevelt's landslide victory—with over 60 percent of the vote— signalled the demise of both the straw-poll method of sampling and of *Literary Digest* itself.

As it happened, 1936 was also the first year that practitioners of the newly developed techniques of "scientific polling" were on the political scene, branching out from the field of market research. Several newspapers had begun syndication of George H. Gallup's survey results, which, in contrast to *Literary Digest,* forecast Roosevelt's victory. Gallup publicly predicted that the *Digest* poll was riding for a fall, and identified the reason: its sample was drawn heavily from higher-income people, many of whom were angered by Roosevelt's social and economic policies and who were thus likely to vote Republican. The guiding principle of the new technique used by Gallup was to select a sample as representative, rather than as large, as possible.

This scientific sampling method has dominated the field since then, with a very successful record. But even it met its match with the 1948 election, when almost every poll predicted that Thomas E. Dewey would defeat Harry S. Truman by a landslide. (It looked so certain to one leading pollster that he stopped taking samples in mid-September.) But even science can prove fallible, and Truman won with 49 percent in a four-way contest.

Some of the other hazards of election forecasting are highlighted by an analysis of what went wrong with the polls in 1948. A committee of the privately financed Social Science Research Council did the analysis.[11] It found that the sampling methods used were sound, but the key error came in assuming that respondents who said they were undecided would wind up voting in the same ratio as those who had made up their minds. In fact, these voters decided much more heavily in favor of Truman—close to 75 percent. The major polls have further refined their methods since that time and today make special efforts to detect late swings to one candidate or the other. It should be noted, however, that they do not even claim to be able to predict divisions within closer than 2 to 3 percent. The margin of victory in several presidential elections has been less than 1 percent, so it is clear that even the most accurate polls cannot furnish a confident prediction of the winner in such elections.

Polling Techniques

How can a sample of as few as 1500 people be used to predict the actions of a hundred million? The answer is complex, but it revolves around a technique which can be summarized in a few basic steps.

Asking the Questions. The goal of a public opinion survey is to get candid replies from a representative sample at a minimum cost. The problem of cost is yet to be overcome, as today's least expensive methods still tend to be the least accurate also. But there are fairly universal guidelines for getting the most candid replies possible and for choosing useful samples.

In finding out what the people think about an issue, the cheapest method is to mail out ballots to a sample and tally the replies, but invariably, the people who are involved enough to make the effort to reply will not be representative of the sample. The same factors which motivate some to respond

---

[11]*The Pre-Election Polls of 1948: Report to the Committee on Analysis of Pre-Election Polls and Forecasts,* Social Science Research Council Bulletin no. 60 (New York, 1949).

while others don't bother also make for opinion differences, as the *Literary Digest* experience showed. Telephone polling can avoid this, but it rarely establishes sufficient rapport to obtain really candid replies. The most dependable method is still the costly face-to-face interview. For reliable results, the interviewers should be carefully selected and trained. But even this method has drawbacks. Because it is costly, it often creates pressure on the pollster to make do with a minimum number of interviews.

The wording of questions so as to avoid leading the respondent toward one conclusion or the other is also an important element in sound polling technique. For example, the question "Should we stop communism in Central America?" will bring more affirmative responses than the question "Should we send troops to fight in Central America?" The pollster must also avoid tones of voice or sympathetic looks that might encourage one response over another—a task that is much harder than it seems. But whereas phrasing and asking opinion questions requires some amount of skill, a problem even more difficult is that of selecting the sample.

Selecting the Sample. In deciding whom to use as the sample, the pollster must make a choice between two major schools of thought. One, the stratified-quota sampling school, tries to include a proportionally representative cross-section of the society. Though the method has an undeniable logic, it is very difficult to carry out in practice. It puts a tremendous burden on interviewers, requiring them to pick and choose among respondents in order to maintain representative ratios as regards to income, sex, race, age, religion, and party preference. The judgments they must make in doing so can easily introduce unintentional errors, as they separate the procedure from a centralized control.

The second major approach is to try for a truly random sample, eliminating all elements of deliberate choice and judgment in deciding which individuals to include in the sample. The ideal method to obtain such a sample would be to put the name of every potential voter in the country in a data bank and have a computer print out several thousand names at random. This method produces more dependable results than the quota system. For telephone surveys, a computer actually dials the numbers nationwide at random, effectively eliminating human choice. The method most often used is to use one hundred to two hundred regular interviewers whom the polling company has hired from different areas around the country, each of whom interviews fifteen to twenty persons in a designated locality. The result is a total sample which is both random and highly representative. The method is called area sampling. It involves an initial decision of which geographic districts should become sample areas, the classification of these districts into groups according to population characteristics, and random selection of both, which categories to use and which people to question from each category. The resulting sample is quite close to that which a completely random selection would obtain and is considerably less expensive.

How Reliable Are the Polls?

The widespread use of public opinion surveys suggests that they have achieved a high degree of public confidence, and this is indeed true. Overall, the opinion research business sells services costing over a hundred million dollars a year in the United States alone, and the number of private polls commissioned by candidates in primary and general elections each year is now in the thousands.

A major limitation of polls, however, especially for election forecasting, is the unpredictability of voter turnout. This presents an extremely difficult problem, because many respondents who say they intend to vote actually will wind up staying home on election day. These voters and the "I don't knows" are quite likely not to divide up the same way as those who are very conscientious about voting. Thus, election results may be very different if there is a heavy voter turnout rather than if only a few show up at the booths. The election-year pollster must adjust raw findings for this factor, but there is no way to be certain how big the turnout will be and what, if any, will be the effect of last-minute events such as rain storms and foreign-policy announcements.

Public opinion is "volatile," able to change quickly under the impact of events. In 1965, as Lyndon Johnson escalated the war in Vietnam, an aide told him that "we have overwhelming public opinion on our side." LBJ, a crafty political pro who had long read the polls, replied, "Yes, but for a very underwhelming period of time." He was right; majority support for the war in 1965 turned into majority opposition in 1968.[12] Nothing is permanent in public opinion; volatility must be taken into account.

Finally, a survey that is accurate in its overall results cannot assure the same degree of reliability when broken down into finer categories. In order to get an accurate reading, the sample must be large enough to average out any quirks. But a sample adequate for a national finding will probably not involve a big enough sample from any one category, such as region, income, or religion, to provide the same degree of reliability.

AMERICAN OPINION

Presidential Popularity

One of the oldest and most important items in U.S. public opinion polls measures the popularity of the president at a given moment. In a technical sense, the question asks "how the president is handling his job as president," not how much the respondent likes the president. In practice, however, the respondent who likes the president will approve of the president's job performance.

---

[12]For a study of how much opinion changed during the Vietnam War among different subgroups, see Hazel Erskine, "The Polls: Is War a Mistake?" *Public Opinion Quarterly* 34 (Spring 1970): 1.

Table 8-1   Highs and Lows of Presidential Popularity

	HIGH	LOW	AFTER 5 YEARS
Truman	87%	23%	37%
event	end of World War II	Korean War	
Eisenhower	79%	49%	60%
event	reelection	recession	
Kennedy	83%	56%	—
event	Bay of Pigs invasion	—	
Johnson	80%	35%	43%
event	election	Vietnam war	
Nixon	68%	24%	27%
event	Vietnam peace	Watergate scandal	
Ford	71%	37%	—
event	takes oath	recession	
Carter	64%	26%	—
event	human rights	Iranian hostage crisis	
Reagan	68%	41%	65%
event	Geneva summit	recession	

Source: *New York Times,* 2 Feb. 1986. Copyright © 1986 by *The New York Times Company.* Reprinted by permission.

President Reagan, for example, was so likeable that citizens perceived him as doing a good job even when some of them disagreed with his economic and foreign policies. At any rate, the term "popularity" has stuck to this poll even if the question was designed to measure performance and not popularity.

Typically, presidents start with high popularity and then decline. During their first year they enjoy a "honeymoon" with the press and the public. The high point of their popularity often comes early in their term of office. After some years, however, problems accumulate: the economy turns sour or foreign policies don't work. This brings a popularity low point. Presidents seldom leave office as popular as they were during their first year.

Almost any major action a president takes produces at least a temporary upturn in his popularity. Americans like their presidents to be decisive, and they rally to expressions of firmness from the White House. Later, after the announced new policy has not produced expected results, popularity may again slump. Some suspect that presidents, especially later in their terms of office, may deliberately try to appear decisive in a dramatic way in order to boost their sagging popularity. Foreign policy provides the natural arena for such dramatic moves and (as we will consider in the next chapter) the best television coverage. A meeting with his Soviet counterpart, a bold strike against terrorists, or the rescue of American hostages provide a welcome lift in popularity for a president. Notice in Table 8-1 how the highest popularity ratings of Presidents Truman, Kennedy, Nixon, Carter, and Reagan came with a dramatic foreign policy event. Even a failure, the 1961 Bay of Pigs attempted invasion to overthrow Castro, caused Americans to rally around President Kennedy. When a humiliating situation lasts a long time, however, presidential popularity sinks, as Carter and Reagan both found in dealing with Iran. Similarly, a war that drags on a long

Table 8-2 The Ideology of Americans

	DESCRIPTION OF SELF	OF REAGAN	OF MONDALE
Very Liberal	5%	4%	14%
Somewhat Liberal	12	10	20
Moderate	48	31	37
Somewhat Conservative	24	26	9
Very Conservative	8	19	5
Don't know	3	9	15

Source: New York Times, 28 Feb. 1984. Copyright © 1984 by *The New York Times Company.* Reprinted by permission.

time destroys popularity; Truman experienced this in Korea and Johnson in Vietnam. Economic recession is also bad for popularity; three Republican presidents (Eisenhower, Ford, and Reagan) were rated low during economic downturns.

Presidential popularity based on one situation tends to spill over into other areas of presidential activity. As might be expected, President Reagan's popularity jumped several points in the wake of the successful U.S. takeover of Communist Grenada and the rescue of American students there in the fall of 1983. At that same time, approval of Reagan's economic policies also climbed, although little in the economy had actually changed.[13]

President Reagan retained his popularity unusually long; after five years in office he was rated close to his high point. But in late 1986 news of an attempt to ransom American hostages by selling arms to Iran brought a drop in Reagan's popularity. Reagan seemed to be going back on his word to never deal with terrorists. As the Iran arms scandal unrolled, he also seemed to be not fully in charge or aware of what his administration was doing; his age seemed to be catching up with him, and his ratings slumped below 50 percent approval.

Liberals and Conservatives

Reagan's personal popularity did not necessarily reorient Americans to a conservative ideology. Americans, politically, continued to distribute themselves unimodally, depicted as the familiar bell-shaped curve, with most people at the center of the curve (Table 8-2). Such a distribution, social scientists find, is virtually the norm for all industrialized democracies, a fact that probably makes democracy possible.[14] During the Reagan years, the percentage of Americans identifying themselves as conservatives did not increase, and more Americans expressed support for environmental and welfare legislation, typi-

[13]Barry Sussman, "Reagan's Broad Gains in the Wake of Grenada," *Washington Post National Weekly Edition,* 21 Nov. 1983, p. 10.

[14]In an interesting 1973 study, West Europeans were asked to place themselves on an ideological scale, one for the most left, ten for the most right. Most of the countries produced neat bell-shaped curves. See Ronald Inglehart and Hans D. Klingemann, "Party Identification, Ideological Preference and the Left-Right Dimension among Western Mass Publics," in *Party Identification and Beyond,* ed. by Ian Budge and others. (New York: John Wiley, 1976).

cally liberal causes.[15] The percentage who thought the poverty programs of the 1960s—one of Reagan's favorite targets—generally made things better actually increased during the Reagan years. Americans had not repudiated the moderate welfare state. The American people liked Reagan, but they did not become Reaganites.

How can we explain this seeming inconsistency: a popular conservative president but no growth in conservatism among the population? Here we return to the difference between economic and noneconomic liberalism discussed earlier in this chapter. Americans are not very clear about what they mean when they say "liberal" or "conservative." Retired people, for example, support Social Security and Medicare—attitudes that might make them economic liberals. But many retired people call themselves conservatives because they oppose the erosion of traditional values. They use "conservative" in the noneconomic sense. College-age people, on the other hand, may disdain the welfare state and celebrate market economics—making them economic conservatives—but they may call themselves liberal in reference to their open-mindedness on social, racial, and lifestyle questions.

This helps explain the Reagan years. President Reagan appealed to both economic and noneconomic conservatives. Some of the economic conservatives who supported him were liberal on other issues such as abortion, foreign policy, and race relations. The so-called "yuppies" were often in this category. Some of the noneconomic conservatives who supported him were liberal on economic policy such as government help for failing industries and for welfare programs. Working-class religious fundamentalists were apt to be in this category. It was Reagan's genius to be able to hold together these two different strands for several years. There had been little overall growth in "conservatism"; rather, Reagan had appealed to the economic conservatism of some and to the noneconomic conservatism of others. There was no guarantee that this coalition would stay together.

Who Pays Attention?

Some decades ago, political scientist Gabriel Almond proposed that there were three American public opinions, not just one:[16]

1. A *general public* that consists of a majority of Americans—people who don't know or care about much beyond their immediate concerns. For example, they show little interest in foreign policy unless the country is in a war or international crisis.

[15]R. W. Apple, Jr., "President Highly Popular in Poll; No Ideological Shift Is Discerned," *New York Times*, 28 Jan. 1986, p. A14.

[16]Gabriel A. Almond, *The American People and Foreign Policy* (New York: Frederick A. Praeger, 1960), p. 138. This book was originally published in 1950. Notice how the three levels of public opinion here correspond to the three types of political culture Almond later discovered in his civic culture study: the parochial, the subject, and the participant cultures. (see chap. 7). Political scientists seem to think in terms of three.

2. An *attentive public* that consists of a minority of Americans—people who are among the better-educated and who follow more abstract political concerns, such as foreign policy. They are the audience the elite plays to; and, in turn, this attentive public passes on views that mobilize the general public.

3. A *policy and opinion elite* that consists of a small number of highly influential people—those who are involved in politics, often professionally. These members of Congress, appointed officials, and top journalists devise foreign and domestic policies and articulate them to the attentive public and to the general public.

Especially in the case of foreign affairs, Almond has made a strong case. Survey after survey finds appalling ignorance of world affairs. Some citizens—even college students—may demand strong action against Libya or Nicaragua but cannot locate these countries on a map. In the case of domestic affairs, the general public has better knowledge and clearer views than they do on foreign policy. They are especially attentive to the state of the economy and react sharply to high inflation or high unemployment—problems no one can escape. Crime is also a widespread concern, and tough police and courts meet with approval. More abstract economic questions—such as the size of the federal deficit—arouse much less interest because they are not matters of personal concern.

The general public is also fragmented because divergent groups are interested in different questions. Farmers are concerned about produce prices, steel and auto workers about imports, women about wage equality, and minorities about job opportunities. Accordingly, the general public rarely speaks with one voice. A time period in which some groups are satisfied may be a time when others are dissatisfied. More affluent whites generally approved of Reagan's economic policies, whereas blacks and poor people, who still suffered from high unemployment levels, didn't approve of Reagan's policies.

The attentive public, although fewer in number, may have more importance politically because they have ideas which they articulate, demonstrating political competence. Sometimes they are capable of rousing the general public. Opposition to the Vietnam war and to South Africa's policy of apartheid started with small numbers of critics who wrote and spoke of their concerns in churches, newspapers, and classrooms. In the mid-1980s, while few people were paying attention, some of the attentive public were raising questions about war in Central America and the refugees from that part of the world. The attentive public can act as "sparkplugs" among the apathetic and slow-reacting general public. This is why all regimes treat intellectuals with caution and sometimes with suspicion. For this reason, Communist regimes expend great effort to ferret out a handful of dissident intellectuals. In Washington, administration officials devote much time and energy in trying to win over the attentive public so as to minimize criticism that might influence the general public and the next election. As we will consider in Chapter 9, relations between the White House and the news media often resemble a cat-and-mouse game. All over the country, the attentive public can offer the general public new ways of looking at issues. And the regime may not like attention drawn to certain issues.

Intensity. The general public's indifference and fragmentation mean their views are often hard to discern and may have relatively little impact on decision making. A member of Congress is apt to think: "Half the people in my district don't care about gun control. A quarter oppose it, and another quarter support it. So whom do I pay attention to?" Chances are, he or she will pay attention to the group with the most intensely held views. Polls show that most Americans would permit abortion, but few are strongly supportive of abortion. The "pro-life" foes of abortion, although a minority nationwide, feel so intensely about the subject that they can often drown out the greater numbers who are not passionately concerned. Intensely held views of a few can offset large numbers of indifferent people.

Jews are less than 3 percent of the U.S. population, but among them are such intense supporters of Israel that most elected officials take a pro-Israel stance. Some Jews and many Christians are indifferent or critical about Israel. But these views do not influence politicians because the indifferent views don't count and the critical opinions are held without passion and intensity. Red hot opinions beat lukewarm ones any day. The same situation occurs with opponents and supporters of gun control. Most Americans favor some form of gun control, but they are mostly lukewarm about the issue. The opponents to gun control are red hot and thus quite influential. The intensity factor means that relatively small groups of citizens can have a great deal of influence.

The disproportionate influence of the attentive public and passionate opinion-holders underscores one of the problems of public opinion. Often there is little "public" opinion, just the opinion of scattered and small groups who pay attention to issues and care intensely about issues. Should their views be excluded as nonrepresentative of the public or should they take on added weight as the views of the only people who really care about the issues? Which is the more democratic approach? Most people would be inclined to say democracy means going with the greatest numbers, even if their views are lukewarm. When it comes to a question that deeply concerns them, however, many people do not wish to have a simple headcount, arguing that the majority view is ignorant or mistaken and should not be heeded. We will consider some of these questions when we discuss interest groups in Chapter 10.

Is Polling Fair?

Polls do not merely monitor public opinion; they help make it. Critics charge that published or broadcast poll results can distort an election. For example, the news media may give considerable attention to polls that indicate one candidate is leading another by 35 percent. Such publicity, underdog candidates claim, can be devastating to their campaigns. Would-be supporters of the underdog candidate may lose interest. They may even jump on the leader's bandwagon. Even more important, campaign funds may dry up because the candidate behind in the polls looks like a loser. Few political scientists think average voters are likely to change their votes because a poll shows their candidate is losing. But it does seem probable that poor poll showings, especially early in the campaign, can act as a self-fulfilling prophecy of defeat for some candidates. Those who lead in the early polls get more donations, more news coverage, and thus more supporters. Those behind in the early polls are sunk at the start. We will consider the problem of media coverge in the next chapter.

One controversy of the 1980s was the effect of "exit polls" that question voters just as they leave the balloting area. With the three-hour time difference between the east and west coasts, exit polls enable television to predict winners in the East while westerners still have hours in which to cast a ballot. Does the early prediction in the East effect the vote in the West? Democrats charged that during the two Reagan landslides many West Coast people were persuaded to not bother to vote because the early East Coast exit polls had already given the contest to Reagan. This development robbed state and local Democratic candidates in the West of votes that might have been theirs if more people had voted. Some urged a delay in broadcasting the results of exit polls, but the television networks, pleading freedom of the press, refused to delay. No evidence was found that exit polls influenced the presidential vote, but they might have influenced other contests for the House, the Senate, or the state legislature. Polls, especially when their results are broadcast so quickly, are not neutral in their impact, but no constitutionally legal way has been found to control them.

Should America be Governed by Polls?

Considering the preceding discussion, it would seem in most cases that America should not be governed by polls. First, public attention varies widely. On many issues, the general public has no knowledge or opinion. In such a situation, the intense concern of a minority might dominate the poll results. Leaders, especially with modern means of communication, can influence public opinion in their direction. This encourages government leaders to try to create the kind of feedback they want to hear. Typically, public opinion follows executive decisions by several months. Public opinion does not usually lead executive decisions.

The wording of the questions and selection of the sample (the people to be polled) can seriously skew poll results. We must be sure that the survey was done by reliable professionals with standardized questions and a random sample. Polls conducted by partisans of a cause or candidate can seriously mislead and should be ignored. Equally serious is the problem of volatility: the changeable nature of poll results. What the public likes one month it may dislike the next. Decisions made on the basis of a given survey may meet with public displeasure when the consequences of the decisions sink in. Accordingly, public officials who are tempted to "go with the polls" and think, "All those voters can't be wrong," may be stepping into a trap that hurts both themselves and their country if they vote on the basis of the polls alone. The polls, if done well, can provide a useful snapshot of public opinion at a given moment. Poll results are no substitute for a careful analysis of the issue and prudent anticipation of the future.

SUGGESTED READINGS

ASHER, HERBERT. *Public Opinion Polling*. Washington, D.C.: CQ Press, 1987. Short, informative introduction to techniques and problems of survey research.

BENNETT, W. LANCE. *Public Opinion in American Politics*. New York: Harcourt, Brace, 1980. Good introductory roundup that includes findings up to 1980.

COHEN, BERNARD C. *The Public's Impact on Foreign Policy*. Boston: Little, Brown, 1973. Finds public opinion follows rather than leads in the formation of foreign policy.

HOLLOWAY, HARRY, AND JOHN GEORGE. *Public Opinion: Coalitions, Elites, and Masses*. New York: St. Martin's, 1982. Delineates and attempts to weigh the several factors that contribute to the makeup of public opinion.

KEY, V. O., JR. *Public Opinion and American Democracy*. New York: Knopf, 1961. An eminent authority on American politics gives a basic statement on public opinion and examines how much it does and should influence governance.

MCCLOSKY, HERBERT, AND ALIDA BRILL. *Dimensions of Tolerance: What Americans Believe About Civil Liberties*. New York: Basic Books, 1983. A sophisticated study that shows markedly greater support for civil liberties among elites.

NIEBURG, HAROLD L. *Public Opinion: Tracking and Targeting*. New York: Praeger, 1984. A more advanced book on techniques for following change and ascertaining the views of subgroups.

PIERCE, JOHN C, ET AL. *The Dynamics of American Public Opinion: Patterns and Processes*. Glenview, Ill.: Scott, Foresman, 1982. Comprehensive overview of long-term change and stability in U.S. public opinion.

QUALTER, TERENCE H. *Opinion Control in the Democracies*. New York: St. Martin's, 1985. Warns of the dangers of government using propaganda to manipulate public opinion.

SIMON, RITA JAMES. *Public Opinion in America, 1936–1970*. Chicago: Markham, 1974. Good summation of the empirical findings of standard survey questions from the beginning of scientific polling.

WORCESTER, ROBERT M., ED. *Political Opinion Polling: An International Review*. New York: St. Martin's, 1983. The history, methods, and problems of polls in ten countries; a rare international comparison.

chapter 9

Political Communication and the Media

The mass media have always loomed large in American politics.[1] In the 1780s, the Federalist Papers were published in daily newspapers throughout the colonies in an all-out effort to win over the people to the idea of a new constitution. Andrew Jackson's victory in 1828 over John Quincy Adams marked the end of one of the most bitter "media campaigns" in America's history. In it, mudslinging reached its high point (or low point) when Jackson and his wife were accused of moral irregularities, and the press played a key role in the exchange of propaganda. In the early twentieth century, we had a media candidate in Teddy Roosevelt: he tailored his rough-and-ready image to fire the imagination of the people, with great success. And Franklin D. Roosevelt used his famous fireside chats on radio, along with hundreds of press conferences, to win support for his policies. In 1987 the media crushed the candidacy of Democratic presidential hopeful Gary Hart with revelations of his alleged "womanizing." Today, the mass media are a recognized component of American politics, and modern campaigns depend on television so much that many critics complain that candidates no longer run for office on issues—instead, professional media consultants package them and sell them like any product.[2]

COMMUNICATION IN POLITICS

Political scientists have long recognized the dependence of political power on communications—as any quick comparison of Abraham Lincoln's power with that of Ronald Reagan will reveal. Karl W. Deutsch, among the first to systematically study the political uses and implications of modern communications systems, claims the rate of modernization of developing nations and the rise and decline of metropolitan areas around the globe can be measured from patterns and flow of mail, telephone calls, and migration paths of the labor force.[3] The political system and the communication system precisely parallel one another, and it is doubtful that one could exist without the other.

Levels of Communication

All political action is a reaction to communication of one kind or another. There are, however, different levels and types of communication. Face-to-face communication is the most basic. It is also the most effective means for altering or reinforcing political opinions, because it allows for dialogue where mass media cannot. Listeners in an auditorium can question or challenge the speaker, and he or she can respond directly to the audience to overcome their resistance.

[1] For a fine historical review, see Thomas C. Leonard, *The Power of the Press: The Birth of American Political Reporting* (New York: Oxford University Press, 1986).

[2] See Kathleen Hall Jamieson, *Packaging the Presidency: A History and Criticism of Presidential Campaign Advertising* (New York: Oxford University Press, 1984).

[3] His basic concepts can be found in Karl Deutsch, *The Nerves of Government: Models of Political Communication and Control* (New York: Free Press, 1966), and *Nationalism and Social Communications: An Inquiry Into the Foundation of Nationality* (New York: John Wiley, 1953).

Until the early 1930s, face-to-face communication was the main method of political campaigning and proselytizing. Nominees for office would stump their districts and address small groups of voters, appealing for their support with the help of ward bosses, precinct captains, and political organizers. However, the rise of television and the complexity of modern society have today largely destroyed the tradition of grass-roots stumping, except as a means of getting free coverage on newspaper front pages and news programs.

The Mass Media. The great advantage of the mass media over face-to-face communication is that they reach an infinitely larger audience, and therefore yield a greater voter or public-opinion return. A speech that gets on television can reach millions of people at once, but a speech given at even the largest rally may be heard by only a few thousand people. If even a small percentage of television viewers respond positively to what the speaker says, that response can become tens of thousands of votes—perhaps enough to swing an election.

But the mass media are essentially a one-way avenue of communication. If a viewer dislikes President Reagan, she can turn the channel; if she disagrees with his message, he can't counter her objections with a custom-made response. Studies of the impact of the mass media on individual thinking and behavior show that mass media can effectively reinforce existing political opinions but can't really convert anyone. Radio and television do have stronger persuasive power than the printed word because they are closer to face-to-face communication, but their impact on the people still depends partly on the influence of chats with friends after the program is over.

The Two-Step Flow of Mass Communications. If most messages bounce off most people without leaving much of an impression, how do the mass media penetrate an audience? Paul Lazarsfeld and Elihu Katz were among the first to perceive a two-step pattern in this process.[4] They found that every community has respected *opinion leaders*—teachers, ministers, community and civic leaders, outstanding businessmen and professional leaders—who follow the media carefully. These people take political cues from the mass media and pass them on to their less attentive friends in normal daily contact. In this way, political messages filter down to everyone. The effectiveness of mass-media appeal depends on these opinion leaders, and it is they whom successful politicians must reach, influence, and convince. Notice the resemblance here to Almond's distinction between the "general" and "attentive" publics discussed in the last chapter.

Television may have somewhat eroded the role of opinion leaders in the community. The TV newscaster has become an opinion leader on a grand scale. Television not only serves by transmitting direct political messages, it also serves indirectly as an instrument of social change by bringing news events into the

---

[4]Paul Lazarsfeld and Elihu Katz, *Personal Influence* (New York: Free Press, 1955); also Elihu Katz, "The Two Step Flow of Communication: An Up-to-Date Report on an Hypothesis," *Public Opinion Quarterly* 21 (1957):61–78.

homes of the people. Most observers agree that the black civil rights movement of the 1960s would not have achieved the success it did without television. Racial discrimination in the South was largely unnoticed—perhaps deliberately unnoticed—in the print media and radio. But TV news of fire hoses and police dogs used to attack peaceful marchers turned most Americans in favor of equal black rights. Likewise, the graphic television coverage of the Vietnam war—the world's first television war—turned many people against the war and against President Johnson.

Who Uses the Media?   Not everybody watches TV, especially TV news coverage. And not everybody reads on subways or buses or listens to the radio while driving to work. The various modern media appeal to different audiences, who can be distinguished by education, income, and age. The better educated individuals are, the more they will use the mass media. College graduates tend to read newspapers, magazines, and books as well as listen to the radio and watch television and motion pictures. But grammar- and high-school graduates, who use the mass media more for entertainment, generally favor television, radio, and motion pictures more than the print media. Likewise, people in high-income brackets read a lot, whereas low-income groups rely more heavily on television and radio for information and entertainment. Ninety percent of the people in high-income brackets are regular magazine and book readers, but only half of the people in low-income groups are.

Age or maturity also affects the use of the mass media. In general, people between the ages of thirty and fifty pay more attention to the editorial and news content of newspapers and magazines than do teen-agers and young adults, who tend to use newspapers for entertainment. Young readers tend to study the sport pages, follow the doings of theatrical celebrities, and pay more attention to feature articles than to hard news stories. The eighteen-year-old who keeps up on the news and editorial opinion is the exception, not the rule.

Modern Mass Media

Newspapers.   In 1910, the United States had more than 2600 daily newspapers, and 57 percent of all American cities had two or more competing papers. Today, fewer than half of these newspapers remain, and they have monopolies in almost every community. Does this decline in competition mean that the people are being denied access to a healthy variety of political and editorial opinion? The charge that the fabled "free press" is little more than a sham is backed up by certain facts. Some 60 percent of U.S. newspapers are owned by centrally controlled syndicates or chains, and corporation ownership of most large newspapers gives them a conservative bias.

But most newspapers do not present the news in an obviously partisan manner. The reasons are both practical and idealistic. Sixty-five to ninety percent of newspaper revenue comes from advertising, and fees from advertisers depend on the newspapers' circulation. Thus, keeping circulation high is the main concern, and the result is usually a middle-of-the-road news policy calculated to please most people.

Journalism itself has a long tradition of objectivity in news reporting (although the editorial page may be another story). The profession's own idealism no doubt influences newspaper people to present the news fairly and honestly. Further, most news printed in the U.S. papers is from a wire service, and wire services take special pains to be objective and to refrain from editorializing.

How much political impact, then, do U.S. newspapers have? Not as much as they used to. Fewer households take newspapers now than half a century ago. The content of newspapers is mostly advertisements (one important reason people read them) and wire-service copy. The editorials of most newspapers carry little weight. There are, of course, some exceptions, and for these we refer to the "elite" media.

The Elite Media. *The New York Times, The Washington Post,* and *The Wall Street Journal* are read by a small fraction of the U.S. population, but they carry by far the most clout. Decision makers in Washington and indeed across the country read them and take both their news stories and their editorials seriously. Leading thinkers fight battles on their "op-ed" pages (opposite the editorial page) or in their letters-to-the-editor columns. That is why these papers have influence out of all proportion to their circulation. They are what is known as the "elite press." The people who read them on average are wealthier and better educated and have more influence than the reader of a hometown paper. The elite press pursues "investigative reporting," looking for governmental and partisan wrongdoing, something the average paper usually shuns. *The New York Times* jolted the nation when it published the "Pentagon Papers" on the Vietnam war in 1971. The dogged pursuit of the 1972 Watergate burglary by *The Washington Post* brought down the Nixon Administration in 1974. The editorials of *The Wall Street Journal* influenced economic decisions in the Reagan administration.

The small-circulation magazines of opinion also qualify as the elite press. The conservative *National Review,* the liberal *New Republic,* the leftist *Nation,* and the neo-conservative *Commentary* have considerable impact on "opinion leaders," the sorts of people who influence others. President Reagan named Jeane Kirkpatrick as ambassador to the U.N. on the strength of an article of hers he had read in *Commentary.* Students are often ignorant of the elite press, but those who themselves aspire to leadership status would be well advised to follow one or more of these journals.

Radio. Like newspapers, radio is not what it used to be. Between the two world wars it zoomed in popularity, and radio news, comments, and political addresses—such as Franklin D. Roosevelt's famous "fireside chats," which served as models for both Jimmy Carter and Ronald Reagan—were quite influential. But with the rise of television in the 1950s, radio became a medium of background music for driving or doing housework. News dwindled into brief hourly spots, much of it "rip and read" from the wire-service printer. Radio now has little political impact. But radio too has an elite exception, the 90-minute radio magazine *All Things Considered* on National Public Radio, full of in-depth explorations of world events, economics, politics, and reasoned opinion. This daily broadcast brought back to radio a portion of the better-educated of all political persuasions.

The Wire Services.   Most hard news in newspapers and on radio, and even a good deal of television's news, is not produced in-house but comes from a printer hooked up to the New York offices of the Associated Press or United Press International. True, the elite press disdains to use wire-service copy, as it's a matter of pride for them to have their own newspersons covering the story. But most papers in America are little more than local outlets for the Associated Press (AP) and United Press International (UPI). Often editors on small-town papers read just the first two paragraphs, so that they can write a headline, and slap the stories into their papers nearly at random.

AP is a cooperative, with members paying assessments based on their circulation. They also contribute copies of local stories to AP, which rewrites them for nationwide transmission. UPI, long in financial difficulties, is privately owned and sells its wire to subscribers. The interesting thing here is that AP and UPI are among the few wire services not owned, subsidized, controlled, or supervised by a government. They are free of governmental influence and proud of it. Britain's Reuters gets discreet government subsidies; France's AFP has government supervision, as does West Germany's DPA; and the Soviet Union's TASS is wholly a creature of Moscow.

The American wire services are free, but they have other problems which limit their quality and influence. First, they move fast; every minute is a deadline. This means they can give little time to digging. Second, the wire services' definition of news is something from an official source. All wire-service stories are carefully attributed to police, the White House, the State Department or Pentagon, and so on. If it's not official, it's not news. This causes the wire services to miss many explosive situations in the world because they do not like their reporters to talk to opposition people, the average man in the street, or the merchants in the bazaar, who might have a completely different—and sometimes more accurate—perspective than the official spokespersons. Most American news media failed to notice the coming of the Iranian revolution for this reason. Often the best news stories are not about a key event or statement but about what people are saying and thinking. The wires don't cover this.

THE GIANT: TELEVISION

When most Americans say "the media," they mean television, for television towers over everything else in terms of impact. Most Americans get their political information from television, and most say they believe information obtained

MEDIA EXECUTION: On February 1, 1968, Associated Press photographer Eddie Adams snapped this photo of South Vietnam's police chief blowing out the brains of a captured Vietcong officer. TV cameras also captured the instant that helped turn Americans against the war.

Wide World Photos

from television more than that in newspapers. Television has touched almost everything in American politics and has changed almost everything it has touched. Election campaigns now revolve heavily around the acquisition of TV time; winners are usually those who can raise the most money to hire the best media consultants. Television has become a suspect in the decline of both U.S. election turnout and political parties. Some observers see television as contributing to the more complete trivialization of U.S. politics, which admittedly was seldom very profound to begin with.[5]

TV News

Television, by very definition, favors the visual. Just talking heads provide no more news than does radio. (Talking heads do provide something very important, though—a sense of personality and hence credibility, a sort of imitation face-to-face communication). TV news producers therefore devote more attention to a news story with "good visuals" than without. As with the wire services, abstract, deeper topics tend to go by with little coverage, whereas dramatic action—if there was camera crew on hand to catch it—gets played up. Television, like most of the rest of the U.S. news media, ignored the deep hatred that was brewing against the Shah of Iran for years, but caught the dramatic return of Ayatollah Khomeini. Television never did explain what the Vietnam war was about, but a brief film clip of a Saigon general blowing out the brains of a Vietcong prisoner in 1968 helped sicken Americans against the war. Just as the wire services are hooked on official sources, television news is hooked on the eye-catching. This makes television inherently a more emotional medium than

[5]For an argument that television has turned politics into show business, see Niel Postman, *Amusing Ourselves to Death: Public Discourse in the Age of Show Business* (New York: Viking, 1985).

the others. Television coverage can go straight to the heart, bypassing the brain altogether; that is its great power.[6]

Unfortunately, TV camera crews are expensive to maintain in the field, especially overseas, so they usually arrive where the action is only *after* having been notified by the wire services. Television prefers to know in advance what's going to happen; then it can schedule a camera crew. This makes TV news lopsided with press conferences, speeches, committee hearings, and official statements. Some critics characterize these happenings as "media events," things that would not have occurred without television coverage. A media event is not fake, but it is planned in advance with an eye to catching the attention of TV crews. Not only do officials understand this, but protest groups, too, stage marches, sit-ins, and mass arrests to get TV exposure for their cause. Chanted protesters at the 1968 Democratic convention in Chicago: "The whole world is watching!" The next time you watch television, count the number of film clips of events that were obviously scheduled in advance as opposed to those that weren't; the former will probably outnumber the latter by a big margin.

Deep analysis is also not television's strong point. An average news story runs one minute; a two- or three-minute story is considered an in-depth report. Walter Cronkite, long dean of TV newspeople, repeatedly emphasized that television news was just a "headline service," meaning that if viewers wanted detail and depth they would have to go elsewhere. Many Americans, of course, don't look deeper and are left with the tardy, the eye-catching, and the media event as their daily diet of information. Thus it is not surprising when polls repeatedly discover that Americans are poorly informed about the great issues of the day.

Television and Politics

All agree that television has changed politics, and in several ways. Incumbency, especially in the White House, has always brought recognition. TV has enhanced this recognition, but not always to the incumbent's satisfaction. Television news is heavily focused on the president and to a lesser extent on the rest of the executive branch. Congress gets much less coverage, the courts even less. This deepens a long-term American tendency to president-worship. The president—especially with the way TV socializes small children—is seen as an omnipotent father figure, a person who can fix all problems. That in itself should make a current president very happy. But then things go wrong; the president doesn't fix the problems; an ultra-critical press implies that his policies may be making them worse. The flip side of being treated as all-powerful is catching all the blame. The media, especially television, whips up president-

---

[6]Although ignored as a charlatan by most communication scholars, Marshall McLuhan offered valuable insights into the power of television. See his *Understanding Media: The Extensions of Man* (New York: McGraw-Hill, 1964); and Marshall McLuhan and Quentin Fiore, *The Medium is the Message* (New York: Penguin Books, 1967).

worship and then whips up mass dissatisfaction with the president's perform-ance. This whip-'em-up-and-let-'em-fall factor may have contributed to the rash of one-term presidencies that followed Eisenhower. Expectations, heightened by the media, are very high, and disappointments are correspondingly bitter. Some critics charge that the media are wrecking the U.S. political system with that kind of coverage, making the country unstable and ungovernable.[7]

Nomination by Television. Television also contributes importantly to the presidential selection process. With all eyes focused on the early presidential primaries—especially New Hampshire—commentators grandly proclaim who is the "real winner" and who is picking up "momentum."[8] The lucky candidate thus designated as frontrunner goes into the remaining primaries and the national convention with a bandwagon effect, enhanced recognition, and lots of TV coverage. In the nominating process, television has become a kind of kingmaker. It is no wonder that candidates arrange their schedules and strategies so as to capture as much TV exposure as possible.[9]

TV coverage of candidates focuses on their personalities, not on issues. Television, with its sharp close-ups and seeming spontaneity, gives viewers what they think is a true glimpse of the candidate's character. Actually, this may not be so; some candidates play the medium like professionals (Ronald Reagan), and others tense up and hide their normal personalities. How a candidate performs on television is a poor index of how he or she will perform in office, but it is the one most American voters use.

While television is playing this major role in nominating and electing candidates, the political party is bypassed. Party organizations and bosses are not very important, as candidates on television can go right over their heads to the voters. Since the leading contender or two have already picked up their "momentum" going into the convention, they don't need party professionals to broker a nominating deal. Politics has come out of the proverbial smoke-filled back rooms and into the glare of TV lights, not always for the better. The party and its chiefs used to know a thing or two about politics and were often capable of putting forward tried and tested candidates. With television, a candidate can come from out of nearly nowhere and win the top national office with little political experience. We must be careful, though, in blaming television for the weakening of the parties. American parties, with the exception of a few urban machines, were never as strongly organized as most European parties. And American parties began declining a long time ago, not just with the advent of television. Further, other factors, such as the rise of special-interest groups,

---

[7]See Austin Ranney, *Channels of Power: The Impact of Television on American Politics* (New York: Basic Books, 1983).

[8]See Leon V. Sigal, "Newsmen and Campaigners: Organization Men Make the News," *Political Science Quarterly* 93 (Fall 1978):3.

[9]Thomas E. Patterson, "Television and Election Strategy," in *The Communications Revolution in Politics*, ed. Gerald Benjamin (New York: Academy of Political Science, 1982).

PRESIDENT REAGAN used his professional abilities to the fullest in his weekly radio broadcasts modeled on FDR's "fireside chats." Decades earlier, Reagan had begun his career as a radio announcer.
Karl H. Schumacher, The White House

political-action committees, and direct-mail solicitation have also undermined party strength. Television is not the sole culprit.

Television and Apathy.   Another "blame-television" charge also has to be taken with a grain of salt: that television has made U.S. voters apathetic and lowered election-day turnouts. True, there is a close coincidence in time; turnout has dropped some ten percentage points since 1960, when TV first established itself as the top means of campaigning. Possibly TV saturates viewers so far in advance that they lose interest. Perhaps this loss of interest has occurred because the top two candidates usually sound so similar that voters see little difference, although this could happen without television. Perhaps it is because the charges and countercharges in political spots come so thick and fast that the voter is "cross-pressured" into indecision and apathy. All of these theories may be true, but it's hard to blame television alone, because the declining U.S. voter turnout also comes at a time of declining party strength and identification. In Western Europe, where paid-for political TV spots are generally prohibited and campaigns are much shorter—usually about a month instead of the year and more in the United States—voter turnout is much higher, sometimes topping 90 percent. But does this high turnout have much to do with television or is it a result of party organization and voter identification?

One thing U.S. television does for sure: It costs candidates a bundle. Depending on the time of day and locale, a one-minute spot can go for $100,000. The cost factor in itself has transformed American politics. Members of

Congress can sometimes get by with little TV advertising, but virtually all senatorial and presidential candidates need it. About half of presidential campaign chests are estimated to now go for television. Political consulting—the right kind of themes, slogans, and speeches presented in the right kind of TV spots—has become a big business. Some critics contend that with enough money, a candidate can, in effect, buy the office through television. That may be an exaggeration, but money in politics has become more important than ever. This heightens the importance of special-interest groups and political-action committees, which in turn has weakened the role of the parties and perhaps deepened feelings of powerlessness among average voters. In the TV age, chances are that the winning candidate has also spent much more, most of it on televised spot advertising.

More and more Americans are ignoring party labels, either calling themselves "independents," splitting tickets, or voting for the other party. The trend, alarming to some political scientists, is called voter "dealignment," citizens *not* lining up with a party. Lacking party identification, these voters are increasingly open to persuasion via the media, especially television.[10] This, some suggest, produces great "volatility" as voters, massaged by media professionals, shift this way and that in response to candidates' televised images.

Television: Ownership and Control

The U.S. government exercises the *least* control of communications of any industrialized country. Since the invention of the telegraph, the American government has stood back and let private industry operate communications for profits. In Europe, by contrast, telegraphy was soon taken over by the postal service, as were telephones. The U.S. government—partly because of First Amendment guarantees of free speech and partly because of the U.S. ethos of free enterprise—simply does not like to butt in. For European nations, with traditions of centralized power and governmental paternalism, national control of electronic communications is as normal as state ownership of the railroads.

The U.S. attitude of nonpaternalism has led to the freest airwaves in the world, but it has also brought some problems. With the rapid growth of radio in the 1920s, the electromagnetic spectrum was soon jammed with stations trying to drown each other out. To bring some order out of the chaos, the Radio Act of 1927 set up a five-member Federal Radio Commission (FRC) appointed by the president to assign frequencies, call letters, and maximum power. Stations had to get licenses and could lose them. Most important, the 1927 act put the government on record for the first time as recognizing that the airwaves were public property and should serve "the public interest, convenience, and necessity." The Communications Act of 1934 superseded the FRC and created the Federal Communications Commission (FCC), which monitors broadcasting to

---

[10]Thomas R. Dye and L. Harmon Zeigler, *American Politics in the Media Age*, 2ed. (Monterey, Cal.: Brooks and Cole, 1986), chap. 6.

this day. The 1934 act recognized the danger of partisanship and now provides for five FCC commissioners appointed by the president and approved by the Senate. The commissioners serve staggered seven-year terms, and no more than three can be members of the same party.

The Wasteland. In theory, the FCC licenses radio and TV stations to serve "the public interest," but in practice no station gets its license revoked. The FCC lays down no rules about program content except for obscenity on the air. Programs can be as trashy or as lofty as the owners want. Most owners, in their appraisals of the viewing audience, emphasize the former. FCC Commissioner Newton Minow decades ago despaired that television was a "vast wasteland," but there was nothing the FCC could do to make programs more cultural, educational, or morally uplifting. Most broadcasting in America is private and profit-oriented. Profits derive from advertising, which depends on audience size. Station owners argue that they automatically serve the public interest in offering the programs most people want. They are also, of course, serving their own interests. If most people want 24 hours of rock-and-roll, that must be the public interest for that area. If most people like violent and sexy detective shows, TV must provide them. Thus do self-interest and altruism happily merge.

Critics bemoan this kind of reasoning, pointing out that broadcasters are not merely *following* public tastes but *setting* them by offering only competing junk. About the only outlet for the critics' frustrations, though, is public broadcasting. During the 1950s, noncommercial FM and television stations, financed by universities and community donations, began to offer programming at higher cultural and educational levels. The Ford Foundation and Congress came in with more support. In 1967, Congress set up the corporation for Public Broadcasting (CPB), with National Public Radio (NPR) and the Public Broadcasting Service (PBS) under it. This is as close as the United States has come to establishing a link between government and broadcasting, and it's not very close. Government funding, especially with the budget cuts of the Reagan administration, accounts for only a minority of NPR's and PBS's finances. Public broadcasting presents all political viewpoints. NPR and PBS are the only exceptions to private ownership and profit-orientation in American broadcasting.

The FCC doesn't supervise the content of programs, but it does have a political impact. Section 315 of the 1934 act, known as the "equal-time provision," tells broadcasters that if they give or sell air time to one candidate, they must do the same for others. Station owners, of course, don't like to give away air time. They also fear that public-interest programs featuring the candidates of the two big parties will lead to minor or frivolous candidates demanding equal time. News broadcasts are exempt from the equal-time rule, so debates between the two leading presidential contenders are conducted by a panel of newspeople to get around the equal-time provision. Broadcasters may also not be too happy about selling air time, for it must go at the lowest rate, which in turn must be offered to the opponents. Broadcasters have repeatedly sought modifications of the equal-time provision.

Another FCC power, more vague than "equal-time," is the "fairness doctrine" first published in 1949 by the commission. Recognizing that broadcast editorials are part of the public interest, the fairness doctrine requires broadcasters to offer air time for those with opposing views to respond. Enforcement, though, is left up to the broadcasters, and many public-spirited interest groups feel that broadcasters simply try to avoid all controversy so that they won't have to make air time available to anyone. The Reagan-appointed members of the FCC proposed abolishing both the equal-time and fairness provisions, arguing that they tended to limit political debate on the airwaves.

The European Experience

The American airwaves are lightly regulated. Could it—or should it—be otherwise? The European experience offers a range of possibilities, all involving greater governmental control or supervision than the United States has. Television in the Soviet Union is strictly government-controlled and is carefully aimed. It is patriotic, upbeat, and positive, calculated to inculcate feelings of loyalty and hard work and to uplift culturally. Instead of the "hands off" American attitude, the Soviet approach to use television as an instrument of education and guidance. Soviet programming accordingly stresses the glorious but trying events of World War II, factories and workers happily producing more and more, and opera and ballet that would be seen only on PBS in the United States. Soviets familiar with American TV regard it as debauchery, an example of capitalism run amok. The concept of giving viewers what they want is alien to them, and Soviet programming has little pop music and light entertainment.[11] Political pronouncements are generally reserved for the party newspaper, *Pravda* (Truth), and its government counterpart, *Izvestia* (News). The Soviets regard newspapers as more authoritative than television.

French television is also government-controlled, although not as heavy-handed as in the Soviet Union. Before he returned to power in 1958, Gen. Charles de Gaulle watched a great deal of television and concluded that it was the perfect way to control a country. As the powerful president of the Fifth Republic, which he created, from 1958 to 1969, de Gaulle did indeed use television as a tool of governance and guidance. In military uniform and with his sonorous voice and superb command of the language, de Gaulle put down two rebellions and won four referendums with his televised calls for loyalty. The governmental office de Gaulle estabished, the ORTF, is still at work today, although many French viewers and journalists are aware that it slants the news. The French left protested this rigging of information, but when the Socialists swept to power in 1981 they did not free up the ORTF, rather they proceeded to slant things *their* way. The trouble with government-controlled broadcasting, though, is that listeners and viewers will try to go elsewhere. In the French case, they tune in to radio and television from Luxembourg and Monaco, which are

---

[11]See Ellen Propper Mickiewicz, *Media and the Russian Public* (New York: Praeger, 1981).

more objective than the French programs. To a certain extent, government-control of radio and television is self-defeating, for these media lose credibility. In 1986, a new conservative French government "privatized" some of the airwaves by selling off the largest of France's three state-owned TV networks, TF1.

The northern European systems are better at putting some distance between the government and broadcasting. The British Broadcasting Corporation, created in 1927, is run by a board of governors who are nonpartisan but are nonetheless named by the government. The BBC is supported by annual licenses that listeners and viewers must buy; it carries no commercial advertising. During Britain's brief (three-week) campaigns, air time is allocated to the three main parties—Conservative, Labor, and the Social Democrat-Liberal Alliance—in proportion to their strength in Parliament. Whereas the nonparternalistic U.S. system lets programming sink to a low level, the BBC system, supervised by cultivated and educated governors, rises high, often too high for the British public; many find it staid and boring. Since 1954, Britain has permitted private, commercial TV in the form of the Independent Television Authority, which offers programs more at the mass level. Swedish and West German broadcasting are mainly financed by user license fees. They are governed by nonpartisan boards of media people, cultural leaders, and civil servants. The West German system has both nationwide and state networks, diffusing control and introducing a certain amount of competition. Advertising is permitted, but grouped into several-minute spots throughout the day. Advertisers do not sponsor programs and have nothing to say about content. Paid political advertising is not permitted, but time is allocated to parties during election campaigns for political messages.

The U.S. broadcast media are, paradoxically, free but expensive. They have practically no government control, but listeners and viewers pay a price in having programing skewed to earn broadcasters the maximum amount of money. The price is junk programming that does indeed leave America culturally, educationally, and informationally underdeveloped.

ARE WE POORLY SERVED?

As may be judged from some of our earlier discussions, the U.S. news media do not serve Americans very well. First, news coverage is highly selective, overconcentrating on some areas while ignoring others. This is called "structural bias." The president and his staff occupy over half the time of news about the federal government. Why is this? The president is inherently more dramatic and eye-catching than the other branches of government. Reporters, editors, and producers are afraid that if they devote more than a little time to Congress and the courts, readers and viewers will become bored. Another reason is that what the president does is visually more exciting than what Congress or the courts do. The president gets in and out of helicopters, greets foreign leaders, travels overseas, or just relaxes at his vacation home; all provide good TV footage. Congress may get some attention when one of its committees faces a tense, controversial, or hostile witness. Then the committee members hurl accusatory questions, the witness stammers back denials, and sometimes shouting erupts. That's good drama; the rest of Congress is pretty dull.[12] And the courts face the biggest obstacle of all: no cameras allowed in most courtrooms. Accordingly, Americans grow up with the notion that the White House does most of the work and has most of the power, whereas Congress and the courts hardly matter.

One part of the U.S. government is especially undercovered: the civil service, in its myriad departments, agencies, and bureaus.[13] Here is where much of the governance of America takes place. But "faceless bureaucrats" make boring interviewees—some are not allowed to be interviewed—and federal regulations are unintelligible. Still, many of next year's news stories are buried in the federal bureaucracy. What agency using what criteria allowed a nuclear power plant to operate? The media don't pay any attention until a Three Mile Island happens. What federal agency using a loophole in the law quietly decided that car manufacturers really didn't need to install air bags or automatic seat belts under a law Congress had passed and the president had signed? (The Supreme Court caught that one in 1983, and said no to the National Highway Traffic Safety Administration.) What federal agency decides that airliner seats have to be covered with flame-resistant fabric? The news media don't even try to cover such things; they wait until something goes wrong and then evince shocked surprise. The very stuff of politics is there in the federal agencies, but few pay attention.

On the world scene, too, the news media wait for something to blow up before they cover it. Except for the elite media mentioned above, there is little background coverage of likely trouble spots. Thus, when revolutions wrack Iran or Central America, most Americans are surprised. They shouldn't be; even moderate news coverage of these places over the years would have kept Americans apprised of the increasing problems. But the U.S. media did not keep reporters in these areas and rarely even sent them on quick visits. Troubled Mexico, with all its implications for the United States, is still largely uncovered. We live in a revolutionary world, but the U.S. media pay little attention until the shooting starts. Providers of "good visuals" rather than analysis and early warning is the way they define their role, and this sets up Americans to become startled and confused.

The biggest problem with the U.S. media is that they do not try to give a coherent, comprehensive picture of what is happening. Operating under tight deadlines, flashing the best action footage, and basing reports heavily on official

---

[12]Michael J. Robinson and Kevin R. Appel found that TV network coverage of Congress was heavily negative. See their "Network News Coverage of Congress," *Political Science Quarterly* 94 (Fall 1979):3.

[13]For a look into the world of Washington reporters and why they cover what they do, see Stephen Hess, *The Washington Reporters* (Washington, D.C.: Brookings Institution, 1981).

sources, the media bombard us with many little stories but seldom weave them together into a big story. They give us only pieces of a jig-saw puzzle. Part of this is due to the nature of any news medium that comes out daily: newspapers and television take events one day at a time. Such news is usually incomplete and often misleading. We see people shooting, but we don't know why. The media world is, in Shakespeare's phrase, "full of sound and fury, signifying nothing."

What Can Be Done?   The mass media—except for the elite media—do not provide *meaning*. Some, such as the wire services, deliberately shun analysis and interpretation in their stories; that would be unobjective or editorializing. Reporters are typically unequipped to explain the historical background or long-term consequences of the stories they cover. Reporters are expected to be generalists, to be able to cover everything and anything. All you have to do is write down what the official source says. It is for this reason that editorials and columns of opinion often contain more usable "news" than the straight news stories, for the former set the news into a meaningful context, whereas the latter just leaves the bits and pieces scattered about. Unfortunately, most Americans make do with the bits and pieces as they make decisions on candidates, economic matters, and sending troops abroad.

Can anything be done about this? Professional newspeople generally agree that the public is ill-informed, and some will even admit that their coverage could be wider and deeper. But the limiting factor, they emphasize, is the public itself. Most people don't want to be well informed, especially about things distant or complicated. Audience surveys usually find that people care least about foreign news and most about local news. Newspapers can go broke pushing too much world news; some, in fact, are going the way of the check-out-counter weeklies with the splashy and the trashy. Most people aren't intellectuals and don't like complicated, in-depth analyses. The shooting they care about; the reasons behind it they don't. Do the media have any responsibility, though, in educating the mass public so that citizens can better comprehend our complicated world? Some idealists in the media do feel a responsibility, but they are usually offset by the hard-headed business types, who have the last word. After a while, the idealists become cynical. We cannot expect any major improvements soon. For you, however, the student of political science who is already among the more attentive, the answer is the elite media. Use the mass media for sports coverage.

The Adversaries: Media and Government

The role of the press as critic in the healthy functioning of U.S. democracy has long been recognized. Wrote Thomas Jefferson in 1787:

> Were it left to me to decide [between government without] newspapers and newspapers without government, I should not hesitate a moment to prefer the latter.

Over the centuries, the press has criticized government.[14] In the late 1960s and early 1970s, however, a new adversarial relationship between media and government emerged that is with us today. To be sure, not all the media entered into the fray; most newspapers with their wire-service stories continued to quote official sources. But the elite media and television often adopted hostile stances toward the executive branch.

The Media and Vietnam. The causes are not hard to see: Vietnam and Watergate. In both episodes the executive branch engaged in considerable lying to the media in order to soothe public opinion. Many media people resented being used in this way and struck back by means of sharp questioning in press conferences and investigative reporting. The presidency of Richard Nixon didn't help matters; he had long feared and hated the press. On losing the governer's race in California in 1962, he slouched off muttering that the press "won't have Nixon to kick around any more." Before presidential press conferences, Nixon used to try to calm his nerves by relaxing in a darkened room before the grilling. Nixon liked to operate in considerable secrecy and then spring his decisions on the public in direct telecasts without any newspeople getting in the way. In turn, the press resented him all the more.

In Saigon, the U.S. military held afternoon press briefings dubbed the "five-o'clock follies" in which the army tried to put its best foot forward with indications of progress in the war. Journalists soon tired of the repetitive, misleading, and irrelevant briefings and took to snooping around themselves. What they found wasn't too pretty: a corrupt, inept Saigon regime that was not winning the hearts and minds of its people; a Vietcong able to roam and strike at will; and tactics and morale inadequate to stop them.[15] One young *New York Times* reporter was so critical of the Diem regime that his stories undermined American confidence in Diem and paved the way for Diem's 1963 ouster and murder by his own generals.[16] Such is the influence of the elite media.

Television, too, showed a picture different from what U.S. officials wanted: the bodies of young GIs covered with mud and blood in full color. Because TV inherently favors the visual, it beamed gory film clips into America's living rooms. TV also developed, perhaps unwittingly, a devastating style of coverage in which scenes of horror were juxtaposed with calm reassurances of top officials. The contrast silently indicated that the officials were either fools or liars. In 1971, CBS News accused the Defense Department, in a documentary, of

[14]One recent history claims that all presidents have disliked the press. John Tebbel and Sarah Miles Watts, *The Press and the Presidency: From George Washington to Ronald Reagan* (New York: Oxford University Press, 1985).

[15]Some critics claim that the U.S. media wrongly portrayed the 1968 Tet offensive as a Communist victory when actually Communist forces suffered great losses. However, Tet did mark the point at which a majority of Americans started opposing the war. See Peter Braestrup, *Big Story: How the American Press and Television Reported and Interpreted the Crisis of Tet 1968 in Vietnam and Washington*, abr. ed. (New Haven, Conn.: Yale University Press, 1983).

[16]See David Halberstam, *The Making of a Quagmire* (New York: Random House, 1965).

REPORTER'S HANDS shoot up insistently at a presidential press conference. Many media people took a critical approach to government in the aftermath of Vietnam and Watergate.

Jack Kightlinger, The White House

spending millions of tax dollars to win public and congressional support. "The Selling of the Pentagon" raised a storm of controversy, with administration accusations of tricky editing that made interviewees look as if they were saying things they weren't. By this time, media and government were in a snarling match.

That same year, another bombshell burst: the "Pentagon Papers" appeared, first in *The New York Times*, then in the *Washington Post.* The papers were a multivolume, top-secret study commissioned by former-Secretary of Defense Robert McNamara to document decision-making on the Vietnam war.[17] Daniel Ellsberg, a former Pentagon official who had turned against the war (and is now involved with antinuclear protests), made photocopies and delivered them to the newspapers. In the age of xerography, there are no more total secrets. The Nixon administration was outraged—although the Papers made the Johnson officials the chief culprits—and ordered their publication halted, the first time the U.S. government ever censored newspapers. The Supreme Court immediately threw out the government's case, and the presses ran again. By this time, there was open warfare between government and the media.

The Media and Watergate.   The next year, 1972, began a process that brought the fall of the Nixon administration and, for at least portions of the media, a new self-image as guardians of public morality. Persons connected to the White House were caught burglarizing and planting telephone "bugs" in the Democratic campaign headquarters in the Watergate office and apartment complex. Dogged investigation by two young *Washington Post* reporters revealed a massive cover-up led by the Oval Office.[18] The more Nixon promised to come clean, the guiltier he looked. Nixon was never impeached. A House special

[17]Neil Sheehan et al., *The Pentagon Papers* (New York: Bantam Books, 1971).
[18]Bob Woodward and Carl Bernstein, *All the President's Men* (New York: Simon & Schuster, 1974).

committee voted to recommend impeachment; then Nixon resigned. The House certainly would have voted impeachment and the Senate probably would have convicted. Would the same have happened without media coverage? Ultimately, the legal moves came through the courts and Congress, but the media made sure these branches of government would not ignore or delay their duties. Did the media bring Nixon down? The Nixon people thought so, but then they always loathed the press. Others have argued that the same would have happened without the investigative reporting, but more slowly and with less media drama. The point is that media and government are so intertwined that they are part of the same process and hard to separate.[19]

Since Watergate, some branches of the media, namely the elite press and the national television networks, have adopted generally adversarial stances toward the executive branch.[20] Criticism of the occasional changes of course under the Ford and Carter presidencies was immoderate and sometimes unreasonable. Carter, like Nixon, claimed the press was out to get him. The policies of the Reagan administration were almost automatically doubted and criticized, but for years nothing stuck on the popular "teflon president." Finally, as the wrongdoings associated with the Iran arms deal emerged, the media seemed to relish reporting the White House contradictions and coverups.

Had the press gone too far? Some people began to get fed up at the high-handedness with which the media impugned all authority. The media seemed to think they were always right, the government always wrong. One favorite target of media criticism was the former U.S. commander in Vietnam, retired General William Westmoreland. CBS News produced a documentary that said Westmoreland and his staff deliberately lied about Communist troop strength. Westmoreland sued and even though he lost, the media world trembled.[21]

What is the proper role of the media in a democracy? That they can and should criticize is clear: this keeps government on its toes. But how much should they criticize? Should they presume wrongdoing and coverup everywhere? Should many reporters model themselves after Woodward and Bernstein of Watergate fame and try to ferret out scandals at every level of government? The press is largely protected from charges of libel, for "public" persons are presumed to be open to scrutiny. This has left some public figures feeling helpless and bitter at the hands of an all-powerful press. Public opinion has grown critical of the too-critical media. Perhaps the United States can find some happy middle ground.

[19]See Gladys Engel Lang and Kurt Lang. *The Battle for Public Opinion: The President, the Press, and the Polls During Watergate* (New York: Columbia University Press, 1983).

[20]Michael Baruch Grossman and Martha Joynt Kumar found that all administrations since 1960 have passed through successive phases of alliance, competition, and finally detachment in their relationships with newspeople. See their *Portraying the President: The White House and the News Media* (Baltimore, Md.: Johns Hopkins University Press, 1981).

[21]See Renata Adler, *Reckless Disregard: Westmoreland v. CBS et al.; Sharon v. Time* (New York: Knopf, 1986).

SUGGESTED READINGS

ABEL, ELIE, ed. *What's News: The Media in American Society.* San Francisco: ICS Press, 1981. Twelve academics and journalists tell what's right and what's wrong with U.S. media.

BAGDIKIAN, BEN H. *The Media Monopoly.* Boston: Beacon Press, 1983. A media critic charges that growing concentration of ownership is skewing and limiting the news.

BARBER, JAMES DAVID. *Race for the Presidency: The Media and the Nominating Process.* Englewood Cliffs, N.J.: Prentice-Hall, 1978. Fine study of the impact of the mass media on how candidates win nomination.

BENJAMIN, GERALD, ED. *The Communications Revolution in Politics.* New York: The Academy of Political Science, 1982. Useful articles on technological politics and communication in government and in international relations.

BERKMAN, RONALD, AND LAURA W. KITCH. *Politics in the Media Age.* New York: McGraw-Hill, 1986. Good and up-to-date introductory survey of the field.

DENTON, ROBERT E., JR., AND GARY C. WOODWARD. *Political Communication in America.* New York: Praeger, 1985. An attempt to define political communication in theoretical terms and apply it to current politics.

GANS, HERBERT J. *Deciding What's News.* New York: Vintage Books, 1980. Careful empirical study of how editors select and present news stories.

GRABER, DORIS A. *Mass Media and American Politics,* 2d ed. Washington, D.C.: Congressional Quarterly Press, 1984. Good summation of much research by a noted specialist.

————, ED. *Media Power in Politics.* Washington, D.C.: Congressional Quarterly Press, 1984. Excellent roundup of recent articles on the many impacts of the mass media on U.S. politics.

HALBERSTAM, DAVID. *The Powers That Be.* New York: Knopf, 1979. The *New York Times* reporter who helped bring down Diem turned a jaundiced eye against his former employer and other leading media.

KERNELL, SAMUEL. *Going Public: New Strategies of Presidential Leadership.* Washington, D.C.: CQ Press, 1986. A fine scholarly study showing how the president uses his media prominence to get his way.

LINSKY, MARTIN. *Impact: How the Press Affects Federal Policymaking.* New York: W. W. Norton, 1986. Empirical study of how media prod decision makers into action.

PARENTI, MICHAEL. *Inventing Reality: The Politics of the Mass Media.* New York: St. Martin's, 1986. A radical critic argues that the media have a conservative bias.

PATTERSON, THOMAS E. *The Mass Media Election.* New York: Praeger, 1980. Balanced, scholarly study of the media in the 1976 presidential election.

RANNEY, AUSTIN. *Channels of Power: The Impact of Television on American Politics.* New York: Basic Books, 1983. A top political scientist sees television's impact as big and mostly bad.

RESTON, JAMES. *The Artillery of the Press: Its Influence on American Foreign Policy.* New York: Harper & Row, 1966. Venerable *New York Times* columnist explains the problems of world news coverage. Old but still good.

chapter 10

Interest Groups

Interest groups are especially numerous, vocal, and visible in the United States, but we have no monopoly on them. They are an element in the political life of every highly organized modern society. Even in countries where social, economic, and political life is dominated by central planning, interest groups exist, though in muted form. In the Soviet Union, for example, citizens have no legal right to organize private associations at will, and all legitimate organizations are controlled, with little independence to criticize or alter government policy. Nonetheless, outside observers have detected interest groups even in the Soviet Union, quarreling, for example, over whether heavy industry or light will be emphasized in economic plans.[1] And opposing the regime, groups of dissidents spring up from time to time despite the Kremlin's efforts to promote uniformity.

WHAT IS AN INTEREST GROUP?

The term *interest group* covers a wide spectrum of people and issues. In his landmark work, *The Governmental Process,* David B. Truman defines an interest group as "a shared-attitude group that makes certain claims upon other groups in society" by acting through the institutions of government.[2] Some interest groups are transient, whereas others are more permanently organized. Many are solely interested in influencing the government's public policy, whereas others are only sporadically concerned with political decisions. Some work directly through the executive or administrative agencies, whereas others work through the judicial or legislative sectors, or even through public opinion. But one crucial factor is common to all interest groups: they are all non-publicly-accountable organizations which attempt to promote shared private interests by influencing public policy outcomes that affect them.[3]

How Interest Groups Differ From Political Parties

It may seem that interest groups resemble political parties. But party leaders are not elected by the general public, nor are they answerable to the people as a whole for their decisions. Parties try to influence public policy. But unlike political parties, interest groups lie outside the electoral process and are thus not responsible to the public. Whereas party leadership is not chosen by the voters, each elected candidate is, and so the survival of the party depends on the people's support. Private interest groups may try to influence the nomination of candidates who are sympathetic to their cause, but the candidates run under the party banner—not the interest group banner.

Goals. The goal of the political party is to acquire power through elections. The interest group, however, is concerned with specific programs and

---

[1]See H. Gordon Skilling and Franklyn Griffiths, eds., *Interest Groups in Soviet Politics* (Princeton, N.J.: Princeton University Press, 1971).

[2]David B. Truman, *The Governmental Process* (New York: Knopf, 1951), p. 37.

[3]This general definition is reflected in Arthur Bentley's work, *The Process of Government* (Orig. ed., 1908; Evanston, Ill.: Principia Press, 1949), considered a forerunner of contemporary political science. The book attempts to tie together the common elements of modern interest groups.

issues and is rarely represented in the formal structure of government. The interest group tries to steer political parties and their elected officials toward certain policies rather than enacting those policies itself. Interest groups often try to win the favor of all political parties. Environmentalists want the support of both the Republicans and the Democrats in their fight to minimize ecological damage. But at times they may take a stand in favor of one party if they are convinced that party will further their objectives with greater vigor. In 1988, for example, environmentalists massively supported the Democrats.

Nature of Memberships. Most political parties want broad enough support to win an election, drawing into their ranks different interests. Their membership is much more varied than that of the interest group. Even the conservative Republican party includes people in all income brackets and occupations, and some of its members are more liberal than many Democrats. The Democratic party, on the other hand, seen as the more progressive party of the working man, also counts all walks of life among its supporters.

Interest groups generally have a more selective membership. Members of a labor union are likely to share similar living and working conditions and to have comparable educational and cultural backgrounds. Interest groups for a specific problem or issue, such as ecology or the banning of nuclear weapons, may draw their members from a wider spectrum, but even they tend to have more similarities than members of parties.

Almost Unlimited Number. The purpose of a party is to nominate and elect its candidates and perpetuate itself in power. For several reasons, including the length of a ballot, the number of political parties must be limited; even in multiparty political systems, all the parties can usually be counted on the fingers of both hands. But interest groups are a different matter. There is no functional limit (such as the length of a ballot) on their proliferation, and some countries seem to offer a particularly fertile environment for their development. The United States has long provided such an environment. As de Tocqueville observed in the 1830s: "In no country of the world has the principle of association been more successfully used or applied to a greater multitude of objects than in America." De Tocqueville is still accurate. Just open a Washington, D.C., phone book to "National . . ." and behold the hundreds of national associations, institutes, leagues, and committees.[4] Much of Washington's prosperity is based on its obvious attraction as a headquarters for interest groups.

Interest Groups: Who Belongs?

In every highly organized technological society, the prevailing mode of life is maintained by a multitude of different industries with separate goods and

---

[4]For a look at the complexity of interest-group activity in Washington, see Jeffrey M. Berry, *The Interest Group Society* (Boston: Little, Brown, 1984).

FARMERS meet with President Reagan and Secretary of Agriculture John Block to air their concerns.

services. Within any society, there are differences in the cultural, economic, educational, ethnic, and religious backgrounds of people. These varied categories of people and enterprises represent the raw material of interest groups.

This characteristic of modern society supplies the basis for David Truman's theory of interest groups: wherever there are divergent interests there exists the potential for an interest group. Interest groups play a central role in a democratic government, and we pay considerable attention to the pressure system of organized special interest groups attempting to influence governmental policies. Because of our highly developed pressure system, the United States is often defined by theorists of Truman's school as a "pluralist democracy" in which a multiplicity of interest groups, all pushing their own claims and viewpoints, creates a balance of opposing interests which prevents any one group from dominating the political system. In this optimistic view, government policy is the outcome of competition among many groups, which represent the varied interests of the people. This is the classic pluralist picture.

The U.S. system does indeed include many rival pressure groups. But, in contrast to David Truman's theory, many observers have noted that the members of these groups tend to be drawn overwhelmingly from the middle and upper classes, and that group activities are dominated by individuals with business-related interests. The mere fact of competition among rival interest groups does not guarantee a democratic system. As E. E. Schattschneider noted, "The flaw in the pluralist heaven is that the heavenly chorus sings with a strong upper-class accent."[5] Many critics of our interest group systems would agree that middle- and upper-class interests are disproportionately represented in comparison to the lower classes, which have relatively little voice in the pressure system.

[5]E. E. Schattschneider, *The Semisovereign People: A Realist's View of Democracy* (New York: Holt, Rinehart and Winston, 1960), p. 29.

Elite theorists argue that, if David Truman's group theory really operated, the poor would begin to organize in groups as soon as they became aware that they were poor and didn't want to be. Yet, with only sporadic exceptions, the poor, who seem to have so much to gain from collective action, have been slow in joining together to promote their common interests. When organizations or aid programs have been developed to tackle the problems of poverty, the ideas, money, and leadership often has come from outside the community. Better-off and better-educated people are much more likely to participate in politics, and this includes organizing and running interest groups. In this area, too, the poor get shortchanged.

Left on their own, the lower classes are more likely to act explosively rather than as organized groups with reasonable approaches. They have a strong sense of grievance which has been demonstrated time after time through history. The storming of the Bastille during the French Revolution is one example of how poverty-nurtured resentments boiled over into violence. In recent U.S. history, the riots of the sixties in large-city ghettos reflected the anger that race-related poverty produced in many black Americans.[6] The ghetto riots, while serving to publicize the grievances and anger that exist in certain poor communities, resulted in great destruction that hurt the people living in those communities more than anyone else. They cost their perpetrators a great deal without offering any real challenge to the power and influence of business and industry, labor unions, or other groups that the poor regard as stumbling blocks in the way of their objectives. Not all sectors of society can effectively form and use interest groups.

Interest Groups and Government

Interest groups try to influence government. But what if there is no government? To take an extreme example, consider Lebanon, where by the 1980s the "government" controlled only a portion of Beirut. There were, to be sure, plenty of groups: a dozen religious denominations, each with its own militia engaging in nearly constant civil war. Would we call these "interest groups"? Probably not. Although some interest groups engage in occasional violence, they do so in a context of trying to influence government. In Lebanon, there was not much government to influence; the groups fought to guard their respective "turfs." Not all clashes of groups automatically qualify as "interest-group activity."

Interest groups presuppose an existing government that is worth trying to influence. Government, in fact, virtually calls many interest groups into life, for they are intimately associated with government programs. There are farm lobbies because there are farm programs, education lobbies because there are education programs, and veterans' lobbies because in years past the government chose to go to war.

---

[6]See Rufus P. Browning et al., *Protest Is Not Enough: The Struggle of Blacks and Hispanics for Equality in Urban Politics* (Berkeley, Cal.: University of California Press, 1984).

To take one example, the 1958 National Defense Education Act (NDEA) put millions of dollars into university foreign-area and language programs. A decade later, as enthusiasm for these subjects waned (partly because of the Vietnam war), a vigorous lobby dedicated to "world education" and funded by universities that received NDEA grants tried to persuade Congress to continue the program. Congress had created a program, the program created an interest group, and then the interest group worked on Congress. This is one reason that programs, once set up, tend to never get terminated, for they develop constituencies with a strong pecuniary interest in continuing the programs. As government has become bigger and sponsored more programs, the number of interest groups has proliferated. By now, virtually every branch and subdivision of the U.S. government has one or more interest groups watching over its shoulder, demanding more grants, a change in regulations, or their own agency. The Departments of Education and Energy were created under these circumstances, and Ronald Reagan vowed to abolish them. He couldn't: the interests associated with them—in part created by them—were too powerful.

Sometimes interest groups participate in government legislation and implementation. In Britain, "interested members" of Parliament are those who openly acknowledge that they represent industries or labor unions. This is not frowned on and is considered quite normal. In Sweden, interest groups are especially large and powerful. Swedish "royal commissions" that initiate most new legislation are composed of legislators, government officials, and interest-group representatives. After a proposal has been drafted, it is circulated for comments to all relevant interest groups. Some Swedish benefits for farmers and workers are administered by their respective farm organizations and labor unions. Some call this "corporatistic," meaning that interest groups are taking on governmental functions.[7] Top representatives of business, labor, and the cabinet meet regularly in Sweden to decide a great deal of public policy. Critics charge that this too-cozy relationship bypasses parliamentary democracy altogether.

Bureaucrats as an Interest Group

Government and interest groups are related in another very important but sometimes overlooked way: the bureaucracy has become one of the biggest and most powerful interest groups of all. Civil servants are not merely the passive implementers of laws; they have a great deal to say in the making and application of those laws. Much legislation originates in the specialized agencies. Many of the data and witnesses before legislative committees are from the executive departments and agencies.

---

[7]Some authors argue that West European interest groups operate in a generally corporatistic fashion. See Suzanne D. Berger, ed., *Organizing Interests in Western Europe: Pluralism, Corporatism, and the Transformation of Politics* (New York: Cambridge University Press, 1981).

Needless to say, these bureaucracies develop interests of their own. They see their tasks as terribly important and so naturally think they need a bigger budget and more employees every year. When was the last time a professional civil servant—as opposed to a political appointee—recommended abolishing his or her agency or bureau? Bureaucrats have a lot of knowledge at their fingertips, and knowledge is power. When the Reagan administration came in, it said it would abolish the Department of Energy (DOE). One of the authors of this book asked a friend, an official of the department, why he wasn't worried. "They won't abolish us," he asserted knowingly. "They can't. DOE manufactures nuclear bombs, and the administration needs the DOE budget to disguise how big the nuclear-bomb budget is." He was right; Reagan did not abolish the Department of Energy.

It was earlier proposed that interest groups were offshoots of society and the economy. That is only partly true, for they are also offshoots of government. Government and interest groups, to paraphrase Thomas Hobbes, were born twins. The more government, the more interest groups.

To say that every political system has interest groups doesn't say very much, for interest groups in different systems operate quite differently. One key determinant in the way interest groups operate is the government. Here we can refine our definition of pluralism discussed in Chapter 5. Pluralism is determined not by the mere existence of groups, each trying to influence government, but the degree to which government permits or encourages the open interplay of groups. Pluralism has a normative component, an "ought" or a "should."

Antipluralism in Europe.   The United States and Britain, for example, are considered highly pluralistic, for interest-group activity is acceptable and desirable. Many observers consider lobbying the normal functioning of a healthy democracy, with nothing dirty about it.[8] In France, on the other hand, interest group activity, whereas it does exist, is frowned on and considered a bit dirty. France is heir to centuries of centralized and paternalistic government. The French are used to Paris ministries setting national goals and supervising much of the nation's economic activity. Further, the philosopher Jean Jacques Rousseau still has a powerful hold on the French mind. Rousseau argued, among other points, that there must be no "partial wills" to muddy and distort the "general will," that which the whole community wants. Rousseau presumed there was such a thing as a general will, something pluralists deny. Accordingly, interest groups are seen trying to pervert the good of the whole community. The French bureaucratic elites pay little attention to interest groups, seeing them as "unobjective." French interest groups operate in a more constrained atmosphere than their American or British counterparts.

The Soviet Union takes this a large step further. Open interest-group activity is taboo. There are, to be sure, plenty of Soviet interests that like to make

---

[8]For an explanation of British and American concepts of interest, see Stephen Miller, *Special Interest Groups in American Politics* (New Brunswick, N.J.: Transaction Books, 1983).

their case, but they must do so quietly, within the confines of party discussions, and must not lay claim to more than their area of professional interest. None dare propose major or systemic change. The way groups function is structured by government, which can permit a lot or very little open activity.

EFFECTIVE INTEREST GROUPS

Political Culture

Interest groups are most likely to flourish in democratic societies where occupational and other contacts put individuals in touch with a wide range of people and where political participation is emphasized. The percentage of people who join organized groups differs greatly from one country to another.

In their study of political cultures, Almond and Verba noted that people in the United States, Great Britain, and Germany were more likely to participate in voluntary associations than were citizens of Italy and Mexico.[9] According to their findings, 57 percent of the respondents in the United States, 47 percent in Great Britain, and 44 percent in Germany were members of groups. In Italy and Mexico, the extent of participation was significantly smaller, amounting to only 30 percent and 24 percent, respectively. Civic participation in every country increased with educational level, and in all except the United States, more men than women were participants. Not all of the groups were political, of course, but some 24 percent of American, 19 percent of British, and 18 percent of German respondents were involved in political associations. By comparison, very few Italian and Mexican respondents participated in politically involved associations. One of the significant findings of the study was that in societies where many join groups, people have a greater sense of political competence and efficacy.

Money: Rise of the PACs

Money is probably the single most important factor in interest-group success. Indeed, with enough money, interests hardly need a group. Money is especially important for elections, and groups try to secure the victory of candidates known to favor their cause. Most democracies have recognized the danger in too close a connection between interests and candidates, the danger that we will have the "best Congress money can buy." Some, such as West Germany and Sweden, provide for almost complete public financing of the major parties in national elections. Spain, which rejoined the democracies only in 1977, subsidizes parties after the election according to how many votes they received and parliamentary seats they won.

[9]Gabriel Almond and Sidney Verba, *The Civic Culture* (Boston: Little, Brown, 1965). Another survey found that 31 percent of the United States population actually belong to organizations that seek to influence public issues. Robert E. Lane, *Political Life* (New York: Free Press, 1959), p. 204.

The United States has been reluctant to go to public financing of campaigns for several reasons. First, there is the strong emphasis on freedom. The U.S. Supreme Court interprets the First Amendment to include dollars as a form of free speech. If a person wants to give a lot of money to a candidate, that is a political statement and must not be restricted. Second, U.S. campaigns are much longer and more expensive than in other democracies, the result of our weak, decentralized parties and nominating system. In West Europe, elections can be short and cheap because the parties are already in place with their candidates and platforms. And third, given these two previous conditions, legislators have not been able to find a formula for public financing that really works in the manner intended. One experiment turned out to have some negative "unforeseen consequences."

We refer to the rise of the political action committees (PACs), the result of 1971 legislation.[10] Congress sharply limited the amount of money that individuals and corporations could contribute to candidates in an effort to curb the influence of "big money" in politics. But there was no prohibition on individuals and businesses organizing committees and donating money to them that in turn would go to desirable candidates. PACs grew like mushrooms, from 600 in 1974 to over 4000 in 1984. In 1984, they spent over $100 million on House and Senate races. Although PACs were originally an idea of labor unions, business PACs now heavily outspend labor PACs. Large corporations, many with defense contracts, are heavy PAC contributors. More interest-group money is being poured into campaigns than ever before; the 1971 law did not work.[11]

Some PACs, in an effort to skirt the law, do not work *for* a desired candidate but *against* his or her opponent. That way they can claim they are not contributing to Candidate Jones but are merely, as public-spirited folks, pointing out to the voters certain things they should know about dastardly Candidate Smith. In 1980, the National Conservative Political Action Committee thus helped unseat several liberal Democratic senators and delivered a Republican-dominated Senate to President Reagan. The tactics were so dirty that some of the winning Republicans said they wanted nothing to do with "Nicpack."

Can or should anything be done about interest groups and money? One solution might be to go to a European-type system in which the parties are well organized and campaigns are short and relatively cheap. But that is simply not in the cards for the United States. Another might be to limit the amount that any company could give to a PAC and that any PAC could give to a candidate. The Supreme Court rejected such limits in 1985. Public financing of all candidates—presidential nominees who gain at least 5 percent of the national vote are already entitled to federal financing—would be terribly expensive. For the foreseeable

[10]For a history of PACs, see Alfred Balitzer, *A Nation of Associations: The Origin, Development, and Theory of the Political Action Committee* (Washington, D.C.: American Society of Association Executives, 1981).

[11]For a thorough study of how PACs operate, see Larry J. Sabato, *PAC Power: Inside the World of Political Action Committees* (New York: Norton, 1985).

future, it will not be possible to break the tie between interest groups and candidates in the United States.

Issues: Rise of Single-Issue Groups

Perhaps the second greatest factor in the influence of interest groups (after money) is the intensity of the issue involved. The right issue can mobilize millions, give the group cohesion and commitment, and boost donations. There have always been American interest groups pursuing one or another idealistic objective, but during the 1970s the rise of "single-issue" interest groups changed U.S. politics. Typically, interest groups have several things to say about issues, for their interests encompass several programs and departments. Organized labor in the form of the AFL-CIO might try to persuade government on questions of Social Security, medical insurance, education, imports and tariffs, and the way unemployment statistics are calculated. The AFL-CIO has a long-term, across-the-board interest in Washington. The same can be said for many business groups.

But to the single-issue groups only one issue matters, and it matters intensely. Typically, their issues are moral—and therefore hard to compromise—rather than material. The most prominent single-issue group is the Right to Life or antiabortion movement. Until 1973, abortion was scarcely a political issue, but in that year the Supreme Court ruled that abortion was legal. Many Roman Catholics and Protestant fundamentalists were shocked, for they believed that human life begins at the moment of conception and that aborting a fetus is therefore murder. "Pro-life" people opposed, for a starter, allowing any state or federal medical funds to be used for abortion, then tried to amend the Constitution to outlaw abortion. They were opposed by the "pro-choice" forces, for abortion rights are linked to the women's movement. Feminists argued that whether or not to have an abortion is a matter for the individual woman to decide and no one else; the right to choose returns to women an element of control over their lives and hence is part of their liberation from second-class status.

The antiabortionists made life miserable for many senators and representatives. They cared about nothing else in a representative's record—where he or she stood on taxes, jobs, defense, and so on. They wanted to know where he or she stood on abortion, and a compromise middle ground—the refuge of many politicians faced with controversial issues—was not good enough. How can you be a "moderate" on abortion? Many elections turned on the abortion issue. Fortunately for some candidates, the pro-choice forces helped offset the pro-life forces.

Other single-issue causes appeared, such as prayer in public school and homosexual rights. Taken together, these two and the abortion question were sometimes referred to as the "morality issue." Gun control grew into a major issue, fanned by the assassinations of John and Robert Kennedy and Rev. Martin Luther King. The powerful National Rifle Association (NRA) opposed such groups as Handgun Control. None of these issues made elected representatives

PRO-LIFE group from Pittsburgh makes its statement on Capitol Hill, linking the nuclear issue with the abortion question.

Catholics for a Free Choice

any happier. They liked to be judged on a wide range of positions they have taken, not on one narrow issue on which it is hard to compromise. For many, politics lost its joy, and there were an increasing number of incumbents who chose not to run again. Of those who did, many silently prayed that the single-issue groups would destroy each other and leave them alone.[12]

Size and Membership

Curious as it may seem, size in terms of numbers of members or supporters is not necessarily the most important element in interest-group strength. Money and intensity are often able to offset sheer size. Groups that claim to speak for large numbers are not appreciated if it is known that only a small fraction of the group is composed of committed members. The National Association for the Advancement of Colored People (NAACP) claims to speak for millions of blacks, but its actual membership is much smaller. All things being equal, a large group has more clout than a small one. But things are never equal.

The socioeconomic status of members gives groups clout. Better-off, well-educated people with influence in their professions and communities can form groups that get more respect. The socioeconomic status of American Jews boosted the impact of the American-Israel Public Affairs Committee (AIPAC) and other Jewish groups. As Japanese Americans climbed educationally and professionally, their Japanese American Citizens' League (JACL) started having more of an impact and won apologies for the highly unconstitutional internment of West Coast Japanese in World War II. JACL then worked on getting compensation. Respect leads to clout. This means, paradoxically and unfairly,

---

[12]For an opposing view, see Sylvia Tesh, "In Support of 'Single-Issue' Politics," *Political Science Quarterly* 99 (Spring 1984):1.

that disadvantaged groups with the biggest grievances are among the least likely to be listened to.

Access

Money, issue, and size may not count for much unless people in government are willing to listen to the group. To be sure, these ingredients help, but it is often the careful cultivation of relationships with congresspersons and civil servants over the years that makes sure that doors are open. When a group has established a stable and receptive relationship with a branch of government, it is said to enjoy, in the words of Joseph LaPalombara, "structured access."[13] Greek American congresspersons and senators are, quite naturally, receptive to Greek arguments on questions concerning Turkey and Cyprus.[14] Michigan legislators are likewise disposed to discuss the problems of the automobile industry. Arab Americans complained bitterly that Jews enjoyed too much access on Capitol Hill and organized their own groups to try to gain such access.

What happens when groups are shut out, have no access? The pluralists tend to think this can't happen in a democracy, but apparently it does. Black and Indian militants argued that no one was listening to them or taking their demands seriously. Only when violence began in certain urban ghettos and on certain Indian reservations did Washington begin to listen. When the wealthy and powerful have a great deal of access, the poor and unorganized may have none. The consequences sometimes lead to violence.

STRATEGIES OF INTEREST GROUPS

Approaching the Lawmakers

Although lobbying is not the only strategy of interest groups, it is the one that receives the most attention. Unfortunately, the unscrupulous dealings of a few individuals have given lobbyists an unsavory image with the public.[15] Incidents of blackmail and bribery do occur (as they do in other areas of human endeavor), but such tactics are anathema to the average lobbyist.

Lobbying Techniques.   The approaches and techniques commonly used by lobbyists vary widely according to the types of interest the lobbyists represent

---

[13]Joseph LaPalombara, *Interest Groups in Italian Politics* (Princeton, N.J.: Princeton University Press, 1963).

[14]For studies of the Greek ethnic group, see Paul Y. Watanabe, *Ethnic Groups, Congress, and American Foreign Policy: The Politics of the Turkish Arms Embargo* (Westport, Conn: Greenwood Press, 1984); and Laurence Halley, *Ancient Affections: Ethnic Groups and Foreign Policy* (New York: Praeger, 1985).

[15]See, for example, E.E. Schattschneider's discussion of the "contagion of conflict" in *The Semisovereign People*, chap. 1.

UNION MADE: This sign at a union hall reminds a Democratic candidate for the Senate where his support comes from. Many interest groups support candidates in the expectation of future consideration.
Michael Roskin

and the way in which they conceive their jobs. In "The Role of the Lobbyist," Samuel C. Patterson identified three types of lobbyists: the "contact man," the "informant," and the "watchdog."[16] The contact man promotes the interests of his group by establishing friendships with legislators to whom he can present his group's case on a person-to-person basis. The informant lobbies in public rather than in private meetings, offering testimony supporting his group's case at legislative hearings and disseminating published materials on the group's behalf. The watchdog keeps close track of what is happening in the legislature so he can alert his group to take action when the time is appropriate.

Criteria for Successful Lobbying. The success of a lobbyist's approach depends on several factors, one of which is the receptivity of legislators. Surveying lobbyists' evaluations of their various techniques, Lester Milbrath found that those which were rated most effective by the lobbyists themselves involved direct communication between the lobbyist and the legislature.[17] The highest-rated strategies included not only the personal presentations of viewpoints and "research results" made by the contact-man type of lobbyist to individual legislators, but also the lobbyist's testimony at legislative hearings.

[16]Samuel C. Patterson, "The Role of the Lobbyist: The Case of Oklahoma," *The Journal of Politics* 25 (February 1963):72–92.
[17]Lester Milbrath, *The Washington Lobbyists* (Chicago: Rand McNally, 1963).

LOBBYISTS descend on Capitol Hill, seeking support for their group, as the 1986 tax reform bill is being debated.

Dennis Brack/Black Star

Rated less effective were the techniques—such as contacts by constituents and close friends, letter and telegram campaigns, public relations campaigns, and publicizing voting records—which involved no personal communication between legislators and lobbyists. The lowest-rated strategies were those of "keeping channels open" between interest groups and legislators. Under this category would fall campaign work, social get-togethers, and financial contributions.

Approaching the Administration

The executive branch of government is also a target for interest group pressure and pesuasion. Antipollution groups, for instance, seek support from the Department of the Interior in their efforts to ban automobiles from the national parks. As a general rule, interest groups will approach a department of the government and not the president, who is not readily accessible to such groups and their lobbyists, although he may be aware of the pressures they apply and may be indirectly involved in deciding how to handle them. Interest groups tend to concentrate their attention on the department that specializes in their own area of interest. Farm groups deal with the Department of Agriculture, public service companies deal with the Federal Power Commission, and so forth. As a rule, each department pays careful heed to the demands and arguments of groups in its area. In fact, at one time or another, many government bureaucracies have been "captured" or "colonized" by powerful pressure groups within their respective spheres of authority.

Techniques of Interest Groups. In dealing with the bureaucracy, interest groups employ about the same tactics they use with legislators, including personal contacts with officials, the supplying of research and factual materials, public relations and publicity campaigns, and entertaining. However, some kinds of pressuring, such as letter-writing campaigns, are less effective with bureaucrats than with legislators, since jobs in government administration are gained by appointment rather than election and many are protected by tenure. One special occasion for interest groups to make their influence felt in the bureaucracy is the time when candidates are up for appointment to top-level government posts, including positions in the president's cabinet. At such times, interest groups may influence the choice of a nominee who is to serve in areas that they regard as sensitive to their own interests. In 1981, President Reagan named to head the Environmental Protection Agency a person with long-time professional interest in developing rather than protecting nature. Anne Gorsuch was so pro-industry that her tenure created a scandal, and she was forced to resign in 1983.

Approaching the Judiciary

In the United States, interest groups also seek to realize their goals through the judicial process. Every year the state and federal courts hear numerous cases filed or supported by such interest groups as the American Civil Liberties Union, the Sierra Club, and the NAACP. The issue of government enforced racial segregation is one of many that have been taken to the courts by interest groups. The legal staff of the NAACP, for example, through its chief attorney Thurgood Marshall (now an Associate Justice of the U.S. Supreme Court), successfully challenged the constitutionality of all state laws requiring racial segregation in public schools. In recent years the U.S. Supreme Court has dealt with several delicate and important social issues brought to it by interest groups, including women's rights, the death penalty, abortion, and school prayer.

Interest groups have generally used two methods to pursue their goals through the judicial process. The first is to initiate suits directly on behalf of a group or class of people whose interests they represent (such suits are commonly referred to as "class actions"). The second method is for the interest group to file a brief as a "friend of the court" (*amicus curiae*) in support of a person whose suit seeks to achieve goals that the interest group is also seeking.

Other Tactics

Government is not the only target of interest-group action. Organized interests may often choose to take their case to the public with peaceful—or not so peaceful—appeals.

Appeals to the Public. Even powerful interest groups realize the importance of their public image. For this reason, many interest groups invest considerable sums in public relations programs and publicity campaigns to explain how they contribute to the general welfare and why their programs and policies are good for the country. U.S. railroads took to television to explain their case for "fair" governmental policies so they could stay alive and compete with trucking. The "right-to-work" lobby placed many magazine ads attacking unions for preventing non-union people from getting or keeping jobs.

Even while investing large sums in publicity, some interest groups maintain what is popularly referred to as a "low profile," preferring to promote their objectives without advertising themselves. In such cases, groups may rely on planted news stories that promote their objectives indirectly and behind-the-scenes pressure to prevent the publication of material that they judge to be detrimental to them. The Tobacco Institute, for example, discreetly funds research that casts doubt on findings that smoking is bad for your health. The American Petroleum Institute seeks no news coverage but lets its officers be quoted as unbiased experts in the field, supposedly above the political fray.

Demonstrations. Whereas certain special interest organizations, such as the American Cancer Society and the Heart Fund, may have access to free advertising space and time, most interest groups do not, and most lack the funds to purchase such publicity. Under these circumstances, a group with limited finances and motivated members may decide to try nonviolent demonstrations as a way of publicizing and promoting their cause. The precedent for such demonstrations in modern times was provided by Mahatma Gandhi, who used this tactic against the British Raj before India gained its independence in 1947. Gandhi, who derived his inspiration for nonviolent protest at least partly from an essay on civil disobedience by Henry David Thoreau, written in protest against the United States–Mexican War of 1946–48, also provided a model for the American black leader Martin Luther King, who headed the nonviolent civil rights movement during the 1950s and 1960s.

Protesters against nuclear power plants, facing the financial and political resources of power companies, felt that marching, picketing, and sometimes blocking plant entrances through sit-ins was their only option. With news media coverage of their protests, they were able to gain adherents, contributors, and sometimes access in Washington. Their powerful opponents, of course, often prevailed, leading some protesters to become frustrated and bitter.

Violent Protest. A group that loses faith in the efficacy of conventional political channels and modes of action often sees violent protest as its only alternative. Although violent protest occurs more than we would like in this country, it is not a mode of action that interest groups normally use. Rather, it is a reaction that requires a psychological buildup, nurtured by such tensions as poverty, discrimination, frustration, and a sense of personal or social injustice. An outbreak of violence usually begins spontaneously as a result of an incident which sparks the pent-up anger of a frustrated group, and the momentum of mob behavior escalates the violence. The riots of the sixties in black ghettos in large cities typify such violence. The more articulate rioters claimed they were simply *opposing* the violence they suffered daily at the hands of police, all levels of government, and an economy that kept them underpaid or unemployed. Did the violent protest work? Perhaps it was no coincidence that the social legislation of the Great Society was passed during this period. The British got out of India and Palestine when outbursts of violence made the areas difficult to govern. The white government of South Africa started offering cautious reforms only when blacks turned to violence. We may not like to admit it, but in certain circumstances, violence works. Americans are certainly no strangers to violence. As black leader H. Rap Brown put it, "Violence is as American as cherry pie."

INTEREST GROUPS: AN EVALUATION

Interest groups are an intrinsic part of every modern democracy. Yet, how well do they serve the needs of the average citizen?

How Well Do Interest Groups Articulate Ideas?

Every question of public policy involves a variety of different, and often conflicting, interests, most of which deserve a hearing in a democracy. Some of these interests are represented in the legislature, but many are not, especially in a two-party system such as that of the United States. Interest groups help represent a wider range of interests in the legislative process.

Many smaller organizations, however, have neither the members nor the money to make an input. Unless they are able to form coalitions, they cannot defend their interests from larger, more powerful groups. The mere fact that interest groups can articulate demands does not mean that the demands will be heeded. Resources are highly unequal among interest groups. Some are rich and powerful and have a lot of "clout." Others get ignored.

There is a further problem in a system where interest groups are accorded a prominent place: What about those individuals who are not organized into groups? Who speaks for them? Many citizens are not members or beneficiaries of interest groups. They vote for elected leaders, but the leaders usually pay more attention to group demands than to the unorganized multitude that elected them. If legislators and executives are attuned to interest groups, who is considering the interests of the whole country? At times, it seems as if no one is. Then we may begin to appreciate Rousseau's emphasis on the "general will" over and above the "particular wills" that make up society.

To try to remedy such defects, the "citizens' lobby," Common Cause, was formed in 1970. Claiming to represent the will of all in promoting good government, Common Cause, funded by voluntary subscriptions, successfully fought for public funding of presidential campaigns, an end to the congressional seniority system, and disclosure of lobbying activities.[18] In a similar vein, Ralph Nader set up several public-interest lobbies related to law, nuclear energy, tax reform, and medical care. Although groups such as these have done much good work, they raise an interesting question: Can a society as big and complex as America's possibly be represented as a whole, or is it inherently a mosaic of groups with no common voice?

Interest Groups as a "Safety Valve".   In almost every nation there are alienated citizens who feel they have been forgotten or discriminated against by the government. Interest groups often help to stabilize society by providing unhappy citizens with a "safety valve"—a legitimate outlet for their complaints and frustrations. Tenants subjected to the indignities of poor plumbing and roaches may organize to voice their complaints rather than vent their frustrations through violence. Of course, anyone who joins an organized group is largely committed to acting within the system. Truly alienated citizens want radical change, and compromises between interest groups and government may not satisfy them.

Defining Issues and Arenas of Conflict.   Individuals with interests in common do not constitute an interest group until they become aware of their shared attitudes, discontents, and problems and are motivated to take action to maintain or improve their position. The women's movement started gathering momentum in the 1960s with books and articles expressing the dissatisfaction of some women with the conditions imposed by society on them. The leaders, ranging from moderates concerned with improving the legal status and employment opportunities of women to extremists who advocated separatism to allow women to "find themselves," gave women a standard by which to measure their own feelings about themselves and the roles assigned to them by society. The movement also made it necessary for government officials and political candidates to develop political stands on the issue.[19] Women's groups organized support not only for such objectives as the ending of job discrimination, but also for the accessibility of birth control information, legal abortions, day care centers, and desegregation of traditionally male restaurants and clubs.

Do such organizations really speak for most of their members, or do they represent the interests of a small but vocal minority within the group? Interest

---

[18]See Andrew S. McFarland, *Common Cause: Lobbying in the Public Interest* (Chatham, N.J.: Chatham House, 1984).

[19]For an overview of the feminist movement, see Ethel Klein, *Gender Politics: From Consciousness to Mass Politics* (Cambridge, Mass.: Harvard University Press, 1984).

group leaders, like leaders of political parties, often have stronger ideas on issues that their followers. But political party leaders, especially in such nations as the United States, must often compromise on issues in order to appeal to the largest possible majority at election time. Interest group leaders, in contrast, must often take stronger or more extreme stands than many of their members would like in order to retain a favorable bargaining position. Strikes called by union leaders do not always have the full sympathy of the workers, many of whom are more interested in collecting their weekly paychecks than they are in bargaining for a new contract. And many women who are in favor of equal pay for equal work find the concept of abortion, as presented by many women's leaders, to be an anathema.

Interest Groups: Educators or Propagandists?

When important issues of public policy are being considered by Congress, it is customary to permit interested parties to offer testimony at committee hearings to support their stands on the issue. Experts who testify at congressional hearings serve the purpose of presenting the legislators with important technical, scientific, and statistical information. Hearings may help Congress to pass fairer laws that are more in tune with public needs. But the argument can also be made that the groups that get a hearing in Congress are those with the influence to gain access to the formal governmental process; grass roots groups often have less access.

In addition to educating the government, interest groups often play a crucial role in developing public awareness and knowledge of issues. Certain groups, such as the Consumers Union, specialize in helping people to use their money more knowledgeably. Others, such as the American Medical Association (AMA) and some insurance organizations, have been sources of advice on such subjects as good health habits, proper nutrition, accident prevention, and planning for financial security. Critics of the interest-group system argue that by disseminating information, the groups are acting as propagandists rather than as educators. No interest group is going to publicize information which puts it in an unfavorable light; the information it offers to government and the public is highly selective.

Stalemating Political Power

Interest groups compete with one another, and in the process they may help to limit the power and influence that any group can exercise within Congress or a governmental agency. However, by dispersing political power, interest groups can also stalemate government action. Certain issues have been aptly characterized as "hot potatoes," because government action in either direction will arouse a loud outcry from one group or another. Typically, such issues are ardently supported and vehemently opposed by competing groups with enough voting power and influence to drive politicians to equivocation.

Government may in effect get "stuck," trapped between powerful interests and unable to move on important national problems. Italy has been called a "stalemate society" for this reason.

Political scientist Samuel Beer believes that this is what happened to Britain. British interest groups became too strong and too closely connected to government programs. Elections became little more than attempts by the two main parties to promise more and more to all manner of interest groups. Because the groups' demands were inherently in conflict, this led to what Beer calls "the paralysis of public choice."[20] Parties were no longer able to articulate overarching policies for the good of the entire nation; they were too intent on winning over this or that group. Beer's analysis explains why many Britons elected and then reelected Margaret Thatcher, for she pointedly ignored the demands of both business and labor groups to do what she thought best for the country. Many Britishers thought it was high time somebody said no to the interest groups. Britain is a case where interest groups may have become too powerful. Is the United States far behind?

Interest Groups: Do They Serve in Our Best Interests?

Interest groups are a part of modern society. They differ from each other in their structures and strategies as much as the people who join them, but they all share a common goal: to promote their needs by influencing the political decisions which affect them. Some interest groups, such as ecology organizations and the Consumers Union, are intended to benefit the general public. Others, such as the AMA and the Bar Association, offer services on a members-only basis. However, the services a group provides for its members are less important to its overall success than other factors, such as financial resources, a receptive social and political environment, an appealing issue, size, cohesiveness, strong leadership, and relations with other groups.

In two-party systems especially, issues tend to be muted by political candidates who try to appeal to as broad a segment of the voting public as possible. The result is a gap between the narrow interest of the individual voter and the general promises of an electoral campaign—a gap which interest groups attempt to fill by pressing for firm political actions on certain issues. But how well do interest groups serve the needs of the average citizen? The small businessman, the uninformed laborer, and minority groups with limited financial resources tend to get lost in the push and pull of larger interests and government. The successful interest groups, too, tend to be dominated by a vocal minority of well-educated, middle- and upper-class political activists. In some cases interest groups have become so effective that they overshadow parties and paralyze policy making with their conflicting demands. The precise balance between the good of all and the good of particular groups has not yet been found.

[20]Samuel H. Beer, *Britain Against Itself: The Political Contradictions of Collectivism* (New York: Norton, 1982), pp. 15–19.

SUGGESTED READINGS

BERGER, SUZANNE, D. *Organizing Interests in Western Europe: Pluralism, Corporatism, and the Transformation of Politics.* New York: Cambridge University Press, 1981. Theory and case studies of the power of European interest groups.

CIGLER, ALLAN J., AND BURDETT A. LOOMIS, EDS. *Interest Group Politics* 2d ed. Washington, D.C.: Congressional Quarterly, 1986. Comprehensive, up-to-date, and readable collection on U.S. interest groups.

ETZIONI, AMITAI. *Capital Corruption: The New Attack on American Democracy.* New York: Harcourt Brace Jovanovich, 1984. Argues that PACs are turning government over to private interests.

KEY, V. O., JR. *Politics, Parties, and Pressure Groups.* New York: Crowell, 1958. Classic analysis of diverse groups in American politics.

LaPALOMBARA, JOSEPH. *Interest Groups in Italian Politics.* Princeton, N.J.: Princeton University Press, 1963. An important work casting doubt on pluralist assumptions of access and detailing the different styles of interest-group action.

LOWI, THEODORE. *The End of Liberalism: The Second Republic of the United States,* 2d ed. New York: W. W. Norton, 1979. A critical, insightful, and stimulating analysis of the consequences of pressure-group politics in the United States.

MILBRATH, LESTER W. *The Washington Lobbyists.* Chicago: Rand McNally, 1963. A study that takes a positive view of the role of lobbyists in the political process.

OLSON, MANCUR, JR. *The Logic of Collective Action: Public Goods and the Theory of Groups.* New York: Schocken Books, 1968. Olson creates an original model of the dynamics of group action and comes to some important conclusions.

SABATO, LARRY J. *PAC Power: Inside the World of Political Action Committees.* New York: Norton, 1985. Perhaps the best book on PACs out so far; comprehensive.

SCHLOZMAN, KAY LEHMAN, AND JOHN T. TIERNEY. *Organized Interests and American Democracy.* New York: Harper & Row, 1986. Good introductory round-up.

SCHULZINGER, ROBERT D. *The Wise Men of Foreign Affairs: The History of the Council on Foreign Relations.* New York: Columbia University Press, 1984. Study of a private group that powerfully influences U.S. foreign policy.

TRUMAN, DAVID. B. *The Governmental Process: Political and Public Opinion.* New York: Knopf, 1951. The role of pressure groups in congressional politics is thoroughly examined.

WILSON, GRAHAM K. *Interest Groups in the United States.* New York: Oxford University Press, 1981. British scholar explains upsurge in U.S. interest group activity.

chapter 11

Political Parties
and
Party Systems

To many Americans, a political party doesn't mean a great deal. The two major U.S. parties often seem to be alike. Both parties share much in the way of basic values, ideologies, and proposals. Elections usually turn on the personality of the candidates rather than party affiliation. Many American political scientists worry that the parties are becoming so weak that they may fail to perform necessary political functions to keep the system running correctly.

This weakness of American parties is curious, for the United States was the first country to develop mass political parties. Mass-based U.S. parties appeared with the presidential election of 1800, decades before parties developed in Europe. The Europeans, however, may have developed political parties more fully. Americans have tended to forget that parties are the great tools of democracy. They are the bridges between the people and the government, or, to use a systems phrase, the major "inputting" devices. As the famous E. E. Schattschneider put it, "The rise of political parties is undubitably one of the principal distinguishing marks of modern government. Political parties created democracy; modern democracy is unthinkable save in terms of parties."[1] If American parties are weakening, it may bode ill for the long-term future of American democracy. For what will take their place? Political action committees? Television campaigns? Neither prospect is appealing.

A *political party,* defined by one leading political scientist, is "any group, however loosely organized, seeking to elect governmental office-holders under a given label."[2] Almost all present-day societies, democratic or not, have some sort of political party system to link citizens to government. Occasionally military dictators—such as Franco in Spain, Pinochet in Chile, or generals in Brazil—try to dispense with parties, blaming them for the country's political ills. But this never lasts, for even dictators find that they need parties. Franco regarded all parties with a snarl but set up a "National Movement" that did the same things parties do. Within two years of Franco's death in 1975, Spain's parties came out into the open to give the country a party system that is not too different from its European neighbors. Similarly, the Brazilian generals tried to set up two obedient and controlled political parties, but when they gave up power in 1985, a genuine party system emerged that resembled the party system they thought they had abolished in their 1964 coup. Pinochet also found that however much he tried to crush Chilean party activity, it persisted underground. Love them or hate them, countries seem unable to do without political parties.

FUNCTIONS OF PARTIES

In democratic systems parties perform several important functions that help hold the political system together and keep it working. Some of these functions, to be sure, coincide with parties in nondemocratic systems, but Communist parties are another species that we will consider separately.

[1]E. E. Schattschneider, *Party Government* (New York: Holt, Rinehart and Winston, 1942), p. 1.
[2]Leon D. Epstein, *Political Parties in Western Democracies* (New York: Praeger, 1967), p. 9.

Aggregation of Interests. If interest groups, considered in the last chapter, were the highest form of political organization, government would be terribly chaotic and unstable. One interest group would slug it out with another, trying to sway government officials this way and that. There would be few overarching values, goals, or ideologies that could command nationwide support. Instead, it would be every interest group for itself. (Some worry that the United States already resembles this situation.) Parties help tame and calm interest-group conflicts by *aggregating* their separate interests into a larger organization.[3] The interest groups then find that they must moderate their demands, cooperate, and work for the good of the party. In return, they achieve at least some of their goals. Parties—especially large parties—are thus coalitions of interest groups. A classic example of this was the Democratic party that Franklin D. Roosevelt built in the 1930s which helped get him elected four times. It consisted of unionized workers, farmers, Catholics, Jews, and blacks. Labor unions, for example, working with the Democrats, got labor legislation they could never have obtained on their own. As long as this coalition held together, the Democrats were unbeatable; since then the coalition has badly decayed. President Reagan, as we considered earlier, attempted in the 1980s to aggregate economic and noneconomic conservative groups into the Republican party.

Integration into the Political System. As the aggregation of interest groups goes on, parties pull into the political system groups that had previously been left out. In reaching out for votes, parties usually welcome new groups into their ranks, giving them a say or input into the formation of party platforms. This gives the groups both a pragmatic and a psychological stake in supporting the overall political system. Members of the group feel represented and develop a sense of efficacy in the system and loyalty to the system. The British Labor party and U.S. Democratic party, for example, enrolled workers with platforms stressing union rights, fair labor practices, welfare benefits, and educational opportunities. Gradually, a potentially radical labor movement learned to play by the democratic rules and support the system.[4] Now, ironically, British and American workers are so successfully integrated into the political systems that many vote Conservative or Republican. In countries where parties were unable to integrate workers into the political system, labor movements turned radical and sometimes revolutionary. U.S. parties have helped integrate successive waves of immigrants and minorities into American political life.

Political Socialization. As parties are integrating groups into society, they are also teaching their members how to play the political game. Parties may

---

[3]For a theoretical explanation of interest group aggregation, see Gabriel A. Almond and G. Bingham Powell, Jr., *Comparative Politics: System, Process, and Policy,* 2d ed. (Boston: Little, Brown, 1978), Chap. 8.

[4]Seymour Martin Lipset stressed the positive function leftist political parties play in integrating the working class into the system. See Lipset, *Political Man: The Social Bases of Politics* (New York: Anchor Books, 1963), pp. 22–24.

introduce citizens to candidates or elected officials, giving citizens the feeling that they can make an input, thus deepening their sense of efficacy within the system. In party activities, people learn to speak in public, to conduct meetings, and to compromise, thus deepening their political competence. If nothing else, parties are the training grounds for leaders with talent. In fostering individual leadership skills, parties in democratic countries are also building up among party members a feeling for the legitimacy of the system as a whole. Historically, some European parties attempted to set up distinct political subcultures—complete with party youth groups, soccer leagues, newspapers, women's sections, and so on. The effort was self-defeating, however, for the more these parties socialized their members to participate in politics, the less the members were drawn to the subcultures. The fading remnants of this effort to build party subcultures can still be found in Italy in both the Christian Democrats and the Communists. Some American parties also provided social services. New York's Tammany Hall served as a welcome wagon for European immigrants, helping them find jobs and housing, while enrolling them into the Democratic party.

Mobilization of Voters.   The most obvious function of parties is getting people to vote. In campaigning for their candidates, parties are whipping-up voter interest and boosting voter turnout on election day. Without party advertising, many citizens would pay no attention to elections. Most political scientists believe there is a causal connection between weak U.S. political parties and low voter turnout. In Sweden, strong and well-organized parties often produce voter turnouts of 90 percent or higher. Some critics object that party electoral propaganda trivializes politics, but even this propaganda has a function. By simplifying and clarifying issues, parties enable voters to choose among complex alternatives.

Organization of Government.   The party's rewards for victory in an election are the governmental jobs and power it uses to try to shift government policy to its way of thinking. The party with the most seats in the U.S. House or Senate appoints the chamber's leaders and committee chairpersons. The occupant of the White House appoints more than 3,000 people to high-level jobs in the executive departments. This allows the victorious party to put its stamp on the direction which governance will take for at least four years. Party control of government in the parliamentary systems of West Europe (discussed subsequently) is tighter than in the United States, for parliamentary systems give simultaneous control of both the legislative and executive branches to the winning party. What a prime minister wants he or she usually gets, and with minimal delay, because party discipline is much stronger in the parliamentary systems of West Europe. In no system, however, is party control of government complete, for the already established bureaucracies of government have considerable power of their own (see Chapter 15). Parties *attempt* to control government; they don't always succeed.

BRITISH Conservative party leader Margaret Thatcher, here addressing the U.N., became prime minister in 1979, and carefully picked a cabinet that would carry out her ambitious program to revitalize the British economy.

UPI/Bettmann Newsphotos

Parties in Democracies

In evaluating party functions, two major factors must be considered: the degree of centralization in the party's organization and the extent to which a party actively participates in government policy.

Centralization. The control party leadership can exert on its elected members varies widely among democratic systems. At one extreme is Israel, whose highly centralized system of candidate selection calls for each party to draw up a national list of nominees to the parliament, or Knesset. Since Israel's system of elections uses proportional representation, 120 candidates are nominated, but only the names listed at the top of the ballot can be expected to win seats. Party chiefs can place tried and trusted people higher on the list; newcomers lower. This helps insure party discipline. West Germany also uses party lists, but the country is divided into ten states in which state parties have the dominant say. Such a system decentralizes party control. In Britain, the parties select their candidates by a process of bargaining between each party's national headquarters and its local constituency organizations. The national headquarters may suggest a candidate who is not from that district—perfectly legal in Britain—and the local party will look the person over in order to approve or disapprove of the candidate. The local party may also run its own candidate after clearing the nomination with national headquarters. The varying degrees of centralization of these systems gives their parties coherence, discipline, and ideological consistency. When you vote for a party in Israel, West Germany, or Britain, you know what they stand for and what they will implement if elected. Once elected, members of these parliaments do not go their separate ways but vote according to party decisions.

Voters have no such assurance of party discipline in the United States. Parties in the U.S. have historically been decentralized and weak. State party organizations may have some power; but, in most cases, candidates have only themselves to rely on. Candidates for the House and the Senate, in effect, create a new party organization every time they run. Between elections, U.S. parties lie dormant. The Republican National Committee and Democratic National Committee may not have many resources to distribute to candidates. Candidates are expected to raise their own money through contributions from individuals and political action committees (Chapter 10). Candidates then appeal directly to the voters by television and other media. Increasingly television advertisements fail even to mention the candidate's party affiliation. Candidates are thus in a position to tell their national parties: "I owe you very little. I didn't get much party help to win, and I won't pay much attention to you now that I'm in office." This makes U.S. parties radically decentralized and often incoherent. Elected officials answer to their conscience, to their constituents, and to their political action committees, and not to their political parties.

Setting Government Policy.   One key to responsible party government is the extent to which the majority party can enact its legislative program. Here, the American party system is exposed to its severest criticism from advocates of strong parties. In parliamentary systems, the majority party must resign when it can no longer muster the votes to carry on its legislative program. In contrast, the problem in the United States is often one of identifying exactly where the majority lies. The platform of the presidential campaign is not binding on the members of the president's party in Congress. What if the party of the president is not the majority party in one or both houses? Furthermore, just what is and who determines the legislative program of a party that may control Congress, yet has no central leader like the president? Does Mario Cuomo, Paul Simon, or Edward Kennedy speak for the national Democratic party? Or, do the elected congressional leaders in each house of Congress have the right to speak for their party members when they are not represented in the White House? These are just some of the problems parliamentary systems don't have.

In the United States, the legislative program is initiated centrally, with the president. But it must be acted on by various majorities within the House and Senate, and by the 535 individual senators and congressmen, each of whom is ultimately responsible for his or her own vote, as he or she is for his or her own reelection. Is the president, then, to be blamed for failing to fulfill campaign promises, or does the fault lie rather with a party discipline that is too loose? Schattschneider argued that because U.S. national parties are so decentralized, not one of them can agree on a strong national platform, and the result is that the American government is "a punching bag for every special and local interest in the nation."[5] But, on the other hand, many of us would prefer our senators and representatives to vote according to their consciences rather than the dictates of a more distant party leadership, as is the style in Europe.

---

[5]Schattschneider, *Party Government*, p. 209.

Party Participation in Government. True, a parliamentary system of government is more conducive to what Schattschneider regards as responsible party government than the American federal system. Our system, with its rigid set of checks and balances, can make it difficult for parties to bridge the separation of powers in order to enact platforms. But this is not entirely the fault of the American party system. It is inherent in the constitutional separation of powers between the executive and legislative branches. Occasionally, when a powerful president controls both the White House and Congress, party platforms may turn into law, as when Lyndon Johnson got his Great Society program through the Democratic Congress of 1965–66. No European parliamentary system had ever passed so many sweeping reforms so quickly.

Still, party participation in government is stronger in Western Europe, for in parliamentary systems the winning party *is* the government, or, more precisely, its leadership team becomes the cabinet. This allows for more clear-cut accountability and voter choice than is available in the American system, where the parties are decentralized and stand for many viewpoints. In both systems, parties participate in government by providing jobs for party activists in the various departments and agencies. In Britain, about one hundred members of the winning party's parliamentary faction take on cabinet and subcabinet positions. Some three thousand Americans receive political appointments when a new president takes office.

Parties in Communist States

The concept of "loyal opposition" is alien to Communist politics. Whereas democratic systems acknowledge the right of differing political groups to try to alter the course of the nation, Communist systems claim that they already know the outcome of history. The party's job is not to question government policy but to govern; its ultimate goal is not to gain control of the policy-making machinery but to guide society from capitalism through socialism and into the classless society.

The Communist party of the Soviet Union (CPSU), unlike Western democratic parties, offers an all-encompassing explanation of human history in the class struggle and an equally dogmatic analysis of social evolution in dialectical materialism. The hierarchy of the party interprets Marxist-Leninist thought and applies it to whatever sociopolitical or economic crisis might arise. The party's cadres go out among the people to enlist their support for the party's policies. Since the party leadership controls every aspect of government, there is a parallel between the structure of government and that of the party. In effect, the Soviet Communist party is a state within a state and a government within a government.[6]

[6]See Ronald J. Hill and Peter Frank, *The Soviet Communist Party,* 2d ed. (Winchester, Mass.: Allen & Unwin, 1983).

CPSU Structure. In the Soviet Union, every level of government has its corresponding party organization. At the local level, each unit of government is controlled by a soviet—a council whose members are elected by the people. For every soviet, there is a Communist party group that nominates all candidates for local government. Higher up, the Supreme Soviet (the national legislature and, according to the 1977 constitution, the highest organ of the state) elects the members of the Presidium (an executive council that governs when the Supreme Soviet is not in session) and theoretically supervises the Council of Ministers, which is equivalent to a Western cabinet. But corresponding to the Supreme Soviet is the Central Committee of the Communist party, which dominates the Supreme Soviet. The Central Committee is theoretically the highest tribunal within the Soviet Communist party. Its members are elected by local, district, and regional party cells and supposedly represent the will of the party's members. Normally, the Central Committee delegates most of its authority to the Politburo, a body of about fifteen top party people, many of whom also serve in "governmental" slots on the Council of Ministers. On top of this, much of the daily administration of the party is handled by the Secretariat, the party's administrative apparatus overseen by the General Secretary. In practice, great power accrues to the general secretary, an office developed by Stalin, for the *Gensec* makes appointments to key posts and thus lines up loyal supporters. The general secretary is understood to be the top Soviet official and usually takes on other governmental titles as well. In the Soviet Union, the person who controls the Secretariat controls the party, and he or she who controls the party rules the nation.

Communist Party Membership. Communist parties around the world do not encourage mass membership for several important reasons. In the first place, party discipline decreases in direct proportion to growth in membership: ten thousand people are easier to control than a million. Moreover, they do not want inactive or rebellious members and periodically purge the party ranks of dead wood. Membership requirements are far more rigid than in Western political parties, and, once admitted, the party member must participate. He or she is responsible for turning out the vote, explaining government policies to fellow workers, and enlisting their support for those policies. Rather than seeking to change government policy, the loyal Communist party worker's job is to sell fellow citizens on the leadership's policies.

Fascist Parties. Mussolini's Italian Fascist party and Hitler's Nazi party resembled the Communist party in organization. Like the Communists, the Fascists and Nazis had a highly centralized, elite party, and no political opposition was permitted. Both had youth organizations in order to recruit future party leaders, both conducted periodic purges to eliminate unreliable members, and both used secret police. Today, neo-Fascist and neo-Nazi parties still exist in Italy and Germany, but they are small and unlikely ever to win control of their country's governments. The fundamental difference between the party system of a democratic nation and that of a Communist or Fascist state is obvious: the former allows parties to compete for political power, the latter doesn't.

CLASSIFYING PARTY SYSTEMS

By Number of Parties

The One-Party System. The one-party system, generally associated with totalitarian regimes of the left or right, is a twentieth-century phenomenon. The Soviet Union, both Chinas, and many of the emerging nations of Africa and Asia are one-party states. All are characterized by a single party that controls every level of government and is the only party legally allowed in the country.

The "people's democracies" of Eastern Europe are not, technically, one-party systems. Communist Poland, for example, has three legal political parties joined in a permanent "national front." But the seats in the *Sejm* (parliament) are so divided that the Communists are assured a majority. The Polish Communists tolerate the other two parties, and Polish election laws do permit a certain degree of competition among individual candidates. But, since the Polish voter can only choose among candidates, not among parties, his or her franchise is essentially meaningless.

The Dominant-Party System. The American South since the Civil War was until a generation ago the closest facsimile to a one-party system that America had to offer. Eleven states in the American South were traditional Democratic strongholds: in these states, for many decades, the Republicans were so weak that they didn't even bother to run candidates for office. Likewise, Republicans traditionally controlled much of New England and the midwestern farm belt. It was rare for the Democrats to capture control of major state offices in these areas, and when they did they were rarely reelected. But a crucial factor separates these dominant-party systems, and their counterparts in India and Japan, from true one-party states: opposition parties in dominant-party systems are free to contest elections. And, of course, U.S. regional politics has changed in the last generation. Now every state has competing parties.

But some democratic nations have dominant-party systems at the national level as well. Since winning independence in 1947, India has been governed mostly by the Congress party. Although the Congress party is regularly opposed by parties advocating a variety of interests, the opposition has generally been fragmented, and it has won a national election only once, when the Congress party itself was in disarray.[7] Similarly, the Liberal-Democratic party of Japan has so consistently won that Japan has been called a "one-and-a-half party system,"

---

[7]See Robert L. Hardgrave, Jr., and Stanley A. Kochanek, *India: Government and Politics in a Developing Nation,* 4th ed. (New York: Harcourt Brace Jovanovich, 1986), Chap. 6.

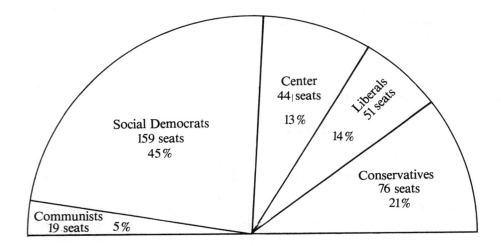

Percent indicates shares of the 1985 national vote.
(Does not add to 100% due to rounding and votes for minor parties.)

Figure 11-1   The Ideological Spectrum in Sweden's Parliament
Sandra Rife

with the much smaller Socialists being the half party.[8] In Mexico, the Party of Revolutionary Institutions (PRI) has also totally dominated since 1929, but not completely democratically.[9] The more conservative National Action party (PAN) has threatened civil disobedience if PRI's voting fraud does not cease. Mexico is a dominant-party system with a touch of single-party dictatorship.

The Two-Party System.   Most familiar to us is the two-party system, a hallmark of the English-speaking world. The United States, Britain, Australia, and New Zealand all have two major parties with a fairly equal chance of winning. Although third parties, such as that of John Anderson's 1980 presidential attempt and Britain's Social Democrat-Liberal Alliance, seldom win, they serve to remind the two big parties of voter discontent. Often one or both of the two main parties will then offer policies calculated to win over the discontented. In this way, even small third parties can have an impact.

The Multiparty System.   On the other end of the continuum from one-party nations are those with several competing parties. The Swedish party system (fig. 11-1) shows how its parties, arrayed on a left-to-right spectrum, receive seats in parliament in proportion to their share of the vote. This system

[8]See Ronald J. Hrebenar, *The Japanese Party System: From One-Party Rule to Coalition Government* (Boulder, Col.: Westview Press, 1987).
[9]See Daniel Levy and Gabriel Székely, *Mexico: Paradoxes of Stability and Change* (Boulder, Col.: Westview Press, 1983).

is often criticized as being unstable. The Fourth French Republic and the current coalition government of Italy are prime examples of the shortcomings of having many parties, as each has been unable to keep any government in power for more than a few months at a time. But whereas it is usually true that the existence of many political parties makes it harder for any one party to win a governing majority, this is not always the case. The Netherlands, Sweden, and Israel generally manage to construct stable multiparty coalitions that govern effectively. The number of parties is not the only reason for cabinet instability. Much depends on the political culture, the degree of agreement on basic issues, and the rules for forming and dissolving a cabinet. Scholars have spent considerable effort debating which is better, two-party or multiparty systems. It's hard to say, for both have fallen prey to indecision and immobilism. In the meantime, there has been a drift in both systems toward a middle ground, "two-plus" party systems.

The Two-Plus Party System.   Many democratic countries now have two large parties with one or more relevant smaller parties. West Germany has large Christian Democratic and Social Democratic parties, but the Free Democratic and Green parties win enough votes to make them politically important.[10] Britain is often referred to as a two-party system, but it has long had third parties of some importance: the Liberals (lately running as the Social Democrat-Liberal Alliance), the Scottish Nationalists, and Plaid Cymru (the Welsh nationalists). Even Spain, which has a history of multiparty fragmentation, emerged from the elections of 1986 with a two-plus party system: a very large Socialist party, a middle-sized rightist Popular Alliance, and a scattering of smaller parties.

To be honest, we should also call the U.S. system two-plus, for it too has long had third parties, some of which we mentioned earlier. In 1912 Teddy Roosevelt stalked out of the Grand Old Party (GOP) with his "Bull Moose Republicans," splitting his party and giving the election to Wilson and the Democrats. In 1948, some Southern Democrats ran as "Dixiecrats." In 1968, Gov. George Wallace of Alabama won nearly ten million votes for his implicitly racist American Independent party. The label "two-party" doesn't do justice to the complexity of U.S. politics.

Degree of Competition

Political scientist Giovanni Sartori, among others, is not completely satisfied with simply counting the number of parties to classify party systems. Also important is the degree and manner in which the parties *compete*. The term "multiparty system" does not differentiate between those that are stable and

---

[10]See Helmut Norpoth, "The German Federal Republic: Coalition Government at the Brink of Majority Rule," in *Government Coalitions in Western Democracies,* eds. Eric C. Browne and John Dreijmanis (New York: Longman, 1982).

those that are unstable. Sartori's scheme does; it delineates party systems of "moderate pluralism" from those of "polarized pluralism."[11]

In the former, there are usually five parties or fewer, and they compete in a "center-seeking" or centripetal manner; that is, their platforms and promises appeal to middle-of-the-road voters. Left-wing parties curb their radicalism and right-wing parties dampen their conservatism, for both know that the bulk of the voting public is somewhere nearer the center. Thus political life in moderate pluralism tends to be calm and stable, with ideological considerations toned down. Sweden is an example of a five-party system of moderate pluralism.

When the number of parties is greater than five, Sartori believes, there is the danger of polarized pluralism. Here the parties compete in a "center-fleeing" or centrifugal manner. Instead of moderating their positions, parties become ideologically extreme and engage in a "politics of outbidding" with their rivals. Many of the parties offer more and more radical solutions, either radical left or radical right. Some of the parties are "antisystem" or revolutionary. Parties that try to stick to the center find themselves attacked from both sides. Such a situation makes for political instability, sometimes leading to civil war, as in Spain in the 1930s, or to military takeover, as in Chile in 1973.

"Relevant" Parties. Sartori includes a useful methodological note: Just what do you count as a party? Every group that calls itself a party? Every group that wins a certain percentage of votes or at least one seat in parliament? We should count as "relevant parties," Sartori argues, those which the main parties have to take into account either in campaigning for votes or in forming coalitions.[12] If a party is so small and weak that no major party needs to worry about trying to win over its adherents, it is irrelevant. Likewise, if it is unnecessary to forming a governing coalition, it is irrelevant. Thus British Trotskyists and Swedish antialcohol Christians are ignored by all and don't count as parties, but Italy's Republicans and Israel's National Religious party, each with only a few percent of the vote, are necessary coalition partners and thus count as relevant parties.

Using Sartori's definition of "relevant" parties, would we include various American third-party efforts? Although the Democrats in 1948 denied the importance of the States' Rights party (Dixiecrats) and in 1968 the importance of Wallace's forces, in both elections they took them into account. In 1968, Democratic nominee Hubert Humphrey visited the South and emphasized that the Democratic party was a "very big house" that could accommodate many viewpoints, a lame attempt to make Southern voters forget the strong civil-rights reforms of the Johnson administration. In 1980, the independent candidacy of John Anderson probably forced President Carter to emphasize foreign and ecological policies he might otherwise have minimized. In these cases, we could

---

[11]Giovanni Sartori, *Parties and Party Systems: A Framework for Analysis*, vol. 1 (New York: Cambridge University Press, 1976), pp. 131–85.

[12]Sartori, *Parties and Party Systems*, pp. 121–25.

say the United States had relevant third parties. The tiny Communist, Socialist Worker, and Socialist Labor parties no one has to take into account, so under Sartori's definition we should not consider them relevant. The jury is still out on the Libertarian party, an extreme free-market party that pledges to deliver what Reagan talked about, the near-dismantling of the federal government.

Parties and the Electoral System

How a given nation gets its party system is often difficult to determine. Much is rooted in its unique historical developments. Some very different countries have similar party systems: Culturally segmented India produced a dominant party system (under the Congress party), as did culturally homogeneous Japan (under the Liberal-Democrats). Single-factor explanations will not suffice, but political scientists generally agree on the importance of the electoral system.[13]

Single-member election districts where a simple plurality wins tend to produce two-party or two-plus–party systems. Such is the case in the United States, Britain, Canada, Australia, and New Zealand—all on the original English model. The reason for this is not hard to understand: small third parties are grossly underrepresented in such systems and often give up trying. There is a big premium in single-member districts on combining political forces to form the party with a majority or at least a plurality. If one party splits, it often throws the election to the party that hangs together. The factions within a party may not love each other, but they know they've got to stay together to have any political future. This factor goes a long way toward explaining why the two big American parties stay together despite considerable internal differences.

Proportional representation allows and perhaps even encourages parties to split. Proportional systems use multimember districts and assign parliamentary seats in proportion to the percentage of votes in that district. In the Anglo-American single-member districts, the winner takes all. In multimember districts, winners take just their percentage. Accordingly, there is not such a big premium placed on holding parties together; a splinter group may decide that it can get one or two people elected without having to compromise with other viewpoints. Israel's proportional representation system helps in this way to produce its many small parties. As we will discuss in Chapter 13, modification of electoral laws can change a country's party system, pushing a country from a multiparty to a two-plus–party system, as in West Germany, or from a multiparty system to a "two-bloc" system, as in France. Interestingly, when France shifted to a proportional system for the 1986 legislative elections, the small, racist National Front won seats for the first time, illustrating how proportional systems encourage minor parties.

---

[13]See Douglas W. Rae, *The Political Consequences of Electoral Laws* (New Haven, Conn.: Yale University Press, 1967).

TYPES OF POLITICAL PARTIES

One of the first scholars to formulate a scheme for classifying political parties was French political scientist Maurice Duverger. His relatively simple scheme put all political parties into one of three descriptive categories: mass, cadre, or devotee. The mass parties include the Western democratic parties, which vie for members by attempting to cut across social-class lines and which seek the largest membership possible. European parties, whereas not as broadly based as the Anglo-American parties, are still mass parties because their membership is open. In contrast, cadre parties, such as the Soviet Communist party and India's Congress party, draw their support from the politically active elite. Generally associated with totalitarian or developing nations, cadre parties have centralized organizations and expect the elite group which makes up their membership to be active within the party. Duverger uses the term *devotee* for parties such as the Nazis under Hitler, where the party's formal structure is built around one man. This type of organization makes the leader as important as the philosophy he personifies.[14]

Maurice Duverger's system is useful for making some distinctions but falls short in many instances. For example, how could Duverger explain the difference between the Democrats in the United States and Labor in Israel? Each is a mass party, but party leadership nominates Labor candidates, whereas rank-and-file Democrats have the most powerful voice in the selection of party nominees. Because of the shortcomings of Duverger's classification scheme, political scientists Kenneth Janda and Fred Riggs devised another way of categorizing party systems.[15] They label parties according to the ways they recruit members, raise funds, and make nominations. The Labor party is leader-oriented because the party leadership alone nominates candidates. A party financed by members' dues is member-oriented, but if most of the support comes from private donors, the party is interest-oriented. In all, Janda and Riggs developed fifteen categories based on the variations and similarities in the internal structure of parties. But again, this classification scheme is imperfect because it fails to take into account variations in ideology or the type of people who make up a party's membership.

Political scientists Richard Rose and Derek Urwin did just this, categorizing parties according to whether the bulk of their membership is religious or anticlerical; blue-collar or middle-class; and united by race and ethnic identity or mixed.[16] The Christian Democratic parties in Western Europe are primarily

---

[14]Maurice Duverger, *Political Parties: Their Organization and Activities in the Modern State* (New York: John Wiley, 1954).

[15] Kenneth Janda, "Retrieving Information for a Comparative Study of Political Parties," in *Approaches to the Study of Party Organizations,* ed. William J. Crotty (Boston: Allyn and Bacon, 1968), pp. 159–216; and Fred W. Riggs, "Comparative Politics and the Study of Political Parties: A Structural Approach," also in Crotty, pp. 45–104.

[16]Richard Rose and Derek Urwin, "Social Cohesion, Political Parties, and Strains in Regimes," *Comparative Political Studies* 2 (August 1969): 7–67.

Roman Catholic. The anticlerical Italian Republican and Socialist parties draw their support from people who object to the political power of the church. Democratic Socialist parties draw heavily on trade union members and other wage earners; other parties attract predominantly the upper middle-class. Parties that are united by racial or ethnic identity are relatively rare in the western world but quite common in Asia and Africa. Mixed parties such as the Democratic and Republican parties in the United States cut across religious, social, and ethnic lines to draw at least some support from every significant group.

The Rise of the "Catchall" Party

Accompanying the general drift of most democracies to two-plus party systems has been the growth of big, sprawling parties that attempt to appeal to all manner of voters. Before World War II, many European parties were ideologically narrow and tried to win over only certain sectors of the population. Socialist parties were still at least partly Marxist and aimed their messages largely at the working class. Centrist and conservative parties aimed at the middle and upper classes, agrarian parties at farmers, Catholic parties at Catholics, and so on. These were called *Weltanschauung* (German for "world view") parties because they tried not merely to win votes but to sell a certain view of the world.

After World War II, Europe changed a lot. As prosperity increased, people began to think that the old ideological narrowness was silly. In most of West Europe, big, ideologically loose parties that welcomed all voters either absorbed or drove out the *Weltanschauung* parties. The late German political scientist Otto Kirchheimer coined the term "catchall" to describe this new type of party. His model was the German Christian Democratic party, a party that sought to speak for all Germans: businessmen, workers, farmers, Catholics, Protestants, women, you name it.[17] The term now describes virtually all ruling parties in democratic lands; almost axiomatically, they've got to be catchall parties to win. The British and Canadian Conservatives, Spanish and French Socialists, Italian Christian Democrats, and Japanese Liberals (who are actually conservative despite the name) are all catchall parties. And of course the biggest and oldest catchall parties of all are the U.S. Republicans and Democrats.

Whereas most political scientists welcome this move away from narrowness and rigidity, another problem has come up. Because catchall parties are big and contain many viewpoints, they are plagued by factional quarrels. Struggles between parties have in many cases given way to struggles within parties. Virtually every catchall party has several factions.[18] Scholars have counted nine factions in the Italian Christian Democrats and five in the Japanese Liberal-

---

[17]Otto Kirchheimer, "Germany: The Vanishing Opposition," in *Political Oppositions in Western Democracies,* ed. Robert A. Dahl (New Haven, Conn.: Yale University Press, 1966).

[18]Frank P. Belloni, and Dennis C. Beller, eds., *Faction Politics: Political Parties and Factionalism in Comparative Perspective* (Santa Barbara, Cal.: ABC-Clio, 1978).

Democrats, parties that resemble each other in their near-feudal division of power among the parties' leading personalities. A good deal of American politics also takes place within rather than between the major parties.

Criteria for Party Categories

Political parties can be classified in several ways, but underlying the categories are usually four broad criteria:

Who Supports the Party? Broad-based parties such as the Democrats and Republicans combine the political demands of different, and often antagonistic, parts of society. Narrow-interest parties, in contrast, articulate the interests of a single group. Catchall parties that draw from all parts of society stand the best chance of winning control of a stable government, because their political appeal is as broad as the community itself. Generally speaking, narrow-interest parties do not have enough support to win power, unallied, through the democratic process. To win control of the government, they must either enter into coalitions or seize power by force.

What is the Party's Membership Policy? Political parties are either "open" or "closed" in their membership requirements. Broad-based parties generally have their doors open to anyone who wishes to join, whereas elite parties operate more like an exclusive club. They carefully screen prospective members, and in some cases require them to complete a period of apprenticeship. Such is the case with Communist parties, especially those in power. Catchall parties, naturally, welcome all as members.

How Are Candidates Chosen? The way in which candidates are chosen varies so widely that meaningful distinctions are difficult. Broad-based parties generally give members the most voice in selecting nominees for office. This doesn't mean that political conventions are totally open, but rather that the party members have some say in who will run on the ticket. Such is the approach of the two big U.S. parties. In Communist parties, candidates are chosen by the party hierarchy. Most democratic parties choose their candidates at party conventions attended by loyal, long-time members, often representing constituency organizations.

What Are the Party's Goals? The parties we are familiar with are concerned primarily with winning office and control of government. However, third parties such as the Liberal party in Britain or Barry Commoner's Citizens party in the United States realize the unlikelihood of their gaining legislative control and have different goals. Their main concern is to "send a message" to the big parties. They exist to articulate a specific opinion and to see that this interest is protected by trading their political support for legislative favors. Finally, revolutionary parties, like the Communist party, are concerned with

CHOSEN: Ronald Reagan and George Bush were selected by the 1980 Republican convention in Detroit to run for president and vice-president respectively.
UPI/Bettmann Newsphotos

teaching the people a way of life, and use government power to change existing norms and established institutions. Their goal is to create a utopian society by employing the power of the state to convince its citizens to accept the party's concept of the ideal society.

Inherent in these broad criteria for classifying political parties is the assumption that the parties are aiming for a permanent standing in the political system. The nature of a party's appeal, its membership policy, candidate selection process, and political goals all center on the fact that the parties must hold some measure of support from the people. This support manifests itself in the form of members and money, both of which are vital to the survival of a party.

RECRUITMENT AND FINANCING

Political party leaders and members come and go, but the party itself strives to remain. How do parties recruit new members? Where do their leaders come from? How do they obtain the financial backing necessary to carry on their activities?

Recruitment

The requirements for party membership vary widely. The United States is unique in the Western world in that, strictly speaking, there is no party membership. One may register locally as a Republican or Democrat, but that doesn't mean much. It allows the person to vote in that party's primary but imposes no other obligations, such as paying dues or helping in campaigns. A citizen may, of course, join a local or state party club or committee, but this simply makes him or her a member of that group. This is not the case in Western Europe, where one may indeed become a party member. Parties set their own membership requirements and impose their own regulations on members. To join the Conservative party in Britain, one must sign a declaration testifying to support of the party's goals and pay yearly dues amounting to about sixty cents. Many British union members are automatically enrolled in the Labor party. Many European unions divert a part of their dues to the labor party in their country. Of course, most union members recruited in this manner are not likely to become actively involved in party affairs.

Incentives to Join. For European union members, joining the labor party is often the path of least resistance. But there are other reasons why people choose to identify themselves with a particular party. Political scientist Samuel Eldersveld found nine major reasons, ranging from the involvement of one's friends or relatives in a particular party to more self-generating motives.[19] Among these reasons lies the possibility that a particular candidate or issue may so capture the attention of a person that he is motivated to political action and so joins the party. Precinct workers may actively recruit party volunteers. Or, a citizen's participation in civic affairs may lead to political dealings with the local government, where one particular party is in office. Ideological commitment can also be a factor in motivating people to identify with a party, though this is true more in Europe than in the United States, where parties are less prone to ideological labels. Finally, people may become active in politics out of ambition for their own personal or professional advancement, or for political power itself.

Recruiting Candidates. Despite Ronald Reagan's jump from Hollywood star to president, most candidates for public office come up through the party ranks. How large a say does the party hierarchy have in deciding who will become a candidate? Lester G. Seligman's study of recruitment methods in the United States reveals that in "safe" districts, where people consistently vote for the same party, party officials do not play much of a role in candidate selection.[20] Usually, such districts have incumbent officeholders who will probably be returned to power, but when an office falls vacant, party factions are allowed to fight it out among themselves for control of the nomination. In "unsafe" districts where the minority faces a difficult battle, party officials must go out and draft people to run. Generally, loyal party workers are given the dubious honor of leading the party to certain defeat, and they run out of a sense of obligation to the party. Seligman finds that in competitive areas, party officials do not dominate in choosing candidates. Here, party leaders as well as factions within

[19]Samuel J. Eldersveld, *Political Parties: A Behavioral Analysis* (Chicago: Rand McNally, 1964), pp. 118–34.

[20]Lester G. Seligman, "Political Recruitment and Party Structure: A Case Study," *American Political Science Review* 55 (March 1961):77–86.

the party tend to support favored candidates in the primaries, but they are often upset by candidates supported by powerful nonparty interest groups.

Three means of choosing candidates exist outside of direct selection from the ranks by the established party leadership. Some candidates are self-recruited: they enter the primary on their own strength. These may be wealthy persons who hope to use massive advertising to compensate for their lack of organizational support, or persons who voice points of view that bring them a popular following but not party backing. Candidates may also be recruited by cooptation: a party may ask a "big name" who is not formally identified with it to run as its candidate. This usually happens when the party has no strong candidate of its own and hopes to capitalize on a popular new face. The Republican party's nomination of Eisenhower for president in 1952 is an example of cooptation. Finally, candidates are persuaded to file for office as the agents of groups who hope to win concessions from the established party hierarchy. Rev. Jesse Jackson's efforts in the 1980s can be seen in this light.

How Representative Are Party Leaders? How do our political leaders differ from each other? Are they representative of the party members who support them? Kenneth Prewitt studied the process by which eighty-seven San Francisco Bay area communities selected their local leaders.[21] His findings stress the role of social bias in the selection of political officials. Across the board, the city councilmen were wealthier and better educated than their respective constituencies. Prewitt found that, consciously or subconsciously, the American political system tends to favor candidates from the upper socioeconomic classes. Other studies have shown that party leaders in both major parties have more money and education than rank-and-file members.

Political Opinions: Party Leaders and Rank-and-File. It is often argued that America's political leaders do not reflect and respond to the needs of their constituents, and that party platforms represent vague attempts to dodge rather than satisfy complaints and issues. Curiously enough, much research suggests just the contrary: that political leaders actually hold stronger ideological views than do their followers, and that it is instead the weak and inconsistent ideologies of the party rank-and-file which prevent the leaders from taking firmer stands on issues.[22]

The leaders of both the Democratic and the Republican parties differ sharply on issues, whereas the broad party memberships often hold almost indistinguishable points of view. Democratic leaders can be counted on—with exceptions, of course—to apply a prolabor, prominority group, and pro-lower-

---

[21]Kenneth Prewitt, *The Recruitment of Political Leaders: A Study of Citizen Politicians* (Indianapolis, Ind.: Bobbs-Merrill, 1970). See Chapter 5 for a discussion of the elite view of American politics, which Prewitt represents.

[22]For a review and summation of elite-mass differences, see Joseph LaPalombara, *Politics Within Nations* (Englewood Cliffs, N.J.: Prentice-Hall, 1974), pp. 489–94.

income group stand to particular issues that arise. And Republican leaders in general favor business and agriculture. Their followers, however, are not as likely to apply such broad ideology to specific issues. Instead, their opinions are more likely to have little relation to their party membership. In terms of political opinion, then, party leaders differ from their followers in that they show a greater political sophistication. Their greater involvement in the political system, their education, and their background in general allow them to maintain a more consistent ideology than the rank-and-file party members hold.

Recruitment of Members in the Soviet Communist Party. In contrast to most Western political parties, the Soviet Communist party (CPSU) does not actively recruit broad memberships to support it at the next election. Instead, the CPSU tries to limit its rolls to those members who will work most efficiently and actively for the cause. Party members are carefully picked for their intelligence, leadership qualities, and ideological suitability and are admitted to the full privileges of membership only when they have proved their worth and reliability. The result is that party membership is drawn heavily from the educated white-collar professional and technical classes. The Communist party needs skilled members with education, intelligence, and motivation far more than it needs broad numerical support at the polls.

Financing the Political Party

Every organization is faced with the task of raising money to finance its activities, and this includes political parties. Imagine the financial problems involved in conducting a nationwide political campaign in the United States. In 1976, an estimated $540 million was spent in all the political campaigns—presidential, congressional, state, and local. Just four years later, in 1980, an estimated $1 *billion* was spent for all political campaigns.[23] The parties have become desperate to raise money. The Republicans are more successful and outspend the Democrats in most contests.[24] Because we have no formal method for financing political parties, American parties are dependent in great part on voluntary contributions from wealthy donors. Many other countries have official methods for raising financial support.

The Party Membership Fee. In Great Britain, India, Israel, and most continental European nations, political party members, like members of a private club, are required to pay dues in order to keep their membership active. To attract as large a membership as possible, the fee is deliberately kept low. Although effective in this sense, the result is that the dues usually do not come

---

[23]Herbert E. Alexander, *Financing Politics: Money, Elections, and Political Reform*, 3rd ed. (Washington, D.C.: Congressional Quarterly, 1984), p. 9.

[24]Gary C. Jacobson, "Party Organization and Distribution of Campaign Resources: Republicans and Democrats in 1982," *Political Science Quarterly* 100 (Winter 1985–86):4.

close to covering operating expenses. Thus, parties must turn to external sources, and so the problem of fund raising, which is so familiar to American parties, is felt on a smaller scale in other nations, too. There are many different solutions. In West Germany and India, candidates are expected to contribute what they can to their own campaigns and their party's coffers. This favors wealthy candidates over politicians of only moderate means. Britain strictly limits the amount of money any single candidate can spend on a parliamentary campaign, holding candidates criminally liable for violations of campaign spending laws. Although raising money still presents problems for political parties of these nations, the scale of their dilemma is nowhere near that of the Republicans and the Democrats. Our presidential campaigns, including the primary elections in the spring, require over a year of speeches, appearances, and attention-getting for at least one of the contenders. In contrast, European campaigns rarely last more than a couple of weeks to a month, so the expense is proportionally lower.

External Support. Japan, Israel, France, and Italy, like the United States, have laws that restrict or sharply regulate political contributions from industrial corporations, labor unions, and similar economic interest groups. West Germany, Spain, Sweden, and Finland use government funds to subsidize political parties in proportion to each party's electoral strength. This system has been criticized for its obvious discrimination against new parties, however. The United States Congress in 1974 passed a similar plan (the Presidential Campaign Fund) which allows taxpayers to authorize the Internal Revenue Service to donate one dollar of their income tax payment to the fund which subsidizes presidential nominees in proportion to the votes they receive, provided they get a minimum of 5 percent of the nationwide vote. About one taxpayer in four authorizes the checkoff, not enough to nearly cover campaign expenses. Political action committees (PACs—discussed in Chapter 10) have filled the vacuum with a vengeance. Now U.S. parties rely more and more on PACs, deepening the influence of interest groups.

The U.S. Party System: Could It Be Different?

There's a great deal of valid criticism of American political parties. Because they are so dependent on affluent donors and PACs, they are open to immoderate special-interest influence. Because they are so weakly organized and so highly decentralized—in effect, every congressional district and state has its own parties, little related to each other—the parties do not cohere at the national level and are rarely able to articulate clear-cut platforms and policy goals. Because there are only two main parties, each usually aiming for the political center, they are not able to offer voters an extensive menu to choose from. Most political scientists agree that U.S. parties, especially in contrast to their West European counterparts, are weak.

Can anything be done about this? Parties and party systems are rooted in their countries' history, society, and institutions. The U.S. Constitution never recognized parties, and the Founding Fathers warned against them. American society is not fragmented; it may not need more than two parties to express the general divisions within the population. And of course the single-member district with a simple plurality win favors a two-party system. Realistically, we can expect no major change in America's two-party system.

But could there be changes in the way the two parties function? Already there may be some move toward party centralization. President Reagan made the Republicans a more thoroughly conservative party with a reasonably clear program. This forced the Democrats to better organize themselves and to better define what they stand for.[25] Some of the "reforms" the Democrats had carried out in the 1970s proved to have weakened and divided the party; the reforms themselves had to be reformed.[26] Technology is helping to centralize the parties. Computerized mailing lists are a powerful inducement for state and local party organizations to cooperate with national headquarters. The national party committees can also channel PAC money to loyal candidates. In the long run, this may make the two parties more cohesive and ideologically consistent.

And there may be a certain advantage in *not* having strong parties. Strong parties may fall into the hands of oligarchic leaders who control too much and stay on too long, getting the party stuck in rigid and outmoded viewpoints. The U.S. system, by virtue of its very fluidity, may be better able to process demands from a wider range of citizens. The lack of programmatic coherence confers the benefit of flexibility.

SUGGESTED READINGS

BEYME, KLAUS VON. *Political Parties in Western Democracies.* New York: St. Martin's, 1985. A comprehensive review of party systems and theories about them.

CROTTY, WILLIAM. *American Parties in Decline,* 2d ed. Boston: Little, Brown, 1984. A good summation of why U.S. parties are in trouble and how little can be done about it.

ELDERSVELD, SAMUEL J. *Political Parties: A Behavioral Analysis.* Chicago: Rand McNally, 1964. Both theory and empirical analysis of the political party in action are discussed.

EPSTEIN, LEON D. *Political Parties in the American Mold.* Madison, Wis.: University of Wisconsin Press, 1986. A masterful review of what has been happening to U.S. parties by a top scholar.

KEEFE, WILLIAM J. *Parties, Politics, and Public Policy in America,* 4th ed. New York: Holt, Rinehart and Winston, 1984. The multifaceted role of U.S. parties and why the American electorate is not too happy with them.

KOLBE, RICHARD L. *American Political Parties: An Uncertain Future.* New York: Harper & Row, 1985. Thorough survey of classic and recent literature on U.S. parties and their problems.

LIPSET, SEYMOUR MARTIN, ED. *Party Coalitions in the 1980s.* San Francisco: Institute for Contemporary Studies, 1981. Considers how far U.S. electoral realignment is likely to go.

McHALE, VINCENT, ED. *Political Parties of Europe.* Westport, Conn.: Greenwood Press, 1983. Encyclopedic handbook detailing all of Europe's parties, including historical ones, by country.

MICHELS, ROBERT. *Political Parties.* New York: Free Press, 1949. The source for the "iron law of oligarchy" as developed in a study of socialist parties.

[25]See David B. Truman, "Party Reform, Party Atrophy, and Constitutional Change: Some Reflections," *Political Science Quarterly* 99 (Winter 1984–85):4.

[26]For a sharp criticism of what the Democrats did to themselves see Nelson W. Polsby, *Consequences of Party Reform* (New York: Oxford University Press, 1983).

PETROCIK, JOHN R. *Party Coalitions: Realignments and the Decline of the New Deal Party System.* Chicago: University of Chicago Press, 1981. A methodologically sophisticated look at long-term trends in U.S. party realignments.

PRICE, DAVID E. *Bringing Back the Parties.* Washington, D.C.: Congressional Quarterly Press, 1984. A broad overview of the health of U.S. parties and their chances for renewal.

SARTORI, GIOVANNI. *Parties and Party Systems: A Framework for Analysis,* vol. 1. New York: Cambridge University Press, 1976. Insightful and provocative study of party systems and their consequences.

SORAUF, FRANK J. *Party Politics in America,* 5th ed. Boston: Little, Brown, 1984. A comprehensive survey of the American party system.

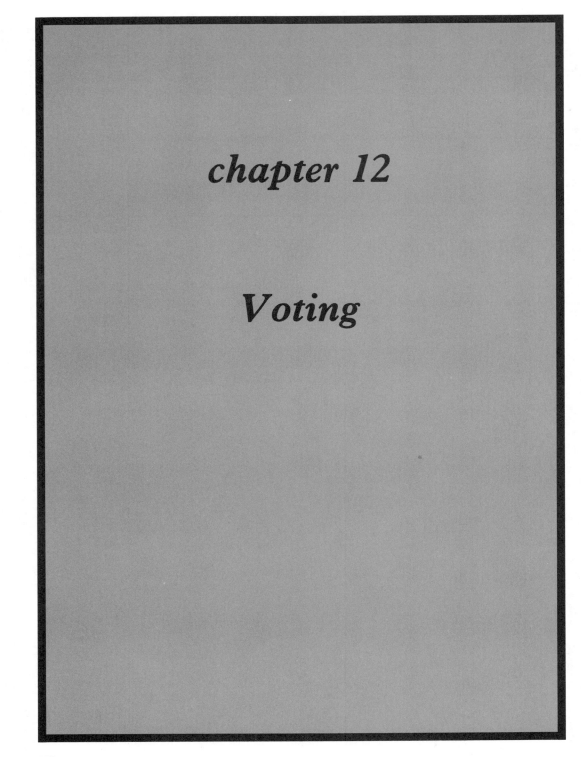

chapter 12

Voting

In this chapter we ask three general questions on voting behavior, each question followed by a more specific question about voting behavior in the United States. First, we ask why do people vote. This leads us immediately to the puzzle of why voting turnout in the United States is so low. Second, we ask how people vote. This brings us to the question of whether party loyalties in the United States are declining or merely shifting. Finally, we ask what wins elections. This takes us to some of the strategies that are applied in U.S. elections.

WHY DO PEOPLE VOTE?

In a nation with a strong commitment to democracy and participation, one would expect citizens to show great interest in politics and voting. Curiously, Americans vote considerably less than citizens of other democracies. In the 1984 election, little more than half those eligible to vote in the United States bothered to cast a ballot. And historically, voter turnout in the United States was never very high; it hit a peak of 63 percent in 1960 but by 1984 had declined to 53 percent.[1] Election turnout in Sweden, West Germany, and Italy sometimes tops 90 percent. Spain in 1977 had not experienced a free election in forty-one years, yet turnout was 79 percent, perhaps a measure of how much Spaniards appreciated the right to cast a democratic ballot.

In nonpresidential elections, U.S. turnout is even worse; perhaps a quarter to a third vote. Why do democratic Americans have such a poor voting record? Apathy and indecisiveness are partly responsible. Typically, more than half of U.S. nonvoters say they aren't interested in or are dissatisfied with the candidates. Many feel their vote won't make a difference; even more feel that none of the candidates are really good. Another part of the reason is the U.S. party system, in which the two large parties do not offer an interesting or clear-cut choice; both tend to stick to centrist positions. Only about one adult American in twenty is involved enough in politics to attend a political meeting, contribute money, or canvass a neighborhood.[2]

Nonvoting in the United States has inspired a major debate among political scientists as concerns both its causes and its meaning. One school views the decline with alarm, arguing that low electoral participation means many Americans are turning away from the political system, which in turn is losing its legitimacy and authority. If this keeps up, democracy itself could be threatened. Another school is more sanguine, arguing that the decline may mean that Americans are basically satisfied with the system, or at any rate not sufficiently dissatisfied to go to the effort of registering and voting. Indeed, countries with very high voter turnouts may be suffering from a sort of political fever in which partisan politics has become dangerously intense.

In West Europe, three-quarters or more of the citizens routinely vote; in the United States little more than half vote. Why the difference? One obvious

[1]For a good—and pessimistic—overview of declining U.S. voter turnout, see Thomas E. Cavanagh, "Changes in American Voter Turnout, 1964–76," *Political Science Quarterly* 96 (Spring 1981):1.

[2]Lester W. Milbrath, *Political Participation* (Chicago: Rand McNally, 1965), pp. 16–22.

reason is that in Europe, registration is automatic. As soon as one reaches the age of eighteen, one is eligible to vote. Local authorities, in effect, do the voters' registering for them. In contrast, America's residency laws and sometimes ponderous registration procedures can present an obstacle to the would-be voter. The citizen, not the government, carries the burden of making sure that any details, such as change of name or residency, are recorded in the official accounts. This involves the inconvenience of a special visit to the official place of registration several weeks before the election. By the time that campaign excitement has begun to mount, the deadline for registration is long past. Further, elections are held on working days (in much of Europe, voting takes place on Sundays), and the lineup of local, state, and national candidates is often enough to baffle all but those who have memorized the sample ballots. These structural factors provide only some of the reasons for low U.S. turnout. We will explore others.[3]

Who Votes?

In his landmark work, *An Economic Theory of Democracy,* Anthony Downs theorized that people will vote if the returns outweigh the costs.[4] If the stakes seem important enough, the voter will go to the trouble of voting. Thus, the person whose property taxes stand to be raised if a new school bond is passed is much more likely to vote on the issue than his or her neighbor who rents an apartment and will not be hurt by the tax. The cost of political information, both financial and personal, is also influential in determining whether a person will vote. The price of a newspaper, the sacrifice of switching from a favorite TV show in order to watch the news, and the time involved in attending a political meeting all tend to prevent political information from being distributed equally to everyone, because each person places a different value on personal time and political awareness.

The result is that the poor and the uneducated in every society are the least likely to vote. According to some studies, the typical American nonvoter is a woman in her twenties, married to a blue-collar worker, with little formal education. Why? Because relatively poor, she has few financial investments and probably feels she has little economic stake in the election outcome. Being poorly educated, the cost of getting political information, in terms of time taken from other interests and chores, is likely to outweigh the benefits she feels she derives from a knowledge of current affairs. Her lack of education also makes her part of a tradition in which her sex has stayed clear of politics. She is therefore likely to take voting less seriously than men do. It should be pointed out that fewer women fit this pattern than before. More and more, women work outside the

---

[3]See Everett Carll Ladd, *Where Have All the Voters Gone? The Fracturing of America's Political Parties* (New York: Norton, 1978).

[4]Anthony Downs, "The Causes and Effects of Rational Abstention," in *An Economic Theory of Democracy* (New York: Harper & Row, 1957), pp. 260–75.

DIVORCE: The referendum in Italy showed marked differences in social categories of voters. Men, better-educated people, younger people, and liberal and leftist party-identifiers tended to support retaining Italy's law permitting civil divorce. Women, religious Catholics, and political conservatives went against it.

Michael Roskin

home, are educated, and are less likely to defer to male political judgments. Accordingly, women's turnout has come to more and more resemble men's. Still, the typical voter in almost every democracy is a middle-aged man, college educated, with a white-collar job. He is more likely to vote in a national election if he lives in a city than if he lives in the country. And he is more likely to vote if he identifies strongly with a political party than if he calls himself an independent.

Within these broad generalizations of characteristics of the typical voter and the typical nonvoter, it is possible to identify several specific factors that are likely to have an influence on whether a person votes or not. Although personality is important, income and education, race, age, sex, and area of residence all act in a predictable manner.

Income and Education.   People who enjoy a large income are more likely to vote than those who are less affluent. And people who are well educated are more likely to vote than those who dropped out of high school. Are they in fact the same individuals? Not quite, for a wealthy person who did not finish high school is almost as likely to vote as a wealthy college graduate. Even though certain voters often combine these characteristics (good education makes it easier to earn a good salary), the two influence voting in rather different ways. One is a matter of having a stake in election outcomes, the other a broader question of interest and sophistication.

According to the Survey Research Center, assembly-line workers living in small towns may see little difference between a Ronald Reagan and a Walter

Mondale.[5] They are accustomed to paying taxes, following rules and regulations, and making a living through hard work. They are likely to see little difference in the way they fare under a Democratic administration as opposed to a Republican administration and therefore feel that they have little stake in the election's outcome. In contrast, presidents of large corporations feel involved in the election. They see a direct cause-and-effect relationship between who wins the election and their personal fortune, which will be affected by changes in international monetary policy, personal and corporate tax reforms, government policy toward organized labor, interest-rate changes, and a score of other complex fiscal policies. Of course, blue-collar workers may be affected by a change in the administration, but they are less likely to be aware of the stakes.

The difference between upper-class voters and working-class nonvoters is primarily a feeling of *efficacy*. Assembly workers feel that their votes will make little difference. Corporation presidents, on the other hand, believe that their participation is important to the political process, and that the difference between one candidate and the next is likely to be significant. Whereas a change in the party in office is likely to have an impact on blue-collar workers, we can see why corporation presidents feel that the stakes are more important. In their experience, they have seen interest groups and private associations succeed in changing government policy, if only by successfully influencing the local school board to expand a school-bus route. In contrast, blue-collar workers are likely to see American political life from the perspective of the "silent majority" subculture. Friends, neighbors, and family have never had any wealth and have never organized to successfully pressure the government.[6]

Many well-educated people have broader interests in elections beyond personal economic stakes in its outcome. More widely read and more sophisticated than the high-school graduate (or dropout), the college-educated person—whether wealthy or not—tends to be more interested, better informed, and more likely to participate in elections.[7] As our discussion in Chapter 7 indicates, schooling helps to provide both a sense of the importance of political participation and a more abstract intellectual curiosity which makes people more likely to read papers, keep abreast of the news, and feel involved in the political events of their nation and local area.

Race.   Despite federal laws and black organizations, black voting rates are lower than white—about 18 percentage points lower in 1984.[8] Still, the gap may be slowly closing. Black income and education levels have risen. The 1965

---

[5]Angus Campbell et al., *The American Voter* (New York: John Wiley, 1960), chap. 17.

[6]According to Seymour Martin Lipset, both organizing skill and a belief in the effectiveness of organization go hand in hand with higher income. See *Political Man* (New York: Doubleday, 1960), pp. 190–203.

[7]Raymond E. Wolfinger and Steven Rosenstone found education to be the major factor in voting turnout. See their *Who Votes?* (New Haven, Conn.: Yale University Press, 1980).

[8]Paul R. Abramson, John H. Aldrich, and David W. Rohde, *Change and Continuity in the 1984 Elections* (Washington, D.C.: Congressional Quarterly Press, 1986), p. 109.

Voting Rights Act overcame many of the barriers placed in the way of black registration, chiefly in the South. Southern black registration rose from 29 percent in 1960 to 63 percent in 1976. In 1984, Rev. Jesse Jackson campaigned doggedly for the Democratic nomination even though he knew he didn't stand a chance; he did it to encourage blacks to register, and they did. Important in this has been the political consciousness-raising blacks have gone through in the last generation. Many have learned the value of participation and of voting. Some previously racist white politicians got the message and became respectful toward their black constituents. Chicanos faced similar problems and also showed low turnouts. Race, accordingly, is still a factor in U.S. election turnout.

Age. Young people—those under 25—typically feel less politically involved than those who are older; accordingly, they vote less. About half of U.S. citizens 18 to 25 years of age are currently not registered to vote. (This is probably not the case in your political science class, first because you are college students and second because you're at least a little interested in politics.) Non-voting among the young parallels our discussion of income and voting. Young people, with lower incomes and little property, don't feel economically involved with election outcomes. When they start paying substantial taxes, they become much more interested. Focused on the concerns of youth, many have no time or interest in political questions which seem abstract and distant.

In 1971 the Twenty-Sixth Amendment lowered the U.S. voting age from 21 to 18. Interestingly, at almost the same time, most other democracies did the same. The results were similar: the newly enfranchised young people didn't vote as much as their elders, and when they did vote, their preferences weren't much different. Middle-aged people are more likely to vote than either youngsters or oldsters, probably because the middle-aged person is at a peak in earning power. The many important issues for the elderly—such as Social Security and Medicare—have brought out older voters in greater numbers, partly offsetting their disinclination to vote.

Sex. Traditionally, men were more likely to vote than women in almost every society. In large part, this was due to the fact that women had only comparatively recently won the right to vote. (Switzerland's female population was enfranchised only in 1971). Since 1920, when female suffrage was granted in the United States, the gap between men's and women's voter turnout has been narrowing steadily. Now the difference in turnout between the two groups is nil.[9]

Area of Residence. City dwellers are more likely to vote than rural residents. This probably reflects the easier accessibility of voting booths in the cities, where a relatively few blocks can comprise a voting district with the same population as a rural district of several square miles. In France, unlike Britain

[9]Ibid., p. 110.

and the United States, rural areas traditionally turn out a higher percentage of voters than do cities. This is because in France, local politics in small towns is conducted on a much more intimate level than the depersonalized politics of the big city.

People who have lived in the same place for a long time are more likely to vote than are transients or newcomers, for long-time inhabitants of any community feel more involved in their neighborhood goings-on, and are therefore more likely to participate in groups and activities that will sustain their community.

Voter turnout in the United States is somewhat lighter in the South than in the North and West, even in urban areas. Traditionally lower participation in the South reflected a number of influences, including a lower standard of living for that region of the nation and a traditional lack of strong party competition in the area due to the once unquestioned predominance of the Democratic party. Many of the traditional characteristics of the South and its politics have recently changed, and now turnout in the South is approaching turnout in other areas of the country. Other nations are also characterized by regional differences in voter participation. In France, the areas south of the Loire River have a lower voter turnout than the northern areas of the country.

HOW DO PEOPLE VOTE?

The reasons that people vote as they do are many and complex. Deep loyalty to a political party, the advice of a friend, fondness for one candidate and distrust of another, and feelings about an issue—each of these can have an overriding effect on a voter's election decision. The influences that determine the way a person will vote can be grouped according to the type of effect they have on the individual voter's political leanings. The result is a pattern of *long-term* and *short-term variables*. For example, many working-class Britons have always been Laborites and will continue to vote Labor for the rest of their years. The same is true of many American Democrats and Republicans. An affiliation with a political party is a long-term influence: it affects the way a person votes for his or her entire lifetime. In contrast, there are short-term variables which may cause a person to vote one way or another for one election year but won't influence his ballot three or four years later. Margaret Thatcher shrewdly called British elections in 1983 to catch the glow of military victory in the Falklands and again in 1987 during an economic upswing and disarray in Labor's ranks. Her Conservatives won both times.[10] Similarly, in 1976 in the United States, Jimmy Carter benefited from a "morality factor" awakened by the Watergate scandal. By the 1980s, however, voters deserted the Democrats and Jimmy Carter for Reagan and the promise of economic recovery. A particular candidate or a

---

[10]See Austin Ranney, ed., *Britain at the Polls, 1983* (Durham, N.C.: Duke University Press, 1984), especially Chap. 7.

specific issue can have the effect of changing a person's vote for one election without causing any permanent shift in party loyalty.

Party Identification

American politics has operated on a two-party system since the mid-nineteenth century. There has been talk of developing an effective and permanent third party, but such a party has not yet come into existence. Indeed, most American voters seem satisfied with the two major parties. For some people, party identification is strong enough to be compared with a religious affiliation. It is heavily influenced by one's parents and is instilled early in life. By the time they reach fourth grade, more than half of all school children consider themselves either Democrats or Republicans. And over half never change the affiliation they inherited from their parents.

Why does party identification remain a stable element throughout many people's lives? One reason is that what we learn as small children has a way of staying with us. Like a preference for certain foods learned in childhood, a preference for one party is difficult to shake. Another reason is that it is easier to vote along party lines. Party identification provides the easiest means of marking the complicated U.S. ballots. It provides a shortcut for election decision-making—a "standing decision." Persons who call themselves Democrats are automatically predisposed toward any Democratic candidate, whether they realize it or not. When asked how they feel about the Republican candidate, they will probably express suspicion of the candidate and his or her views.

Party ID, as it's called, is an important element in electoral stability. People who stick pretty much to one party are like a foundation, allowing politicians to anticipate what people want and try to deliver it. Weak party ID produces great "volatility" in voting, as citizens, like ships without keels, blow this way and that in the political winds. It is with some concern, then, that political scientists notice a decline in the number of party identifiers in the United States, a topic we shall explore presently.

Party Identification in Europe.
Whereas American political parties have some effect on the way most people vote, most European parties are more influential in determining an individual's election choice. Since World War II, Britain has been characterized by a consistent split between Labor and Conservative supporters.[11] The "swing" from one major party to another during national elections ranges from only about 1 percent to 5 percent. In voting for representatives to Parliament, one study of the midsixties showed that 71 percent of British voters could be counted on to return the same party to Commons.[12]

---

[11]See David Butler and Donald Stokes, *Political Change in Britain,* rev. ed. (New York: St. Martin's Press, 1976).

[12]Jorgen Rasmussen, "The Implications of Safe Seats for British Democracy," *Western Political Quarterly* 19 (September 1966):516–29.

Great Britain and the United States both have two-party systems. What effect does party identification have in nations where there is a healthy competition among several political parties? One study compared party identifiers (as opposed to all voters) in the multiparty system of Norway with those in the American two-party system to determine how influential party identification was in determining voter decisions.[13] As could be expected, Norwegian identifiers were significantly more likely to vote along party lines than were American Democrats or Republicans. The smaller political parties of Norway represent more tightly knit points of view. Thus, party identifiers in Norway are more able to express a personal ideology through their vote, unlike Republicans or Democrats in the United States. Not all European systems with several competing parties are characterized by high party identification. A comparative study of French and American voters found that while 75 percent of Americans classified themselves as either Republicans or Democrats, less than 45 percent of Frenchmen were members of one of their nation's political parties.[14] The French party system, unlike that of Norway, is characterized by many short-lived parties. The authors of the French-American study felt that the confusion caused by this ever-changing system was one reason for France's low degree of party identification. Their findings indicate that multiparty systems don't necessarily mean high voter identification with political parties.

Does party identification influence the European voter differently than the way it influences the voter in the United States? Leon D. Epstein argues that it does.[15] Whereas a relatively high percentage of American voters identifies with a political party, Epstein feels that this party identification means something different in the American, as opposed to the European, setting. Many Americans are registered with a party, but they cannot always be counted on to vote according to their party registration. On the other hand, Europeans, few of whom are party members, are more likely to vote according to their party memberships once they have established such loyalties.

Who Votes How?

No one can predict with absolute accuracy the voting in a free and fair election; but, using the same social categories we discussed in Chapter 8 (on public opinion) and earlier in this chapter (on voting turnout), political scientists can arrive at a general description of what kinds of people tend to identify with the various parties. Bear in mind that no social category votes 100 percent for a given party; people are highly individualistic and often like to go their own way, disregarding group norms. This accounts for some poor Republicans and some rich Democrats. If more than half of a given social category supports and votes

---

[13]Angus Campbell and Henry Valen, "Party Identification in Norway and the United States," *Public Opinion Quarterly* 25 (Winter 1961):505–25.

[14]Philip E. Converse and Georges Dupeaux, "Politicization of the Electorate in France and the United States," *Public Opinion Quarterly* 26 (Spring 1962):1–23.

[15]Leon D. Epstein, *Political Parties in Western Democracies* (New York: Praeger, 1967), pp. 78–85.

for one party, we probably have a significant relationship between the social category and the party. If three-quarters identifies with a party, we have a very strong relationship. We are making statements here that indicate a *tendency,* not an absolute relationship. Political scientists learn to say things like, "Jews *tend* to vote Democrat," and not "All Jews are Democrats." Notice in Table 12–1 that two-thirds of Jews in 1984 voted for Mondale, but the other third voted for Reagan. Beware of absolute statements.

Once practicing politicians (and sometimes political scientists) detect a tendency in a group to identify with a certain party, they call it a *voting bloc.* The candidates' strategy is then to secure enough blocs to deliver a majority of the electorate, and they tailor their campaign to win over the blocs most likely to vote for them. The concept of voting blocs is an oversimplification, however, for there is no such thing as a solid bloc. Consider, for example, the "working-class vote."

Class Voting. As we discussed in Chapter 8, social class is one determinant of party identification and voting behavior. Even in the United States, where class distinctions are blurred, blue-collar workers tend to register and vote Democratic. This tendency is especially strong in families where the breadwinners are union members. Notice in Table 12–1 how "union households" were

Table 12-1   Who Voted How in 1984

	REAGAN	*MONDALE*
Overall	59%	40%
Men	62	37
Women	56	44
Whites	64	35
Blacks	9	89
College graduate	58	41
High school graduate	60	39
Less than high school	49	50
18–29 years old	56	43
30–44 years old	57	42
45–59 years old	59	39
60 and older	60	39
White Protestant	72	27
Catholic	54	45
Jewish	31	67
Union household	46	53
Professional or manager	62	37
White collar	59	40
Blue collar	54	45
Student	52	47
East	52	47
Midwest	58	40
South	64	38
West	61	37

one of the few categories that went for Mondale in the 1984 election. In most European countries, this tendency is stronger, for unions are often connected to social-democratic or labor parties. This relationship doesn't always work to deliver the vote, however. The gigantic Swedish union, LO, can reliably deliver the labor vote to the Social Democrats in Swedish elections. But in the 1983 British elections only 39 percent of union members voted Labor.[16]

The middle and upper classes tend to have more conservative political leanings. In 1984, the higher the family income, the greater the tendency to vote for Reagan.[17] Better-off Britons and Swedes are also more likely to support their respective conservative parties. Two things muddy class voting. Some working-class people—because they consider themselves middle class, have a family tradition, or have individual convictions—vote for conservative parties. A majority of the U.S. and British working class voted, respectively, Republican in 1984 and Conservative in 1983. Conversely, some middle and even upper class people—because they are of working-class origins, have a family tradition, or have individual convictions—vote for parties on the left. Such people are especially important in providing working-class parties with educated leadership. Most of Europe's labor, social-democratic, or socialist parties are led by middle-class intellectuals. This two-way crossover—working-class identifying with conservatives and middle class identifying with the left—dilutes class voting until it virtually disappears in some elections. In hard economic times, however, class voting can reappear as a major factor.

Regional Voting. Some regions identify strongly with certain parties. Often these are areas that have been conquered and subjugated centuries ago, and the inhabitants still harbor resentments. South of the Loire River, the French tend to vote Socialist. Scotland and Wales vote heavily Labor. And in the U.S., the southern states used to be solidly Democratic. By 1984, regional loyalties had so shifted that the South was the strongest area for the Republican Reagan; and the East—which following the Civil War had been a Republican bastion—was weakest for Reagan.

Religious Blocs. Religion can have an even deeper impact than region. In France, for example, devout Catholics vote mostly conservative; nonreligious people vote mostly left.[18] The same applies to Italy, where the largest party, the Christian Democrats, was founded by and is still linked to the Roman Catholic Church. The Catholic areas of Germany are more likely to vote Christian Democrat than are the Protestant areas. In the United States, Catholics and Jews

---

[16]By the editors of *The Economist, Political Britain Today* (New York: Cambridge University Press, 1984), p. 6.

[17]Abramson, Aldrich, Rohde, *Change and Continuity*, pp. 136–37. One writer argues that the Reagan elections brought a return of class voting. See Thomas Byrne Edsall, *The New Politics of Inequality: How Political Power Shapes Economic Policy* (New York: Norton, 1985).

[18]Howard R. Penniman, ed., *France at the Polls: The Presidential Election of 1974* (Washington, D.C.: American Enterprise Institute, 1975), p. 203.

have tended to be Democrats, whereas white Protestants have tended to be Republicans.

Age Groups. It's not necessarily true that younger people are more radical than their elders. Rather, they tend to catch the tide that is flowing in their youth and stay with it. Young people socialized to politics during the Depression tended to identify with the Democratic party all their lives. By the same token, Republicans hope that the enthusiasm for Reagan among young voters in the 1980s will give them a permanent sense of identification with the Republican party. Age groups react in part to the economic situation. Many young voters felt that Reagan's policies of growth would lead to jobs, but many retired voters feared Reagan's cuts in Social Security. In 1984 this led to retired voters being slightly more liberal than young ones.

Gender Gap. It also used to be assumed that women were more traditional and conservative than men, but that tendency has been reversed in the United States. Women voted for Mondale in 1984 by 5 percentage points more than men. Although Geraldine Ferraro, Mondale's running-mate, was the first woman to run for vice-president, women did not necessarily vote Democratic because of her. Women have been voting more for the Democrats for some time. Furthermore, young and better educated women voters tend to vote more Democratic than older women. Women tend to like the Democrats' support for welfare measures and the Equal Rights Amendment and to dislike the Republicans' emphasis on military spending.

Racial Minorities. Blacks are the most loyal Democrats by far; 90 percent of those who voted went for Mondale in 1984. A majority of Hispanic and Asian-American voters also identify with the Democrats. The affinity of racial minorities for the Democrats, however, may have cost the party some white votes. Republicans were delighted to portray the Democrats as the party of minorities, feminists and labor unions—and to portray themselves as the party of everyone else.

Urban Voting. One of the few laws political science can offer is that big cities vote liberal or left-wing. This is explained, partly, by the concentration of the working-class vote in cities—for big cities have big factories. In addition, cities are also centers of education and sophistication, places where intellectuals are often drawn to liberal and leftist causes. Country and suburban dwellers tend to embrace conservative values and vote for conservative parties. England votes overwhelmingly Tory, but not the city of London. West Germany's Bavaria is a conservative stronghold, but not the people of Munich. Italy is dominated by the Christian Democrats, but not Italy's urban population. The mayors of most large American cities are Democrats; even the Reagan landslide of 1984 failed to alter the voting tendencies of U.S. cities.

Electoral Realignment

For some decades political scientists have debated a theory of *critical* or *realigning elections*.[19] Typically people retain their party identification for a long time, sometimes all their lives. But, according to this theory, in several watershed presidential elections, the party loyalties of many voters are destroyed, and they establish new, durable party identities. These "critical elections" do not determine how every vote will be cast, but they set the terms of debate and the main topics to be debated. They give one party dominance, although not absolute control. The critical or realigning elections in U.S. history are usually seen as the following:

1800, the emergence of Jefferson's Democratic Republicans
1828, the emergence of Jacksonian populist Democrats
1860, the emergence of Lincoln's Republicans
1896, the emergence of business Republicanism
1932, the emergence of Roosevelt's New Deal Democrats

Between these critical elections, party identifications are stable and most people vote according to them. This is called the "normal vote" or "maintaining elections."[20] Occasionally, enough voters will disregard their party identification to elect the weaker party: Democrat Grover Cleveland in 1884 and 1892, Democrat Woodrow Wilson in 1912 and 1916, and Republican Dwight Eisenhower in 1952 and 1956. These have been called "deviating elections" because the party shift was only temporary; afterwards voters went back to their long-term party ID.[21]

A Reagan Realignment?   Republicans anticipated that the Reagan sweeps of 1980 and 1984 marked a realignment in party identification in their favor. Party registration rose for Republicans and declined for Democrats until the parties were about equal in size. Young people, in particular, who are the future of any party, registered and voted Republican. Even more important, Reagan and his intellectual supporters restructured the ideological debate in a conservative direction (see Chapter 6). It was no longer fashionable, as it had been from the election of Franklin D. Roosevelt to the election of Jimmy Carter, to talk about using the powers of government to fix social ills and provide welfare programs. Instead, the political debates concerned how to lower taxes,

---

[19]The founder of the theory was the great V. O. Key with his article, "A Theory of Critical Elections," *Journal of Politics* 17 (February 1955):3–18. Many others have explored the topic, including Walter Dean Burnham, *Critical Elections and the Mainsprings of American Politics* (New York: Dodd, Mead, 1968) and James L. Sundquist, *Dynamics of the Party System: Alignment and Realignment of Political Parties in the United States*, rev. ed. (Washington, D.C.: Brookings Institution, 1983).

[20]See Angus Campbell et al., "The Concept of the Normal Vote," *Elections and the Political Order* (New York: John Wiley, 1966), chap. 2.

[21]Campbell and others, *The American Voter*, pp. 531–38.

cut government spending, limit government regulation, reduce the federal deficit, and restore growth through free enterprise. Before Reagan, even Republicans went along with the welfare state, and some of the biggest expansion of welfare programs occurred under Nixon. After Reagan, even the Democrats demanded fiscal responsibility.

But realignments don't come with name tags. It might not be possible to tell if there has been a realignment until some decades later. Furthermore, it may be difficult to spot the precise election in which realignment occurred. Looking at the results of the 1968 election, which brought Nixon to the White House, and carefully dissecting regional trends, Kevin Phillips concluded in 1969 that a Republican majority was emerging.[22] Which then was the critical election, 1968 or 1980? If it were 1968, it would mark Carter's election in 1976 as a "deviating election"; and, indeed, Carter's victory was largely the result of the Watergate scandal. What was missing from the Nixon years, however, was the ideological conservatism that came with Reagan. We might say that the ingredients for a realignment in favor of the Republicans came with the 1968 election but did not fully coalesce until 1980. What we have then is not a single "critical" election but a time period in which realignment occurred.

Further, if there were a Republican realignment it did not extend to congressional races. Even during the Reagan landslides, the House of Representatives stayed in Democratic hands, and in 1986 the Senate moved back under Democratic control. Congressional contests, heavily focused on local interests, are relatively insulated from the tides that turn presidential elections. Voters typically look to their Representative for services and economic benefits. Often, in these situations, Democrats are better able to deliver than Republicans, who preach (but do not always practice) cutting government programs.

How then can we tell if there has been a realignment? If the Republicans keep winning the presidency, and if they are able to extend their power to Congress, then there has been a realignment. If, however, an economic downturn during a Republican presidency and an attractive Democratic candidate produce one or more Democratic presidential victories, the theory of electoral realignment will have to be reexamined. If voters react mostly to current situations and candidates' personalities, the basic supposition of party identification will have to be reconsidered. Perhaps party ID is not as important as it once was. Instead of realignment, we may be seeing *dealignment*.

Electoral Dealignment

Since the mid-1960s, the number of voters committed to neither party has increased sharply. In 1948, under 20 percent of U.S. voters called themselves independents. In 1980, one poll showed an amazing 40 percent calling themselves independent, exceeding the 37 percent who were Democratic and

---

[22]Kevin B. Phillips, *The Emerging Republican Majority* (New Rochelle, N.Y.: Arlington House, 1969).

the 24 percent who were Republican.[23] More recently, the number of self-styled independents has subsided, but it still runs around one-third. What happened to produce this major change, and what does it mean for American politics?

Studies in the 1950s indicated that people calling themselves independents tended to be least involved in and least informed about politics. This is no longer the case, as many independents are now well-informed and politically concerned. Independents tend to be young and college-educated. They also came of age during extraordinary times. In 1964 they heard the Democratic candidate for president promise not to send Americans to fight in Vietnam. In 1974 they saw a Republican president resign in shame. Their faith in conventional party politics was considerably shaken; both major parties appeared dishonest. This was also the time when the postwar "baby boom" came of age, swelling the numbers of young people who were disillusioned.

Governing the United States had become more difficult. Inflation, unemployment, slow economic growth, and the pressing demands of various groups contributed to discontent and sometimes anger at both parties, which struggled with these problems without much success. Some political scientists noticed that this process coincided with three trends: (1) declining voter turnout, (2) declining party loyalty, and (3) declining trust in the government in Washington.[24] Do the three items hang together? Which causes which? Declining political trust is probably the underlying cause, giving rise to the other two.

If things keep on like this, is there a danger for U.S. democracy? There well could be. Presidents are not voted in by a majority of those eligible, only by a majority of those actually voting. With only about half voting, that means presidents often win with not much over one-quarter of the total electorate behind them, hardly a claim for an impressive mandate. Further, the high numbers of independents, when they decide to vote, easily shift their loyalties more on the basis of mood and candidate personality than according to issues. This voter volatility makes the country hard to govern, for it deprives elected officials of stability and predictability. Voters become too fickle for any president to please them. Interest groups and media replace parties.

Fortunately, such decline need not be permanent. Some surveys show an uptick in both trust in government and party identification.[25] The slowdown of inflation under President Reagan produced a calming and stabilizing effect. Republican identifiers increased until the two main parties and the independents each constituted roughly a third of the electorate. Political scientists generally mark increased party identification—for either main party—as a healthy trend. But much depends on circumstances and presidential decisions. Renewed

[23]Everett Carll Ladd, "The Brittle Mandate: Electoral Dealignment and the 1980 Presidential Election," *Political Science Quarterly* 96 (Spring 1981):3.

[24]Paul R. Abramson, *Political Attitudes in America: Formation and Change* (San Francisco: Freeman, 1983), pp. 3–15.

[25]See Arthur Miller, "Is Confidence Rebounding?" *Public Opinion*, June/July 1983, pp. 16–20.

economic difficulties or American involvement in another war in the Third World could put the country on the road to dealignment again.

WHAT WINS ELECTIONS?

Short-Term Variables

Which is more important to the voter—Margaret Thatcher's economic program or the fact that she heads the Conservative party? Ronald Reagan's personality or his membership in the Republican party? The answer to what determines a vote depends largely on the divisiveness of the issues of an election year and on popular feeling about the candidate. Party affiliation provides election guidelines for the voter when immediate variables don't intervene, but if the voter feels strongly enough about the opponents or the setting of one specific election, he or she is likely to disregard party membership and vote for the opposition.

In every election, some voters will cross party lines and vote for a candidate or candidates in the opposite camp. Dividing one's vote among candidates of more than one party is called ticket-splitting. Analyses of ticket-splitting in presidential elections in the United States show that this has been a growing trend. Some surveys find half of the voters casting ballots for candidates of more than one political party. Among the highest groups of ticket-splitters are the well-educated, the upper classes, young voters, and independents. In 1984, in spite of Ronald Reagan's landslide, the Democratic party was able to draw enough support to keep control of the House of Representatives.

What are the reasons behind ticket-splitting? Cross-pressures created by countervailing motives is the principal factor. Republicans opposed to a U.S. military role in Central America had to make a choice in 1988 between their party and their principles: they might have decided to vote according to principles on the national ticket and according to party in state and local contests. The committed Democrat who thought women unsuitable for high office had to make a tough decision in 1984; many decided to vote for all the Democratic candidates except for president and vice-president. The general rule is that the less committed party identifiers are more likely to divide their votes.

Although there are many variables that cause voters to divide their votes between parties, political analysts have found that most of the factors that lead to ticket-splitting and to a departure from long-term party identification are related either to the particular issues of a campaign or to the individual candidate.

Issue Orientation. In 1900, William Jennings Bryan based his candidacy on the Populists' call for a silver standard for the dollar, identifying himself so strongly with that issue that even now the mention of his name brings the response "cross of gold." Bryan lost, but the case illustrates an election where one issue dominated voter decisions.

A political issue is a question about policy which causes conflict. Any government action or proposal will foster some conflict; the degree depends on the dimensions of public reaction. The issues that are the most decisive to any election are the ones which affect the most people the most directly, and the way different issues affect different voters is a good measure of the diversity of the people. In the American presidential election of 1988, some young men of draft age voted for the candidate they thought would not lead the country into a war. Many black people voted for the candidate they saw as most likely to further racial equality, whereas a large number of workers in organized labor based their choice on the degree of sympathy they thought the candidates had for organized labor. Domestic issues have traditionally had much more impact on voter decisions than foreign affairs, although several elections (including Lyndon Johnson's victory over Barry Goldwater in 1964) have been influenced by foreign policy questions. America's seeming impotence overseas, symbolized by the Iran hostage crisis in 1980, swung votes to the candidate who promised to restore U.S. strength, Ronald Reagan. In 1984, issue voting was weak. In fact, voters on average saw Mondale's position as a trifle closer to their own, but they still preferred Reagan.[26]

Candidate Image.   Charles de Gaulle of France, Pierre Elliott Trudeau of Canada, Willy Brandt of Germany, and John F. Kennedy of the United States are some of the more charismatic political figures of recent times. Each inspired either strong loyalty or sharp distrust; few people had neutral feelings about them. Candidate orientation refers to a voter's attitudes about a particular candidate apart from feelings about issues or regular party affiliation. Candidate orientation is sometimes very important in determining an election, although candidate orientation is seldom the sole reason for voting a certain way.

Some elections hinge largely on who the candidates are. Dwight Eisenhower's winning smile deserves much of the credit for Republican control of the White House in the fifties, just as Charles de Gaulle's and Konrad Adenauer's personalities dominated the politics and elections of France and West Germany for several years. Even in parliamentary democracies, where prime ministers are elected only indirectly by parliament, elections have become increasingly dominated by the personalities of the leading contenders almost as if they were presidential elections. In Spain, Britain, West Germany, and elsewhere in Europe, election posters feature pictures of the candidate for prime minister, much as in U.S. presidential contests.[27] Televised election campaigns have heightened candidate orientation throughout the world.

Incumbent Performance.   Most people do not carefully evaluate issues in a presidential election, but they do accumulate an overall evaluation of the

---

[26]Abramson, Aldrich, and Rohde, *Change and Continuity,* chap. 6.

[27]See Michael Roskin, "Spain Tries Democracy Again," *Political Science Quarterly* 93 (Winter 1978–79):643–44, and *Countries and Concepts: An Introduction to Comparative Politics,* 2d ed. (Englewood Cliffs, N.J.: Prentice-Hall, 1986), pp. 186–88.

JIMMY CARTER, here a candidate for the Democratic nomination in 1976, moves through a crowd in a small Pennsylvania city as if they were the folks back home in Georgia. Carter's campaign strength was his natural rapport with small-town America.

Michael Roskin

performance of an incumbent president. That is, they feel the president has done a good job or a poor one. Especially important is their perceptions concerning the health of the economy and government steps to boost economic growth.[28] The accumulated or package views of voters toward incumbent presidents has been termed "retrospective voting" because it views in retrospect a whole four years of performance in office.[29] When voters think the government in general is doing a good job they reward the incumbent's party: Johnson in 1964, Nixon in 1972, and Reagan in 1984. When they think the government in general is doing a poor job they punish the incumbent's party: Humphrey in 1968, Ford in 1976, and Carter in 1980.

Retrospective voting is colored, naturally, by party identification, issues, and candidate personality. A strong Republican is likely to find little good to say about a Democratic administration. For those with weak party identification, plus the many independents, the feeling of overall performance is apt to be the most powerful determinant of voting. Further, if an administration scores well in the minds of such people in restrospect, they may start identifying with that party. Voting behavior is complex. When people say they "like" candidates, what does it mean? Do they like the candidates' party affiliation, their stands on issues,

[28]For the link between economics and voting, see Heinz Eulau and Michael S. Lewis-Beck, eds. *Economic Conditions and Electoral Outcomes* (New York: Agathon Press, 1985).

[29]See Morris P. Fiorina, *Retrospective Voting in American National Elections* (New Haven, Conn.: Yale University Press, 1981).

their personal images, or the sum total of their performance in office? Unraveling such puzzles is the crux of campaign strategy.

Candidate Strategies: A Practical Application of Voting Behavior Studies

Campaign strategies are geared toward two goals: keeping "one foot on home base" by not alienating the normal party supporters, and at the same time trying to win over votes from the undecided and from as many of the opposition as possible. There are many forces at play in the ultimate decision of the voter. The political and economic events of an election year—war, depression, treaties—also contribute to both the dimension and the direction of voter reaction. In a year when a major crisis has occurred, voter turnout is likely to be high; in a year when things have gone rather smoothly, voters may be relatively apathetic.

How does the candidate use these variables to plan campaign strategy? In most cases, the campaign is designed to fit the opinions and needs of the constituency. Thus, the candidate must be aware of pockets of party strength and resistance, what city dwellers are thinking versus the opinions of people in the suburbs, what districts contain the lowest rates of participation (and will therefore yield the smallest numbers of votes), and which stands on issues are likely to inflame large groups of people against his or her candidacy. Only when the candidate has some awareness of the direction and intensity of voter opinion will he or she be able to plan an effective campaign. Important in this is a knowledge of "voting blocs."

Voting blocs fall into roughly the same categories as the public opinion blocs discussed in Chapter 8. Class, religion, and geographic characteristics are the most important influences in opinion formation, and these provide general guidelines for predicting voting behavior. Urban and rural voters will oppose each other on a mass-transit bond; blacks and whites may vote differently on a school-busing issue. Every election victory is the result of a major coalition formed by several smaller blocs of voters. On a national scale, the Democrats used to represent a coalition of labor, blacks, Catholics, Jews, and urban voters; the Republicans received their support from a coalition of rural and farm voters, the remaining Protestants, and nonunion workers. By the 1960s, though, these traditional blocs had begun to break up, and neither party has managed to reconstruct them.[30] The breakup of the blocs, it should be noted, coincides with the declining voter turnout and party loyalty discussed earlier.

Once a candidate recognizes opinion patterns and the strength of the support from various blocs, he or she can use this knowledge to plan strategies more effectively. In 1984, Ronald Reagan reached large numbers of farmers

---

[30]Some scholars, journalists, and practicing politicians believe new voting blocs are emerging. See Seymour Martin Lipset, ed., *Party Coalitions in the 1980s* (San Francisco: Institute for Contemporary Studies, 1981).

who he knew would be receptive to his message through early-morning radio commercials. Black newspapers and "soul stations" carry political advertising to large numbers of black voters. In this way, the candidate can use even the mass media to aim a particular message toward a specific bloc of voters.

Through a knowledge of characteristic voting patterns of different regions, presidential candidates may recognize that no matter how much time they spend in a state, they won't have a chance of carrying it—or that a few more visits may be able to bring that state over. An understanding of voting behavior can thus perform an immeasurable service in helping a candidate recognize which groups support them, which groups might, which won't even vote, and which will not budge.

SUGGESTED READINGS

ABRAMSON, PAUL R., JOHN H. ALDRICH, AND DAVID W. ROHDE. *Change and Continuity in the 1988 Elections*. rev. ed. Washington, D.C.: Congressional Quarterly Press, 1987. A superb examination of the 1984 elections, including congressional, that puts the Reagan victory into historical perspective.

ALFORD, ROBERT R. *Party and Society*. Chicago: Rand McNally, 1963. Voting patterns and preference in the United States, Great Britain, Canada, and Australia with the author's "index of class voting."

BERELSON, BERNARD, PAUL F. LAZARSFELD, AND WILLIAM N. MCPHEE. *Voting*. Chicago: University of Chicago Press, 1954. One of the first of the behavioral-socio-political studies of the American electorate. Based on a survey of Elmira, New York.

CAMPBELL, ANGUS, ET AL. *The American Voter*. New York: John Wiley, 1960. A pathbreaking work on American voting behavior that forms that basis for other contemporary studies.

CHUBB, JOHN E., AND PAUL E. PETERSON, EDS. *The New Direction in American Politics*. Washington, D.C.: Brookings Institution, 1985. An excellent collection that sees considerable party realignment as a result of the Reagan victories.

CONWAY, M. MARGARET. *Political Participation in the United States*. Washington, D.C.: Congressional Quarterly Press, 1985. Exploration of varieties of citizen participation, including a discussion of the voter turnout question.

DALTON, RUSSELL J., ET AL., EDS. *Electoral Change in Advanced Industrial Democracies: Realignment or Dealignment?* Princeton, N.J.: Princeton University Press, 1985. A welcome comparative study that finds major electoral alignment shifts in other countries.

LADD, EVERETT CARLL. *Where Have All the Voters Gone? The Fracturing of America's Political Parties.*

New York: Norton, 1978. A worried and insightful look into declining voter turnout by a master of survey research.

NIE, NORMAN H., SIDNEY VERBA, AND JOHN R. PETROCIK. *The Changing American Voter*, enlarged ed. Cambridge, Mass.: Harvard University Press, 1979. An update and a reply to Campbell's classic study.

POLSBY, NELSON W., AND AARON WILDAVSKY. *Presidential Elections: Strategies of American Electoral Politics*, 6th ed. New York: Scribners, 1984. An impressive summation by two top political scientists of the many shifts in U.S. presidential politics.

POMPER, GERALD M. *Voters, Elections and Parties: The Practice of Democratic Theory*. Rutgers, N.J.: Transaction Books, 1987. A top elections scholar synthesizes his previous research to come up with a theory of democracy.

ROKKAN, STEIN. *Citizens, Elections, Parties*. New York: David McKay, 1970. The social patterns of electoral support in Western politics.

ROSENSTONE, STEVEN J. *Forecasting Presidential Elections*. New Haven, Conn.: Yale University Press, 1983. Offers a complex predictive model of voting that factors in all manner of variables.

SUNDQUIST, JAMES L. *Dynamics of the Party System: Alignment and Realignment of Political Parties in the United States*, rev. ed. Washington, D.C.: Brookings Institution, 1983. A penetrating analysis of voter-party alignment in the United States and the prediction that dealignment will reverse.

VERBA, SIDNEY, NORMAN H. NIE, AND JAE-ON KIM. *Participation and Political Equality: A Seven-Nation Comparison*. New York: Cambridge University Press, 1978. An important cross-national study of how and why people participate in politics.

chapter 13

The Basic Structures of Government

WHAT IS A POLITICAL INSTITUTION?

The word "institution" is apt to conjur up an image of an impressive building with stately columns, home of a legislature or executive department. True, many institutions are housed in imposing structures—it bolsters their authority—but architecture is not what political institutions are about. *Political institutions,* rather, are established and durable relationships of power and authority.

The U.S. Supreme Court, for example, even if it met in a tent, would be an important institution as long as its decisions were obeyed. As we will consider later, it was not clear what the powers of the Supreme Court were to be when it began, but forceful personalities and important cases slowly gave it power. Like most institutions, the Supreme Court *evolved* into importance.

In Chapter 1 we looked at authority as a fluid thing that requires continual maintenance. A political institution can be looked at as congealed or partly solidified authority. Over time, people have become used to looking to political institutions to solve problems, decide controversies, and set directions. Institutions, because they are composed of many persons and (if they're effective) last many generations, take on lives of their own apart from the people temporarily associated with them. This gives the political system stability; citizens know where they stand.

Institutions are bigger than individual leaders. When President Nixon resigned under a cloud of scandal in 1974, the institution of the presidency was scarcely touched. If there had been a series of such presidents, and if they had refused to resign, the institution itself would have been severely damaged. Sometimes dictators have tried to make themselves into "institutions." But it hasn't worked, for no matter how powerful dictators are during their lifetimes, the institutions they have tried to build unravel upon their deaths. Francisco Franco ruled Spain—sometimes with an iron hand—for thirty-six years. He attempted to insure the system he had set up would survive after him, but it was too much based on himself. Within three years of his death, Spain had established a democracy, a new constitution, a multiparty system, a free press, and many other rights and liberties which Franco had hated. Dictators seldom build lastingly; they are rarely able to *institutionalize* their personal power.

Powerful inhabitants of an office, however, can sometimes put their personal stamp on the institution. George Washington set standards and precedents that his successors felt compelled to follow even though his actions were not specified in the Constitution. Washington retired after two terms, and, until Franklin D. Roosevelt, no president tried to serve longer. Washington had put something into the institution of the presidency that was not codified into law until the Twenty-Second Amendment in 1951. In another example, the first chancellor of the Federal Republic of Germany (West Germany), Konrad Adenauer, offered such decisive leadership that the institution of the chancellor has been powerful ever since.

One way to approach the study of institutions is to try to locate the most powerful offices of a political system: "Who's got the power?" Studying constitutions may help locate power, but sometimes they do not tell the whole story. Reading the U.S. Constitution, for example, you might think the executive and the legislative powers were in equal balance. This is what the Founding Fathers intended, but over the past two centuries power has gravitated into the hands of the president. The French constitution, set up by Charles de Gaulle in 1958, seemed to give the presidency near-dictatorial powers. But the French legislative elections of 1986 brought a conservative parliament and prime minister to face a Socialist president who had been in office since 1981. The Socialist president, sensing he had lost public support, gave way and permitted the conservatives to repeal much of what the Socialists had earlier enacted. It was hard to predict how French institutions would handle the problem of the legislative and the executive branches being under the control of different parties. The French constitution was unclear on this point. But now the situation is clearer, and it turns out the French presidency has less power than was previously thought. Constitutions are themselves institutions, gradually evolving in practice if not in wording.[1]

MONARCHY OR REPUBLIC

An example of such evolution is the modern constitutional monarchy. Calling a country a monarchy or a republic is to describe its "form of state." A *republic* is simply a form of state which does not have a monarch. The word *republic* does not imply "good" or "democratic." All but a few countries in the world are republics. Most of the remaining monarchies are figurehead constitutional monarchies such as those of northwest Europe—Britain, Norway, Sweden, Denmark, Holland, and Belgium. The king of Spain still has an active political role. He restrained the army from pulling off a coup in 1981, thus becoming a bulwark of Spanish democracy. The traditional, working monarchies still found in the Arab world—Morocco, Saudi Arabia, Jordan, Kuwait—are likely doomed unless they can accomplish the extremely difficult task of turning themselves into limited constitutional monarchies. Failure to do so has in recent decades led to the overthrow of traditional monarchies and their replacement by revolutionary regimes in Egypt, Iraq, Libya, Ethiopia, and Iran.

The limited constitutional monarchies of northwest Europe pose an interesting question. How is it that these countries can combine an old form of state with a modern democracy? Indeed, the countries mentioned are some of the freest and most democratic in the world. The answer seems to be that monarchies perform an integrative function, holding together divergent social groups during the delicate modernization phase. The traditional sectors of society—the clergy, the army officers, the great landowners—usually oppose democracy and may be tempted to carry out coups to stop democratization. But these sectors are also monarchist in orientation, and, if the king goes along with democratization, the traditional sectors will probably support it also. The monarch thus serves as a bridge between the traditional political system of the

---

[1]For a classic essay on this subject, see Karl Llewellyn, "The Constitution as an Institution," *Columbia Law Review* 34 (January 1934) 1.

Middle Ages and the modern participatory system, easing the way from one to the other.[2]

Consider the histories of countries that retained their kings—gradually limiting the monarch's powers until they were figureheads. Then consider those countries that deposed their monarchs. Britain temporarily deposed its monarchy in the seventeenth century, but it was soon reestablished. Since then Britain's political evolution has been mostly peaceful and gradual. The French Revolution repudiated monarchy and alienated French conservatives. Since then French politics has been a nasty tug of war between conservative and radical forces with rare periods of stability. Sweden retained its monarchy and evolved into a model social-welfare state. Germany lost its monarchy after World War I, when the Kaiser abdicated and fled to Holland; and, after the shaky fourteen years of the Weimar Republic, Hitler took over with his Nazis. It has been suggested that this might not have happened if Germany had stayed a monarchy with a moderate Kaiser (such as Prince Max of Baden) that all sectors of society could trust. Monarchs can confer legitimacy on new democratic institutions. When Juan Carlos of Spain blocked a military coup in 1981, the head of the Spanish Communist party announced his support for monarchy. The king of Spain had thus bridged most sectors of Spanish society, even those which had previously been revolutionary and antimonarchist.

New republics, such as those of the Third World, have to face the multiple crises of nation-building (discussed in Chapter 2) without a dominant institution that can confer legitimacy. If their fragile new institutions can survive the first decades, they gradually gain legitimacy. In time, respect for republican institutions may succeed in uniting most elements of the society, as has happened in the United States. As Edmund Burke pointed out two centuries ago, in the world of institutions, old is good, for an institution that has survived and adapted over a long time has also implanted itself into citizens' hearts and minds.

Monarchs are *heads of state;* symbolically representing their nations by receiving foreign ambassadors and giving restrained speeches on patriotic occasions. In republics, their analogues are presidents, some of whom are also little more than figureheads. The republics of West Germany, Italy, and Israel, for example, have presidents as heads of state, but they don't do much in the way of practical politics. The *head of government* is the real working executive, and, in most systems, is called prime minister (as we shall explore in subsequent chapters).

UNITARY OR FEDERAL SYSTEMS

Another basic institutional choice concerns the territorial structuring of the nation. There are really only two choices: unitary or federal. A unitary system accords its component areas little or no autonomy; most governance is done

---

[2]This point is well made in Seymour Martin Lipset, *Political Man: The Social Bases of Politics* (Garden City, N.Y.: Anchor Books, 1963), pp. 65–66.

from the capital city. The subdivisions—departments in France, provinces in Italy, counties in Sweden—are largely for administrative convenience. Federal systems are composed of units that have considerable political lives of their own: U.S. and Brazilian states, Soviet and Yugoslav republics, and Swiss cantons. These units cannot be legally erased or easily altered by the central power.

There is, theoretically, a third alternative: the confederation, a group so loosely formed that the component parts can override the center. Confederations tend to have short lives; they either fall apart or become federations. This was the fate of the United States under the Articles of Confederation. Similarly, the Confederate States of America demonstrate the difficulty of the structure: each state had such independence that they could not jointly coordinate their efforts during the Civil War. Switzerland still calls itself a confederation (Confederatio Helvetia), but it is actually a federal system. Perhaps the European Common Market—or, as it likes to call itself, the European Community—is the only current example of a confederation, with the weak powers of its headquarters in Brussels easily blocked by the vetoes of individual member countries.

Unitary Systems

Unitary governments have significant control over local authorities. They usually touch people's daily lives in more ways than a federal government would. For example, in France, elementary school curricula are drawn up by the central ministry in Paris in order to reduce regional differences. Most unitary states have a national police force and control over local militia units. Generally, there is only one court system, whose judicial officers are appointed by the national government.

Even in a unitary state, the central government cannot run all local affairs. In Great Britain, for example, local governments maintain substantial authority.[3] All the counties and boroughs (cities) elect councils with standing committees for each area of administration. The councils control policing, education, and health and welfare matters. Parliament can always step into local affairs and override these officials; in practice, however, it intervenes only in emergencies, because the British people place a high value on local autonomy.

Local nationalism grew in several unitary systems during the 1970s, and for several reasons. Economics was one. Local nationalists usually claim their region is shortchanged by the central government. The region may have a distinct language or culture that its people want to preserve. Many feel that important political decisions are not under local control, that they are made by distant bureaucrats. Often regions harbor historical resentments at having long ago been conquered and forcibly merged with the larger nation. Several unitary systems grope for solutions to the regional problem.

---

[3]Our discussion follows H. Finer, *English Local Government* (London: Methuen, 1950); and E. C. R. Hadfield and J. C. MacColl, *British Local Government* (London: Hutchinson's University Library, 1948).

Devolution in Britain.   The Celtic Scots and Welsh, pushed to the peripheries of Britain centuries ago by the invading Angles and Saxons, retain a lively sense of their differences from England. Many Scots and Welsh resent being ruled by London. The Scots wanted to retain a bigger share of the North Sea oil revenues—"It's Scotland's oil!" was their cry—whereas the Welsh wanted to make their Cymric language equal to English in schools and on television. During the 1970s, the Scottish and Welsh Nationalist parties grew until they won several seats in Parliament. In 1977 Commons passed "devolution" bills that would have given considerable home-rule powers to Scotland and Wales. The devolution plans had to be approved in a referendum by 40 percent of *all* eligible Scottish and Welsh voters, a higher threshold than a simple majority. Only one-third of the Scots and one-fifth of the Welsh voted yes, and the plan failed. Many thought local nationalism was a nice, romantic idea but impractical. In more recent elections the nationalist parties have lost support as both Scotland and Wales have continued their strong pro-Labor orientation. Whereas the highpoint of Scottish and Welsh nationalism seems to have passed, the problems of these distinct cultures within Britain remains.

Decentralization in France.   France is actually a more unitary system than Britain. Everything is—or, until recently, was—run from Paris. Both monarchs and republicans pursued centralization with single-minded determination. Many of France's ninety-six *départements* were named after rivers to try to erase the historical memories of the old provinces. It didn't completely work, for France, like Britain, has distinctive regional subcultures: the Celtic Bretons (who fled from Britain centuries ago to escape the Saxons), the southerners of the Midi, whose speech is still flavored with the ancient *langue d'oc,* and the Corsicans, who still speak an Italian dialect.

In 1960, to better coordinate economic development, President de Gaulle decreed twenty-two regions consisting of two to eight *départements* each. These were mere administrative conveniences, however. Starting in 1981, Socialist President François Mitterrand instituted genuine decentralization. Certain economic-planning powers were transferred from Paris to the regions. The Paris-appointed prefects lost some of their powers, especially on economic matters. The hitherto powerless departmental legislatures picked up some of these powers. Elected regional assemblies were initiated. France has thus reversed five centuries of steady centralization.

Autonomy in Spain.   Spain, too, decentralized its highly centralized system. Here the problem was more urgent, for regional resentments, long buried under Franco's rule, started appearing in a dangerous manner in the 1970s. Spain's regional problems are among the most difficult in Europe. Basques and Catalans, in the north of Spain, speak non-Castilian languages and are intensely proud of their distinctive cultures. In addition, many areas of Spain were granted *fueros* (local rights) in medieval times which they treasured for centuries. On top of great regional diversity, Spanish centralizers attempted to plant a unitary system on the French model. The result was great resentment that appeared whenever Spain experimented with democracy. Breakaway movements appeared in 1874 and in the 1930s, only to be crushed by the Spanish army, which regards the unity of the country as sacred.

With this background, Spain held its breath in the late 1970s and 1980s as the post-Franco Spanish democracy instituted 17 regional governments called "autonomies." The big problem was in the Basque country, where a terrorist movement, Euzkadi ta Azkatasuna (ETA), demanded complete Basque independence. To appease regionalist feeling, which also appeared in more moderate forms in Catalonia, Galicia, Andalusia, and other areas, the Madrid government allowed regions to become autonomous, with regional parliaments, some taxation power, language rights, and control over many local matters.

Pros and Cons of Unitary Systems. The concentration of authority in unitary states may lead to the feeling among citizens that it is pointless to become active in local affairs, since all power radiates downward from the capital; this feeling can turn into widespread alienation from the government and national political institutions, as in Italy. Furthermore, with national leaders so far removed from community problems—and citizens too disenchanted to make their views known—wise policy making may prove difficult.

On the other hand, the centralization of power in a unitary state can be a significant advantage in facing the problems of modern society. Clear lines of authority can be useful. In unitary systems, the central government can marshal economic resources and coordinate planning and development; its broad taxation powers make the task of financing social welfare legislation much easier. This may explain why many federal nations have become more centralized in recent years. In the United States, India, and West Germany, the federal governments have established national economic policies and have bankrolled social welfare programs.

Federal Systems

Federalism preserves local diversity while simultaneously allowing the central government enough power to run the country. However, there is a great deal of variation in the *governing* of federal nations.[4] Some countries, such as the Soviet Union and Mexico, have become so centralized that some scholars wonder if they can still be called federal. Many political scientists agree that a true federal government must meet ten tests. If it fails more than two or three, it is questionable whether it can properly be called a federal state.[5]

---

[4]The best comparative studies are Arthur W. Macmahon, ed., *Federalism: Mature and Emergent* (New York: Doubleday, 1955); Valerie Earle, ed., *Federalism: Infinite Variety in Theory and Practice* (Itasca, Ill.: Peacock, 1968); and William H. Riker, *Federalism: Origin, Operation, Significance* (Boston: Little, Brown, 1964).

[5]Ivo D. Duchacek, *Comparative Federalism: The Territorial Dimensions of Politics* (New York: Holt, Rinehart and Winston, 1970), pp. 114–19.

1. The government has exclusive control over foreign policy.
2. Member states may not secede or unilaterally break their ties to the national union.
3. The national government may exercise its authority independently of the states and can impose its will without their direct approval or resources.
4. The constitution cannot be amended without the approval of the states.
5. The national government may not unilaterally change the boundaries of a member state.
6. Some significant powers must be reserved for the states.
7. The national legislature is bicameral, and the states are equally represented in at least one house.
8. A dual court system exists; each level of government has courts to enforce its own laws.
9. A national court interprets the constitution and can decide conflicts between state and national governments.
10. Authority is divided between federal and state governments.

A true federal government, according to these standards, rests on a delicate balance between centralized power and local autonomy. This balance is being severely tested in many nations by the demands of contemporary society.

There are several reasons for starting a federal union. The first is to escape the danger of military attack. By combining their resources, a number of small and weak states can defend themselves against a more powerful nation. On the other hand, federations are sometimes formed because member states are interested in aggressive expansion. The pooling of diplomatic and military resources of the states made Bismarck's Germany a major power. Federal unions can serve economic purposes as well, as the United States discovered in creating a continent-wide market without tariff barriers, a feat the European Common Market tried to duplicate. In some cases, a particular social class within a nation will prefer a federal system in the hopes of gaining economic advantage. Charles Beard saw America's Constitution of 1787 as an attempt by the Founding Fathers to defend their property interests by strengthening the central government.[6] Finally, federalism is often the only way to protect national unity. After the termination of British colonial rule, India set up a federal system that allowed such states as Bengal, Punjab, Marathastan, and Rajastan to maintain their own cultures while joining in the Indian nation. These states were jealous of their identities and would not have entered the federal union without a guarantee of local autonomy.

The Units of Government in a Federal System.   Federalism protects local autonomy by creating different levels of government, each with its own responsibilities. In many federal states, there are three levels: the national (or federal)

---

[6]See Charles A. Beard, *An Economic Interpretation of the Constitution* (New York: Macmillan, 1935). A criticism of Beard's thesis is A. C. McLaughlin, *A Constitutional History of the United States* (New York: Appleton-Century, 1935).

government, the state or provincial governments, and local governments. These units often form a pyramid: there are many local governments at the base, fewer state governments above them, and one central authority at the top. Countries with unitary systems are often divided similarly, but the lower levels of government wield little power.

The basic units of local government, the county and the city, are generally created by the states or provinces. They operate under the terms of a charter granted by the state legislature, which outlines their structure and responsibilities. Generally, these charters can be amended by the state legislature. For example, a state government can force a city to build a new sewer system or give police a salary increase.

Local government has five basic functions: (1) public safety, including maintenance of police and fire departments and public health offices; (2) assistance programs for the aged, handicapped, chronically ill, and needy children; (3) regulatory functions, such as zoning, consumer protection, and traffic safety; (4) public services, including schools, parks, and libraries; and (5) proprietary functions, such as owning and operating gas and electric utilities.

There are both advantages and disadvantages to making decisions on a local level. One advantage is that citizens are closest to their local government; they may influence officials and can see how a decision is made and what its effects are. Local governments can often experiment with new programs more easily than larger units; the costs of failure are likewise lower. On the other hand, local governments may lack the money to finance social welfare programs, and their officials are sometimes poorly trained and occasionally corrupt. Local decision-making can lead to duplication of services and poor coordination. When this happens, the responsibility for straightening out the bureaucratic mess may fall on the state government.

The relationship of the states or provinces to other levels of government varies in different federal systems. Generally, these units have their own governments and handle local problems within the limits of federal law. In West

UNITS OF GOVERNMENT: President Reagan meets with county officials at their national convention. Much local governance in the United States takes place at the county level.

Bill Fitz-Patrick, The White House

Germany, each of the ten *Länder* (states) has its own constitution and government.[7] The Landtag (state legislature) can affect the conduct of foreign policy because it elects members of the Bundesrat (the upper house of the national legislature). The Landtag can also legislate on all local matters. States in the Indian federation are given control over certain legislative areas, including education, agriculture, public health, forests, and fisheries.[8] There are also many areas (including marriage and divorce, civil law, and bankruptcy) in which states and the national government share authority. India is unique among federal states because its national government can proclaim a state of emergency, suspend the constitution, and take over the government of any state. Several times "president's rule" has been declared after riots and disorders in various states.

Each of America's fifty states has its own government which can legislate in any area not reserved to the federal government or to the people. Usually, education, welfare, civil law, property taxes, and licensing of professions are all state functions. However, in recent years, the federal government has expanded its activity in the areas of civil law, welfare, and economic regulation. Increasingly dependent on federal grants and revenue-sharing, the states find themselves having to meet federal standards in many areas. New legislation, for example, threatened to withhold federal highway funds if states did not make 21 the legal drinking age.

Originally, the national government in a federal union was expected to handle problems the states could not solve themselves. Thus, central governments today regulate the nation's economy, control national defense and foreign policy, and guarantee the civil rights of citizens. All federal governments insist that national law take precedence over state law. Members of the national legislature are usually elected directly by the people, rather than by members of state governments. The national executive is not under the control of the state government officials either.

From its very beginning, the United States has engaged in a long and stormy debate over the proper role of the federal government. Southern attachment to "states' rights" led to a clash with President Lincoln over the issue of slavery, and the nation erupted into civil war. In the 1960s, controversial U.S. Supreme Court decisions prompted a campaign to curb the power of the federal courts. Some political leaders insist that the concentration of power in Washington is perverting American federalism and endangering the well-being of the nation. At the same time, local governments and citizens continue to rely on a strong federal government for help in solving complex—and expensive—problems.

---

[7]See Arthur B. Gunlicks, *Local Government in the German Federal System* (Durham, N.C.: Duke University Press, 1986).

[8]See M. V. Pylee, *India's Constitution,* 3rd rev. ed. (New York: Asia House, 1980); and Richard L. Park and Bruce Bueno de Mesquita, *India's Political System,* 2d ed. (Englewood Cliffs, N.J.: Prentice-Hall, 1979).

Soviet Federalism. On paper, the Soviet Union is a highly decentralized federation: the fifteen constituent republics have the right to conduct their own foreign policy and to secede at will. The central government is given control over national defense, foreign trade, and economic planning and development, whereas all other functions are left to the republics.

Anyone who has read the Soviet Constitution might be convinced that Russia has a weak central government and strong regional governments. In fact, the opposite is true. The Presidium of the Supreme Soviet (the highest government body) can veto any policy or law adopted by any republic. In addition, none of the republics has an independent source of tax revenue, and they may not appropriate or spend money without approval from the central government. Thus, in spite of what the constitution says, Moscow has almost complete control over the republics. In the meanwhile, many of the Soviet Union's nationalities chafe under Kremlin rule and resent the ethnic Russians, who are topdogs in the Soviet system. The nationalities problem is one of the Soviets' worst.[9]

Yugoslav Federalism. Yugoslavia is also Communist, but it has a more liberal variety of communism, and its federalism is genuine. In fact, Yugoslav federalism may have gone so far that Belgrade does not have sufficient power. Yugoslavia's six republics—plus two autonomous provinces carved out of the largest republic, Serbia—really do run local affairs. Each republic sends equal numbers of representatives to both houses of parliament, and the collegial presidency has one member from each republic. It is as if Yugoslavia were governed by three senates, two on the legislative side and one on the executive side. This can make coordination and integration difficult, as each republic jealously guards its rights. There is considerable national feeling, especially among Croats, many of whom would like to see an independent Croatia. Constantly hovering in the background, to be sure, is the Yugoslav Communist party, which tries to make sure national feelings do not get out of hand. But even the party is organized along republican lines and sometimes has to be purged of local nationalists. Yugoslav federalism came in with the Communists after World War II as a device to appease national sentiments and yet still hold the country together. It has not been completely successful.[10] Tito, while he lived, was a symbol and the cement of national unity, but no one has replaced him.

Canadian Federalism. Canada is another country with strong centrifugal tendencies. Quebec is not alone in talking of separating itself from the federation; so do some of the western provinces. The problem goes back to the eighteenth century, when the British ousted France from North America but

---

[9]See S. Enders Wimbush, ed., *Soviet Nationalities in Strategic Perspective* (New York: St. Martin's, 1985).

[10]See Pedro Ramet, *Nationalism and Federalism in Yugoslavia, 1963–1983* (Bloomington, Ind.: Indiana University Press, 1985).

allowed the French-speaking Quebeckers to keep their language. Over the ensuing two centuries the francophones became second-class citizens, poorer than other Canadians and discriminated against because practically all private and governmental business was conducted in English.

In the 1960s the nationalistic Parti Quebecois (PQ) sprang up, dedicated to Quebec's independence from Canada. To appease them, the Ottawa government in 1969 declared Canada bilingual, with French and English having equal rights.[11] This wasn't enough for the PQ, which made French the only official language of Quebec, turning the English-speaking minority into second-class citizens. PQ strength declined after a 1980 referendum by Quebeckers rejected a plan for independence. Meanwhile, English-speaking western Canada felt Ottawa had gone too far in trying to make the PQ happy. Further, western Canada votes largely Conservative and resents the Liberal east, which dominates the federal government. Alberta and Saskatchewan have oil and natural gas, which they want to price and control themselves, without regulation by Ottawa. Making things even more complicated was the fact that Canada's constitution was until 1982 the British North America Act of 1867. It contained no amending provision. Prime Minister Pierre Trudeau's strategy to "patriate" (bring back to Canada) its full constitutional powers created a political row that for a time threatened to split Canada apart.[12]

The problem with federalism, exemplified in the foregoing discussion, is the difficulty in finding the right balance between central and state governments. If power is too much on the central side, the system loses some of its federal characteristics and becomes a sort of veiled unitary system, as in the Soviet Union, Mexico, and Brazil. If power is too much on the state side, the system starts turning into a confederation or even begins to break up, as in Yugoslavia and Canada. The United States is still searching for its correct balance.

The Balkanization of Government.   There are approximately eighty thousand local governments in the United States, plus fifty state governments and the national government. These governments often get into each other's way, and the taxpayer is frequently a prime victim. The multiplicity of governments is called, half in jest, "balkanization," after the many little countries that emerged in the Balkans as the Turks were pushed out in the last century. Balkanization in the United States has led to immoderate jurisdictional conflicts over whose rules apply in which situation.

One difficulty is the size of American cities and counties. Since World War II, much of the middle class has moved from cities to suburbs, leaving the cities with a shrinking tax base precisely when poorer people—who cannot pay much in taxes but need many social services—are moving in. If the entire

[11]Milton J. Esman, "The Politics of Official Bilingualism in Canada," *Political Science Quarterly* 97 (Summer 1982):233–42.
[12]See John Fitzmaurice, *Quebec and Canada: Past, Present, and Future* (New York: St. Martin's, 1985).

metropolitan area had a single government, then the affluent suburbs (many of whose residents earn their livings in the city) could be taxed to share the burden. But suburbs, with their own representatives in state and federal legislatures, block such moves, and the cities get poorer, more blighted, and more desperate. Some parts of New York City look as if they've been destroyed in a war. Instead of solving their own problems on a metropolitan basis, the cities have to go hat in hand to Washington to ask for financial help. The "fiscal crisis" of U.S. cities seems to be permanent and self-reinforcing. As things get worse, more of the middle class and more of industry moves out, deepening the problems.

The Growth of Federal Power

The Founding Fathers would have difficulty recognizing the balance of powers between state and federal governments today. They expected, first, that the amount of actual governing would be small, and second that most of it would be done by the states under their "reserved" powers. For most of the nation's history this was so. States and localities raised their own revenues and spent them on modest programs; federal help was minor. As late as 1932, federal grants were less than 3 percent of state and local revenue.

But things were changing. The passage of the Sixteenth Amendment in 1913 allowed the federal government to tax income. Although little used at first, it meant that Washington had at its disposal an extractive power much stronger than the states'. Soon small federally funded programs for highways, education, and public health appeared. With Franklin D. Roosevelt's New Deal in the 1930s, federal programs increased in number and funding. With Lyndon Johnson's Great Society in the 1960s (Johnson was a great admirer of Roosevelt), federal programs exploded. Now, close to $100 billion flows from Washington to state and local governments. States and localities have come to depend on federal grants for a quarter of their revenues.

State and local governments often don't like being dependent on Washington, but they need the money.[13] It's easier for the federal government to collect taxes through its progressive income tax (the richer you are, the bigger percentage you pay) than it is for states and cities through their small income, sales, and property taxes. The public demand for services has outstripped the financial ability of most states. Theoretically, states and cities could decline federal grants, but no one likes to turn down offers of money, even if there is some red tape involved.

The net impact is a growth of federal power. Because it provides money, it can set standards. The content of school lunches; design and construction of hospitals, highways, and airports; and women's collegiate athletics come under federal supervision. Some have suggested that this makes the United States less

[13]For an introduction to the problem, see Richard P. Nathan, "State and Local Governments under Federal Grants: Toward a Predictive Theory," *Political Science Quarterly* 98 (Spring 1983):1.

federal than it used to be. Perhaps so, but there seems no way to reverse the process. Should toxic and nuclear waste disposal be left to state discretion? Is education a purely local concern? If it were, standards and dollar support would vary wildly across the fifty states, leaving the U.S. population inadequately educated.

The New Federalism. The federal grants process is terribly complex, consisting of some five hundred different grants. Firms offer computerized grant-finding services, and states, cities, hospitals, and universities hire people for their "grantsmanship"—their ability to locate and win grants. Further, most of these grants are "categorical," aimed at a specific problem. This takes control and discretion away from state and local authorities. Funds for flood control cannot be used for sewage processing; funds for school books cannot be used for athletic equipment. State and local officials have complained of being locked into federal programs that don't take local needs into consideration.

Presidents Nixon and Reagan thought they had the answer: move away from the categorical grants to broader "block grants" and "revenue sharing." Both presidents called their programs the "New Federalism," connoting a return of some power and control to the states. The federal government had become too powerful, they argued, so power should be given back to the states. It didn't quite work that way.

Congress, under President Nixon's leadership, designated $6.9 billion a year to go directly from the federal treasury to the states as revenue sharing, which states could spend as they needed without federal guidelines or supervison. The trouble was that this made states and cities *more* dependent on Washington, not less. Further, because revenue sharing is distributed by formula, it goes to rich cities and poor cities alike. One city may desperately need it to keep up police and fire services, whereas another may use it just to improve its parks. Because revenue sharing gives money with practically no strings attached, it erodes federal control. Revenue sharing isn't "aimed" at problems; it leaves that up to state and local officials, who mostly use the money for general budget (police and fire departments, streets and schools).

An intermediate ground between categorical grants (too narrow) and revenue sharing (too wide) appeared in 1974 with the block grants. These take several related categorical grants, roll them into one, and let state and local officials use them within the general category.[14] President Reagan, for example, reduced dozens of categorical grants into a few block grants and called this the New Federalism. There was a catch. Whereas the block grants were simpler and had fewer federal strings attached, they also provided less money.[15] In 1978, for every $100 state and local governments raised on their own, they received $32 in

---

[14]See Timothy J. Conlan, "The Politics of Federal Block Grants: From Nixon to Reagan," *Political Science Quarterly* 99 (Summer 1984):2.

[15]See Richard P. Nathan and Fred C. Doolittle, "Federal Grants: Giving and Taking Away," *Political Science Quarterly* 100 (Spring 1985):1.

federal funds. By 1985 federal funding was down to $24 and by 1987 to below $20 for every $100 raised by state and local governments. This left many states and municipalities desperate for funds. The question of how much federal money to give and how to give it is a permanent problem of U.S. federalism, for it is one facet of the problem we discussed earlier, that of the proper balance between central and state governments in federal systems.

The Unitary-Federal Mixture

No country is perfectly unitary nor is any perfectly federal. Even strongly unitary systems have certain elements of local input and control. And federal systems keep considerable power (and sometimes increase this power) for the center. The interesting trend of our time is the tugging of unitary systems in a somewhat federal direction while some federal systems move slowly in a more unitary direction. Britain offered devolution to Scotland and Wales, and, although the referendum failed, the issue is by no means over. France breathed life into its twenty-two regions, and Spain granted regional autonomy, offering us two examples of highly centralized governments moving to quasifederalism. In the United States, the previously limited powers of Washington over the states and cities have grown over the decades. Money led the way: federal funds meant federal standards and supervision. In so doing, the United States took on some of the characteristics of a unitary system.

It would be premature to say that eventually the two systems will meet in the middle, for both unitary and federal systems carry with them centuries of institutional and cultural baggage. If a unitary system moves too quickly to a sort of federalism, it arouses opposition, such as that of the Spanish army. If a federal system moves too much toward central control, it arouses the anger of the component states. Our task is not to simply classify countries as "unitary" or "federal," but to see how they actually operate in practice. Then we will find all manner of interesting deviations from the model, borrowings, and attempts to modify systems that no longer match a given country's needs.

ELECTORAL SYSTEMS

Americans are fond of contrasting elections in the United States with those in the Soviet Union in order to point up the differences between free and fake elections. But Russians argue that Soviet elections also represent the "will of the people." Is there a model of a free election with which American and Soviet elections can be compared?

Two or More Competing Political Parties. In order to have a meaningful choice, the voter must be permitted to choose freely between candidates with different stands on various issues. The Soviet Union, where only Communist party candidates are allowed to run for office, fails to meet this basic requirement. Some leftist thinkers criticize the American party system on similar grounds; they argue that our elections do not offer a meaningful choice because both Democrats and Republicans support the capitalist economic system. True, but their stands on domestic and foreign policy questions often differ, so that voters have a choice. And there are socialist and other minority parties on the ballot.

Freedom to Campaign and Debate. In a free election all political parties and legally qualified candidates must have the opportunity to air their views and seek the support of the public. In practice, this means that newspapers, magazines, radio, and television must make advertising space and time available to all parties.

The question of "equal opportunity" to campaign has prompted some political theorists to suggest that truly democratic elections require some sort of financial subsidy to parties and candidates that are too poor to compete with the major parties and their candidates. Money counts in U.S. elections, especially in buying TV time, and this gives well-financed candidates a big edge. There is now some federal support for presidential candidates, but many West European countries cover a considerable part of election expenses in order to minimize the effects of special-interest money. In all of these, though, the catch is that government support is proportional to votes received. Accordingly, small and weak parties derive little help from such subsidies and complain they can't get their message across. Opportunity to campaign does not mean equal financial resources, something that simply cannot be helped.

Universal Adult Suffrage and Equal Weighting of Votes. Democracy requires that the right to vote be universal (within limitations), with every person's vote counting equally in choosing representatives. All nations restrict the right to vote to some degree, even if only to keep convicted murderers from the polls. Most of these restrictions do not violate basic democratic principles, but some do. South Africa, which denies the vote to blacks, cannot be considered to have free elections. Nor is it permissible to give one person two votes (as was done in Britain for a time) simply because he or she is better educated or wealthier than the average voter. All electoral districts must be roughly equal to all other electoral districts within the jurisdiction of the state.

Free Choice and an Honest Count. Absolutely crucial to a free election is the right of the voter to cast his or her ballot without fear of reprisal. Before the introduction of the secret ballot, or Australian ballot, in the 1870s, American voting was often in public view and thus open to pressure. Elections must also be honestly administered. To avoid fraud (such as voting several times in several different precincts, or "voting the graveyards"), there are lists of all registered and legally qualified voters. And when the polls have closed, election results must be honestly counted and publicly posted. (Today, more votes in the United States are tabulated by machines which make the count more reliable—but even machines sometimes fail.) Crooked vote tabulations in the 1986 Philippines election led to the removal of President Marcos.

The Candidate Can Claim a Mandate. In the United States, the candidate who wins a presidential election (even if he or she does not obtain a majority of the popular vote) claims to have received a mandate to carry out the party platform. For an election to be meaningful the winning party must have the backing of a large portion of the people. In European nations using proportional representation, it is more difficult for any one party to win a "working majority." To control a legislature, a party must often enter into a coalition with other parties. This can dilute the claim to a clear mandate, and the result is sometimes an ineffective government.

A Contrast: The Soviet Electoral System

Using these five criteria as a model of a free and meaningful election, we can see that the United States and West European nations generally meet the requirements. How does the Soviet Union differ? According to its constitution of 1977, all citizens are guaranteed the right to vote, and 99.9 percent of eligible voters participate in national elections. On paper, at least, no system could be more democratic than the Soviet Union's. But is it so democratic in operation?

One-Party Control. The Supreme Soviet is the highest governing authority in the Soviet Union, and election laws specify that its candidates may be nominated by Communist party cells, collective farms, unions, youth organizations, and cultural societies. In practice, it is only the party members who do the nominating. Except for the lowest levels of government, the Soviet nominating system produces only a single candidate for each office, usually a member of the Communist party. Once nominated, candidates campaign actively, but there is really no contest. If a voter approves of all the candidates, he or she folds his or her ballot and drops it in the box. But if he or she disapproves of one or more candidates, he or she must retreat behind a screen in order to scratch out the name of the person disapproved of. As only the bravest voters would draw attention to themselves by doing this, most candidates win 99 percent of the vote.

In Western eyes, Soviet elections seem a waste of time, but the Soviets defend them. The Communist party, they argue, truly represents the will of the Soviet people, and since no one has the right to oppose the people's will, no one should oppose the party. If one accepts this somewhat circular reasoning, then the Soviet electoral system is democratic, and Soviet elections renew and strengthen the Communist party's popular mandate. But the Western idea of democracy and popular elections is quite different. How do democratic elections work?

Choosing the Candidates: The First Step in an Election

In choosing which candidates to put before the public the party is crucial. If hundreds of candidates were to put themselves on the ballot, the voter would be faced with a meaningless jumble and the result would be more chaos than democracy. Such procedures may have been possible in the face-to-face setting of the city-state, but not in the modern nation. A certain irony comes in here. To make elections democratic and meaningful we must have parties do the nominating, but in placing this task in the hands of parties we are letting in an undemocratic element, namely, domination of the process by party leaders and the disproportionate influence of party activists. This cannot be helped. No party is internally perfectly democratic; all are dominated to greater or lesser degrees by elites. Some political scientists argue that parties need not be completely democratic internally, that the crux of a democracy is competition between parties in which voters choose. How the parties select candidates is their business; we only need two or more to choose from. Accordingly, one should not expect perfect democracy in the way parties pick candidates; the overall system may still be democratic.

Nomination by Petition.   Great Britain, France, Japan, Canada, Australia, and New Zealand use petitions to nominate candidates. In Britain almost any citizen is free to run for election to the House of Commons. All he or she must do is obtain a nomination petition listing his or her name, address, occupation, and the parliamentary district; register the signatures of ten legally qualified voters from that district; and make a deposit of £150. The fee is returned to the candidate if he or she polls at least one-eighth of the vote in the general election; otherwise, it is kept by the government. This is to discourage frivolous candidates.

Getting on the ballot in Britain is easy, but without party endorsement the effort is doomed. What counts is getting selected by the Conservative, Labor, Liberal, or Social Democratic parties (the last two ran jointly in 1983 and 1987). This is done by local party organizations in consultation with national headquarters. Most candidates are local people, but the national party can suggest promising outsiders to constituency organizations. There are no national nominating conventions or primary elections in Britain, or indeed in most of the world.

Nominations in the United States.   Most candidates for office in the United States are nominated by direct primary elections—with the exception, of course, of the presidential and vice-presidential candidates, who are nominated by delegates at a national convention. Three-quarters of the delegates to this convention are now elected in primaries (just as candidates may be nominated in primaries), but this varies from state to state. Since election laws are made and enforced by each state, there is no one national procedure.

Before the direct primary was introduced around the turn of the century, the *party caucus* was the chief means of selecting candidates at all levels and choosing delegates to state and national conventions. Party organizations would caucus in private meetings, usually held behind closed doors, to select these candidates and delegates. Today, although precinct and county caucuses are still widely used, especially in choosing delegates, the state caucus is not nearly as powerful as it once was and has been largely replaced by the primary elections. In most states, candidates for the House, the Senate, governships, and other offices must win a plurality in a *primary election* before becoming official candidates. To enter a primary, a candidate must file a petition with the signatures of a specific number of party supporters. Two types of primaries are used in the United States. The closed primary is used in Illinois, Florida, New York, and many other states. It allows only registered members of the party to participate. The open primary, used in Wisconsin and several other states, allows any voter to participate in any party primary: Republicans may cross over and vote in the Democratic primary, and vice-versa. The main problem with the open primary is that if voters decide to cross over in large enough numbers, one party could determine the outcome of the other's primary election. Therefore, the open primary cannot be relied on to reflect the true feelings of the party rank-and-file.

The direct primary is the chief means by which the major American parties select their standard-bearers, and in some ways it helps to democratize our system of nominations. A candidate who opposes the party line can frequently upset the party organization's candidate if he or she is able to exploit a sensitive public issue. Primary elections allow presidential hopefuls to enlist grass-roots support in their bid for candidacy, thus bringing the people—at least ideally—into the candidate-selection process.

But the primaries have their drawbacks too. First, they impose a heavy financial burden on both the candidates and the party. To mount an effective campaign, a candidate must buy office space, billboards and bumper stickers, and media time. Access to wealth is almost a prerequisite for a successful primary campaign. Second, the primaries have weakened the parties. By appealing directly to the rank-and-file voters, candidates need not depend on official party support and can thus be independent. Neither the Democratic nor the Republican party can effectively discipline wayward candidates or officials who ignore official policy decisions. Weaker parties mean weaker voter identification with parties, and this leads to lower voter turnouts. Thus primaries, by trying to be very democratic, may indirectly contribute to the weakening of democratic institutions. Some political scientists began to wonder if the reforms of the early 1970s, with their expansion of primaries, hadn't gone too far.[16]

Delegates to national presidential conventions may be legally bound or personally committed to a particular candidate, united behind a favorite son or daughter, or uncommitted. Generally, a "committed delegate" is committed on the first ballot only, and is free to vote as he or she pleases thereafter.

Nomination at the national convention hinges on winning a majority of delegates' votes. It is quite possible that when the convention opens, no candidate will have the number of committed delegates required to win the nomination on the first ballot. In this case, it may take several votes before one of the front-runners—or in the case of a tie, a compromise "dark horse"

[16]See Nelson W. Polsby, *Consequences of Party Reform* (New York: Oxford University Press, 1983).

candidate—is chosen to head the ticket. In 1844, for example, James K. Polk was nominated to lead the Democratic party on the ninth ballot—even though Martin Van Buren had come to the convention with most of the delegates committed to support his own nomination. In the past, coalitions and behind-the-scenes bargains often played an important part in settling on a compromise candidate. Today, support is usually arranged before the first ballot, so that voting rarely continues to a second or third one.

The Election: Frequency and Timing

Once the candidates have been nominated, the formal campaign can begin. Here, too, the United States holds the record: it not only spends the most money on its political campaigns, it also has the longest campaigns of any Western democracy. Most European nations limit their campaigns to three or four weeks, but American primary elections, conventions, and eight weeks of formal campaigning force presidential hopefuls to spend over a year on the campaign trail. Suggestions are regularly made that American election campaigns be shortened. Yet the campaign has become an American institution, and it is unlikely that it will be greatly revised.

Election Timing in Presidential Democracies. In presidential democracies such as the United States and Brazil, elections are fixed at regular intervals by constitutional law. In general, members of the lower house of the national legislature are elected for the shorter period of time. In America, a new House of Representatives is elected every two years, on the theory that representatives should remain close to constituents. A short term of office gives the people the chance to remove any member of Congress who drifts too far from their needs. Members of the upper house are elected for a longer term. The original rationale is that their distance from the people allows them to stabilize the actions of the lower house, which might be carried away by momentary concerns. United States senators, therefore, are elected for six-year terms, with one-third of the Senate up for election every two years.

In the United States, the president may serve only two full consecutive four-year terms. Franklin Roosevelt's more than twelve years in office caused complaints of "monarchy" and demands for reform, so that Americans today are assured a new administration every other presidential election year. The French president serves for seven years and may be reelected without limit, although after seven years many French voters want a change.

Elections in Parliamentary Democracies. Great Britain, and the many nations who pattern their governments after it, has a far more flexible system. A general election to select a new parliament (and hence a new administration) must be held at least once every five years (every four years in Germany), and may be held at any time *during* that period. An incumbent government's ability to call an election when it wishes gives it a marked advantage over the opposition party. In 1983, for example, Prime Minister Margaret Thatcher called British elections more than a year early to take advantage of the popularity she had won in the brief war with Argentina over the Falkland Islands. Earlier in her term, her tough economic policies had made her Conservative party unpopular; it would have been suicide to have called an election then. In Britain, the timing of an election is crucial.

Which system works best—presidential elections at set intervals, or parliamentary systems at varying intervals? Each has its advocates. Many political scientists argue that the parliamentary system is superior: if a national scandal or crisis develops and the prime minister's party can no longer control parliament, then new elections must be held and a new mandate must be sought. Government is always on its toes and responsive to the people. In presidential democracies, only impeachment can hasten the demise of a corrupt or incompetent government, as Americans discovered in the two years of agony and partial governmental paralysis of Watergate. In a parliamentary system, a prime minister involved in a major scandal would be out in a week or two. Moreover, national elections in presidential democracies often fall during lulls—periods of apathy between national crises, when no crucial issues exist. The two systems have both strengths and drawbacks.

Indirect Elections: The Electoral College

Americans are so used to the idea of directly electing their public officials that they often forget that they do not directly elect the most important officer of their government. Switzerland, Brazil, and the United States all elect their chief executives indirectly, by means of electoral colleges. And France, Holland, and West Germany choose the upper houses of their national legislatures indirectly. In indirect elections, people vote for electors who in turn vote for the candidates.

The American citizen who voted for Ronald Reagan or Walter Mondale in the 1984 presidential election did not actually cast his ballot for the man whose name appeared on the party ticket. Instead, he or she voted for a slate of electors who were pledged to vote for the candidate whose name appeared on the ticket. Each state has an electoral vote equal to its total number of representatives and senators in Congress,[17] and the candidate who receives the most popular votes in each state normally receives *all* the electoral votes of that state. As a result, candidates' campaigns tend to focus on the large states with the most electoral votes.

Is the use of the electoral college instead of direct popular voting compatible with democracy? The question has raised serious concern in recent years. In 1860, Abraham Lincoln received only 40 percent of the popular vote, but was elected by a majority of the electoral college. And in 1968, Richard

---

[17]With the exception of Washington, D.C., which has in effect three electors assigned to it by the 23rd Amendment.

Nixon finished only half-a-million votes ahead of Hubert Humphrey in one of the closest popular elections in American history, yet won the electoral college hands down—301 to 191. The electoral college vote often bears little numerical relationship to the actual popular vote. A second major objection to the electoral college is that the electors are only morally—not legally—committed: they can conceivably throw their support to any of the candidates listed on their state's ballot. (In 1968, a South Carolina elector who was supposed to vote for Nixon actually cast his ballot for Wallace.) And finally, in the event of an electoral tie, the House of Representatives is obligated only to choose one of the *three* highest finishers, with no obligation to choose the candidate with the most popular votes.

The electoral college was originally intended to reduce the president's dependence on the masses and to allow the educated elite to choose the best-qualified man for the presidency. But whereas this rationale is logical from the perspective of eighteenth-century thought, it doesn't fit nearly as well with modern democratic thinking. The electoral college is in many ways an anachronism, and many feel that it should be abolished and the president elected by popular vote.

Single-Member Districts

The simplest electoral system is the Anglo–American *single-member district,* wherein one member of parliament or one member of Congress is chosen to represent the entire district by winning a plurality (not necessarily a majority) of the votes. This system puts pressure on interest groups and political factions to coalesce into two big parties. If there were, say, four parties who received 25, 25, 24, and 26 percent of the vote for their candidates, respectively, the last party would win the election. Under these circumstances, at least two of the losing parties recognize it is to their advantage to combine forces for the next election. The other two parties would also be forced to combine. For this reason, countries tend to be two-party systems which have single-member districts and have elections decided by a plurality of the vote. Usually one party is somewhat liberal or leftist, and the other is conservative or rightist.

United States	*Democratic*	*Republican*
Britain	*Labor*	*Conservative*
Australia	*Labor*	*Country and Liberal*
New Zealand	*Labor*	*National*
Canada	*Liberal*	*Progressive Conservative*

Third parties can and do exist in such systems, but without much hope of winning. They continue as protest groups or as pressure groups on the big parties. The British Liberal party has long won nearly one vote in five, but because they are dispersed rather evenly throughout the country the Liberals have rarely won more than a dozen seats. Single-member systems are unkind to third parties.

Advantages of Single-Member Districts. Single-member districts do have certain advantages. The two parties they tend to produce usually stick to the center of the political spectrum, for this is where the votes are. This inhibits the growth of extremism. If, for one election, leaders out of touch with mainstream views should capture control of the party, the party is apt to lose. After the election the party will probably soon dump the extremists. This is what happened with the Republicans under the conservative Goldwater in 1964, the Democrats under the liberal McGovern in 1972, and the British Laborites under left-wing Michael Foot in 1983. As was mentioned in Chapter 8, public opinion in most democracies arrays itself as a bell-shaped curve. Parties that depart too far from the center penalize themselves.

A further advantage of such systems is that they generally give a parliamentary majority to one party. Coalitions are rarely necessary. Victories are magnified in single-member systems. A relatively small "swing" of votes from one party to another can translate into many parliamentary seats, perhaps enough to form a parliamentary majority and a new government. This gives the majority party a clear and stable mandate to govern until the next election. The United States, with its constitutionally mandated separation of powers, muddies the advantage of this system by frequently giving the White House to one party and the Congress to another.

Disadvantages of Single-Member Districts. Single-member districts create a somewhat artificial majority in the parliamentary body which makes governing easier. In so doing, such systems do not fairly or accurately reflect actual public opinion or voting strength. In each district the winner takes all. The losing party, even if it received 49 percent of the vote, gets no representation. This is particularly unfair to third parties, especially if their supporters are not sufficiently concentrated to form a plurality in a few districts, as is the fate of the British Liberals.

Single-member districts teach parties a sort of golden rule about sticking to the political center. This can make politics safe but dull. The two big parties, in trying to win over the many votes in the middle, often end up sounding rather alike. The resulting voter boredom helps explain the low voter turnout in U.S. elections, discussed in the last chapter. The European multiparty systems have much higher voter turnouts, partly because voters can choose from a more interesting menu of parties.

Proportional Representation

Proportional-representation (PR) systems overcome the disadvantages of single-member systems but bring in problems of their own. PR systems are based on multimember districts; that is, each district sends several representatives to parliament, not just one as in single-member systems. In the small lands of Holland and Israel, the entire country is one big district. In Sweden the district is a county, in Spain a province. If the district is entitled to ten seats, each party offers voters a party list of ten candidates. Each voter picks one list, and the party gets seats in proportion to the vote it receives. If the party won 60 percent of the votes in a ten-member district, it would send the first six names on its party list to parliament. A party with 20 percent would send its first two names.

Mathematical problems immediately appear. Rarely does the vote divide itself as neatly as 60 percent, equal, in our example, to six seats. A more typical situation might be one party winning 42 percent of eleven seats. Would the party get 4.62 seats? How do you send a fraction of a person to parliament? There are a couple of ways to handle this. The most common is the d'Hondt system which uses a mathematical formula to divide the seats; it tends to overrepresent the larger parties at the expense of smaller ones.[18] Sweden also uses a mathematical formula plus an interesting provision for nationwide seats. Its twenty-eight districts elect only 310 of the Riksdag's 349 seats. Naturally, mathematical discrepancies appear, so the remaining 39 seats are parcelled out to rectify any variances from the parties' national percentages.

To minimize the problem of splinter, nuisance, or extremist parties, some PR systems require parties to win a certain percent of the vote in order to obtain any seats at all. These are called "threshold clauses." West Germany requires a party to get at least 5 percent of the vote nationwide; Sweden requires 4 percent.

Advantages of Proportional Representation. The chief advantage is that the country's legislature accurately reflects the main currents of public opinion and party strength. Parties are not quite so dominated by the need to capture the middle of the electoral spectrum as is the tendency in Anglo-American systems. Parties can thus articulate their ideologies and principles more clearly because they aren't trying to please everybody. If a small part of the population—as low as one percent in Israel—really believes in something, they can run as a party and win a few seats. They are not forced to amalgamate into bigger parties and dilute their views, as would happen in the Anglo-American system.

Disadvantages of Proportional Representation. PR systems tend to encourage party splintering, or, more accurately, where political views are splintered it permits small groups to organize as parties and win seats in parliament. This tendency, however, is waning, and two-plus party systems have emerged even in PR systems. Sweden, Spain, and France have one or two large parties plus a few smaller ones. Their political systems are not terribly splintered. Israel, on the other hand, is plagued by splinter parties; fifteen parties were elected to the Knesset in 1984. If the chief party falls short of half the seats in PR systems it must form a coalition with other parties. These coalitions are often unstable, as is the case in Italy. It's not true that multiparty systems are always unstable.

---

[18]For the mathematically inclined, the d'Hondt and other systems are explained in Douglas Rae, *The Political Consequences of Electoral Laws,* rev. ed. (New Haven, Conn.: Yale University Press, 1971), chap. 2.

Where one party is big enough to govern alone, they are quite stable. Nonetheless, the Anglo-American systems confer an almost automatic majority and thus stability.

West Germany: A Hybrid. One interesting system combines the best of both worlds. West Germans elect their lower house, the Bundestag, on the basis of both single-member districts and proportional representation. On a split ballot, a West German votes for both an individual to represent his or her district and a party to represent his or her *Land* (state) in proportion to the votes received. Overall strength in the Bundestag is set by the second vote, the one for parties, so seats are always proportional to votes. Half of the seats, though, are reserved for the 248 winners of the district contests. The net effect of West Germany's split representation system has been to produce a "two-plus" party system (discussed in Chapter 11) and great governing stability. The West German system is a modification of the PR system that was designed after World War II to prevent a repetition of the weak and unstable Weimar system, which had proportional representation that treated the country as one big district, and it has succeeded magnificently.

CHOOSING INSTITUTIONS

Political institutions are, in large measure, artificial creations. Most of them, of course, have evolved over time, but at key points in a nation's history, people have had the opportunity to choose their institutions. This brings an element of creativity into politics. Institutions neither fall from heaven nor rise from earth. They are crafted by a handful of people who can do a good job, or a poor one. They are guided by both past experience and by reason. Often they are taking a leap in the dark. The Founding Fathers had little in the way of precedent when constructing a presidential federal republic. Modified by time, usage, amendments, statutes, and court decisions, their handiwork has endured. The drafters of Germany's Weimar constitution in 1919 were less fortunate. On paper, the Weimar constitution looked like a perfect democracy, but some of the institutional choices were poor: no monarch, a weak president, a PR electoral system that treated the entire country as one district and encouraged splinter parties and cabinet instability, and a provision for emergency powers that could be misused. One wishes we could have warned them of their fateful choices.

When political science was young, it focused heavily on constitutions, as if selecting the right institutions could confer moderation and stability on a political system. Well, often the right choices can help. We may wonder if political science, in trying to imitate the natural sciences, has strayed too far from its origins. There was something noble and challenging about trying to devise workable, durable constitutions. In a tumultuous world, there can be few higher tasks than the development of effective political institutions.

SUGGESTED READINGS

BOGDANOR, VERNON AND DAVID BUTLER, EDS. *Democracy and Elections: Electoral Systems and Their Political Consequences.* New York: Cambridge University Press, 1983. A skeptical view, backed up by extensive data from Western Europe and Japan, that different electoral systems matter.

CROTTY, WILLIAM J., AND JOHN S. JACKSON. *Presidential Primaries and Nominations.* Washington, D.C.: Congressional Quarterly Press, 1985. Probably the best book on the subject, by two noted specialists.

DICLERICO, ROBERT E., AND ERIC M. USLANER. *Few are Chosen: Problems in Presidential Selection.* New York: McGraw-Hill, 1984. A critical review of the U.S. presidential selection process with a good chapter on the electoral college.

DUCHACEK, IVO D. *Comparative Federalism: The Territorial Dimension of Politics,* rev. ed. Lanham, Md.: University Press of America, 1987. Thorough cross-national overview of how states are organized geographically.

EARLE, VALERIE, ED. *Federalism: Infinite Variety in Theory and Practice.* Itasca, Ill.: Peacock, 1968. Studies of federalism in several countries.

HOWITT, ARNOLD M. *Managing Federalism: Studies in Intergovernmental Relations.* Washington, D.C.: Congressional Quarterly Press, 1984. Solid and readable case studies of the federal-state-local policy tangle.

LIJPHART, AREND, AND BERNARD GROFMAN, EDS. *Choosing an Electoral System: Issues and Alternatives.* New York: Praeger, 1984. Several experts present the pros and cons of various electoral systems.

NATHAN, RICHARD P. *Revenue Sharing: The Second Round.* Washington, D.C.: Brookings Institution, 1977. Evaluation by one of the acknowledged specialists in the field.

PADDISON, RONAN. *The Fragmented State: The Political Geography of Power.* New York: St. Martin's, 1983. Compares and contrasts unitary and federal solutions in a number of countries.

RAE, DOUGLAS W. *The Political Consequences of Electoral Laws,* rev., ed. New Haven, Conn.: Yale University Press, 1971. A contemporary analysis of how rules and institutions affect representation.

REAGAN, MICHAEL R., AND JOHN SANZONE. *The New Federalism,* 2d ed. New York: Oxford University Press, 1981. Impact of Nixon's decentralization efforts.

SUNDQUIST, JAMES L. *Constitutional Reform and Effective Government.* Washington, D.C.: Brookings Institution, 1986. Noted specialist cautions that major reforms may be neither feasible nor desirable.

chapter 14

*Legislatures
and Executives*

Political institutions, it is theorized, become more specialized and differentiated as they become more modern. Primitive hunting bands may have nothing more than a single leader who decides everything. Tribes may add councils of elders to debate major problems and adjudicate disputes. The Athenian assembly combined legislative, executive, and judicial roles. The Romans developed a senate, but it, too, combined several roles, and its powers declined as Rome went from republic to empire. In the Middle Ages, the prevailing feudal system was a balance among a king, nobles, and leading churchmen, and it is in feudalism that we first get a glimpse of the "balance of power." Pledged the nobles of Aragon (in northeast Spain) to a new king, "We, who are as good as you, swear to you, who are no better than we, to accept you as our king and sovereign lord provided you observe all our statutes and laws; and if not, no."[1]

Ambitious monarchs, who were often at war, desperately needed revenues. Some of them started calling assemblies of notables to levy taxes. In return for their "power of the purse," some of these assemblies were allowed a modest input into royal policies. Such were the beginnings of the British Parliament, which is divided into two houses (Lords for peers and church leaders and Commons for knights and burghers) and the Swedish Riksdag, which originally had four chambers (for nobles, clerics, burghers, and farmers). The French Estates General, with three houses (for nobles, clerics, and commoners), got off to a weak start and was soon forgotten as French monarchs gathered more and more personal power in what became known as absolutism.

In Britain, Sweden, and some other European countries, though, legislatures slowly grew in power and were able to resist the absolutist demands of monarchs. In Britain in the sixteenth century, Henry VIII, who broke with Rome because he wanted a divorce, developed a partnership with Parliament because he needed its support in passing laws to get England out of the Catholic Church and the Church out of England. By the seventeenth century, Parliament considered itself coequal to the monarch and even supreme in the area of taxes. The English Civil War was a quarrel between royalists and parliamentarians over who had top power. In 1649 Parliament decided the issue by executing Charles I.

John Locke, the English philosopher who lived through this momentous period, extolled the power of the "legislative" as the most basic and important.[2] During the Age of Enlightenment in the eighteenth century, political theorists such as Montesquieu, Voltaire, and Jefferson declared that liberty could only be secured if government were divided into three distinct branches, each having the ability to check and balance the others. With few exceptions, modern governments are divided into these three branches. Theoretically, at least, the legislature enacts laws (rule initiation) that allocate values for society; the executive branch enforces the statutes (rule application) passed by the legislature; and the judicial branch interprets the law (rule adjudication) and imposes sanctions on those who violate it. But these responsibilities often overlap, and the separation of powers is rarely clear-cut.

[1]Cited in William C. Atkinson, *A History of Spain and Portugal* (Baltimore, Md.: Penguin, 1960), p. 80.
[2]John Locke, *Second Treatise on Civil Government* (1690), chap. 11.

PRESIDENTIAL AND PARLIAMENTARY

Presidential democracies most clearly show the separation of power between the executive and legislative branches. The chief hallmark of these systems is that the president is not just a figurehead but also a functioning *head of government*. He or she is elected more-or-less directly by the people (in the United States, of course, the quaint Electoral College mediates between the people and the actual election), is invested with considerable powers, and cannot be easily ousted by the legislative body. In parliamentary systems, the *head of state* (figurehead monarch or weak president) is a distinct office different from the head of government (prime minister, premier, or chancellor). In this system, the prime minister is the important figure.

Notice (see fig. 14–1) that in parliamentary systems voters elect only a legislature; they cannot split their tickets between the legislature and executive. The legislature then elects an executive from its own ranks. If the electoral system is based upon proportional representation (see the last chapter), chances are there will be several parties in parliament. If no one party has a majority of

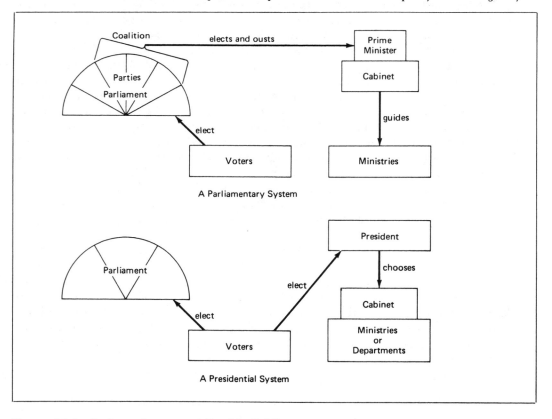

Figure 14-1 Parliamentary versus Presidential Systems

the seats, two or more parties will have to form a coalition. In the late 1980s, the Spanish Socialists had the advantage of a majority of seats and could form a *monocolor* (one-party) cabinet without having to share power with any other parties. At the same time, in Italy, no party was big enough to govern alone, so *five* parties had to form a coalition. Whether one party or several, a majority of parliament must support the cabinet. Usually a monarch (as in Britain and Spain) or weak president (as in West Germany or Israel) "asks"—there's no real choice in the matter—the head of the largest party to "form a government." In these countries, the words "cabinet" and "government" are used interchangeably. The prime minister, after consulting with the parties likely to support him or her, names a team of ministers (called a cabinet or government) who are themselves members of the parliament.[3] These ministers then guide the various ministries or departments of government which form the executive branch. The prime minister and cabinet are "responsible" (in the original sense of the word, "answerable") to the parliament. (Prior to democratization in the nineteenth century, ministers were responsible only to the king.)

Presidents in presidential systems are not responsible to legislatures. The close connection between the legislative and executive is broken. Presidents are elected on their own and choose cabinet ministers or department secretaries from *outside* the ranks of the legislative body. In the United States, of course, top executive and judicial officers must be approved by the Senate. The two branches of government cannot control, dissolve, or oust the other, as can happen in the two branches in parliamentary systems. This gives presidential systems great stability. The president may be unpopular and face a hostile Congress, but he or she can still govern with existing constitutional and statutory powers already in hand.

Advantages of Parliamentary Systems

The United States takes great pride in its separation of powers, the famous "checks and balances" that the Founding Fathers insisted on. Under this system, no branch of government should accumulate too much power. Having just won independence from George III and his feared executive dictatorship, they set one branch of government as a check against the power of another. It was an extremely clever arrangement, and it has admirably preserved America from tyranny. But it is a terribly slow and cumbersome arrangement, an "invitation to struggle" between the executive and legislative branches.[4] Rarely does either branch get everything it wants. The two branches can effectively stymie each other. Congress can fail to pass something the president wants, and

---

[3]For a good description of government formation in parliamentary systems, see G. Bingham Powell, Jr., *Contemporary Democracies: Participation, Stability, and Violence* (Cambridge, Mass.: Harvard University Press, 1982), pp. 133–51.

[4]This well-known phrase is from Edward S. Corwin, *The President: Office and Powers, 1787–1948* (New York: New York University Press, 1948), p. 208.

the president can veto something Congress wants. Some scholars think executive-legislative *deadlock* is virtually the norm for the U.S. presidential system.[5]

Important legislative matters, such as tax reform, can get stuck for years between the two branches of government. The president cannot dissolve Congress and hold new elections, which are set by the calendar. Congress cannot oust a president except by the impeachment procedure. Only one president, Andrew Johnson in 1868, has ever been impeached, and he was not convicted by the Senate. Richard Nixon resigned before the House of Representatives could vote to impeach him. For much of U.S. history, the two branches of government have sat there glaring at each other.

West Europeans consider the American system inefficient and unintelligible, and actually, they are equipped with more modern systems that evolved after the U.S. Constitution was devised. Their parliamentary systems have a *fusion of power* that does not set the branches against each other. In fact, it's sometimes hard to distinguish between legislative and executive branches, for the top executives are themselves usually members of parliament. In the British, West German, Japanese, and Israeli systems, the prime ministers must be elected to parliament, just like an ordinary legislator before he or she can become head of government. As leaders of the biggest parties, they are formally called upon (by the monarch or figurehead president) to form a government. The individuals forming this government or cabinet then transfer from the parliament to the executive departments in order to run them. They must report back nearly continuously to the parliament. At any time, about a hundred British MPs (members of Parliament) also serve at various levels in the executive ministries and departments. Thus executives are also legislators. The cabinet, in effect, is a committee of parliament sent over to supervise the administration of the executive branches of government.

When parliament is in session, the cabinet members are present and must answer questions from their fellow members of parliament. Britain's House of Commons holds a Question Hour every afternoon at the beginning of the session. The members of the two main parties sit facing each other across an aisle on, respectively, the "government benches" and "opposition benches." The front bench of the former is reserved for cabinet ministers, the front bench of the latter for the opposition's "shadow cabinet," who are the MPs who would become ministers if their party should win the next election. MPs without any executive responsibilities sit behind the cabinets and are called "backbenchers." Most questions to the prime minister and his cabinet come from the opposition benches; first written questions and then oral follow-ups. The questions elicit government answers on policy. The answers are criticized, and the opposition generally tries to embarrass the government with an eye to winning the next election. Most parliamentary systems have analogs to the British Question Hour. In the U.S. system, with its separation of powers, committees of the Senate or

---

[5]See James MacGregor Burns, *The Deadlock of Democracy: Four-Party Politics in America*, rev. ed. (Englewood Cliffs, N.J.: Spectrum, 1963).

House can summon cabinet members and other officials of the executive branch to committee hearings. But appearing before a committee is not the same as a grilling before the entire legislative body. The president, of course, as equal to and separate from Congress, cannot be called to testify.

There are several advantages to the parliamentary system. The executive-legislative deadlock which happens frequently in the American system cannot occur, for both the executive and legislative branches are governed by the same party. If the British Conservatives win a majority of the seats in the House of Commons, the leaders of the party are automatically the country's executives. When the Conservative cabinet drafts a new law, they send it over to the House of Commons to get it passed. There is rarely any difficulty or delay in getting the law passed, because the Conservative MPs almost invariably obey the wishes of the party's leaders. If, by some strange circumstance, members of the governing party should disagree with their own leaders in the cabinet, they can withdraw their support and render a vote of "no confidence" in the government. The government then "falls" and must be replaced by a new leadership team that commands the support of a majority of the House of Commons. If a new election gives the opposition party the numerical edge in parliament, the cabinet resigns and is replaced by the leaders of the newly victorious party, formerly known as the "shadow cabinet." Either way, there cannot be a long disagreement between executive and legislative branches; they are fused into one.

The prime minister and cabinet can be speedily ousted in parliamentary systems. Any important vote in parliament can be designated a vote of confidence. If the prime minister loses, he or she takes it as a signal of lack of parliamentary support and resigns. There is no agony of impending impeachment of the sort that paralyzed Washington for more than a year under President Nixon. A new prime minister can be voted in immediately. If the government makes a major policy blunder, parliament can get rid of the cabinet without waiting for its term to expire. When many Americans became unhappy with President Carter's policies, there was nothing the system could do to remove him from the White House earlier than January 1981. Many Americans felt they were stuck with an unpopular president; parliamentary systems don't get stuck with unpopular prime ministers.

Problems of Parliamentary Systems

Parliamentary systems have other difficulties, however. First, because members of parliament generally obey their party leaders, votes in parliament can be closely predicted. The parties supporting the government will vote for a bill the cabinet has drafted. Parties opposing the government will vote against it. Floor speeches and corridor persuasion have little impact; the legislators vote the way their party instructs. Members of a parliament in such systems have lost their independence, and their parliaments have become little more than rubber stamps for the cabinet. The passage of legislation is more rational, speedy, and efficient, to be sure; but the legislature in such systems can no longer "talk back" to the executive or make independent inputs. This makes West European parliaments rather dull and less important than Capitol Hill in Washington, where legislators often oppose the president, even when he is of their own party. Many European legislators are jealous of the spunky independence and separate resources that American representatives and senators enjoy.

Second, depending on the party system and electoral system, parliamentary democracies often have many parties, with no single party controlling a majority of seats in parliament. This means the largest party must form a *coalition* with smaller parties in order to command more than half the seats. Typically, the head of the largest party is prime minister, and the head of the second largest party is foreign minister. Other cabinet positions, or portfolios, are assigned by bargaining. Italy and Israel are current examples of coalition governments, and they illustrate what can go wrong: the coalition partners frequently quarrel over policy. Eventually one or more parties withdraw from the coalition, bringing it below the required majority in parliament. The government then "falls" for lack of parliamentary support, with or without a formal vote of no confidence. This leads to instability, frequent cabinet changes, and loss of executive authority. Italy, for example, has had some four dozen governments since the end of World War II.

This is not as bad as it sounds—remember, the "government" simply means "cabinet"—and Italian cabinets are usually put back together again after bargaining among the same coalition partners. The trouble is, prime ministers must concentrate on not letting the coalition fall apart, and thus they hesitate to launch new policies that might alienate one of the member parties. The Italian problem is not one of too much change but of too little: the same parties putting together the same coalitions and getting stuck over the same issues. Israel has a similar problem but not as severe. *Immobilism,* the inability to decide major questions, is the danger of multiparty parliamentary systems. Notice how this parallels the problem of deadlock in presidential systems.

Not all parliamentary systems, to be sure, suffer from immobilism. Britain, West Germany, Sweden, and Spain have cohesive and effective cabinets because they have to share little or no power in coalition governments. The largest parties in these countries are big enough to govern either alone or with only a little help from like-minded parties. The West German coalition has fallen only once, in 1982, when the small Free Democratic party abandoned the Social Democrats and went over to the Christian Democrats to form a new coalition. The fall of a cabinet due to defection is equally rare in Britain: since World War II it happened only once, when the small Scottish Nationalist party withdrew its support from the minority Labor government in 1979. The Swedish Social Democrats, short of a majority in the Riksdag, stay in power with the tacit support of the small Communist party. Previously the "bourgeois bloc" of Center, Liberal, and Conservative parties was in power in Sweden from 1976 to 1982, but the cabinets of this coalition sometimes quarreled and fell apart. (For the strengths of Sweden's parties see p. 222.) In general, the more parties in a coalition, the less stable it tends to be.

THE ROLES OF THE LEGISLATURE

The main purpose of legislative bodies, in theory, is to formulate the laws that govern society. In practice, the degree to which the legislature acts as law-initiator varies among political systems and is generally believed to be in decline. Ideally, legislatures initiate laws, propose constitutional amendments, ratify treaties, control tax revenues, and act as a check on the other branches of government.[6]

Lawmaking

The chief job of democratic legislatures is supposed to be that of rule initiation: making the laws that govern society. How does a bill become law? The first step is to draft and introduce the proposed bill. In the West German Bundestag, individual legislators may not introduce bills on their own but must join a *Fraktion* (a group of fifteen members) to propose legislation. But in most democratic legislatures, any member may introduce a bill. Rule initiation often originates in the executive branch, with an agency drafting a proposal and finding a sympathetic legislator to introduce the bill in Congress. When a senator or representative wants to propose a bill of his or her own, his or her staff usually does the actual writing, with the Office of the Legislative Council checking to ensure proper wording. In parliamentary governments, the executive branch may introduce legislation directly, since cabinet members hold seats in the legislature. The Swiss save time by introducing all bills in both houses simultaneously, and whereas this is not always the case in the United States, here, too, high-priority bills are usually introduced in both houses at the same time.

Formal introduction of a bill in the U.S. Congress begins when the proposal is registered with the clerk of the House or Senate and referred to the appropriate committee. Most bills are tabled, or laid aside by the committee after brief consideration, never to be heard of again. However, when the committee thinks a bill has merit, it is sent to a subcommittee for further investigation. Public hearings, which can last for months if a controversial measure is up for discussion, may be held on very important bills. When staff investigations or public hearings are concluded, the bill is then reviewed by the full committee. At this point, the committee may modify certain sections of the bill before voting for or against its passage. If the bill is approved, it goes to the House Rules Committee or Senate majority leader and is then placed on the calendar of the appropriate house for floor consideration.[7]

Once on the floor, the bill is again debated, amended, and revised before it is voted on by the House or Senate. If a majority of each house carries the bill, the Senate and the House then create a conference committee, where differences between the two versions are ironed out. The agreed-on bill then goes back

---

[6]See K. C. Wheare, *Legislatures* (New York: Oxford University Press, 1963).

[7]For an insider's view of the functioning of Congress, see Abner J. Mikva, *The American Congress: The First Branch* (New York: Franklin Watts, 1983).

STATE OF THE UNION address every year is one of the few times U.S. presidents come before Congress under the separation of powers in the U.S. Constitution. Here, President Reagan speaks to the joint houses of Congress.

Bill Fitz-Patrick, The White House

to the House and Senate for a routine revote, where it rarely encounters any controversy. The legislation is then signed by the heads of both houses and sent to the president for his action. If he signs the bill, it becomes law. If he rejects it, Congress needs a hard-to-achieve two-thirds majority to override his veto. If the president neither signs the bill nor vetoes it, it automatically becomes law in ten days—if the Congress is still in session. But if Congress adjourns before the ten days have elapsed, the bill does not become law. This latter approach is known as the "pocket veto."

Although legislatures *pass* laws, few of them *originate* laws. This is why we must take their "rule-making function" with a grain of salt. In a highly technical age, much legislation actually originates in governmental departments and agencies, comes to the attention of cabinet officers, and is sent on to the legislature, which may alter it somewhat. In highly developed parliamentary systems, where one party controls both the executive and legislature (as in Britain and Sweden), the cabinet gets what it wants. Committee work and parliamentary debate don't count for much, because party discipline makes sure that members of the ruling parties will nearly automatically vote the way their party leaders instruct them to vote. Votes in such legislatures are highly predictable along party lines; some observers say such parliaments have become rubber stamps for the executive. The U.S. Congress, with its weak and decentralized party system, represents at least a partial rejection of this. Party discipline is weak, and members frequently buck their own party on key votes. But even in the United States, notice how much of the legislative agenda is determined by items sent over from the White House: new weapons systems, use of troops overseas, expanding or cutting domestic programs, and setting new criteria for pollution or auto safety. Even the budget, the original "power of the purse" that gave legislatures their importance, is now an annual congressional *reaction* to the budget produced by the White House budget office. Accordingly, "lawmaking" is not the only nor perhaps even the most important thing that legislatures do.

Constituency Work.   U.S. congresspersons spend a prodigious amount of time helping constituents.[8] They have staffs in their districts and Washington offices to answer letters, make sure people get their Social Security checks, and generally show that the congresspersons really care. Often the "lawmaker" is so busy with constituency casework—which is important in getting reelected—that he or she pays little attention to making laws. The situation is similar, although perhaps not as extreme, in other democracies. In effect, elected representatives have partly transformed themselves into *ombudsmen,* specialists who intervene with government on behalf of people with complaints. Is there anything wrong with this? Is it not a perfectly valid and necessary role for legislators to play? It is, but at the same time something gets lost: the wider view that a representative of the people should have in helping guide the country. A legislator immersed in constituency work has no time for or interest in bigger questions, so the initiative goes more and more to the executive branch. What then will become of democracy?

Supervision and Criticism of Government.   The potentially more important role of modern legislatures is keeping a sharp and critical eye on the executive branch. Even if they don't originate much legislation, legislatures can powerfully affect the work of government by monitoring government activity to make sure it is in the nation's interest, uncorrupt, and effective. The Reagan administration, for example, found it had to modify its policies on South Africa, environmental pollution, judicial appointments, and strategic weapons, all because Congress had raised difficult and sometimes embarassing questions, even though it had passed little legislation on these matters.

In Britain, the Question Hour allows members of Parliament to grill ministers, sometimes with devastating results. Even if the British cabinet knows that it cannot be toppled in a vote of no confidence—because it controls the largest party in Commons—its members must be very careful in answering these questions. If they give a bad, unconvincing answer to a difficult question, or, even worse, if they try to cover up by lying, it can cost the ruling party dearly in the next election. In the 1963 Profumo affair, a Tory minister was caught lying (about his affair with a call girl) in Parliament; Labor charged the government with laxity on national security and with covering up for one of its

---

[8]See John R. Johannes, *To Serve the People: Congress and Constituency Service* (Omaha, Neb.: University of Nebraska Press, 1984).

"old boys." Labor won the 1964 election in large part because of the Profumo scandal.

In Israel in 1983, the Begin government had to partly pull out of Lebanon because of criticism in the Knesset that the campaign was lasting too long, costing too many lives, and not producing a stable solution. In 1987, congressional investigations of White House dealings with Iran and Nicaraguan contras shook the Reagan administration. Keeping the government on its toes is one of the best things a legislature can do, even if it doesn't pass any laws.

Education.   One of the less-noticed functions of legislatures is their ability to inform and instruct the citizenry on the affairs of government; they are not merely passive inputting devices, taking mass demands and channeling them into government. Legislatures also create mass demands by calling public attention to problems. In the mid-1960s, Senator J. William Fulbright (D-Arkansas), then chairman of the Senate Foreign Relations Committee, educated many Americans about the Vietnam war by televising his committee's hearings, in which a series of experts and governmental officials variously defended and criticized U.S. policy. In Britain and in countries based on its "Westminster model," such as Australia and India, much parliamentary debate is carried in the press nationwide.

Representation.   One of the chief functions of legislatures is to represent people. Although nowhere is there a close match between the characteristics of legislators and those of the people they represent, nonetheless most legislators in most democracies feel they must consider the interest of all their constituents. Even in the U.S. South, now that blacks are voting in considerable numbers, congresspersons generally take care not to offend blacks. A large part of representation is psychological; people like to *feel* they're represented. When they don't feel represented, they become resentful of governmental power. Government loses legitimacy. "No taxation without representation," chanted the American colonials. One may wonder if some members of Parliament representing the thirteen colonies might not have headed off the Declaration of Independence. The laws of South Africa, passed by a whites-only House of Assembly, evoke little support and much disobedience from the black majority of that country. Curiously, Communist systems understand the psychological importance of representation, even though their legislatures meet only a few days each year to rubber-stamp the measures the government and party place before them. Communist "legislators" are much more representative of their populations; relatively high percentages are women, workers, and minority-group members. The controlled press often makes much of the "representativeness" of these delegates and ignores their lack of power.

The foregoing are some of the roles performed by legislatures. Note that only one of them is lawmaking, and that is usually just a follow-up on ideas initiated by bureaucrats and executives. Still, if legislatures fulfill the other roles mentioned, they're doing a lot.

THE STRUCTURE OF PARLIAMENTS

Bicameral or Unicameral

Some two-thirds of the legislative bodies in the world have two chambers, an upper house (the U.S. Senate, the British House of Lords, or the West German Bundesrat) plus a lower house (the U.S. House of Representatives, the British House of Commons, or the West German Bundestag). These are called *bicameral* (two chambers) legislatures. Despite its name, the upper house usually has less and sometimes much less power than the lower house; only the two houses of the U.S. Congress are coequal. A smaller number of parliaments are *unicameral* (one chamber), such as China's National Peoples Congress, Sweden's Riksdag, and Israel's Knesset. Yugoslavia once experimented with a five-chambered parliament. South Africa has a curious (and probably temporary) three-chambered parliament with one house each for whites, mixed-race peoples, and East Indians. The majority black population is unrepresented in the national parliament of South Africa.

The reason for two chambers is clear in federal systems (see the previous chapter). The upper house represents the component parts of the federal

SWEDEN'S RIKSDAG has been unicameral since 1971 when it concluded that the bicameral parliament served no useful purpose. Typically, parliaments are arrayed in a semi-circle.

Lasse Hedberg

system, and the lower house represents districts based on population. This was the great compromise solution incorporated in the U.S. Constitution: the Senate represented the states and the House the people. A federal system axiomatically requires an upper chamber. West Germany's Bundesrat, for example, represents the ten *Länder* (states) and is coequal to the lower house on constitutional questions. On other issues, however, it can be overriden.

The utility of an upper house in unitary systems, however, is unclear. Britain's House of Lords (its members or "peers" are chosen by either heredity or by lifetime appointment) is mostly an elderly debating society that sometimes catches errors in laws passed too quickly and obediently by the House of Commons. Otherwise the Commons overrides any objection from the House of Lords with a simple majority vote. This is also true of the French *Senat,* an indirectly elected body that largely expresses farming interests. The New Zealanders, Danes, and Swedes— all with unitary systems—came to the conclusion that their upper houses served no purpose and abolished them in recent decades.

The Committee System

Virtually every legislature has a number of standing or permanent committees and may from time to time create special ad hoc committees to study urgent matters. The British House of Commons has five standing committees plus several new specialized committees. These committees are much less important than their U.S. counterparts, for the fusion of powers of the British system means that Parliament is not supposed to carefully review, criticize, or reject bills the cabinet has submitted. Operating within the framework of the separation of powers, it is in the U.S. Congress that the committee system has been most fully developed.[9] The House of Representatives has twenty-two standing committees—the Senate, sixteen—and they often make the news. We often hear of the more prestigious of these committees, such as the House Ways and Means and Foreign Affairs, and we know that a good committee assignment is a boon to the career of a freshman member of Congress.

What purposes do these committees serve? Their major function, of course, is to screen the thousands upon thousands of bills that are introduced at every session and pick out the few that merit serious study and consideration. Second, legislatures are so large that bills cannot be drafted by the entire membership; in order to work out an agreement on the precise wording and scope of legislation, proposals must be referred to relatively small groups of lawmakers who will iron out differences and submit polished bills for the consideration of the whole membership. It should not be surprising, therefore, that the bulk of legislative work is not performed on the floor of the House or Senate but is done in committee and subcommittee rooms. The committees are "where the action is."

---

[9]Woodrow Wilson's study points out the power and distinctiveness of the U.S. committee system. See *Congressional Government: A study in American Politics* (Baltimore, Md.: Johns Hopkins University Press, 1981).

Further, each committee usually has several specialized subcommittees; the two houses have a total of about 250 subcommittees. Changes in the 1970s weakened what were considered to be the tyrannical powers of committee chairpersons by making it easier to establish subcommittees. It worked; committees and their chairpersons are not what they used to be. But now, critics charge, subcommittees and *their* chairpersons have decentralized and fragmented power too much, weakening Congress as an institution.[10] A cure for one problem produced new problems, the story of many political reforms.

These same reforms of the 1970s broke the power of appointment of the senior House and Senate leaders of both parties. Committee chairs and membership were generally assigned on the basis of seniority. Now, when the parties caucus at the beginning of a session in each house, members vote for committee chairpersons by secret ballot, effectively breaking the seniority system. Party committees in each house make committee assignments and usually try to take members' interests and expertise into account. Capitol Hill is now more open and democratic than it used to be, but interestingly, this has not enhanced its power vis-à-vis the executive branch.[11]

Standing Committees. In Great Britain and France, standing committees are not as specialized and lack the political influence of their American counterparts. The standing committees in the British Parliament are designed to be flexible and broad, and have traditionally played a less critical role than the American committees. They work out the details of a bill after the House of Commons has approved it, rather than sitting in judgment on the bill before it reaches the Commons floor. However, the age of specialization has been felt in Britain too, and parliamentary reforms have increased the degree of committee specialization. Education, overseas aid and development, race relations, science and technology, nationalized industries, and Scottish affairs all rate permanent committees in Commons. The counterpart in the French National Assembly is the commission—again not as compartmentalized as the American committee. In studying a bill, the commission assigns only one member—called the rapporteur—to the task, rather than working collectively as in the United States and Britain. In the United States, specialization is the name of the game. The larger committees, such as the Senate Foreign Relations Committee, may have a dozen subcommittees.[12]

[10]Charles O. Jones, "Can our Parties Survive our Politics?" in *The Role of the Legislature in Western Democracies,* ed. Norman J. Ornstein (Washington, D.C.: American Enterprise Institute, 1981).

[11]Lawrence C. Dodd is deeply pessimistic about any reforms reversing this trend; they seem to make it worse. See his "Congress, the Constitution, and the Crisis of Legitimation," in *Congress Reconsidered,* 2d ed., ed. Lawrence C. Dodd and Bruce I. Oppenheimer (Washington, D.C.: Congressional Quarterly Press, 1981).

[12]For a thorough overview of congressional committees, see Barbara Hinckley, *Stability and Change in Congress,* 3rd ed. (New York: Harper & Row, 1983), Chapter 6; and Steven S. Smith and Christopher J. Deering, *Committees in Congress* (Washington, D.C.: Congressional Quarterly Press, 1984).

Standing committees in Congress are balanced so that they will represent both political parties and the states or geographic regions with the greatest interest in the committee's area of specialization. For example, Nebraska has someone on the Agricultural Committee, and New York is usually represented on the Education and Labor Committee. Each standing committee is bipartisan, made up of Democrats and Republicans in direct proportion to each party's representation in that house of Congress. If the House is 60 percent Democratic, the House Ways and Means Committee will be, too. Italy adds an interesting power to its standing committees, which also reflect proportional representation of the whole chamber. Italian committees, meeting *in sede deliberante,* can actually pass legislation without bringing it to the full house. This can speed up much routine legislation. Given Italy's disciplined parties, the vote in committee duplicates the vote of the whole chamber, so nothing is lost but delay.

Legislative Leaders

Whereas committees receive more attention in the U.S. Congress than in other legislatures, presiding officers are the center of power in almost every democratic legislature. Most presiding officers are chosen by their colleagues and hold positions with substantial political influence. They recognize speakers, rule on procedures, place motions before the legislature, and have a say in what committee considers a given piece of legislation as well as a significant voice in who serves on a particular committee.

Majority Leaders. The majority leaders of the U.S. House and Senate are the spokespersons of the controlling party in each house, and both are elected by party caucus. They formulate party stands on upcoming legislation, determine the order in which bills come to the floor, negotiate compromises, and have a considerable voice in committee appointments.

Minority Leaders. The U.S. House and Senate minority leaders are also elected by party caucus and serve as spokespersons for the party with the minority of legislative seats. They also formulate party stands and strategies, but they are not as powerful in the legislature as the majority leaders, whom they often criticize.

Speakers. In the United States, the Speaker of the House is its presiding officer. In Great Britain, the Speaker of the House of Commons is chosen by both major parties in the legislature. Once elected, he or she must sever all party connections and refrain from taking part in debates. The Speaker of the U.S. House of Representatives, in contrast, is expected by both parties to use his or her considerable powers to partisan advantage. Yet, as presiding officer, he or she must rule impartially on points of order and give the minority party equal chance to voice their views. The Speakers of most European legislatures are far less partisan than their American counterparts.

Whips. Both the U.S. House of Representatives and the Senate have majority and minority *whips*. In English fox hunting, the "whipper-in" keeps the hounds from straying from the pack; in the legislature, the party whip keeps discipline within the party ranks and rounds up support for party policies. The accuracy of the whip's vote-count for a given piece of legislation will often determine whether a bill will ever make it to the floor. Senate whips are chosen by party caucuses, which endorse the choices of the party leaders. In the House, Democratic whips are chosen directly by the floor leaders, and Republican whips by the Committee on Committees. British whips command compliance from their parties' members in the House of Commons. When "the whip is on," MPs know they must be present for a vote. A backbencher's "refusing to take the whip" means a break in party discipline.

THE RISE OF THE EXECUTIVE

By the late nineteenth century, observers began to notice that parliaments were not working the way they were supposed to.[13] Contrary to Locke's expectations, legislatures seemed to be losing power to the executive. Most political scientists would agree that the trend has continued and perhaps worsened.[14] Some, however, such as Jean Blondel, hold that the original Lockean expectations were too high to begin with and that some parliaments provide useful checks on the executive even though they do not originate much legislation.[15]

Structural Disadvantages. There are many reasons why legislatures do not fulfill the Lockean ideal. Structurally, the executive has built-in advantages. In parliamentary systems, party discipline is strong, and legislators obey party whips. Members of the legislative body are rarely moved by speeches or debates to vote against their party. If they do, they can lose their party's endorsement and be dropped from the party list at the next election. In effect, they are fired from parliament. Gilbert and Sullivan summed it up in the words of a successful British politician in *H.M.S. Pinafore:* "I always voted at my party's call and never thought of thinking for myself at all." In European parliaments we can usually predict within a vote or two how the issue will be decided: most often in favor of the government because the government (or cabinet) commands a majority of seats. In such systems, there's not a great deal for an individual member of parliament to do. No special excitement is evident in the press and public about parliamentary affairs. Only when coalitions break up or when members of one

[13]Lord Bryce, *The American Commonwealth* (London: Macmillan, 1888), I, 165–232, and A. B. Lowell, *Governments and Parties in Continental Europe* (Cambridge, Mass.: Harvard University Press, 1896). Bryce made explicit his worry about the "decline of legislatures" in his *Modern Democracies* (London: Macmillan, 1921), I, 367–77.

[14]See Gerhard Loewenberg, ed., *Modern Parliaments: Change or Decline?* (Chicago: Aldine-Atherton, 1971).

[15]Jean Blondel, *Comparative Legislatures* (Englewood Cliffs, N.J.: Prentice-Hall, 1973).

party defect to another (a rare occurrence) do things get unpredictable and therefore interesting. The European parliaments really are more rational and efficient than the U.S. Congress, but they are also less powerful and less interesting. Efficiency has led to atrophy.

The U.S. Capitol Hill has no such problem with efficiency. Its near feudal dispersion of power with weak party discipline, and its tendency to deadlock with the executive have made it most inefficient. Yet it is precisely these impediments that keep Congress lively and important. In few other countries can the national legislature as a whole "talk back" to the executive and even override a presidential veto. In parliamentary systems, the opposition parties criticize the government party, but the government party does not criticize its own cabinet in power. Nevertheless, even in the United States power has drifted to the executive. The president speaks with one voice, Congress with many. Congress is fragmented into committees and subcommittees—with chairpersons vying for media attention—and this delays and often prevents agreement. Congress expects and even demands presidential leadership and usually gives presidents most of what they want after some controversy and debate. Even the Democrat-controlled House followed Reagan's legislative program.

One case illustrates Congress's dependency on the president and his power. Despairing of ever being able to cut the huge spending budget, Congress attempted to hand over the power to an appointed congressional official in the 1985 Gramm-Rudman Act. The Supreme Court, more aware of the Constitutional issues than most members of Congress, immediately threw out this provision in the law. (Congress had been warned in advance that giving up its power of the purse would be unconstitutional.) So Congress next attempted to hand the power to cut the budget to the White House! It was almost as if Congress were saying, "We give up; we're too divided. So here, Mr. President, you take over our constitutional duties." The astonishing thing about the U.S. Congress, the last Mohican of independent legislatures, is that it *wants* to surrender power to the executive.

Lack of Expertise. Few legislators are experts on technical, military, economic, or social problems. Of the 535 Senators and Representatives in the 100th Congress, nearly half (246) were lawyers.[16] European nations have fewer lawyers in their parliaments and more schoolteachers, journalists, and full-time party people. But hardly any technical experts appear in legislatures. Much legislation nowadays involves technical knowledge. Few legislators are professionally equipped to deal with such technical matters as nuclear power, strategic weapons, medical care, international currency fluctuations, and environmental pollution. Accordingly, legislators must rely chiefly on experts sent over from the executive departments. Much legislation originates with these specialists, and they are often called as witnesses to committee hearings. The ensuing legislation

---

[16]Characteristics of the 100th Congress," *Congressional Quarterly Weekly Report* 44 (27 Dec. 1986) 52:3175.

usually grants these executive specialists considerable discretion in applying the law.

Most parliaments have little or nothing in the way of independent research support; their data come either from the government or from private interest groups. Only the U.S. Congress—again, based on the idea of separation of powers—can generate its own data. The General Accounting Office (GAO), Congressional Research Service (CRS), Office of Technology Assessment (OTA), and Congressional Budget Office (CBO) are all part of the legislative branch. They attempt to provide independent evaluations and data to lessen Congress's dependence on the executive. No other legislature in the world has a fraction of this research capability. Still, it remains to be seen if the research agencies of Congress can counterbalance the massive information advantage of the executive branch.

Psychological Disadvantages. The citizenry of any country is more impressed with their presidents or prime ministers than with their parliament. There may be a deep human need to respond to a single leading personality. A president can have charisma, but whoever heard of a charismatic legislature? American children are socialized to revere the president but to disdain members of Congress. As was mentioned in Chapter 12, even in parliamentary systems voters now respond to the personalities of the candidates for prime minister. Television, by giving a great deal more air time to chief executives than to any other political figure, heightens this tendency. People come to see their president or prime minister as a parental figure, calmly guiding the country toward safety while the silly parliamentarians squabble among themselves. U.S. school textbooks often depict the president as a sort of "daddy." This leads to what some political scientists fear is "president worship."

In summation, compared to executives, legislatures were never very strong. Our modern, technological age gives the executive a further edge. This drift has serious implications for the survival of democracy. The great function of parliaments has been to check and limit arbitrary executive authority. Could legislatures grow too weak to carry out their role as a counterbalance to executive power? Is the trend toward stronger executive power reversible?

Who is the Executive?

In the United States, we hail to only one chief. Our president makes all cabinet appointments (with Senate approval) and has final and ultimate responsibility for all policy decisions. Most Latin American countries also give all executive power to one person. Two countries have plural executives or "collegial presidencies." Switzerland is guided by a seven-member Federal Council elected to a four-year term by the legislature. Yugoslavia has a nine-person presidency, with one person from each republic and autonomous province. In both cases, the presiding officer rotates every year.

Cabinet Government. The most common executive structure is the cabinet. Great Britain's system is a classic example. Technically, it is a plural executive with decision-making powers shared by the prime minister, the ministry, and the cabinet. But in practice it operates like the single-executive system.[17]

The monarch, as official head of state, initiates the new administration by formally inviting the leader of the largest party in the House of Commons to become prime minister and form a government. As such, he or she appoints the two dozen executive department heads, the parliamentary secretaries, the legal officers, the ministers without portfolio, and the parliamentary whips. They are all members of the prime minister's party and are usually chosen to represent every significant group within the party. The cabinet is charged with the formulation of government policy. Theoretically, the prime minister is *primus inter pares* (first among equals) and must carry out decisions reached by the whole cabinet even when personally opposed. But, like an American president, the prime minister can dismiss a cabinet member at any time, and those who oppose his or her decisions are expected to resign. Conceivably, a cabinet that is strongly united against the prime minister could force a change in government policy or even the prime minister's resignation. But this happens rarely, and hasn't occurred since Neville Chamberlain was ousted from party leadership in 1940.

The chancellor of West Germany is even stronger than the British prime minister. The chancellor, too, is majority leader in the lower house (Bundestag). But cabinet appointments are not subject to legislative confirmation, and, once in office, the chancellor doesn't necessarily have to resign just because the Bundestag has voted "no confidence" in his or her government. The West German constitution requires the Bundestag to vote in a replacement cabinet before ousting the old one. This is called "constructive no confidence," and it has contributed a lot to the stability of Bonn's governments. It's much harder to replace a cabinet than just oust it; as a result, constructive no confidence has succeeded only once, in 1982, when the small Free Democratic party defected from the Social Democrat–led coalition to the opposition Christian Democrats. A prime minister supported by constructive no confidence is a more powerful figure than one without it, as one might see in a comparison of the average tenures of Italian and West German cabinets (several months as compared to several years).

The Roles of the Executive

Richard E. Neustadt, a leading authority on the American presidency, has written that "from outside or below, a President is 'many men' or one man wearing many 'hats,' or playing many roles . . . the President himself plays every

---

[17]For a comparison of leadership in presidential and parliamentary systems, see Richard Rose and Ezra N. Suleiman eds., *Presidents and Prime Ministers* (Washington, D.C.: American Enterprise Institute, 1980).

'role,' wears every 'hat' at once."[18] Not only the president, but most modern chief executives wear more than one hat. The unique powers of the presidency, however, put the occupants of the White House in an uncommonly strong position. They are elected independently of the legislature and, as such, are the direct choice of the nation as well as of their party. In addition, they have several exclusive roles: official chief of state, head of government, party leader, commander-in-chief of the armed forces, chief diplomat, chief executive, and chief legislator. These powers reinforce each other to make the presidency the most respected office in the nation. Great responsibility also comes with these broad powers. And, in the last analysis, there is no one to whom presidents can pass the blame for mismanaged affairs. As the sign on Harry Truman's desk so aptly put it, "The buck stops here." Since 1789, the powers of the president have grown enormously,[19] as have those of the chief executives of all other nations.

Chief of State.   Presidents are the surrogates and spokespersons for the American people. They are the visible symbol of the nation and must perform numerous ceremonies usually saved for monarchs and figurehead presidents in other nations. Whereas the vice-president or the president's wife are sometimes sent to dedicate major public work projects or christen boats, tradition still demands that the president greet visiting dignitaries, entertain the diplomatic corps, and represent their country at important international conferences.

Head of Government.   Every head of government—president, prime minister, or chancellor—is responsible for carrying out decisions. He or she must also supervise the bureaucratic machinery at the national level, which makes the responsibilities of the job staggering. The president is responsible for thirteen major departments of government, more than one hundred executive bureaus, five hundred administrative offices, and six hundred divisions employing three million civil servants. One American worker in sixty is a federal employee (compared to one in two thousand in Washington's day), and the president is—at least in theory—each federal worker's boss. To aid the president in this enormous task, the Executive Office of the President, now employing some 1700 full-time workers, was formed in 1939 to conduct the day-to-day supervisory functions of running the bureaucracy.

Party Chief.   Although the president is chosen directly by the people, he is still leader of his political party, as are the British, French, and Spanish heads of government. The chief executive is expected to take the lead in raising campaign funds and in endorsing and campaigning on behalf of his or her party's candidates for local, state, and national office. More important, he or she is expected to play a major role in formulating the party's legislative program.

---

[18]Richard E. Neustadt, *Presidential Power* (New York: New American Library, 1964), p. viii.
[19]Our discussion follows in part Louis W. Koenig, *The Chief Executive*, 5th ed. (San Diego, Cal.: Harcourt Brace Jovanovich, 1986).

The president is not as powerful a party leader as the prime minister in a parliamentary government because of the lack of centralization and discipline in the American party system.

Commander-in-Chief. The U.S. Constitution specifies—and the Supreme Court has upheld—the right of presidents to deploy the country's armed forces as they see fit. Congress has long been exasperated with this power and has tried, never successfully, to curb it. Congress fears that the president's power as commander-in-chief infringes on its power to declare war. In the late 1930s, Congress passed a series of Neutrality Acts designed to keep the country out of the coming war, but President Roosevelt managed to circumvent them. In 1973 Congress, which was too timid to move when the Vietnam war was at its height, passed (over President Nixon's veto) the War Powers Act, which limits the president's use of troops in overseas combat situations to 90 days unless Congress approves an extension. This did not prevent President Reagan from sending U.S. troops into Lebanon, Grenada, or Central America.

Chief Diplomat. Likewise, presidents can do almost anything they want in diplomacy without congressional approval. This holds for most prime ministers as well. Chief executives can grant diplomatic recognition to foreign countries, negotiate trade deals, and conclude "executive agreements" that are almost like treaties. Treaties themselves, those most-important international contracts, must be ratified by the countries' legislatures. In the United States, that means a two-thirds assent from the Senate. The Supreme Court has upheld presidential preeminence in foreign relations,[20] and Congress has gone along with it.

Dispenser of Appointments. Since the introduction of the merit system into the U.S. Civil Service at the turn of the century, the power of patronage has been considerably diminished. All federal judges and legal officers are appointed by the president, as are diplomatic officers and upper-echelon management personnel in the federal departments, agencies, offices, bureaus, and divisions. All in all, the president still has thousands of jobs to dispense every year. One of the key ways a president can enforce party discipline within the congressional ranks is through influence in patronage appointments. Although the power of patronage is not as important as it once was, it carries enough weight so that few legislators willingly incur the wrath of the party leadership.

To a large extent, the success of a president's program is determined by the kind of people appointed to office, for those appointees can bring either creative leadership or routine administration to their jobs. In making appointments, a president considers a candidate's experience, talent, and temperament

---

[20]The landmark case is considered to be *U.S. v. Curtiss-Wright* (1936). For the Supreme Court decision, see Alpheus T. Mason et al., *American Constitutional Law: Introductory Essays and Selected Cases,* 7th ed. (Englewood Cliffs, N.J.: Prentice-Hall, 1983), pp. 118–21.

to manage the responsibilities of office. The decision is also influenced by how many votes an appointee will bring to the administration, the political debts he or she must pay, and the responsibility to call on prominent political and national leaders to serve the office of the president.

Chief Legislator. The president is not only responsible for executing the laws passed by Congress but also has—as has already been discussed—considerable lawmaking powers. Congress gives the chief executive broad discretionary powers in interpreting and implementing law. In many cases, Congress passes very general legislation and leaves it up to the president to fill in the details. Finally, the president initiates legislation. The State of the Union message and National Budget spell out the general direction of the administration for the coming year and suggest programs and laws the president believes are in the best and most urgent interests of the nation.

An Imperial Presidency?

"The accumulation of all powers, legislative, executive, and judiciary, in the same hands," James Madison wrote in *The Federalist,* no. 47, "may justly be pronounced the very definition of tyranny." The Founding Fathers held that power must be balanced internally to prevent one man or group of men from seizing all political control. Checks and balances, John Adams declared, are as effective as "setting a thief to catch a thief," and he was confident that interbranch jealousies would ensure that each branch would confine the other to the political limits set down in the Constitution. In recent years, many political scientists have voiced the fear that the breadth of responsibility required to run a modern nation has caused the office of the presidency to become too powerful. How valid are these fears? Certainly, the relationship between Congress and the president has changed profoundly in the last century.

Samuel P. Huntington noted some startling statistics. From 1882 to 1909, Congress was responsible for shaping more than half (55 percent) of all significant pieces of legislation; between 1910 and 1932, the figure dropped to 46 percent; and from 1933 to 1940, Congress was primarily responsible for initiating a mere 8 percent of all major laws. "Since 1933," Huntington wrote, "the initiative in formulating legislation, in assigning legislative priorities, in arousing support for legislation, and in determining the final content of legislation enacted has clearly shifted to the executive branch."[21] This situation has significantly altered the traditional separation of powers between the legislative and executive branches and has produced a variety of studies both decrying the fall of Congress and defending the increased legislative responsibilities of the presidency.

[21]Samuel P. Huntington, "Congressional Responses to the Twentieth Century," in *The Congress and America's Future,* ed. American Assembly (Englewood Cliffs, N.J.: Prentice-Hall, 1965), pp. 23–24.

The imbalance is even more extreme in European parliaments, where practically no legislation is introduced on members' initiative. It should be remembered that, on a world scale, the U.S. Congress is the most independent and lively legislature. This is the positive side to the weakness of U.S. parties and built-in conflict between the legislative and executive branches. It is Congress's very lack of discipline that gives it the autonomy many European parliamentarians envy. The price the U.S. system pays for this is slowness. With the fusion of powers of the parliamentary system, legislation moves quickly. With the separation of powers between the White House and Capitol Hill, legislation can take a long time, although the president usually prevails in the end.

As the Vietnam war was winding down and Watergate was boiling up, a noted historian produced a book that captured the worried feeling of the time—*The Imperial Presidency,* by Arthur Schlesinger, Jr.[22] Lyndon Johnson had taken the country into a major war without a declaration of war from Congress. Richard Nixon had expanded that war into Laos and Cambodia, again without a declaration of war. Nixon also "impounded" appropriations made by Congress; he simply refused to spend funds in certain areas, in effect exercising an item veto after bills had been signed into law. Was the president overstepping constitutional bounds? Were we on our way to an imperial presidency, going the way of ancient Rome, from republic to rule by the Caesars? Many thought so.

Congress attempted to reassert some of its authority, passing the War Powers Act in 1973 and moving toward impeachment of Nixon the following year. It looked like the beginning of a new era, with Congress and the president once again in balance. But this didn't really happen, for the U.S. system *needs* a strong president to function properly.

When Jimmy Carter took office in 1977, he attempted to deimperialize the presidency, but this simply led to an ineffective White House. Carter, catching the spirit of the time, ran against Washington in 1976. He billed himself as the average American who was not part of the establishment. Symbolically, on his inauguration day he and his family walked down Pennsylvania Avenue instead of riding in the presidential limousine. As an outsider, though, Carter was ignorant of the ways of Washington and quickly alienated a Congress that was dominated by his own party. His important legislation stalled on Capitol Hill and was often diluted by amendments, especially his crucial energy proposals. By the 1980 election, much of the American electorate—and perhaps even some people in Congress—wished for a more forceful and experienced chief executive.

Congress's reassertion of independent authority in the 1970s proved brief, for with the arrival of Ronald Reagan in the White House in 1981, the president once again had a fair degree of command over Capitol Hill.[23] But this,

---

[22]Arthur Schlesinger, Jr., *The Imperial Presidency* (Boston: Houghton Mifflin, 1973).

[23]For a review of the Reagan presidency, especially his relations with Congress, see *Congress and the Nation,* vol. 6, 1981–1984 (Washington, D.C.: Congressional Quarterly Press, 1985), pp. 843–57.

too, did not work for long. In late 1986 it was revealed that officials of the president's National Security Council totally bypassed Congress in selling arms to Iran and using the money to fund *contras* attempting to overthrow the Nicaraguan government. Even President Reagan's supporters in Congress turned angry and subjected his appointees to pointed questions in committee hearings. Once again, a Congress disappointed with alleged executive misuse of power was trying to assert a check over an executive branch it had repeatedly invested with enormous powers.

An Inevitable Trend?

Worldwide, power has been flowing to the executive, and legislatures have been in decline. The U.S. Congress has put up some good rear-guard actions, but it, too, has been generally in a slow retreat. Some observers have argued that this can't be helped, that a number of factors make this shift of power inevitable. If this is true, what can we do to safeguard democracy? Democracies still have a trump card, and some say it is enough: electoral punishment. As long as the chief executive, whether president or prime minister, has to face the electorate at periodic intervals, democracy will be preserved. The "rule of anticipated reactions," of which we spoke in Chapter 5, will keep them on their toes. Perhaps the concept of checks and balances was a great idea of the eighteenth century that doesn't fit the twentieth. Maybe we will just have to learn to live with executive dominance.

Even if we admit that, however, there is another problem. Within the executive, power has been flowing to the unelected civil servants, the bureaucrats. What can protect us from them? For further discussion of this question, let us turn to the next chapter.

SUGGESTED READINGS

BARBER, JAMES DAVID. *The Presidential Character: Predicting Performance in the White House,* 3rd ed. Englewood Cliffs, N.J.: Prentice-Hall, 1985. A psychological theory that accurately predicted Nixon's reactions to Watergate.

BLONDEL, J. *Comparative Legislatures.* Englewood Cliffs, N.J.: Prentice-Hall, 1973. A magisterial overview in cross-national perspective of the role, power, and performance of legislatures.

BURNS, JAMES M. *The Deadlock of Democracy.* Englewood Cliffs, N.J.: Prentice-Hall, 1963. A major argument that Congress and the president are caught in a paralyzing stalemate.

CAMPBELL, COLIN. *Governments Under Stress: Political Executives and Key Bureaucrats in Washington, London, and Ottawa.* Toronto: University of Toronto Press, 1983. This rare comparative effort shows some differences and much similarity between presidential and prime-ministerial decision making.

CRABB, CECIL V., JR., AND PAT M. HOLT. *Invitation to Struggle: Congress, the President, and Foreign Policy.* 2d ed. Washington, D.C.: Congressional Quarterly Press, 1984. Details how Congress tries, but does not always succeed, in making a policy impact.

DODD, LAWRENCE C., AND BRUCE I. OPPENHEIMER, EDS. *Congress Reconsidered,* 3rd ed. Washington, D.C.: Congressional Quarterly Press, 1985. Excellent collections of essays by knowledgeable specialists.

FISHEL, JEFF. *Presidents and Promises: From Campaign Pledge to Presidential Performance.* Washington, D.C.: Congressional Quarterly Press, 1985. A methodologically sophisticated review of how well recent presidents have kept their election promises.

FISHER, LOUIS. *The Politics of Shared Power: Congress and the Executive,* 2d ed. Washington, D.C.: CQ Press, 1987. An official of the CRS demonstrates the complex interactions and conflicts of the two branches with recent case studies.

KELLERMAN, BARBARA. *The Political Presidency: Practice of Leadership from Kennedy through Reagan.* New York: Oxford University Press, 1984. Case studies emphasizing the effect of personality on how recent presidents have led or failed to lead.

LOWI, THEODORE J. *The Personal President: Power Invested, Promise Unfulfilled.* Ithaca, N.Y.: Cornell University Press, 1985. A worried look at the growth of presidential power and public expectations that the president cannot meet.

NEUSTADT, RICHARD E. *Presidential Power: The Politics of Leadership from FDR to Carter.* New York: John Wiley, 1980. Plea for presidential effectiveness.

ORNSTEIN, NORMAN J., ED. *The Role of the Legislature in Western Democracies.* Washington, D.C.: American Enterprise Institute, 1981. Symposium with U.S., British, and German legislators and scholars. Good comparative perspective.

POLSBY, NELSON W. *Congress and the Presidency,* 4th ed. Englewood Cliffs, N.J.: Prentice-Hall, 1986. Thorough review by an acknowledged master.

REEDY, GEORGE E. *The Twilight of the Presidency.* New York: NAL-World, 1970. A pessimistic warning on the growth and misuse of presidential power by a Johnson press aide.

RIPLEY, RANDALL B. *Congress: Process and Policy,* 3rd ed. New York: Norton, 1983. A major statement on how congressional fragmentation structures the way the Hill works.

SCHLESINGER, ARTHUR, JR. *The Imperial Presidency.* Boston: Houghton Mifflin, 1973. Worried view that recent presidents had overstepped their bounds.

SULEIMAN, EZRA N., ED. *Parliaments and Parliamentarians in Democratic Politics.* New York: Holmes & Meier, 1986. Seven countries show different and changing powers of parliaments and relations with executives.

SUNDQUIST, JAMES L. *Constitutional Reform and Effective Government.* Washington, D.C.: Brookings Institution, 1986. A long-term specialist on Congress casts a thorough but skeptical eye at reforming the U.S. system.

chapter 15

Administration
and Bureaucracy

When the term *bureaucracy* is mentioned to the average citizen, he or she thinks of the red tape that must be cut through to obtain a service or information. Actually the term refers to any large-scale organization of appointed officials whose primary function is to implement the policies of the decision makers. Ideally, a bureaucracy is a rational system or organized structure designed to permit the efficient and effective execution of public policy. In order to do this, a bureaucracy operates in accordance with a fixed set of rules and procedures. It has a clearly recognized chain of command (or hierarchy of authority) through which responsibility flows from the top down. The job of the bureaucracy is to apply policy guidelines to particular situations. It is a method of organization that enables government to operate with some uniformity—and, therefore, predictability—and in a manner that is rational and subject to internal supervision and control.

Bureaucracy is by no means confined to government. At a time when most Western governments were little more than loose confederations of feudal powers, the Roman Catholic Church had an impressive and influential administrative system. Through a chain of command, authority flowed from the pope down to parish priest. Until the advent of strong monarchies, this organizational pattern was the envy and model of secular rulers. Armies are also characterized by their rigid bureaucratic structures which are based on the military chain of command. Bureaucracy is equally pervasive in most civilian institutions, including schools, hospitals, large corporations, and so on. Corporations such as Exxon and General Motors have clearly defined chains of command, and they organize their necessary functions into specialized departments and offices.

The Organization of the Federal Bureaucracy in the United States

Fewer than 18 percent of the civil servants in the United States are federal. Of our 16.4 million civil servants, 9.6 million are employed by local governments, 3.9 million by state governments, and only 2.9 million (not counting military personnel) by the federal government. Remember, most government services—schools, police, and fire protection—are provided by local governments.

The Cabinet Departments. In the United States, the thirteen cabinet departments—employing between 85 and 90 percent of all federal civil servants—share a common anatomy, even though they may differ in size and scope of operations. Each is headed by a secretary who is appointed by the president (with the consent of the Senate) and serves at his pleasure. The undersecretaries and assistant secretaries are also political appointees. This differs from, for example, the British system, where officials up through the equivalent of our undersecretaries are members of the permanent civil service.

The basic function of the cabinet departments is to carry out legislative and executive policies. For example, the Department of Agriculture is charged with enforcing congressionally mandated farm-price supports. This is no simple matter, however, for the departments must determine how to interpret the intent of Congress. Very often, when a controversial issue is involved, the only way Congress can muster even the barest majority to pass the legislation is by couching it in the most general and politically nonoffensive terms. Thus, the legislation that a department must enforce often only sets broad guidelines for action and the bureaucracy has latitude to establish specific working policy that suits its own interests or those of the chief executive.

The cabinet departments are subdivided into bureaus that are headed by career civil servants rather than political appointees. For example, the Bureau of Labor Statistics is part of the Department of Labor, and the Bureau of the Census is part of the Department of Commerce. Here the day-to-day work of the departments is carried out, and bureau chiefs possess a great deal of discretionary authority, even though they must work within the framework of statutory law and executive policy. In addition, the cabinet departments maintain local offices in each state and, ideally, uniform policies prevail at all departmental levels.

Federal Agencies.   Some independent agencies of the federal government, like the departments, are accountable to the president. Each is headed by a single administrator whom the president appoints and can remove. Sometimes created in response to a particular lobby, the agency performs a single, highly complex function that may be more political than administrative. For example, the United States Information Agency (USIA) is frankly ideological; its function is to portray the United States in a favorable light to win foreign support for American policies. At the other end of the spectrum is the National Aeronautics and Space Administration (NASA), which was organized to coordinate America's explorations into space.

Federal Corporations.   Government-owned corporations are combinations of government agencies and private business enterprises which serve vital needs that private enterprise cannot meet.[1] Although corporation heads are appointed by the president and, in many cases, confirmed by the Senate, they exercise a good deal of autonomous power. They can, for example, use their own judgment to handle and reinvest the funds that the legislature has appropriated. The United States Postal Service, the Tennessee Valley Authority (TVA), the St. Lawrence Seaway Development Corporation, and the Export-Import Bank are a few of the more important federal corporations. The TVA and St. Lawrence Corporation undertook massive public works construction that few private corporations could have financed. Similarly, no private corporation would be willing to risk the Post Office's deficits. Federal corporations operate under the basic guidelines set down by Congress, and, since few of them are

---

[1]For an excellent brief introduction to problems of U.S. government corporations, see John T. Tierney, "Government Corporations and Managing the Public's Business," *Political Science Quarterly* 99 (Spring 1984):1.

CIVIL SERVANTS: Technically, this NASA space shuttle team of pilots and scientists, including the first U.S. woman astronaut, are federal civil servants.

NASA

profitable, they depend on annual legislative appropriations. They are therefore liable to congressional criticism of their organizational structure and policies.

Independent Regulatory Agencies. These agencies are charged with economic regulation of private businesses that directly affect the public welfare. They have quasijudicial and quasilegislative authority that derives from Congress. For example, Congress has given the Nuclear Regulatory Commission (NRC) the power to shut down nuclear power plants it deems unsafe. Such decisions are enforceable in the courts and are not often overturned by the judiciary.

These agencies have been the target of a great deal of criticism. Ralph Nader and others charge that they are overly influenced by the very industries they should be controlling. Many commissioners are drawn from the ranks of private industry and, critics say, are more concerned with preserving certain vested interests than with protecting the public. The Federal Power Commission, for example, is often under attack by those who feel it is staffed solely by representatives of industry rather than of consumer interests. There is a measure of truth in this criticism, but it must be acknowledged that agency employees need a technical understanding of the industries they regulate if they are to do their jobs. There can be little doubt that the responsiveness of the various agencies has increased since critics have brought agency deficiencies to the attention of the public.

Bureaucracies in Other Nations

As formidable as our federal bureaucracy may seem to us, government bureaucracies in some other countries are even more pervasive in both scope and authority.[2]

Communist Countries. The Soviet Union is one of the most bureaucratic nations in the modern world, but its bureaucracy is tied to the Communist party. Although according to Communist dogma, a dictatorship of the proletariat has no need for a Western-style bureaucracy, immediately after the Russian Revolution the Soviets instituted bureaucratic management in their developing industrial society.

Upper-echelon Soviet bureaucrats form a privileged elite; their salaries and lifestyles are far superior to those of the average citizen. Special shops, a house in the country, and Western clothes are regular features of the high-level bureaucrat's life.[3] To rise in the hierarchy, one must be a party member, for party loyalty is all-important. The members of the bureaucracy are drawn from the university graduates, who, in return for their free educations, must work in a state agency for three years following graduation. After that period, many of them choose to remain.

Each department is headed by a minister who is a member of the Council of Ministers (which is roughly equivalent to a Western cabinet). This council—the highest executive authority in the government—is composed of high-ranking party members, some of whom are also members of the Politburo (the innermost ruling authority of the party). Not only do the ministers control their departments, but, wherever possible, loyal party members are placed strategically in subordinate positions in an effort to make sure that policy is carried out to party specifications.

France. Many European countries pattern their bureaucracies on the French model.[4] Most of Europe shares traditions of Roman (code) law and centralized rule. After the French Revolution destroyed the monarchy, Napoleon restored central control of the bureaucracy and, by making it more rational and effective, increased its power. Napoleon, with the *intendants* of Richelieu as his model, created the prefects to carry out government policy at the local level.

Since then, merit and technical expertise have been the primary considerations in the appointment of French bureaucrats. Most career civil servants are graduates of one of the "Great Schools," such as the *Ecole Polytechnique,* an engineering school, or, since World War II, the *Ecole Nationale d'Administration,*

[2]For a broader, theoretical view of bureaucracies, see B. Guy Peters, *The Politics of Bureaucracy: A Comparative Perspective,* 2d ed. (New York: Longman, 1984).

[3]See Michael Voslensky, *Nomenklatura: The Soviet Ruling Class* (New York: Doubleday, 1984)

[4]See F. F. Ridley and J. Blondel, *Public Administration in France,* 2d ed. (London: Routledge and Kegan Paul, 1969).

which was specifically created to train government officials. The severe instability of the Third (1871–1940) and Fourth (1947–1958) Republics increased the bureaucracy's power, because it had to take on the responsibilities of initiating and enforcing policy if the day-to-day business of government was to proceed at all. In many cases, permanent civil servants called *directeurs* (roughly equivalent to American bureau chiefs) had to operate independently. The Fifth Republic brought greater stability and stronger ministerial control, and the bureaucracy has become more consistent in the day-to-day administration of French government.

The American concept of decentralization has only recently come to France; the French viewed local levels of government primarily as administrative conveniences. The French national government still centrally controls the country's bureaucratic network. From the American viewpoint, this centralization was often carried to an extreme. For example, at any given moment in the school day, all schoolchildren in a particular grade throughout France were likely to be engaged in the same activity. Local conditions, problems, or initiatives were secondary considerations in bureaucratic decisions. The Socialists, who swept to power in 1981, included in their proposed program the decentralization of France. A 1982 law reduced the powers of the prefects to little more than police and firefighters and retitled them "commissioners of the Republic." Elected councils in the ninety-six *départements* and twenty-two regions got policy and taxation powers in education and economic development. Decentralization reversed five centuries of centralized French administration.

West Germany.   Prussia and its ruling class, the *Junkers,* put their stamp on German administration. Obedient, efficient, hard-working—these are the qualities the aristocratic *Junkers* cultivated. They were also a state nobility, dependent on Berlin and controlling all its higher civil-service positions. Frederick the Great of Prussia, who ruled from 1740 to 1786, had a passion for effective administration and established universities to train bureaucrats. When Germany united in 1871, under Prussia's leadership, Prussian administrative styles permeated the new nation. Democracy counted for little among German administrators; loyalty to the emperor was more important. One of the reasons the short-lived Weimar Republic (1919–33) failed, it is believed, was because the civil-servant class had little but contempt for democracy. With the Third Reich, they eagerly flocked to Hitler.

The current West German government has a strongly federal structure that limits Bonn's administrative powers.[5] Theoretically, it is responsible for controlling foreign affairs, collecting taxes, defense, transportation, the postal service, some social insurance programs, and intelligence activities. But in practice, the federal government controls only one domestic program—unemployment insurance. It also operates jointly with the *Land* (state) governments to

---

[5]See K. Konig et al., eds., *Public Administration in the Federal Republic of Germany* (Hingham, Mass.: Kluwer Academic, 1983).

collect taxes; all other domestic programs are administered by the *Länder,* under federal guidelines. If we followed this system in the United States, the state governments rather than the Department of Labor and the Justice Department would be charged with enforcing the Taft-Hartley Act. Today's West German civil servants are committed to democracy. Trained in law—throughout Europe this is at the undergraduate level—at various universities (there is no equivalent of the French Great Schools), Bonn bureaucrats tend to bring with them the mentality of Roman law, that is, law neatly organized into fixed codes rather than the more flexible U.S. and British Common Law, "judge-made" law. Used throughout Europe, Roman law (mostly the updated Napoleonic Code version) gives civil servants a somewhat rigid, by-the-book mentality.

Great Britain.   Britain, unlike France, has strong traditions of local self-government and dispersion of authority. This pattern of administration, which is also common to the United States, relates to the Anglo-American experience with representative government, which encouraged legislative control of administrative authorities. During the nineteenth century, the growth of British government at the local level also encouraged the dispersion of administrative authority; it was not until the twentieth century that the central government began to participate in local affairs.

Curiously, Great Britain was rather late in developing a modern bureaucracy. Until the Northcote-Trevelyan Report calling for major reform was issued in 1854, the bureaucracy was rife with corruption and nepotism. Positions in the bureaucracy (for instance, military commissions) were openly bought and sold. By 1870, however, a merit civil service based on competitive examinations had been established.

British ministers are accountable to Parliament for the conduct of their departments and, along with their cabinet colleagues, make departmental policy. However, real bureaucratic power is in the hands of the "permanent secretary" (a career administrator) and the career deputy secretaries, undersecretaries, and assistant secretaries who serve at lower ranks. Thus, even though the British and American bureaucracies share the same tradition of decentralized administrative authority, control over the bureaucracy is tighter in Britain than in America.[6] English bureaucrats feel that their primary loyalty belongs to their departments rather than to a political party or leader; and so they faithfully carry out the ministry's policies and seldom initiate policy on their own.

Characteristics of Bureaucracies

Bureaucrats have often been pictured as plodding counters of paper clips who spend their time passing the buck and figuring out how much their pensions will amount to. As is the case with most caricatures, this one contains

---

[6]For a good account of the British bureaucracy, see J. R. Greenwood and D. J. Wilson, *Public Administration in Britain* (Winchester, Mass.: Allen & Unwin, 1984).

some germs of truth. The first scholar to make a systematic analysis of bureaucracy and bureaucrats was the German sociologist Max Weber (1864–1920). His classic studies provide the starting point for a current examination of bureaucracy.

Weber's Characteristics of Bureaucracies. Weber's analysis was based on the German bureaucratic model, but his principles can be applied worldwide. Weber's criteria for defining bureaucracy were:[7]

1. Administrative offices are organized hierarchically.
2. Each office has its own area of competence.
3. Civil servants are appointed, not elected, on the basis of technical qualifications as determined by diplomas or examinations.
4. Civil servants receive fixed salaries according to rank.
5. The job is a career and the sole, or at least primary, employment of the civil servant.
6. The official does not own his or her office.
7. The official is subject to control and discipline.
8. Promotion is based on superiors' judgment.

Weber felt he was studying something relatively new. Some of the above characteristics could be found in classic China, but not all. Like the nation-state, bureaucracies started in western Europe around the sixteenth century but were reaching their full powers—which Weber distrusted—only in the twentieth century.

Goodnow and Wilson. At the turn of the century, Frank J. Goodnow and Woodrow Wilson made significant studies of the American bureaucratic system.[8] Bureaucracy in the United States, they noted, must work within the framework of our democratic society. But how can professional civil servants, who are not directly accountable to the electorate, be reconciled with the goals of democracy? Wilson and Goodnow set up the theoretical base that allowed turn-of-the-century political scientists to accept the ideals of democracy together with the efficiency of a professional civil service. They made a distinction between political (policy making) and administrative (enforcement) officials. In order to ensure that our democratic system is always run by elected officials, Goodnow concluded that the political officials must always control the administrative officials. This subordination must be clearly defined on an individual and agency level. Administrators, then, never initiate policy: they merely follow the policy guidelines laid down for them by the political leaders.

Political scientists today feel that these distinctions are not applicable to modern government. Administrative officials, they note, when given only the

[7]This is a paraphrase of Weber's criteria. See Robert K. Merton et al., eds., *Reader in Bureaucracy* (Glencoe, Ill.: Free Press, 1952), pp. 21–22.

[8]Frank J. Goodnow, *Politics and Administration* (New York: Macmillan, 1900); and Woodrow Wilson, "The Study of Administration," *Political Science Quarterly* 2 (June 1887):197–222.

broadest policy guidelines by Congress and the president, do make policy decisions. Many of these decisions are made on the basis of the administrators' expertise in their fields, which, because of our highly specialized government, political leaders do not always have.

The overlapping of administrative and political functions, therefore, is a result of the demands of modern government and not of the desire for power of professional civil servants. It is clear that the United States of the 1980s can no longer look to Weber or to Goodnow and Wilson for an analysis of modern bureaucracy. We must go further.

Beyond Weber. Weber's bureaucracy served a highly stratified, authoritarian society—one in which the average citizen did not "talk back" to bureaucrats. Late–twentieth-century America is a far different place, and private citizens and legislators do not hesitate to criticize bureaucrats or call them before investigating committees to explain their actions. These investigations, however, can be carried to extremes, as the excesses of Senator Joseph McCarthy in the 1950s illustrate. McCarthy's almost fanatical crusade against communism eliminated from public service such people as an entire generation of experts on China. Bureaucrats in sensitive political posts try to keep themselves attuned to prevailing public and congressional opinion. They do not—indeed, they cannot—function solely on the basis of precedent and paper rules and procedures.

Further, anyone who has had to deal with a bureaucracy can testify to the fact that it is not as impersonal, predictable, and precise as the Weberian ideal would have it. Bureaucrats are psychological beings and seldom act in the sterile manner implied by Weber. In a bureaucracy, as in other organizations, improvisation, informality, and entrepreneurship in the decision-making process are common.

Additionally, some political scientists have noticed the tendency for bureaucratic agencies to become interest groups themselves. Far from being neutral and passive administrators, bureaucrats are active participants in the formation of laws and policies. Elected and appointed executives are often entirely dependent on the data and ideas that career civil servants provide them with. Leaders, in effect, become followers. Civil servants frequently lobby legislators to get the programs they want. The danger here, some feel, is government of the bureaucrats, by the bureaucrats, and for the bureaucrats. It is startling to realize that no government, East or West, democratic or dictatorial, civilian or military, has managed to fully control its bureaucracy.

ROLE OF BUREAUCRACY IN MODERN GOVERNMENTS

General Functions

The functions of modern government bureaucracies include administering, servicing, regulating, licensing, information gathering, and "housekeeping" chores. All government bureaucracies perform at least two of these basic functions, with some bureaus specializing, and some carrying out multiple functions.[9]

Administration. The primary function of most government bureaus can be defined, simply, as the execution and enforcement of the laws enacted by the legislature and the policies promulgated by the executive. For example, the United States has a policy of channeling federal funds to the states to defray the cost of various welfare programs. The Department of Health and Human Services administers this policy by deciding how much federal money each state is entitled to and seeing to it that the money is used for its intended purpose. Britain has a policy of providing free medical care to citizens. Its National Health Service administers this policy by overseeing medical training, assigning patients to doctors, running the hospitals, and so on. Administration, therefore, is the implementation of public policy, and because it involves policy decisions, it also entails rule making. In conjunction with their administrative duties, departments often initiate campaigns to publicize their work and to educate the public as to a program's benefits and purposes. In many countries there are also continuous programs of education in such areas as traffic safety, fire prevention, and conservation of natural resources.

Patterns of administration vary from country to country. In the Soviet Union, for example, the party serves as a watchdog over the bureaucratic network. Virtually all Soviet officials in decision-making positions are party members, and all offices have party people in them. What the party calls its *kontrol* function keeps Soviet bureaucrats on their toes. If their unit doesn't run right or if they are egregiously crooked (and many are), they can be fired, demoted, or transferred to a remote area. This tends to make them extremely cautious and to go by the book. Indeed, lack of innovation is a hallmark of the Soviet system. The Soviet bureaucracy is huge, including some fourteen million persons, partly because it also supervises the economy. Party *kontrol* is probably indispensable for such a system. Note that the West does not have a comparable mechanism for supervising and checking its bureaucracies.

In Britain, executives and administrators oversee the day-to-day operations of their departments, and higher administrative officials help draft proposed legislation as well as help their ministers answer questions from members of Parliament. Since Britain, like France, has a partially nationalized economy, such basic services as steel plants, coal mines, railroads, and telegraph and telephone lines are run by government-controlled corporations that make policy decisions normally reserved to the private sector in the United States.

Services. Many government agencies are created to serve the general public or specific groups. The U.S. Weather Bureau is, perhaps, the best

---

[9]The following section is based on Charles E. Lindblom, *The Policy-Making Process,* 2d ed. (Englewood Cliffs, N.J.: Prentice-Hall, 1980); Harold Seidman, *Politics, Position, and Power: The Dynamics of Federal Organization* 3rd ed. (New York: Oxford University Press, 1980); and Peter Woll, *American Bureaucracy,* 2d ed. (New York: Norton, 1977).

example of a service agency. Although those of us who have been caught without an umbrella on a day when the Weather Bureau promised no rain may not think much of the service, it is nevertheless vital to farmers and fishermen. The U.S. Department of Agriculture conducts research in pest control, land management, and livestock improvement, dispenses surplus food to the poor, and provides information about nutrition to the general public. In Britain, most health care is dispensed by the government. In Sweden and West Germany, the government runs extensive job-finding services. And in the Soviet Union, the government provides free education at all levels for those who qualify.

Regulation.   The regulatory functions of government are also designed to safeguard the general public's welfare. In the United States, the Securities and Exchange Commission, for example, protects investors by establishing guidelines for the registration of new issues as well as the buying and selling of stocks and bonds. Britain has had legislation on the books since 1819 regulating working conditions in factories, and similar legislation exists in most industrialized countries. This legislation is enforced by particular agencies. The U.S. Department of Labor, for example, oversees elections in unions to make sure that they are conducted fairly. The election of a reform candidate to the scandal-ridden United Mine Workers' Union shows how successful the Department of Labor's regulating powers can be. In Germany, the enforcement of federal law by the Land governments is supervised by the Bundesrat (the upper house of the national legislature), and federal administrative courts are empowered to compel Land governments to enforce national law. In all instances, the regulation powers are backed by the potential of force. In the United States, for example, regulatory agencies can issue "cease and desist" orders. Although offenders may challenge these orders in court, most voluntarily choose to comply.

Licensing.   Licensing is closely related to regulation. It enables governments to impose minimum standards and qualifications in certain areas. For example, if you want a license to drive a car, practice medicine or law, sell real estate, teach in the public schools, or work as a barber, you must meet certain government standards. In the United States and other federal countries, these standards are usually set by the individual states. In countries such as France or Great Britain, the national government sets the standards and administers the tests. Even in the United States, however, some licenses are issued by the federal government. For example, an FCC license is needed to operate a radio or television station.

Information Gathering.   Information is needed for two major purposes: to determine whether a law has been violated and to make policy decisions that are rational and based on factual evidence. For example, if a U.S. citizen complains that his or her civil rights have been violated, an investigation— usually by the Civil Rights Division of the Justice Department—has to be made before any action can be taken. And the Environmental Protection Agency must know the exact state of air and water pollution before it can issue orders concerning violations. Similar investigations are conducted by all modern states. The French government made an extensive study of the nation's energy needs before plunging into a massive nuclear-energy program.

Some agencies act only when there has been a complaint. Others, like the Food and Drug Administration (FDA), are constantly making investigations on their own initiative. The FDA does not allow a drug to go on the market—regardless of whether a complaint has been made—until it is satisfied that the product is safe and effective. Sometimes the problem of invasion of privacy arises when organizations, such as the Federal Bureau of Investigation (FBI), investigate the activities of alleged subversives and question their friends, neighbors, and family members. The line between investigation necessary to protect the public interest and invasion of privacy is a fine one, and it is often difficult to tell where one leaves off and the other begins.

THE TROUBLE WITH BUREAUCRACY

The world does not love bureaucrats. The very word has a slightly pejorative connotation. In France and Italy, hatred of the clerk or official on the other side of the counter or desk has become part of the political culture. The United States, with its long-standing theories of minimal government and individual self-reliance, is pleased to hear every major candidate—from both parties—denounce the bureaucracy. One of the funniest experiences is to ride a commuter train or bus into Washington, D.C., and overhear career civil servants complain about "those damn bureaucrats." The paradox of the modern state is that whereas bureaucratic administration is a necessity, it is also often an impediment to the fulfilment of national goals.[10]

Incoming U.S. administrations, particularly Republican, usually vow to bring business-type efficiency to public administration. They rarely make a dent in the problem and sometimes make things worse. "Efficiency" is much harder to apply in public affairs than in private industry. A businessperson can calculate profits and productivity; a civil servant doesn't make any profits and productivity, too, is hard to measure. Governmental offices are sometimes overstaffed, but it is difficult to pick out which workers should be gotten rid of.

At its worst, bureaucracy can show signs of "Eichmannism," named after the Nazi official who organized the death trains for Europe's Jews and later calmly assured his Israeli judges that he was just doing his job. Nazi bureaucracy connotes treating people like things, a problem not limited to Germany. On the humorous side, bureaucracy can start to resemble Parkinson's Law: work

---

[10]This discussion owes much to Joseph LaPalombara's lively "Bureaucratic Pathologies and Prescriptions," in *Politics Within Nations* (Englewood Cliffs, N.J.: Prentice-Hall, 1974), chap. 8.

expands to fill the staff time available for it.[11] Parkinson never called himself a humorist, and many who have worked in featherbedded, purposeless, paper-shuffling agencies agree that Parkinson's Law is accurate.

Bureaucracy and corruption are intertwined. Whenever there are rules to be carried out by public officials, there is a constant temptation to bend them for friends and benefactors.[12] The more regulations, the more bureaucrats, and the more corruption becomes possible. Only a few countries with a strong ethos of public service—Britain and Sweden, for example—have been able to maintain uncorrupt public administration into the modern age. Most countries in the world are corrupt, some a little and some egregiously. In much of the Third World, to be a public official means to take money on the side.[13]

Perhaps the most serious problem with bureaucracy, alluded to above, occurs when it becomes interlocked with and sometimes replaces other branches of government.

The Bureaucracy: Administrator or Policy Maker?

The early theorists of bureaucracy (Weber, Goodnow, Wilson) assumed that professional bureaucrats would never make public policy, but merely execute the will of elected officials. And, indeed, nonpartisan administration was the original motivation behind the development of a merit civil service. However, as Guy S. Claire warned many years ago, most Western nations have developed—however unwittingly—"administocracies" (defined as an aristocracy of administrators) whose personnel are not publicly accountable, but who nevertheless make policy.[14] Whereas a return to the nineteenth-century spoils system is neither possible nor desirable, the question of whether a democracy can afford to allow nonelected and nonresponsible administrators to make decisions that will affect the lives of the people must be considered. First it is necessary to define the specific ways in which bureaucracies affect policy making.

Adjudication.   Many regulatory agencies maintain administrative courts that operate much like regular courts and whose edicts and awards are enforceable in the regular courts. Most states, for example, have administrative tribunals that grant workers' compensation awards. All parties to such an action are entitled to legal counsel and may offer evidence. The FDA can order a drug off the market, and the SEC can ban trading in a particular stock. Two major questions have been raised in this connection. Some maintain that these tribunals' cease-and-desist orders, edicts, and so on should be made by the regular courts: if a cosmetic is harmful, should not the courts—and not the

---

[11]C. Northcote Parkinson, *Parkinson's Law* (Boston: Houghton Mifflin, 1957).

[12]See James C. Scott, *Comparative Political Corruption* (Englewood Cliffs, N.J.: Prentice-Hall, 1972).

[13]For a survey of Third World bureaucracy, see Krishna K. Tummala, ed., *Administrative Systems Abroad*, rev. ed. (Lanham, Md.: University Press of America, 1984).

[14]Guy S. Claire, *Administocracy* (New York: Crowell-Collier, 1934).

FDA—make this decision? Proponents of the administrative courts answer this objection by pointing out that the courts, by their own admission, often lack the expertise to judge highly technical matters. The second question is raised by those who doubt the wisdom of giving so much power to the administrators. These critics feel that even though the law has empowered an agency or department to "regulate in the public interest, convenience, or necessity," the creation of administrative courts means that Congress has given administrators a blank check.

Discretionary Implementation. When a legislature enacts a law, the bureaucracy must enforce it, and when statute law is specific, this is a relatively simple matter. However, this is not usually the case. For example, the U.S. Congress passed a law requiring that toxic dump sites be cleaned up. The law enabled the Environmental Protection Agency (EPA) to do whatever necessary to achieve this goal. The EPA made certain decisions, because every dump cannot be cleaned up at once, and each one entails different ecological, economic, and political problems. Deciding how to go about achieving the general goal became the responsibility of the EPA. When agencies are granted the prerogative of deciding how to implement a law or policy, they are in effect being permitted to make law for society.[15] Defenders of discretionary implementation point out, however, that no code of law can anticipate all circumstances that might arise and that administrators must therefore have some leeway. Furthermore, administrators can always be overruled by public or legislative pressure or by executive edict.

Rule Making. The rule-making authority of regulatory agencies is related to discretionary implementation. For example, higher rates for telephone use must be approved by the Public Service Commission (PSC).

One of the best examples of bureaucratic rule making was the fight to force cigarette manufacturers to place health hazard warnings on their cigarette packages and to include them in advertisements. For several years, the Federal Trade Commission (FTC) and the Public Health Service had been urging such practices. Congress had been reluctant to go along, however, primarily because of pressure from the tobacco industry. In 1965 the Advisory Committee on Smoking and Health and the surgeon general (the nation's chief public health officer) concluded that heavy cigarette smoking increased the likelihood of contracting lung cancer and shortened one's life span considerably. The report disturbed the public, and public pressure on Congress increased. Since 1966 cigarette manufacturers have been required to print danger warnings on all packs.

Meanwhile, the tobacco industry tried, unsuccessfully, to discredit the surgeon general's report, and organizations such as the American Cancer Society were agitating for still firmer antitobacco legislation. In 1967 the FCC

---

[15]See Gary C. Bryner, *Bureaucratic Discretion: Law and Policy in Federal Regulatory Agencies* (New York: Pergamon, 1987).

entered the crusade. Citing the fairness doctrine, it ordered all radio and television stations accepting cigarette commercials to make free time available for antismoking commercials. Soon the American Cancer Society was producing one-minute antismoking announcements.

In 1969 the FCC banned cigarette advertising on radio and television. And, in 1971 President Nixon signed an FTC-sponsored bill requiring cigarette companies to print health warnings on all advertising copy as well as on every pack of cigarettes. Political scientist A. Lee Fritschler reached the following conclusion:

> The initiation and continuation of the cigarette controversy were possible because of both the political power and delegated authority possessed by bureaucratic agencies. Had the decision on cigarettes and health been left to Congress alone, it is safe to assume that the manufacturers would have triumphed, and no health warnings of any kind would have been required. The cigarette-labeling controversy is a clear example of agencies' power to influence and even formulate public policy.[16]

Here was a vivid case of federal agencies openly lobbying for a particular policy and getting it.

Advisory Roles. The growing complexity of modern life has caused legislatures and executives to rely more and more heavily on the technical expertise of bureaucrats. Congress may decide that unsafe mines should be shut down, but only mining experts can determine exactly what conditions make a mine unsafe. Many laws require administrative interpretation. For example, Congress may outlaw deceptive advertising, but the determination of what *is* deceptive is made by the FTC. Bureaucrats do not usually have to convince legislators to take their advice; the lawmakers are often only too happy to have the technical assistance of specialists. This is yet another way in which bureaucrats influence the formulation of public policy.

Conflicts can arise, however. For example, Kennedy's Secretary of Defense, Robert McNamara, a political appointee, was intent on cutting costs where possible. He ran into a wall of opposition from military men, who claimed that they alone knew the technical side of security needs. McNamara's relationship with the military high command was frequently stormy. Similarly, in 1948, President Truman was under intense pressure by State Department experts not to recognize Israel when it became an independent state. Both McNamara and Truman realized that some decisions are, by their very nature, political and that only a politically responsible official ought to make them.

The bureaucracy's role of advisor is not peculiar to the United States; rather, it is an inevitable feature of the modern industrial state. In France, for example, laws and presidential decrees are drawn up and promulgated with the

---

[16]A. Lee Fritschler, *Smoking and Politics: Policymaking and the Federal Bureaucracy*, 3rd ed. (Englewood Cliffs, N.J.: Prentice-Hall, 1983), p. 142.

active assistance of the bureaucracy (particularly the Council of State), and career executives thus have the opportunity to shape policy. Bureaucrats play a large role in the framing of legislation in West Germany. Since federal bureaucrats do not have to supervise field or branch offices, they can devote their energies to policy matters. In fact, they are often successful in convincing their political superiors to accept their way of thinking on issues.[17]

What To Do with Bureaucracy?

Bureaucracy in the twentieth century has become big, powerful, rigid, unresponsive, and intrusive. Some contend it has taken on a life of its own, divorced from the needs of the citizens and governments that first gave it birth. Can anything be done about this?[18] As Joseph LaPalombara has observed, most of the ideas offered to cure bureaucracy entail adding more bureaucrats. Here are some suggested remedies:

Ombudsmen. The ombudsman is Sweden's contribution to the art of governance. Established by the 1809 Swedish constitution, the *Justitieombudsman* (literally, agent of justice) is named and paid by the parliament, not the executive. This is important, for no government agency can be its own ombudsman; that must come from outside. An official who says, "Bring all complaints to me. I'm my own ombudsman," doesn't understand the concept. Absolute independence is necessary for an ombudsman to work effectively. The ombudsman is a government lawyer who intervenes on behalf of citizens treated wrongly by the bureaucracy. The ombudsman has subpoena power, and a reprimand to errant officials is usually enough to set things right. Denmark, Norway, Britain, and New Zealand have set up similar institutions.

Some have suggested the ombudsman concept for the United States. In a sense, we already have it: the congressperson, whose constituency work is much like that of the ombudsman. It might further be argued that since the United States is already overrun with lawyers, no citizen has far to go to find one. Poor people can often obtain free legal assistance. Where the ombudsman idea works is in countries with a tradition of respect for law and a political and moral climate in which a simple reprimand is enough. The American context is not precisely as law-abiding, and an ombudsman might have difficulty working effectively.

Legislative Checks. Whereas an ombudsman system might be difficult to implement in the United States, we have some other mechanisms to oversee the bureaucracy. The U.S. Congress has the General Accounting Office (GAO),

---

[17]See Joel D. Aberback, Robert D. Putnam, and Bert A. Rockman, *Bureaucrats and Politicians in Western Democracies* (Cambridge, Mass.: Harvard University Press, 1981).

[18]For a study on possible ways to control the U.S. Civil Service, see Douglas Yates, *Bureaucratic Democracy: The Search for Democracy and Efficiency in American Government* (Cambridge, Mass.: Harvard University Press, 1982).

Congressional Research Service (CRS), and Congressional Budget Office (CBO). The GAO looks to see that federal funds are spent correctly and effectively; the CRS tries to give Congress the expertise needed to check on the executive-branch specialists; and the CBO, established only in 1974, consolidates Congress's budget-making functions in order to reply to the White House's powerful Office of Management and Budget. In effect, what the United States has done is set up competing bureaucracies—one executive, the other legislative. This does not save money or reduce the number of bureaucrats; it is simply an effort to keep the executive side tied to the national purpose as represented on Capitol Hill.

Cutting.   Americans dream of some golden yesteryear in which there were no bureaucrats on their backs. Politicians often promise to cut the bureaucracy, but they rarely succeed. Cutting bureaucrats means cutting programs, and most citizens soon find their favorite programs getting the ax. They meant to cut *other* people's wasteful programs, not the necessary and prudent expenditures they benefit from. Once a welfare state has been built, it is terribly difficult to dismantle, because so many people have a stake in its bounties. In the 1980s, the Reagan administration tried a different track: keep the programs on the books but fail to fund or staff them adequately.[19] Many federal offices, especially those providing services the president and his supporters disliked, found themselves operating with reduced budgets and manpower, unable to carry out their legislated mandates. At a time of massive federal budget deficits, Congress found it difficult to restore these cuts. In highly public areas such as education and environmental pollution, however, irate citizens and their interest groups demanded attention, and President Reagan had to partially back down. He did not, for example, abolish the Department of Education as he had promised during the 1980 campaign. The meat-ax approach to bureaucracy is tempting but hard to carry out in practice.

Decentralization.   For highly centralized systems, as in France and Italy, decentralization offers some improvement. Decisions can be made closer to home, in consultation with the people they will affect. Decentralization can solve some problems but create others. It brings bureaucratic decision-making closer to the local level, but this can *increase* corruption and inefficiency. Without Paris or Rome looking over their shoulders, who knows what those bureaucrats in the provinces will do? For most of its history, the United States has had a decentralized education system. The result has been a great deal of freedom and local control but also extreme unevenness of quality and blatant racial segregation. Many Americans wish they could go back to strict local control, but they don't want to do without federal dollars. True decentralization means that localities have to raise their own taxes, something they dislike doing.

---

[19]For a study of the effects of the Reagan cuts, see Irene S. Rubin, *Shrinking the Federal Government: The Effect of Cutbacks on Five Federal Agencies* (White Plains, N.Y.: Longman, 1985).

Decentralization may entail widely varying standards and problems of coordination. With West Germany's strongly decentralized federal system, it took years to get the different *Länder* to agree on a program and standards to clean up the seriously polluted Rhine river. Each state saw its environmental responsibilities differently and didn't want its authority eroded.

Further, decentralization does not mean reducing the number of bureaucrats, just placing them at different levels. As such, it may actually seem to put more bureaucrats on the people's back, not fewer.

Politicize the Bureaucracy. Most governments are proud that they have moved to a nonpolitical, neutral, professional bureaucracy. In the United States, we disdain the corrupt "spoils system" of the last century in which political bosses would place their people in choice jobs. But maybe we've gone too far with the career, neutral, detached bureaucrat. Perhaps it's time to reinject a certain amount of political control into the system. Political appointees bring fresh approaches, innovative plans, and a mandate from the people and elected officials for improvement. Bureaucrats live by routine and hate to rock the boat; they are not capable of changing their own system. Only outsiders, appointed from other walks of life for a few years, can do that.

Communist systems are monstrous bureaucracies, but they would be much worse without the party to oversee them. The old U.S. urban machines, such as that of the late Mayor Daley in Chicago, were decried for their corruption, but they were generally responsive to citizen needs and often worked better than the reform administrations that succeeded them. A new American president has some three thousand appointive positions to fill, a very high number compared with the numbers in other countries. Some say this is too many, that we should use career civil servants to fill more of these slots. But it is this appointive power that gives a president what little leverage he or she has over the U.S. bureaucracy.[20] Decrease it and the civil service will be less responsive.

Bureaucracy and Society

For all our dislike of bureaucracy, we must remember that it was not visited upon us from an alien planet. It was set up, funded, and given its duties by our representatives. They did this for reasons, and, although agencies sometimes take on lives of their own, the initial reasons still apply. Do you think a lot of red tape is involved in getting a driver's license? Imagine a society where drivers weren't required to be licensed. Do you think bureaucrats interfere too much with private industry? What would happen if we rolled back our standards on foodstuffs, drugs, and product safety? Do Equal Opportunity bureaucrats harm a white person's chances to get into law school or a good job by ensuring

---

[20]See John W. Macy and others, eds., *America's Unelected Government: Appointing the President's Team* (Cambridge, Mass.: Ballinger, 1983).

preference to minority candidates? It wasn't bureaucrats who set up these laws; it was Congress. Congress, to be sure, was vague and sloppy, leaving administrators too much leeway in drawing up guidelines and then dropping the whole thing on the courts.[21] But the bureaucrats themselves have only the smallest part of the blame.

We live in a complex society. We may try from time to time to make it simpler, to do away with what appear to be burdensome regulations and officious bureaucrats. But when we do, we discover anew that the regulations and civil servants were put there for a purpose. Whereas we may—indeed must—attempt to improve our rules and the agencies that implement them, we are unlikely to eliminate them unless we are prepared to return to a simpler age, a time without nuclear power, automobiles, telecommunications, or employment security. Until then, we are stuck with our unlovely bureaucrats, for in the final analysis, they are us.

SUGGESTED READINGS

CROZIER, MICHEL. *The Bureaucratic Phenomenon.* Chicago: University of Chicago Press, 1964. A leading French sociologist takes a jaundiced look at bureaucracy, especially French bureaucracy.

DOWNS, GEORGE W., AND PATRICK D. LARKEY. *The Search for Government Efficiency: From Hubris to Helplessness.* New York: Random House, 1986. Argues that government is not so inefficient and that it is possible to improve it.

FESLER, JAMES W. *Public Administration: Theory and Practice.* Englewood Cliffs, N.J.: Prentice-Hall, 1980. Good overview by a long-time specialist in the field.

FRITSCHLER, A. LEE. *Smoking and Politics: Policy Making and the Federal Bureaucracy,* 3rd ed. Englewood Cliffs, N.J.: Prentice-Hall, 1983. Important and innovative study on the powers of the federal agencies.

GRUBER, JUDITH E. *Controlling Bureaucracies: Dilemmas in Democratic Governance.* Berkeley, Cal.: University of California Press, 1987. Theories and case studies of how a democracy might control its bureaucracies.

LAPALOMBARA, JOSEPH, AND FRED W. RIGGS, EDS. *Bureaucracy and Political Development.* Princeton, N.J.: Princeton University Press, 1963. Excellent collection on how bureaucrats may impede or enhance national development.

MOSHER, FREDERICK C. *A Tale of Two Agencies: A Comparative Analysis of the General Accounting Office and the Office of Management and Budget.* Baton Rouge, La.: Louisiana State University Press, 1984. Interesting study of two parallel agencies, one congressional and the other executive, that look at the same subject from different angles.

RIPLEY, RANDALL A., AND GRACE A. FRANKLIN. *Congress, the Bureaucracy, and Public Policy,* 3rd ed. Homewood, Ill.: Dorsey Press, 1984. Solid study of how congressional-bureaucratic interactions tend to preserve the status-quo.

ROURKE, FRANCIS E. *Bureaucracy, Politics, and Public Policy,* 3rd ed. Boston: Little, Brown, 1984. Good introduction to the field as a whole.

SIMON, HERBERT A. *Administrative Behavior,* 3rd ed. New York: Free Press, 1976. By a political scientist who won a Nobel prize in economics, this study lays the foundation for much contemporary work on bureaucracies.

STARLING, GROVER. *Managing the Public Sector,* 3rd ed. Chicago: Dorsey, 1986. Good roundup text that includes Reagan's efforts to fix the bureaucracy.

SULEIMAN, EZRA N., ED. *Bureaucrats and Policy Making.* New York: Holmes & Meier, 1984. Collection of essays on how civil servants get their way in several countries.

WEBER, MAX. *Theory of Social and Economic Organization.* Glencoe, Ill.: Free Press, 1958. One of the earliest and perhaps most influential studies of public administration.

WILDAVSKY, AARON. *The Politics of the Budgetary Process,* 4th ed. Boston: Little, Brown, 1984. A specialist in the budget process examines how it operates.

WILSON, JAMES Q. *The Politics of Regulation.* New York: Basic Books, 1980. A conservative takes a critical look at government regulation.

[21]See Gary Bryner, "Congress, Courts, and Agencies: Equal Employment and the Limits of Policy Implementation," *Political Science Quarterly* 96 (Fall 1981):3.

chapter 16

Legal Systems and the Courts

The yearning for "equal justice under law" is one of the human race's oldest aspirations. Justice Oliver Wendell Holmes once remarked, "My freedom to swing my arm stops where the other man's nose begins." Because humans are social beings, their freedom of action must have its limits if the freedom of all is to be preserved. But who decides what these limits are? Without a legal system, force alone would settle disputes. Even in primitive societies, two parties who disagree often look to an objective third party to provide a solution. Modern nations depend on laws to regulate human relations, and courts help to maintain order by enforcing these laws.

However, courts and laws may favor certain groups over others. In recent decades, the United States has become concerned with ensuring equal treatment under law for men and women of all races, religions, and economic means. Both lawmakers and courts play important roles in establishing this equality.

For example, federal laws have eliminated lynching, which was fairly common in the southern states at the turn of the century and in which 85 percent of the victims were black. Similarly, racial segregation gradually gave way to the persistent and patient legal work that ended in the Supreme Court's landmark ruling in *Brown v. Board of Education of Topeka* (1954). This decision, the first of many to establish the principle that racial segregation is a violation of the U.S. Constitution, produced a revolution in American race relations. Some violence did take place, and the battle is by no means over. But to appreciate the importance of law to the civil rights movement, compare the position of the American black to that of the South African black. In South Africa, the whole legal system supports segregation, making violence the only avenue of change.

The law does more than resolve private conflicts among individuals and social groups, granting rights and privileges and imposing duties and responsibilities. Law is also an expression of society's goals and aspirations. The passage of child labor laws, for instance, expressed society's determination to eliminate a practice it had come to regard as a social evil. Changes in the law—in regard to the legality of labor unions, for example—indicated changes in the thinking of the people as a whole with respect to specific questions. Although the law is often slow to catch up with changing mores, it usually does catch up with them in democratic societies because the legislators, who represent the people who elect them, change the laws to suit the voters' new goals and desires. Not everyone agrees about using law to bring about social change, however. Some suggest that Americans place too much of a burden on the law and endanger its status by expecting it to resolve all social and political problems.

THE NATURE OF LAW

What is Law?

For our purposes, law may be defined as "that which must be obeyed and followed by citizens, subject to sanctions or legal consequences."[1] Terms such as *higher law* or *natural law* have appeared in political and social philosophy since

[1] *Black's Law Dictionary*, 5th abridged ed. (St. Paul, Minn.: West Publishing, 1983).

the beginning of recorded civilization. In the Western tradition, the concept of a "higher law" grew out of a mingling of Stoic philosophy and the Judeo-Christian tradition. Higher law was attributed to God or the Creator and was thus higher than laws made by humans. Our own system depends on the idea that people are "endowed by their Creator" with the rights to life, liberty, and the pursuit of happiness, and the right to own property and enjoy the fruits of one's labor—rights that no just government can take away. Many argue that this so-called higher law takes precedence over the laws enacted by humans, and some justify their defiance of society's laws by citing the higher law of nature. Mahatma Gandhi in India and Martin Luther King, Jr., in the United States claimed that their actions, which were violations of existing man-made laws, were morally correct because they conformed to the higher edicts of natural law. However, to focus our discussion, we will restrict ourselves to the definition of law given at the beginning of this paragraph.

Types of Law

Our complex society requires many types of law. There are five major branches of law:

Criminal Law.   In these days when fear of crime is a persistent feature of our lives, it is the workings of the criminal law system that we hear, read, and think most about. Modern criminal law is largely statutory (or code) law and covers a specific category of wrongs committed against persons or institutions. Acts defined as criminal are considered social evils and are threats to the entire community because they disturb the public order or threaten the public welfare. Consequently, the state rather than the aggrieved party is always the prosecutor (plaintiff). Offenses are usually divided into three categories. Petty offenses, such as traffic violations, are normally punished by a fine. Offenses that are somewhat more serious but not major (for example, gambling and prostitution) are known as *misdemeanors* and are characteristically punishable by larger fines or short jail sentences. Major crimes, called *felonies* (for example, rape, murder, robbery, extortion), are punished by imprisonment. In the United States, some criminal offenses (such as kidnapping and interstate car theft) are federal in nature; others (murder, rape, and mugging) are mainly state concerns; and a few (bank robbery and drug traffic, for instance) violate both state and federal criminal laws.

Civil Law.   Many legislative acts (statutes) govern civil rather than criminal matters. Marriage and divorce, custody of children and inheritance, and bankruptcy and the conduct of business are civil concerns. Not every contingency is covered by a statute, however, and in the English-speaking countries, statutory law is supplemented by common law (judge-made law based on precedent) and equity law. Civil law is distinguished from criminal law in that it provides redress for private individuals or corporations who feel that injuries have been done to them. Because a breach of civil obligation is not regarded as endangering the peace or welfare of the community, private individuals conduct most civil litigation.

Unfortunately, both common law and statutory law have one major drawback: they can only provide redress (usually a monetary award) after an injury has been done; they cannot prevent it. Equity (or chancery) law was developed in England to remedy this defect. Arising as an appeal to the "king's conscience," it traditionally dealt with property matters (for example, estates, inheritances, and real estate). Only one feature of it, the injunctive process, is still used widely. An injunction is a court order requiring the person or persons to whom it is directed to do or not to do a particular thing. Equity law can therefore provide a preventive mechanism.

Constitutional Law. Written constitutions are usually general documents that describe the organs of government, their powers, and individual guarantees of freedom. General legislation and court interpretation must fill in the details. An important role of the courts, under a constitutional system of government such as ours, with the recognized authority of judicial review, is to make sure that statutory laws and their administrative interpretations do not violate the spirit or meaning of the constitution. Constitutional law in the United States is mainly composed of the judicial decisions which interpret the various sections of the Constitution.

In the United States, with its tradition of judicial review, the ultimate responsibility of interpreting the Constitution rests with the U.S. Supreme Court. The Supreme Court's interpretations of the Constitution change with time. The cliché, "The Constitution is what the Supreme Court says it is," is not unfounded. In 1896, for example, the Court ruled, in *Plessy v. Ferguson,* that state laws requiring racial segregation in public transportation did not necessarily violate the Fourteenth Amendment, which provides for equal protection under the laws, as long as the transportation facilities for whites and blacks were physically equal. Fifty-eight years later the court reversed itself and ruled that separate public education facilities for whites and blacks are *inherently* unequal, even if physically alike. The Constitution didn't change, but society's conception of individual rights did. Constitutional law (indeed, law itself) is not static, but a living, growing institution.

Administrative Law. A relatively recent development, administrative law includes the regulatory orders enacted by appropriate government agencies. Administrative law develops when regulatory agencies interpret the statutes that Congress has enacted. For example, a federal statute prohibits "unfair or deceptive acts" in commerce. But what business practices are "unfair or deceptive"? The Federal Trade Commission must decide. As the agencies interpret the meaning of Congress's laws, they begin to build up a body of regulations and case law that guides the commission in its future decisions. Administrative rulings may be appealed to the federal courts. The federal government now codifies administrative regulations, and a fairly substantial body of administrative law has grown up in the past half century.

International Law. International law consists of international treaties and conventions and long-established customs recognized by most nations. It is a very special body of law, because it cannot be enforced in the same way as national law. Treaties and agreements among nations may be signed, but their effectiveness depends mainly on voluntary compliance, reciprocal benefit, and threat, coercion, or deprivation. More important, neither domestic nor international courts are always able to ensure that judicial decisions will be executed. Matters are further complicated by the fact that not all states subscribe to existing rules of law. For example, whereas the United States and the USSR comply with the limited Nuclear Test Ban Treaty, which they and several other nations signed in 1963, neither France nor China is a party to the treaty and each continues nuclear testing in the atmosphere. Hence, New Zealand can do no more than protest the radioactive effects of French tests. To be sure, there is an International Court of Justice at the Hague, but it hears only those cases that states bring to it voluntarily. Thus, the system can work only when the individual nations respect the rules. For example, when the court ruled against the United States in 1985 for aiding the Nicaraguan *contras* in their war against the Managua regime, the United States just ignored the verdict and there was nothing to be done. International law is a legal system in that it has built up a fairly uniform body of law over the centuries, but it lacks the cohesion and enforceability we are accustomed to in domestic law.

Legal Systems

Legal systems consist of two major elements used to govern society: a recognized body of law and an enforcement apparatus. In primitive cultures the system is oral and consists of the mores, traditions, and beliefs that govern behavior. In modern society, legal systems are largely codified, that is, embodied in written laws. Committing the systems to writing makes them more precise in intent and, thus, usually more uniform in application.

Legal codification began in ancient times and has been a major feature in the development of civilization. The Ten Commandments and the Code of Hammurabi—still influential—are among the earliest examples of law codes. However, the supreme legal code of the ancient world was Roman law. Its details, covering all aspects of social life, were based on the idea that "right reason" should govern man's affairs. They were so universal, flexible, and logical that they are still in use in much of the world today.[2] Roman law was incorporated by the Catholic church in its *canon law,* and in the East by the Byzantine Emperor Justinian. The

---

[2]See W. W. Buckland and A. D. McNair, *Roman Law and Common Law* (New York: Oxford University Press, 1936); and B. Schwartz, ed., *The Code Napoleon and the Common Law World* (New York: New York University Press, 1956).

celebrated Code of Justinian *(Corpus Juris Civilis),* based on Roman law and dating from approximately A.D. 533, is the foundation that Europe's modern legal systems (with the important exception of Britain's) were built on. After a long intermediate period during which the more primitive Germanic and Salic systems were used, Roman law was revived in the twelfth century, partly because of the work being done in medieval universities by legal scholars. Modern European law, then, is mostly an amalgamation of Roman, feudal, and ecclesiastical law.

The English Common Law

Development. The English common law, originally based on the customary usage of the Angles and Saxons who settled Britain, developed after the Norman Conquest in 1066 and during the reign of Henry I (1100–35).[3] At this time, feudal lords and the Church dispensed justice. Henry began the practice of tightening royal control over the administration of justice. In this way, he made it more uniform and less subject to the whims of the barons. It was Henry II (1154–89), however, who did the important work of legal reform. New legal remedies (such as trial by jury), new modes of litigation, and new forms of action were created. The principles of the grand jury were also developed at this time. Itinerant royal judges began traveling throughout the kingdom, and the feudal and ecclesiastical courts thus lost influence. Over time, the itinerant judges came to use similar principles to decide similar cases in different parts of the kingdom, and there emerged a judge-made body of law which was "common" to all of England. Eventually, the new system led to a regular system of royal courts.

By the opening of the thirteenth century, this entire structure of royal justice rested on the shoulders of the humble "JP." A local citizen appointed by the Crown, the justice of the peace (JP) was supposed to take custody of prisoners until the king's judges arrived to try them. As time passed, the JP began to take on limited judicial functions. For example, he had authority to try minor infractions of law and supervise local police functions; later he was allowed to perform civil marriage ceremonies. The traveling royal justices, the common law courts, and the JPs laid the foundation for the development of English common law.

Features. In administering justice, the judges and courts were forced to improvise. Most of the early judges had a clerical education and were familiar with Roman law as interpreted by the Church. Accordingly, when royal law proved inadequate to the case at hand, the judges applied Roman and canon law provisions. If these were not applicable, they relied on their own common sense and judgment as well as the common practices of the English people. Over the centuries, a substantial body of common law developed—an amalgam of Roman law, church law, and local English customs.

[3]Good histories are T. F. T. Pluckett, *A Concise History of the Common Law,* 2d ed. (New York: Lawyer's Cooperative, 1936); and Oliver Wendell Holmes, Jr., *The Common Law* (Boston: Little, Brown, 1881).

Common law has three distinctive features. First, it is *case* law. That is, it is based on individual legal decisions rather than on a comprehensive code of statutes. Second, common law was made by *judicial decision* (it is "judge-made" law), and thus has great flexibility. Judges can easily reinterpret or modify previous rulings and principles to fit new social and economic circumstances and institutions. Third, common law relies heavily on *stare decisis,* or precedent. Because no two cases are exactly alike, a judge can pick on the smallest point of difference to justify a ruling that breaks precedent. In this way, common law is kept relevant to changing social needs. With the rise of Parliament as a dominant institution in seventeenth-century England, statute law supplemented (and in some cases supplanted) specific provisions of the common law. Today, when the two conflict, statute law always takes precedence.

Significance. Despite the fact that common law has declined somewhat in importance, its influence is still considerable. It has remained important in the legal systems of England, the United States, Canada, Australia, New Zealand, and a number of former British colonies. In many instances, statute law is formal enactment, with minor modifications, of existing common law provisions. A pervasive effect of the common law is that it shaped the development of English society and politics and gave distinctive habits of thought to all English-speaking societies.

Code (Roman) Law

Development. The legal systems of continental Europe (France, in particular) developed very differently from that of England. Feudalism was stronger in France than anywhere else, and until the thirteenth century the feudal lords were virtually independent of royal control. Unifying the country was a long, drawn-out process, with the local lords resisting the central government. The process was finally completed under Louis XIII's reign (1610–43), mainly because of his brilliant advisor, Cardinal Richelieu. Roman law, meanwhile, was enjoying a revival because of the work of legal scholars and changing conditions in Europe. Central governments were asserting themselves throughout Europe, and commerce was reviving on a large scale. It was becoming obvious that some form of centralized justice would be needed for this new age. French jurists, in particular, saw the value of Roman law. It was universal and written. If this law could work so well for the ancient world, why not introduce it into France? Many of its principles, in fact, were already in use because of canon law. The job that remained was codification.

Codifying the law was Napoleon's lasting contribution to the rationalization of justice for France and, eventually, for most of Europe. The Code Napoleon (1804) was the first modern codification of European law. Feudal laws were bypassed, and the emancipation of civil law from religious influence— begun during the French Revolution— was maintained. Although it preserved many of the gains of the revolution, such as the elimination of torture and arbitrary arrest and imprisonment, as well as the guaranteeing of civil liberty and civil equality, it also reflected Napoleon's authoritarian views. These views are seen in the provisions concerning family life: the father's authority was firmly established, and the status of women was depressed. Nevertheless, the code was a great step forward, and Napoleon's invasions of Belgium, Spain, Italy, and Germany brought the code to these countries; their legal systems are still based on it. It is also in use in Louisiana, and European colonists carried it to Asia and Africa later on in the nineteenth century. The tight centralization of French life today is a reflection of its basic philosophy.

Features.   Today, most of the Western world lives under some form of Roman law as interpreted by the Code Napoleon.[4] Most code law is detailed, precise (more so than the written laws in the common-law countries), comprehensive, and understandable by laypersons. Judges are not expected to "make" law, merely to apply it. Precedent carries less weight. Another feature of Roman law is that the judiciary is not independent of the executive (as it is in the Anglo-American system). Therefore, its powers of judicial review are quite limited—either shared with the legislative branch or assigned to a special national court. In Italy, for example, only the *Corte Costituzionale* can rule on the constitutionality of legislation, and the regular supreme court must assume that laws are constitutional unless this court rules otherwise.

Common Features of Both Legal Systems

The differences between the common law and the Roman system are self-evident. The former is general and largely judge-made, and it relies on precedent and custom. The latter is specific and is largely the product of legislation. It is interesting to note that both systems developed to serve the needs of modernizing and centralizing monarchs—Henry I and II in England and Louis XIII and Napoleon in France.

The differences between these two systems should not obscure their similarities; in fact, they are becoming more and more alike. As the volume of statute law increases in the English-speaking nations, the importance and relevance of common law decreases. More and more, the details of legislative enactment are being outlined by administrative agencies, whose regulations are now an integral part of the legal system. In both systems, the law is relatively uniform in its application, universal in its scope, and amenable to change.

THE COURTS, THE BENCH, AND THE BAR

As legal systems developed, so did judicial systems, for it is these systems that handle the day-to-day administration of the law. The organization of a judicial system is always hierarchical, which means that the courts are ranked in a specific

---

[4]Schwartz, *The Code Napoleon and the Common Law World.*

order. The different courts have specific jurisdiction; that is, they generally hear different kinds of cases and have authority in specific geographical areas.

The U.S. Court System

Our court system is unique, consisting of fifty-one judicial structures: the national system, composed of the federal courts, and fifty state systems. A confusing element is that the federal system overlaps that of the states. The federal courts hear many cases in which the issue is one of state laws but where the parties to the litigation are citizens of different states, the so-called "diversity jurisdiction." Also, of course, they hear cases involving the application of federal laws. Conversely, issues of federal law (constitutional or statutory) may arise in the course of a litigation in state court. In that situation, as considered below, the Supreme Court of the United States (SCOTUS) has jurisdiction to review the state court's judgment insofar as it turns on a determination of the federal question.

The National Court Structure. The federal district court is at the base of the national court system.[5] Congress has divided the nation into ninety-four federal court districts employing over 500 judges. The district court is a trial court and hears a wide variety of civil suits arising under federal law as well as criminal cases involving federal infractions. It also exercises the "diversity" jurisdiction noted above. In many criminal cases, where the accused is charged with violating state law as well as federal law, the defendants are turned over to state criminal courts for trial. Bank robbery, kidnapping, and auto theft are examples of offenses that often have interstate ramifications and hence may violate both state and federal laws.

Federal district court decisions can be appealed to a U.S. court of appeals. There are thirteen courts of appeals presided over by 132 judges. Besides hearing appeals from the district courts within its circuit, a court of appeals may also review the rulings of administrative tribunals and commissions, such as the Federal Trade Commission, the Federal Aviation Administration, and the Food and Drug Administration. Each court of appeals consists of three or more judges, depending on need, and arguments are heard by panels of three judges. For the most part, these courts do not question the facts of the case, but consider only whether or not the law has been misinterpreted or misapplied. The court of appeals bases its majority-vote verdict on the appeal primarily on the briefs submitted by the attorneys for both parties to the dispute; oral arguments are quite limited.

At the pinnacle of the federal court system stands the United States Supreme Court, consisting of one chief justice and eight associate justices. Its jurisdiction is almost entirely appellate. The nation's highest court, unlike a

[5]See Robert A. Carp and Ronald Stidham, *The Federal Courts* (Washington, D.C.: Congressional Quarterly Press, 1985).

U.S. SUPREME COURT: Eight associate justices flank Chief Justice William Rehnquist.

Supreme Court Historical Society

court of appeals, is not obliged to hear every case presented to it, and it accepts for a review only a small fraction of the petitions for review that it receives. The Supreme Court will generally not agree to hear a case unless it involves a substantial constitutional question, a treaty, or some significant point of federal law. Here we see the importance of precedent, because the Court's ruling will establish a basis for future decisions. In addition to hearing cases arising in the lower federal courts, the Supreme Court will review cases that come from the state supreme courts if a substantial federal question, constitutional or statutory, is presented. For example, if a state supreme court declares a federal statute unconstitutional, it is almost certain that the U.S. Supreme Court will hear the case.

The State Court System.   Each of the fifty states maintains and operates its own court system. Perhaps 90 percent of the nation's legal business is handled in the state courts. Most of the cases that come before them are civil in nature. Generally, state trial courts operate at the county level, although a number of sparsely populated rural counties may be combined into a single court district. These courts have original jurisdiction in all civil and criminal cases and can hear appeals from local justice of the peace courts and magistrate's courts.

At the local level, justice of the peace courts in rural counties try minor matters and criminal infractions. In urban areas, there are magistrate's or police courts that have jurisdiction over minor traffic cases, violations of city ordinances, and misdemeanors such as public drunkenness. For the most part, these local courts operate without juries because serious cases are handled by the state courts. Most of the penalties they impose are fines or short jail terms.

Judges

The Federal Judges. Federal judges are nominated for the federal bench by the president and are appointed with the advice and consent of the Senate. Federal judges hold their positions during "good behavior," which generally means that they serve for life unless impeached and convicted for criminal behavior. The purpose of a "lifetime" appointment is to free the judges from executive and other political pressure.

Federal judges are invariably lawyers. Some undoubtedly owe their appointments to political favors, but they are usually knowledgeable in the law. The attorney general will draw up a list of eligible candidates; as vacancies occur, the president selects a few names from that list. Before the names are made public, it has been the practice for the president to consult with the American Bar Association (ABA), which rates the judges. Although the president is not obliged to take the ABA's advice, he is usually influenced by it. At the same time, the FBI inquires into the candidates' past and present activities. The Senate must approve all federal judges, and sometimes this generates controversy. Appointees of Nixon and Reagan, charged by Senate Democrats as marginally qualified, withdrew from consideration. In 1986, the vice-president broke a Senate tie to confirm the appointment of a controversial individual as a federal judge.

Some presidents—Eisenhower, for example—have argued that the federal judiciary should be nonpartisan, or at the very least bipartisan. Eisenhower appointed some Democrats to the federal bench (including Supreme Court Justice William J. Brennan) and made an effort to achieve a balance between judicial liberals and judicial conservatives. Most presidents, however, appoint men of their own political party who share their judicial philosophy. President Johnson, for example, appointed Thurgood Marshall—a liberal who believed that the Court should take an active role in promoting social justice—to the Supreme Court. President Nixon, in contrast, appointed four justices whose general political philosophy was conservative and who believed that the Warren Court of the 1950s and 1960s went too far in protecting the rights of the individual, to the detriment of society as a whole. President Reagan followed the Nixon example with the appointment of a conservative who happened to be a woman, Sandra Day O'Connor, the first female on the Court.

The State Judges. State judges are popularly elected or appointed, for terms ranging up to fourteen years. Both parties often nominate the same slate of judges, so that the judicial elections have become largely nonpartisan affairs; only rarely do party fights for a judicial office take place. In a 1986 referendum, Californians ousted their state chief justice, Rose Bird, who had been totally opposed to the death penalty. California justices are appointed but later have to be confirmed by voters.

COMPARING COURTS

What role should judges play? Should they act as umpires, passively watching the legal drama, confining their responsibility to simply ruling on disputed points of procedure? Or should they actively direct the course of the trial, question witnesses, elicit evidence, and comment on the proceedings as they unfold? The idea of judges playing such a role would undoubtedly seem strange—if not harmful—to those of us who have been raised within the common law framework. Yet, in code law countries, judges play just such an active role, and this is one of the crucial differences between the common law and code law systems.

The Anglo-American Adversary and Accusatorial Process. English and American courts are passive institutions in that they do not look for injustices to correct, and they do not apprehend or search out lawbreakers. Instead, they wait until a law is challenged or broken by someone, and the case then works its way up the court system.

The Anglo-American system of justice operates on a set of principles that, together, make up the adversary and accusatorial process. In the adversary process, two sides (plaintiff and defendant) are vying for a favorable decision from an impartial court. The operating principles are as follows. First, the courts will not accept a case that does not involve a real conflict of interest; in other words, the plaintiff must demonstrate how, and in what ways, the defendant has caused damage. Second, once a case has been accepted for trial, the presiding judge acts as an umpire. Both parties present their evidence, call and cross-examine witnesses, and try to refute each other's arguments. The judge rules on the evidence and testimony to be admitted, sees that proper legal procedures are followed, and rules on disputed points of procedure. After both sides have presented their cases, the judge rules on the basis of the facts and the relevant law. If a jury is hearing the case, the judge will instruct the members as to the weight of the evidence (those factors that they may or may not consider). The judge makes an appropriate decision after the jury gives its verdict on the factual issues.

In criminal cases, the police investigate and report to the public prosecutor, who must decide whether prosecution is warranted. The actual trial proceeds much like a civil one: the government is the plaintiff, the accused the defendant, and the court controls the proceedings. Unless a jury has been waived, the jury determines the ultimate issue of guilt under instructions from the judge as to the governing law.

Many decisions of the Warren Court led to increased protection of the rights of the accused in situations where the investigating police officers were alleged to have invaded constitutional rights in gathering evidence. Some people felt the Warren Court's decisions threatened the rights of law-abiding citizens by making it easier for criminals to avoid conviction. With the conservative appointments of Nixon and Reagan, the Burger Court and the Rehnquist Court refined and modified some of these decisions to give a little more power to law officers.

The British Court System

The court system in operation in Britain today was established by the Judicature Act of 1873. For the most part, the system continues common law traditions and is divided into civil and criminal branches.

Selection and Tenure of Judges.   All British judges are appointed by the monarch on the advice of the prime minister, whose choices are based on recommendations of the lord chancellor, who presides over the House of Lords and is usually a cabinet member. To encourage independence, British judges are given lifetime tenure. By tradition, the English bench is supposed to be above party politics and is not supposed to make policy—a tradition bolstered by the fact that there is no judicial review of the constitutionality of legislation in Britain. Judicial review would be difficult in Britain because there is no written constitution. English courts, moreover, are less disposed to review administrative decisions to determine whether they are consistent with statutory grants of authority. The British judiciary is therefore weaker in relation to both the legislative and executive branches than in the United States.

Lawyer's Role.   Although the United States and Britain share a common legal heritage, there are important differences between their systems. One of the biggest distinctions is that in Britain the Crown hires lawyers to prosecute crimes. There are no professional prosecutors to parallel the district attorneys in the American system. Another difference is in the ordering of the legal profession. American lawyers, once they have passed the bar exam, may take on any type of legal work, in or out of the courtroom. British *solicitors* handle all legal matters except representing clients in court. That is reserved to a small number of lawyers called *barristers* who are specialists in courtroom procedure.

The French Court System

French courts, unlike the English courts, are not divided into separate criminal and civil divisions. Instead, France maintains separate systems of regular and administrative courts.[6] French judges sit as a panel to rule on points of law and procedure, but at the conclusion of the trial they retire *with* the jury to consider the verdict and the sentence. Obviously, there is great pressure on

---

[6]See René David, *French Law: Its Structure, Sources, and Methodology*, trans. Michael Kindred (Baton Rouge, La.: Louisiana State University Press, 1972).

the lay jurors to go along with the superior—or at least professional—knowledge and wisdom of the judges. Verdicts require at least an eight-to-four vote, which means that three judges and five of the jurors must agree. American jury decisions, by contrast, must be unanimous in most states.

Role of Judges in Adjudication: The Inquisitorial Process.

In code law countries—that is, throughout most of Europe—judges play a more active role than in common law countries. The prosecutor *(procureur)* is a police official who forwards evidence to an investigating judge *(juge d'instruction)*, a representative of the justice ministry who conducts a thorough inquiry *(enquête)*, gathering evidence and interrogating those involved. There is no parallel to the investigating judge in the Anglo-American system. The French (and Italian) judge first makes a preliminary determination of guilt *before* sending the case to trial, something that is quite out of bounds under the common law.

The major differences between Anglo-American and French criminal procedures are that (1) the decision to indict is not made by a grand jury but by a judge, and (2) the weight of evidence is not controlled by the adversaries (plaintiff and defendant) but by the court, which can take the initiative in acquiring needed evidence.

Another major point of difference in the two systems is that in the Anglo-American system the accused is presumed innocent until proven guilty; in France the assumptions are reversed. In an American or English court, the burden of proof is on the prosecution, and the defendant need not say one word in his or her defense; the prosecutor must prove guilt "beyond a reasonable doubt." In code law countries, the accused bears the burden of having to prove that the investigating judge is wrong.

Lawyer's Role.

Unlike a British or American trial lawyer, the French *avocat* does not question witnesses (the court does that). Instead, he or she tries to show logical or factual mistakes in the opposition's argument or case, attempting to sway the sympathy of the lay jury as in the summation argument of an American trial lawyer. For the most part, the role of the French lawyer is not as vital or creative as that of the English or American, for the court takes the initiative in discovering the facts of the case.

Law in the Soviet Union

The Legal System.

The basic concepts of Soviet law and the workings of the Soviet judicial process are quite different from those of the Western democracies, even though they are similar in strictly criminal—as opposed to political—matters.[7] Soviet law starts with Marx's idea that law exists to serve the ruling class. Capitalists naturally have bourgeois laws designed to protect private

---

[7]See John N. Hazard, *The Soviet Legal System,* 3rd ed. (Dobbs Ferry, N.Y.: Oceana Publications, 1977).

property. Proletarians, who are supposed to be in power in the Soviet Union, have socialist law to protect state property, the property of all society. Much Soviet law is concerned with state property, and those who steal or divert it can be executed by firing squad. Another part of Soviet law deals with sedition and subversion, areas of extremely minor importance in the West. Soviet citizens can receive harsh sentences to Siberia for "antistate activities" or "slandering the Soviet state," areas in which U.S. citizens would be protected by the First Amendment.

Cases with no political overtones are generally handled fairly under Soviet law. Prosecutors with powers similar to French investigating judges gather evidence and bring cases to court but sometimes take into account mitigating social factors and ask for lighter sentences. Defense attorneys are permitted, but they merely advise their clients on points of the law and do not challenge the prosecutor's evidence. There are no jury trials. Courts are organized federally and hierarchically up to the Supreme Court of the USSR. So far as is known, all judges in the Soviet Union are party members.

Some politically sensitive cases never come to trial, for the Soviets want to avoid bad publicity around the world. Obedient Soviet psychiatrists will diagnose dissidents as "sluggish schizophrenic" and put them in prison-like hospitals with no trial. Nobel Prize-winning writer Alexander Solzhenitsyn was simply bundled onto a plane for West Germany in 1974 with no trial. Likewise, dissident physicist Andrei Sakharov was banished to a remote city in 1980 to get him away from Western newsmen. The Committee on State Security (KGB) is so powerful, it sometimes acts independently of Soviet courts.

THE ROLE OF THE COURTS

In the United States, we look to the courts to strike down laws that violate the terms of the Constitution, and we expect the justices to leave their personal feelings and beliefs out of their interpretations. Judicial review is more highly developed in the United States than in any other country, and Americans expect more of their courts than do other peoples.

However, this function is not completely absent from the courts in other Western democracies. In Switzerland, for example, when cases from the cantonal (state) courts come before the Federal Tribunal (their supreme court), the tribunal determines whether a cantonal law violates the federal constitution. However, the tribunal does not pass on the constitutionality of laws passed by the Swiss parliament. The West German Constitutional Court reviews statutes to make sure they conform to the Basic Law, as Bonn's constitution is called.[8] The court, located in Karlsruhe, was included in the Basic Law partly on American insistence after World War II; it was a new concept for Europe. The Karlsruhe

---

[8]D. P. Kommers, *Judicial Politics in West Germany: A Study of the Federal Constitutional Court* (Beverly Hills, Cal.: Sage Publications, 1976).

court is composed of sixteen judges, eight elected by each house of parliament, who serve for nonrenewable twelve-year terms. The court decides cases between *Länder*, protects civil liberties, and outlaws dangerous political parties. Its decisions have been important. In the 1950s it found that both neo-Nazi and Communist parties wanted to overthrow the constitutional order and declared them illegal. It found that a 1974 abortion bill was in conflict with the strong right-to-life provisions of the Basic Law. Because the Constitutional Court operates with the more rigid Roman law, its decisions do not have the impact of U.S. Supreme Court decisions, which, under the common law, literally are the law of the land.

U.S. Supreme Court

The United States Supreme Court's power to review the constitutionality of federal legislative enactments is not mentioned specifically in the Constitution, and throughout much of our history the doctrine that the Supreme Court has this prerogative has been vehemently challenged.

The doctrine was first considered and debated at the Constitutional Convention of 1787. Delegates to that convention suggested that, when in doubt, legislators might call on the judges for an opinion on a proposed law's constitutionality. James Madison stated that a "law violating a constitution established by the people themselves would be considered by the judges as null and void." However, this position was challenged by those who believed that such a power would give the Court a double check and compromise its neutrality. Others felt it would violate the principle of separation of powers. Elbridge Gerry stated that it would make "statesmen of judges," a prophetic remark. At the close of the convention, judicial review had not been explicitly provided for. However, Alexander Hamilton supported the idea and, in *The Federalist* no. 78, which was written to promote ratification of the Constitution, he specifically stated that only the courts could limit legislative authority. John Marshall (chief justice of the Supreme Court from 1801 to 1835) agreed with this position; in fact, he went on record in favor of it nearly fifteen years before the landmark decision *Marbury v. Madison* (1803). Therefore, his assertion of the doctrine of judicial review in that case should have come as no surprise.

The doctrine has never been universally popular, however. Strong-willed presidents have tried to resist the authority of the Court. Thomas Jefferson, Andrew Jackson, Abraham Lincoln, and Franklin D. Roosevelt all differed sharply with equally strong-willed judges.

Marbury v. Madison. The background to *Marbury v. Madison* is as follows.[9] President John Adams, a Federalist, had appointed William Marbury, a

---

[9]Robert K. Carr, *The Supreme Court and Judicial Review* (New York: Holt, Rinehart and Winston, 1942); Robert H. Jackson, *The Struggle for Judicial Supremacy* (New York: Vintage Books, 1941), pp. 24–28; and Robert G. McCloskey, *The American Supreme Court* (Chicago: University of Chicago Press, 1960), pp. 40–47.

Washington, D.C., justice of the peace shortly before leaving office. For some unknown reason, however, Secretary of State John Marshall had neglected to deliver the commission to Marbury. Marshall's successor, the Republican[10] James Madison, refused to deliver the commission. Marbury brought suit in original jurisdiction before the Supreme Court, asking the Court to issue a writ of *mandamus* commanding Madison to deliver the commission. This presented the Court with something of a dilemma. If Chief Justice Marshall and the Supreme Court issued the writ, and Madison refused to deliver the commission, the prestige and authority of the Court would be dealt a severe blow. If, however, Marshall refused to issue the writ, he would in effect call into question the legitimacy of the hasty judicial appointments given to Federalists in the final days of the Adams administration. Marshall's solution was nothing short of brilliant, for it not only criticized Madison and Jefferson, but also established explicitly the principle of judicial review. On the one hand, Marshall ruled that Marbury was entitled to his commission and that Madison should have given it to him. On the other hand, however, he stated that the Supreme Court had no authority to issue a writ of *mandamus* in a case brought to it in original jurisdiction and that, because Section 13 of the Judiciary Act of 1789 implied otherwise, that part of the act was unconstitutional. The decision infuriated President Jefferson, for he understood all too well how cleverly Marshall had escaped the trap and asserted the authority of the Court into the bargain. He realized that the precedent for judicial review had been laid, and called it "both elitist and undemocratic."

From 1803 to 1857, the Supreme Court did not invalidate any act of Congress. In the latter year, it threw out the Missouri Compromise of 1820 that had barred slavery in the old Northwest Territory. This touched off a political storm that was to make Abraham Lincoln president. In the twentieth century, the doctrine has been used extensively. The court itself, however, has always been divided on how it should be used. Judicial "activists," led by Hugo Black,[11] William O. Douglas and Earl Warren, have argued that the Supreme Court must be vigilant in its protection of the Bill of Rights' guarantees. Advocates of judicial "restraint," such as Oliver Wendell Holmes, Felix Frankfurter, and Warren Burger, have argued that only Congress should make public policy, and that unless a legislative act clearly violates the Constitution, the law should stand. The Warren Court (1953–69), named after its chief justice, was markedly activist, issuing decisions in the areas of racial segregation, reapportionment, and rights of the accused that had substantial impacts on U.S. society. The Burger Court that followed was more cautious, reflecting the fact that seven of its members were appointed by conservative Republicans.

---

[10]The Republican party of 1803 was not the Republican party of today, which dates only from 1860. The former, roughly equivalent to the English Whigs of that time, was more liberal than the Federalist party.

[11]Black was an activist on Bill of Rights issues, not across the board.

The Supreme Court's Political Role

In this country, the Supreme Court's rulings have often become political issues. This is not true in other countries, simply because their courts do not have the authority and independence that our courts have. When the Supreme Court of Franklin Roosevelt's day ruled that many New Deal laws were unconstitutional, he referred to the justices contemptuously as "nine tired old men." Richard Nixon, in the 1968 campaign, charged that the Warren Court's liberal decisions had added to the crime problem and, by implication, had endangered the safety of society. It should be obvious by now that the justices do play important political roles. Moreover, the appointment of just one new justice can make an enormous difference. Suppose the Court frequently splits its decisions five to four. A new justice who sides frequently with the minority obviously turns it into a majority. Therefore, it is important to know whether, and to what extent, judges let their personal beliefs interfere with their decisions. Are their ideological views incompatible with the idea of the Court as an "impartial dispenser of justice"?[12]

The Views of Judges

However conscientiously judges may try to keep their personal beliefs out of decisions, their own outlook and background no doubt play some part in their work. Most Supreme Court justices are and have been white, Protestant, male, and from upper- or upper-middle-class families, most of whom can trace their origins to the British Isles. Those critics who claim that the judicial system is too conservative state that the judges cannot possibly identify with the needs of the poor or racially oppressed. But others argue that selecting judges from lower-class and minority groups will not ensure fairness; it will merely replace one set of prejudices with another.

There are other, more concrete factors that affect a judge's rulings. Southern jurists have been, traditionally, more conservative on racial matters. However, there are exceptions. One of the strongest champions of civil rights was Alabama's Hugo L. Black, who had been a member of the Ku Klux Klan during his youth. Similarly, eastern judges are expected to be more responsive to the needs of large industry than judges from farm states. Occupational background may also affect decision making; for example, former corporation lawyers may be more sympathetic than others to the problems of business. Some justices, like Louis D. Brandeis (one of five Jewish justices) and Thurgood Marshall (the only black justice), were active in reform and civil rights causes and brought their liberalism to the bench. Others who have served on state courts believe that the states' rights should be strengthened.

[12]For discussions of the political roles of the courts—especially the Supreme Court—see Glendon Schubert, *Judicial Policy-Making* (New York: Scott-Foresman, 1974); Donald L. Horowitz, *Courts and Social Policy* (Washington, D.C.: Brookings Institution, 1977); and Robert H. Birkby, *The Court and Public Policy* (Washington, D.C.: Congressional Quarterly Press, 1983).

The two most important influences on voting, however, seem to be political party affiliation and the justice's conception of the judicial role in the American system of government. Although we should be wary of generalizations, studies indicate that Democratic justices are much more likely to support liberal stands than are Republican justices.[13] Democrats tend to be judicial activists and to see the Supreme Court as a defender of oppressed minorities and economic groups. They are more likely to distrust state power and to favor an increase in federal authority, while also seeking to protect individual rights under the Fourteenth Amendment against state authority. Republicans, on the other hand, usually favor judicial restraint, are more likely to uphold state authority within the federal system of government, and are less likely than Democrats to apply Bill of Rights guarantees. There are, of course, exceptions to this pattern. When President Eisenhower appointed California Governor Earl Warren in 1953, he thought he was picking a good Republican with a "middle-of-the-road philosophy" as chief justice. Later Eisenhower called the choice "the biggest damned-fool mistake I ever made."[14]

Supreme Court justices are undoubtedly influenced by changing public attitudes. However, many justices see the Court's role as standing firm on certain constitutional principles, despite fluctuations in public opinion. Justice Jackson put it this way: "One's right to life, liberty and property, to free speech, a free press, freedom of worship and assembly, and other fundamental rights may not be submitted to vote; they depend upon the outcome of no election."

In the 1936 election, after the Court had struck down several important laws designed to alleviate the Depression, President Roosevelt was given the greatest mandate in the nation's history. In the following year, he submitted legislation that would have had the effect of expanding the Supreme Court to fifteen members and would have allowed every sitting justice over the age of seventy to retire at a sizeable pension. The plan failed because the people felt that Roosevelt was going too far in attacking the constitutional principle of an independent judiciary, but it did force the Court to look beyond its own narrow world and accept the fact that change could not be postponed indefinitely. Most legal scholars believe that the election of 1936 and the controversy over "court packing" led directly to the Court's becoming more restrained in dealing with New Deal legislation.[15] As one jokester put it, "A switch in time saves nine."

Still another influence on a Supreme Court justice is his colleagues' opinions. Both Chief Justices John Marshall (1801–35) and Earl Warren (1953–69) were able to convert some of their colleagues to their judicial

---

[13]For an unscholarly—and perhaps conjectural—look at the political viewpoints of Supreme Court justices, especially the shift from the Warren to the Burger Court, see Bob Woodward and Scott Armstrong, *The Brethren: Inside the Supreme Court* (New York: Simon and Schuster, 1979).

[14]Quoted in *The Supreme Court: Justice and the Law*, 3rd ed. (Washington, D.C.: Congressional Quarterly Press, 1983), p. 163.

[15]C. H. Pritchett, *The Roosevelt Court* (New York: Macmillan, 1948); and E. V. Rostow, *The Sovereign Prerogative* (New Haven, Conn.: Yale University Press, 1962).

philosophies by the force of their personalities as well as their judicial reasoning. In short, many factors—not all of them knowable—influence a given decision. Perhaps one factor overshadows all others, the fact that Supreme Court justices are appointed for life. They are independent and relatively immune to congressional, White House, and private-interest pressures. This may change them, and in unpredictable ways. Liberals may turn into conservatives, activists into restrainers, and vice versa. The seriousness of their position and the knowledge that their votes may alter the structure of America makes justices think deeply and sometimes change viewpoints. In the Supreme Court, as well as many other places, the office in considerable part makes its occupant.

Political Impact of the Court

Our legal system—in theory and practice—poses a basic conflict. On the one hand, justices are expected to be impartial; on the other hand, the importance of the Court gives them considerable political power. And in the twentieth century, this power is increasing. Earl Warren's court was as active as it was controversial, and in three key areas—civil rights, criminal rights, and legislative reapportionment—it substantially rewrote constitutional law.[16] In the opinion of some, as ninety-six southern members of Congress put it, the Court overturned "the established law of the land" and implemented its "personal political and social philosophy."

Civil Rights. The Supreme Court's decision in *Brown v. Board of Education of Topeka* (1954) led to crucial changes in American race relations. In a unanimous ruling, the Court accepted the sociological argument of Thurgood Marshall (then attorney for the NAACP) that segregated public school facilities were "inherently unequal" because they stigmatized black children and thus deprived them of the Fourteenth Amendment's guarantee of equal protection of the law. One year later, in *Brown* II (1955), the process of desegregation in the public schools was ordered to proceed "with all deliberate speed." Southern whites vowed massive resistance.

America's blacks, encouraged by this legal support, attempted to gain equal treatment in other areas. By 1963, passive resistance had given way to massive confrontation. In *Lombard v. Louisiana* (1963), the Warren Court supported by implication the sit-in tactic, ruling that blacks who had refused to leave a segregated lunch counter could not be prosecuted where it appeared that the state was involved in unequal treatment of the races, relying on the command of the Fourteenth Amendment that no state may deny any person the equal protection of the laws. The sit-in had become a major weapon in the civil rights struggle. In 1964 Congress followed the Court's lead when it passed the

---

[16]For good accounts of the Warren Court's decisions, see Archibald Cox, *The Warren Court* (Cambridge, Mass.: Harvard University Press, 1968), and Bernard Schwartz, *Inside the Warren Court* (New York: Doubleday, 1983).

Civil Rights Act, which barred segregation in public accommodations such as hotels, motels, restaurants, and theaters.

Criminal Justice. The Warren Court's rulings in the area of criminal justice and procedural rights in state criminal cases were even more disturbing to many Americans. An important case in this area was *Mapp v. Ohio* (1961), in which the Court ruled that except in exigent circumstances, evidence seized by police without a warrant was inadmissable in a state court. In 1963, *Gideon v. Wainwright,* the Court held that unless they waive the right, indigent defendants charged with misdemeanors or felonies must be provided with legal counsel. In *Escobedo v. Illinois* (1964), in a five-to-four decision it ruled that a suspect could not be denied the right to have a lawyer during police questioning and that any confessions so obtained could not be used in court. One of the Court's most controversial rulings came in 1966 in the case of *Miranda v. Arizona.* The majority (five to four) ruled that as soon as a suspect is detained by the police, he or she must be told of the right to remain silent and to have a lawyer present during police questioning. Once again the Court had upset local criminal procedures, and once again its ruling was unpopular.

Legislative Reapportionment. Equally controversial was the Supreme Court's "one man, one vote" ruling. Until 1962, state legislative districts had been gerrymandered notoriously, and yet the Supreme Court had consistently maintained that only the states and Congress had the right to draw electoral boundaries. This meant that in many states rural districts were grossly over-represented and cities underrepresented. In a series of decisions in 1962 and 1964, the Warren Court found that unequal representation denied citizens their Fourteenth Amendment (equal protection) rights. The Court ordered that state legislatures apply the principle of "one man, one vote" in redrawing electoral lines.

Much of this angered people who felt they had been hurt: segregationists who didn't like to share schools or other accommodations with blacks, police who felt hampered in dealing with suspects, and rural people who wanted a more-than-equal vote. There were billboards shouting "Impeach Earl Warren," and Nixon in 1968 ran as much against the Supreme Court as against Hubert Humphrey. The Warren Court overthrew Jim Crow laws, rewrote the rules for criminal procedure, and redrew legislative maps. With the possible exception of the Marshall Court, it was the most active, ground-breaking Court in U.S. history.

The Burger Court. The Burger Court was characterized as conservative, an effort to roll back some of the decisions of the Warren court. Actually, the Burger Court was not so clear-cut. Overall, there probably was a conservative drift, but an unpredictable one. On affirmative-action programs to help blacks, for example, the Court seemed to contradict itself. In the 1978 *Bakke* case, the Burger Court found that reserving quotas for black applicants to medical school violated equal protection for whites.[17] The following year, though, in *Weber,* the Court found that it was all right to have quotas to help black workers attain skilled positions. In criminal procedure, the Burger Court became increasingly hard-line. It found in *Arkansas v. Sanders* (1979) that police needed a warrant to open the suitcase of a suspected drug dealer—the kind of decision the Warren Court might have come out with. On the other hand, in *Rhode Island v. Innis* (1980), it allowed police to use "subtle compulsion" to get a murder suspect to incriminate himself by telling police where he put his shotgun. The Warren Court, following its own *Miranda* decision, probably would have called *Innis* interrogation without counsel. The Burger Court found in *Gregg v. Georgia* (1976) that capital punishment is not necessarily "cruel and unusual" if the rules for applying it are fair. In 1984 the Court added a "good faith exception" to the rule excluding wrongfully seized evidence, tilting the law a bit more toward the police and against the accused. In sum, the Burger Court seems to have modified rather than repudiated the Warren Court.[18] The Rehnquist Court bids to become much more conservative.

Limitations on the Court

Despite the fact that the Court's decisions made basic changes in American society, the Supreme Court cannot just rewrite the law. Institutional as well as noninstitutional checks on its authority do exist. For one thing, the Court hears only a handful of the cases brought before it. Once the Court has ruled, moreover, Congress can propose—and the states may enact—constitutional amendments to reverse Court rulings. The Sixteenth Amendment, for instance, reversed a Supreme Court ruling that said that the federal income tax was unconstitutional. Congress can also redefine the authority of the Supreme Court, removing whole areas of litigation from the Court's appellate jurisdiction. In addition, the Court must rely on the chief executive to enforce its rulings, and he can always refuse. In the famous words of Andrew Jackson, "John Marshall has made his decision, now let him enforce it." If Eisenhower had not sent federal troops to Little Rock in 1958, its schools would not have been desegregated despite the Court's 1954 ruling. Moreover, lower federal courts have been known to ignore or evade Supreme Court rulings with which they disagree. Finally, no law and no court order can be enforced well, or for long, unless it has substantial popular support. The Supreme Court cannot afford to get too far ahead or too far behind public opinion. The Court's leftward swing in 1937 and the Rehnquist Court's rightward swing illustrate the importance of public opinion to the Court.

The federal courts are thus an integral part of the policy-making apparatus of government—not just mechanical interpreters of law. They are

---

[17]See Timothy J. O'Neill, *Bakke & the Politics of Equality: Friends & Foes in the Classroom of Litigation* (Middletown, Conn.: Wesleyan University Press, 1985).

[18]See Vincent Blasi, ed., *The Burger Court: The Counter-Revolution That Wasn't* (New Haven, Conn.: Yale University Press, 1983).

involved in the political process in three distinct ways. First, judges are selected on the basis of their political party affiliation and judicial philosophy. Second, judicial decisions in such areas as civil rights and economic matters are influenced by politics. Groups whose welfare depends on the Court's decisions will try to influence the Court to adopt their point of view; and groups that do not succeed with the president or Congress hope that they will have better luck with the courts. Finally, Supreme Court decisions *technically* bind only those parties in the case decided by the Court. By extension, however, such rulings set precedents for similar cases, but the lower courts must decide how and in what ways previous rulings affect the cases that they are considering.

SUGGESTED READINGS

ABRAHAM, HENRY J. *The Judicial Process,* 5th ed. New York: Oxford University Press, 1986. Introduction to the U.S. judicial process from a comparative perspective.

BAUM, LAWRENCE. *The Supreme Court,* 2d ed. Washington, D.C.: Congressional Quarterly Press, 1984. Excellent introduction that includes recent trends.

BERGER, RAOUL. *Government by Judiciary: The Transformation of the Fourteenth Amendment.* Cambridge, Mass.: Harvard University Press, 1977. A noted authority looks at the uses of the equal-protection amendment.

CAPPELLETTI, M., AND W. COHEN. *Comparative Constitutional Law: Cases and Materials.* Indianapolis, Ind.: Bobbs-Merrill, 1979. Rare comparative look at constitutional law, the sort of thing political scientists used to do.

COX, ARCHIBALD. *The Warren Court.* Cambridge, Mass.: Harvard University Press, 1968. A legal scholar, the special Watergate prosecutor fired by Nixon, assesses the activist Supreme Court under Earl Warren.

DWORKIN, RONALD. *Law's Empire.* Cambridge, Mass.: Harvard University Press, 1986. A literate and sophisticated argument for judicial activism.

FRIENDLY, FRED W., AND MARTHA J. H. ELLIOTT. *The Constitution: That Delicate Balance.* New York: Random House, 1984. Lucid, readable introduction to the Supreme Court's great cases by a former TV newsman.

JACOB, HERBERT. *Law and Politics in the United States: An Introduction.* Boston: Little, Brown, 1986. Good review and synthesis of U.S. legal system and its impact on politics.

JOHNSON, CHARLES A., AND BRADLEY C. CANON. *Judicial Policies: Implementation and Impact.* Washington, D.C.: Congressional Quarterly Press, 1984. Explores how judicial trends impact on various sectors of the U.S. population.

MASON, ALPHEUS THOMAS. *The Supreme Court from Taft to Burger.* Baton Rouge, La.: Louisiana State Press, 1979. Top authority charts changes in the Court's decisions and philosophies.

MASON, ALPHEUS THOMAS, WILLIAM M. BEANEY, AND DONALD GRIER STEPHENSON, JR. *American Constitutional Law: Introductory Essays and Selected Cases,* 7th ed. Englewood Cliffs, N.J.: Prentice-Hall, 1983. Excellent compilation covering all major decisions.

O'BRIEN, DAVID M. *Storm Center: The Supreme Court in American Politics.* New York: Norton, 1986. A worried look at the growth and fragmentation of the Supreme Court under Burger.

PELTASON, J. W. *Corwin and Peltason's Understanding the Constitution,* 10th ed. New York: Holt, Rinehart and Winston, 1985. Latest update of a classic.

SILVERSTEIN, MARK. *Constitutional Faiths: Felix Frankfurter, Hugo Black, and the Process of Judicial Decision Making.* Ithaca, N.Y.: Cornell University Press, 1984. Intellectual portraits of two highly influential justices.

STRUM, PHILIPPA. *Louis D. Brandeis: Justice for the People.* Cambridge, Mass.: Harvard University Press, 1984. Readable account of the liberal Supreme Court Justice and his progressive causes.

TRIBE, LAURENCE H. *Constitutional Choices.* Cambridge, Mass.: Harvard University Press, 1985. A critical analysis of the Burger court finds too much pragmatism and too little philosophy.

WITT, ELDER. *A Different Justice: Reagan and the Supreme Court.* Washington, D.C.: Congressional Quarterly Press, 1986. How Reagan has reshaped the Supreme Court to take a less-interventionist stance.

chapter 17

Public Policy

Everything we have discussed so far serves as a prelude for our consideration of public policy. We have looked at the various inputs into politics and how they are processed by the institutions of government. Now we are at last going to focus on the output of the machine: policy. For a long time, political scientists scarcely bothered to look at what came out of the system; they were interested only in the *process*. The actual content of policies was without great meaning. With the cries of the 1960s for "relevance," however, political scientists began to look more closely at the actual content of policies, and soon a new subfield, "public policy" or "policy analysis," was born. By now, most political science departments consider policy analysis a worthwhile branch of the discipline.

What is Policy?

Political scientist Thomas R. Dye, noting that whole books have been written in an effort to define the word "policy," offers his own short and sweet definition: "Public policy is whatever governments choose to do or not to do."[1] This is good, but it raises some questions. Does government always "choose" to do what it does? Many policies come into being as the result of incremental change in bureaucratic practice. In most cases, no one sits down and figures out what should be done; the policy just grows as administrators react to events. Perhaps Dye's definition would be improved if we were to drop the word "choose" and just say that policy is whatever government *does*.

Dye's definition also is at variance with the common governmental use of the term. Government officials use the word "policy" to indicate their intentions, not what they actually do. This gap is especially glaring in foreign policy, where the administration's stated policy usually includes proclamations of peace, understanding, and brotherhood while its actual behavior may be considerably less idealistic. President Reagan sent Marines into Lebanon in 1982 as "peace-keeping" forces, but by 1983 they had become embroiled in war. What was the Reagan policy, peace or war? White House spokespersons, emphasizing the *intentions* of the policy, said "peace." Critics in Congress, emphasizing the combat situation, said "war." Who was right? If we were to use the Dye definition, we would probably have to side with the latter group and ignore the stated intentions. But aren't intentions a component of policy as well as actual performance? Perhaps we could define policy as what government is *trying* to do.

Should we consider *results* in defining the word "policy"? If a given economic policy is intended to produce prosperity but instead produces a recession, would we say that the government's policy is recession? Some policy analysts separate results from policy and call them "policy impact." But can a policy be divorced from its impact? Isn't the net result the true definition of what government is doing? Perhaps we could define policy as a relationship between what government is trying to do and what actually happens. Good policy making would include the recognition that policies need to be continually modified to take account of new problems, some of which may have been created by the

---

[1]Thomas R. Dye, *Understanding Public Policy*, 6th ed. (Englewood Cliffs, N.J.: Prentice-Hall, 1987), p. 2.

previous policies. This process of continual modification and adjustment can be seen in U.S. economic policy over the last two decades.

ECONOMIC POLICY

Economics undergirds everything else in public policy. Virtually all policy choices have economic ramifications, and these are often sufficient to make or break the policy. A policy designed to protect the environment that causes a slowing down of industry and loss of jobs is probably not going to last very long. An energy policy aimed at squeezing fuel from oil shale or tar sands and delivering a barrel of petroleum at three times the cost of Saudi crude can continue only if the government is willing to subsidize it for, say, national security reasons.

With a growing economy, a country can afford to play around with new welfare measures, as the United States did in the booming 1960s. With a stagnant economy, an administration may have to cut back on welfare expenditures and devise policies to spur the economy into greater production. Whatever the issue—environment, energy, welfare, you name it—the policy will be connected to the economy. Some of the worst policy choices are made when decision makers forget this elementary point. Accordingly, economic policy

RESULTS: Federal funds helped build this walkway at a cost of over $400,000 to encourage urban redevelopment. But little development occurred, and the walkway was practically unused. The city finally sold it for $1 just to get it removed, after which major development occurred.

Michael Roskin

takes priority, and it overshadows all other policies. Every political scientist should be to some degree an economist.[2]

Government and the Economy

Nowadays, no one, not even a good conservative, expects the government to keep its hands off the economy. Everyone expects the government to induce economic prosperity, and if it doesn't, then voters will punish the administration at the next election.[3] Earlier in the century this was not the case. Many European governments, as well as Washington, followed the "classic liberal" doctrines discussed in Chapter 6 and pretty much kept their hands off the economy. With the outbreak of the Great Depression in 1929, however, the hands-off policies tended to make things worse, and people began to demand government intervention.

A book by the English economist, John Maynard Keynes, helped chart the way.[4] Keynes argued that the free market by itself may reach a balance of supply and demand only with unacceptably high unemployment. The solution, he suggested, was for government to increase "aggregate demand" by spending on public works and welfare. Some say the "Keynesian revolution" brought us out of the Depression. Others say Franklin D. Roosevelt's New Deal never fully applied Keynesianism; only the massive defense spending of World War II did that. Still others doubt that the New Deal achieved anything lasting except inflation. After World War II, government leaders all over the world, even those who disliked Keynes's theory, turned to Keynesian methods to correct their economies. As vice-president during the 1950s, Richard Nixon denounced Keynesian economics as a Democratic trick. In the White House in the 1970s, however, Nixon announced that he was "now a Keynesian" and could "fine-tune the economy." (He didn't.)

What are some of our leading economic problems and government responses to them? Consider the approximate sequence of events the United States has gone through since the 1960s.

Inflation. Until 1965, the U.S. inflation rate was low, but as President Johnson escalated the Vietnam war in that year it kicked up. War spending pumped some $140 billion into the U.S. economy but not a corresponding amount of goods and services to buy with it. Too many dollars chased too few goods, the classic description of demand-pull inflation. The inflation engendered by the Vietnam war took on a life of its own and lasted into the 1980s. LBJ thought he could win in Vietnam quickly and cheaply, before the war had had much economic impact. He

---

[2]See Michael J. Boskin and Aaron Wildavsky, eds., *The Federal Budget: Economics and Politics* (San Francisco: Institute for Contemporary Studies, 1982).

[3]See D. Roderick Kiewiet, *Macroeconomics and Micropolitics: The Electoral Effects of Economic Issues* (Chicago: University of Chicago Press, 1983).

[4]John Maynard Keynes, *The General Theory of Employment, Interest and Money* (New York: Harcourt, Brace, 1936).

failed. Many economists say that LBJ could have avoided the worst of the inflation if he had been willing to raise taxes to pay for the war.

Tax Hike.   President Johnson was reluctant to ask for a tax increase to pay for the Vietnam war for two reasons. First, he had just gotten a tax cut through Congress in 1964; it would have been embarrassing to reverse course the following year. Second, LBJ did not want to admit to the country that he had gotten it into a long and costly war. By the time Johnson and Congress had changed their minds and introduced a 10 percent tax surcharge in 1968, it was too late; inflation had taken firm hold. The moral is that if you must go to war, you should be sure to increase taxes simultaneously; if you don't there will be the devil to pay with inflation.

Balance of Payments.   Starting in the late 1950s, the United States spent more abroad than it sold. With the war-induced prosperity of the 1960s, America sucked in growing imports without exporting enough to cover them. U.S. industries invested heavily overseas, and American tourists spent freely. A gigantic balance-of-payments deficit grew. The too-high value of the dollar in relation to foreign currencies meant it was cheaper to buy foreign goods but harder to sell ours in foreign markets. Japanese products, especially, took a large share of the U.S. market. American dollars flooded the world; they were too plentiful.

Gold Standard.   In an effort to stem this outflow in 1971, President Nixon cut the link between the dollar and gold, letting the dollar "float" to a lower level in relation to other currencies. In effect, he devalued the dollar by about one-fifth. The dollar went back up, however, and U.S. trade and payments deficits soared even higher.

Wage-Price Freeze.   At the same time, Nixon froze wages and prices to try to knock out the inflationary psychology that had taken hold. The 1971 wage-price freeze was popular at first, but then some people began to complain that there was no corresponding freeze on profits, so that businesses were benefitting unduly. A bigger problem with wage-prices freezes, however, is that when they are removed, pent-up inflationary pressures push inflation higher than ever. Many economists think Nixon's year-and-a-half freeze just set the stage for even greater inflation. Some (mostly liberal) economists supported the idea of wage and price controls—called "incomes policy"—but now, few economists of any stripe want to try them again.

Oil Shocks.   International oil deals, like most international trade arrangements, are made with U.S. dollars. The dollar's loss in value meant that the oil exporters were getting less and less for their black gold. The price of oil in the 1960s was ridiculously low. As a result of the 1973 Mideast war, the members of the Organization of Petroleum Exporting Countries (OPEC) were able to do what they had been itching to do: quadruple oil prices. In 1979, in response to the revolutionary turmoil in Iran, they increased prices again. World oil prices had soared from $2.50 to $34 a barrel. The impact on economies around the world was devastating.

Stagflation. During the 1970s a new word appeared—*stagflation*—to describe a new phenomenon, inflation with stagnant economic growth. Previously, economists had seen a connection between economic growth and inflation; as one went up, so did the other. In the 1970s, this connection was broken. Inflation hit double-digit levels (10 percent or higher), but the economy shrank and joblessness increased. The biggest single culprit was believed to be the massive increase in oil prices that affected every corner of the economy, from agriculture and transportation to manufacturing and construction. The United States was especially hard hit, for Americans had gotten used to cheap energy and had based their industry and lifestyle on it. The manyfold increase in petroleum prices produced inflation everywhere while simultaneously depressing the economy.

Interest Rates. President Jimmy Carter attempted to stimulate the economy, but this made inflation worse than ever; in 1980 it was 13.5 percent. The chairmen of the independent Federal Reserve Board, who are appointed by the president for four years but cannot be fired, took it upon themselves to stem inflation by means of "monetary policy," control of the growth of the U.S. money supply. The Board (also known as "the Fed") can force banks to raise or lower their interest rates on loans. High interest rates mean slower economic growth and a dampening of inflation. Economist Paul A. Volcker, appointed by Carter in 1979 and reappointed by Reagan in 1983, brought interest rates to record levels; at one point they were over 20 percent. It was painful medicine. Inflation did cool, but at the cost of the greatest rate of unemployment (over 10 percent) since the Depression. Americans became aware of how important the Fed is in our economic life and began to wonder if Reaganomics wasn't less important than Volckernomics.

Tax Cut. Again trying to stimulate the economy, President Reagan turned to an approach called "supply-side economics," which focuses on investment and production rather than on consumer demand, as Keynesian policy would. The inspiration of supply-siders was the Kennedy idea that lowering tax rates stimulates economic growth and ultimately generates more tax revenue. Too-high taxes discourage effort and investment.[5] Congress bought the idea and cut income taxes 25 percent over three years. Actually, this scarcely offset the "bracket creep" that American taxpayers had suffered as a result of inflation; their purchasing power had stayed the same, but they found themselves in ever-higher tax brackets. The Reagan tax cut did stimulate the economy, but it also helped produce another problem.

[5]For a nontechnical explanation of supply-side economics, see Jude Wanniski, *The Way the World Works: How Economies Fail and Succeed*, rev.ed. (New York: Touchstone Books, 1983).

UNEMPLOYMENT soared in 1982 as record interest rates slowed the U.S. economy. Michigan's unemployment rate—over 16 percent—was the nation's highest. Here Detroit jobless seek unemployment compensation.

UPI/Bettmann Newsphotos

 Budget Deficits. The Vietnam war produced the biggest budget deficits (expenditures exceeding revenue) since World War II. The ambitious social programs of LBJ's Great Society expanded spending and made the deficits worse. The massive increase in defense spending by the Reagan administration—at precisely the time it was cutting taxes—shot deficits to over $200 billion a year, the biggest federal deficits in history. A curious reversal of economic positions took place in the early 1980s. The traditionally free-spending Democrats had for decades argued—after Keynes—that budgetary deficits are not so important, that they are in fact needed to stimulate the economy. Republicans had argued that having the government pump money into the economy was a prescription for inflation; they stressed a balanced budget. Reagan campaigned on a balanced-budget promise, but once in office, events made him adopt the old Democratic line, that deficits don't hurt. The Democrats (and many Republicans) meanwhile expressed horror at the size of the deficits and urged trims in defense spending plus a tax increase to narrow the gap before inflation soared again. This brings us back to the subject with which we started—inflation—and the fear that the cycle could be starting over again.

 This brief review of some U.S. economic problems and policies illustrates that policy is never a finished business. A policy useful for dampening one problem may give rise to other problems. What's good one year may be bad the next. Government officials are not necessarily doing policy flip-flops; they may be adjusting policies for new situations. Indeed, flexibility is the mark of a good policy maker and rigidity the mark of a poor one.

ENERGY POLICY

Until late 1973, Americans lived in an energy paradise, or, perhaps more accurately, an energy dream world. The country's gigantic industrial expansion had been based on cheap energy. Energy efficiency was one of the last things

Americans cared about in designing or buying cars, homes, and appliances. In mid-1973, gasoline sold for about 38¢ a gallon, and even then some service stations gave away steak knives or car washes with a fill-up.

Then this happy world changed abruptly. The members of OPEC took advantage of the October 1973 Arab-Israeli war to raise their prices fourfold. Other world oil producers eagerly followed. For a time, Arab producers refused to ship oil to the United States because of its support of Israel. In percentage terms, the shortfall in U.S. petroleum was small—well under 5 percent—but in psychological terms, the shortfall was great: near-panic ensued. Gas lines formed. Motorists suddenly demanded small, economical cars to replace their "gas-guzzlers." People started insulating their homes. Americans congratulated themselves on having "learned the lesson" in time to make changes.

But within a few years, the lessons of the 1973–74 oil shock were forgotten. Gasoline prices rose, but only to about 60¢ a gallon. Americans decided they preferred big cars. In 1979, revolution toppled the Shah of Iran, and in the chaos, Iran's oil production dropped. Again, the actual shortfall in the United States was small, for we import relatively little oil from the Persian Gulf, but again gas lines formed. Americans, it seems, need to be hit with an energy crunch every few years to get their attention. Gas prices peaked in 1981 at $1.38 a gallon, and Americans learned to conserve. Part of the "conservation" was actually the result of a world-wide recession caused by the high oil prices and high U.S. interest rates. In a recession, industry and consumers use less energy. An "oil glut" appeared as the combined demand for oil by economies all over the world dropped below what was being produced. Americans relaxed. The price of gas dropped below $1 a gallon, and Detroit couldn't produce enough big cars. Isn't this where we came in? Can a third, perhaps more devastating energy shock (resulting from an event such as the closure of the Persian Gulf) be long in coming?[6]

Control or Free Market?

What was U.S. policy in all of this? None of the choices were pleasant. The big question was whether to implement governmental controls to guide the economy through the energy crisis or to let the free market—through its price-adjustment mechanism—do the job. The former approach was first adopted under Nixon; the controls were increased under Ford and reached a high point under Carter. The latter approach was implemented under Reagan. Both approaches have plusses and minuses.

Controls came in the 1970s precisely because the free market in energy, especially in oil, had led the nation to a dangerous impasse. The free market did indeed hold down energy prices. Because oil was so cheap—it could be produced in Saudi Arabia for as little as 25¢ a barrel—the United States had turned

---

[6]For a clear warning to get ready, see Don E. Kash and Robert W. Rycroft, *U.S. Energy Policy: Crisis and Complacency* (Norman, Okla.: University of Oklahoma Press, 1984).

massively to oil for its fuel needs. U.S. petroleum consumption doubled during the 1950s, then doubled again during the 1960s. We became oil "junkies," dependent on foreign producers for more than a third of our supplies.

The free market worked to expand the U.S. economy and lifestyle with bargain-priced oil. But the free market can't plan very far ahead; it simply reacts to *current* supplies and demands. The oil shocks of 1973 and 1979 indicated that some government planning was needed to cushion the economy against future oil stoppages. In November 1973, President Nixon announced "Project Independence," which was to break U.S. dependence on foreign petroleum. Congress gave the president a Federal Energy Administration (FEA) to deal with short-term energy crises by allocating fuel supplies among the states, an Energy Research and Development Agency (ERDA) to promote technological improvements, expanded daylight-savings time, and a 55-mile-per-hour national speed limit.[7]

Shortly after taking office in 1977, President Carter, clad in a cardigan and sitting by a wood fire, called the United States' need to confront its energy problems "the moral equivalent of war," an expression borrowed from William James. Carter received something Nixon had proposed, a Department of Energy, which grouped together many scattered energy agencies. New laws required utilities to shift from oil and natural gas to coal. Homeowners got tax credits for insulating. Detroit automakers were required to meet steadily higher miles-per-gallon requirements or pay fines. Controls on the price of petroleum and natural gas were gradually lifted, but producers had to pay a "windfall profits" tax on oil and gas from old wells. (To encourage exploration, there was no such tax on oil and gas from new wells.) The development of "synfuels" was subsidized.

The Reagan White House found these complicated laws, controls, taxes, and agencies just plain silly. U.S. energy consumption dipped as energy prices went up, teaching people to conserve. The government didn't need to mandate conservation; the price of energy would take care of that automatically. Reagan promised to get rid of the two departments Carter had founded, Energy and Education. In trying to eliminate the Department of Energy, he learned that the manufacture of nuclear bombs is under the DOE's supervision and disguised in its budget. He therefore decided to let the department stand but, in effect, gutted its regulatory capabilities by cutting its budget and staff—the general Reagan approach to curbing Washington's power without having to go before Congress to repeal existing legislation. Without enforcement capability, many of the congressionally mandated controls became dead letters.

Did the Reagan approach work? Initially, it seemed to. The price of gasoline and home-heating oil dropped during the 1980s. The United States became somewhat less dependent on foreign oil imports. But other things were happening during this time period which clouded the picture. The country,

---

[7]For a review of Nixon's energy policies and how difficult they were to get through Congress, see *Congress and the Nation*, vol. 4 (Washington, D.C.: Congressional Quarterly, 1977), pp. 201–86.

indeed the world, went through a major recession which depressed energy consumption as well as prices. The oil pipeline from Alaska's North Slope was completed and began supplying the West Coast with much of its petroleum, raising domestic-production figures and correspondingly lowering the percentage of U.S. demand satisfied by imported fuel. The very success—or apparent success—of the Reagan program contained the seeds of later trouble: namely, that Americans, once again grown used to plentiful fuel at reasonable prices, would forget about conserving.

Which Energy Path?

Much energy-policy discussion—perhaps too much—focuses on oil. At times, energy policy is little more than oil policy. This is a mistake, for there are other forms of energy which should be considered, and which indeed may soon have to be considered.[8]

Oil.   U.S. petroleum production peaked in 1970, and most experts agree that there is not much new oil left to find in the United States. Accordingly, imported oil provided almost half of U.S. consumption by 1977, an amount that has declined since then but one that still leaves the United States vulnerable. Actually, the United States imports little from the Persian Gulf—West Europe and Japan depend on the Gulf—and instead draws mostly from Mexico, Venezuela, and Nigeria. Even though these supplies are under no threat, any disruption in the Persian Gulf ripples through the world oil market and raises prices for all. Further, and more basic, all petroleum reserves are finite; sooner or later they are going to run out, probably sometime in the next century. Accordingly, long-range planners would like to gradually move us away from petroleum, now the source of about 45 percent of U.S. energy. Natural gas provides about 27 percent, but it, too, is finite.

Coal.   Coal used to be king in the United States, and we have coal reserves that will last for centuries. We are, as an energy expert put it, "the Arabs of coal." But after World War II, U.S. coal usage declined, replaced by cheap oil, until now coal provides only about one-fifth of our energy. Coal burning is dirty—producing soot and acid rain—and coal is bulky and hard to transport and handle, so that power companies, factories, and homeowners gladly switched to fuel oil. Instead of having to stoke a coal furnace, all one had to do was flip a switch. With the oil shocks of the 1970s, however, some began to wonder if we couldn't get back to coal. New laws forbade further construction of oil-fired power plants. Ideas for transporting coal by "slurry" (pulverized coal mixed with water) pipeline were proposed to overcome the high transportation costs of the fuel.

---

[8]For an excellent overview, see Walter A. Rosenbaum, *Energy, Politics, and Public Policy*, 2nd ed. (Washington, D.C.: CQ Press, 1987).

Coal is plentiful, but it has drawbacks. Mining it gouges up the landscape and produces acid runoff, with disastrous effects on the local environment. Burning it throws out pollutants into the atmosphere. Some of the worst of these pollutants can be curbed by smokestack "scrubbers," but these are expensive and power companies fight laws requiring their installation. Every year dozens of miners are killed in accidents. Furthermore, the burning of fossil fuels—especially coal—worldwide is putting tons of carbon dioxide into the atmosphere and creating a "greenhouse effect" that is gradually warming the earth, altering the weather and melting the polar ice caps.

Nuclear.   Touted as clean, economical ("too cheap to meter"), and safe, nuclear energy—in the form of nuclear-fired electricity generating plants—was to be the postwar energy future. The events of recent years, however, have led to the questioning of each of the above three attributes. The power plants themselves may produce some pollution, and safe storage of nuclear wastes, which remain dangerous for thousands of years, is a major problem. Supposedly "safe" disposal containers have been found to leak. In late 1957 a nuclear dump at Kyshtym in the Soviet Ural Mountains exploded, killing perhaps hundreds and forcing closure of the area.[9] Is it any wonder that few states want nuclear dump sites?

The cost of nuclear-produced electricity has soared, and now it is the same as that of coal-produced electricity. Investors learned to shun the stocks of power companies that were going nuclear; the cost overruns were enormous. Safety, however, was the biggest question. The nuclear industry claimed its plants were perfectly safe, but the partial meltdown at Three Mile Island in Pennsylvania in 1979 made people wonder. Relatively little radioactivity was released, but the sheer incompetence of the people running the unit suggested that something much worse could happen soon. The Chernobyl reactor explosion in the Soviet Union in 1986 was much worse and persuaded people the world over that nuclear was not the way to go. Since the Three Mile Island accident, no new U.S. nuclear power plants have been ordered, and their contribution to U.S. electricity remains less than one-sixth. Few foresee major growth in nuclear power.[10]

"Soft" Paths.   The above energy sources—oil, coal, and nuclear—are, in the words of some ecology-minded critics, all "hard," that is, they rely on costly concentrations of hardware. These critics advocate "soft" paths: solar energy, wind, and biomass, all of which can be used by individuals or small groups on a decentralized, self-help basis.[11] Soft-path energy sources are all renewable and

[9]Andrew Cockburn, "The Nuclear Disaster They Didn't Want to Tell You About," *Esquire*, 25 April 1978, pp. 39–43.

[10]Particularly scathing in speaking of nuclear power is environmentalist Barry Commoner in *The Politics of Energy* (New York: Knopf, 1979).

[11]The originator of the concept of "hard versus soft paths" is physicist Amory B. Lovins, who has written *Soft Energy Paths: Toward a Durable Peace* (New York: Harper Colophon, 1977).

THREE MILE ISLAND, scene of a partial nuclear meltdown in 1979, was still being repaired almost a decade later.
Michael Roskin

do not pollute. The price for soft-path energy keeps coming down, whereas the price for hard-path energy keeps going up. Some homeowners have already turned to solar energy for space and water heating (as did the ancient Greeks and Romans when wood became scarce). Devices to convert sunlight to electricity are getting more and more practical. Methane is already generated from animal wastes, wood and crop residue, and other forms of biomass in some farming communities. New windmill designs are making an old American form of energy feasible once again. The power companies, naturally, scoff at such efforts, but a few are experimenting with the use of wind and solar energy. Once futuristic, soft energy paths have become increasingly plausible.

ENVIRONMENTAL POLICY

Environment and energy are closely related, for energy generation is the biggest source of environmental pollution. For centuries, Americans paid little attention to the environment; America was a big country, and there was always room to dump wastes. During the 1960s, however, concern with possibly irreversible environmental contamination began to grow and an ecology ethic and movement began (see the discussion in Chapter 6). By Nixon's first term (1969–73), environmental concerns were at a peak, and Nixon and Congress responded to them. (In Sweden and West Germany, an appreciable "Green" vote has a considerably bigger political impact.)

In 1970 Nixon established the Environmental Protection Agency to consolidate scattered antipollution programs. The Clean Air Act of 1970 required automobile manufacturers to drastically reduce engine emission of carbon monoxide, nitrogen oxides, and unburned hydrocarbons within a few years. The car you drive and gas you burn today are different because of this act. Some environmental legislation went farther than Nixon wanted. In 1972 Congress overrode Nixon's veto of a water-pollution act that made clean water a national goal and allowed citizens to sue polluters and the government over water-borne pollution. America's lakes and streams became a lot cleaner; some dead bodies of water returned to life.

Not everyone was happy, though. Industry found it had to respond to myriad regulations which, it claimed, retarded growth and hurt the economy. With the 1973–74 oil shock, the energy industries in particular claimed that environmental restrictions—many of them unnecessary—blocked Nixon's goal of energy independence. The labor movement was never ecology-minded, and the economic slump of the mid-1970s made it less so. "See that smoke?" asked one steelworker. "That means jobs." The soot-laden air of the steel towns around Pittsburgh cleared up beautifully—as the steel industry shut down, leaving thousands unemployed. "I pursue the goal of clean air and pure water," said President Ford, "but I must also pursue the objective of maximum jobs and continued economic progress." Environmental concerns were placed on the back burner.[12]

During the Carter presidency, new environmental problems came to the fore: toxic wastes. Scientists discovered that some synthetic materials and their wastes caused cancer and other illnesses. Formaldehyde, PCBs, and dioxin were among the most frequently mentioned. The Love Canal incident underscored the problem. In 1978 more than 200 families had to be evacuated from this Niagara Falls, N.Y., subdivision because the land had been a chemical dump site and poisonous chemicals were seeping into their basements. In 1980 an abandoned chemical dump in Elizabeth, N.J., caught fire and pumped out a column of poisonous fumes just five miles from Manhattan. It was revealed that toxic-waste disposal was handled casually and sometimes illegally, some of it by "midnight dumpers" or organized crime. As America has turned more and more to synthetics—plastics, textiles, fuels—the problem has gotten worse and worse. Some 150 million tons of toxic wastes are produced every year, and only a fraction of them, according to the EPA, are disposed of safely.

In 1980 Congress passed the Hazardous Substance Response Trust Fund, better known as the "Superfund," and President Carter signed it into law.

---

[12]For an urgent cry to put environmental concerns on the front burner, see Walter A. Rosenbaum, *Environmental Politics and Policy*, 2d ed. (Washington, D.C.: Congressional Quarterly Press, 1987).

Starting with $1.6 billion, most of it from the chemical industry, the EPA-administered Superfund was to pay for cleanup of damage caused by hazardous chemicals. That same year, Congress empowered the EPA to treat the dumping of toxic wastes as a felony; previously, it had just been a misdemeanor. By 1985, there were 2000 dump sites slated for Superfund cleanup, but only six such dumps had been successfully cleaned up thus far.

Loopholes and lax enforcement abounded in toxic-waste disposal. Outright lying was punished by a $250 fine in New Jersey, where some hazardous wastes had been dumped directly into the Raritan River. Some wastes were (and are) mixed with fuel oil and burned in heating boilers, discharging poisons into the air. To prevent such things from happening requires tighter laws and many more enforcement officials.

The Reagan Administration was not willing to make this extra effort. Industry fought strict enforcement, and the Reagan White House was intent on cutting the domestic budget, not expanding it.[13] The leadership of the EPA became highly political, and some of its top people resigned amidst charges of favoring industry and using the Superfund for electoral impact. As in other areas, the Reagan strategy seemed to be to leave agencies underfunded and understaffed so they couldn't do their regulatory jobs, which was precisely the intention of the Reagan people, who opposed governmental regulation on principle.

But environmental problems won't go away. New contaminated areas are discovered all the time. Even when the hazardous wastes were dumped years ago, the current Washington administration may catch the blame if it appears indifferent to environmental pollution. The environment has become a permanent issue in national politics, and administrations ignore it at their peril.

WELFARE POLICY

A generation ago, in the mid-1960s, President Lyndon B. Johnson launched his War on Poverty, aimed at creating a Great Society by eliminating poverty. LBJ, who had long been Senate majority leader, got Congress to deliver almost everything he wanted. Then the Vietnam war, amidst rising costs and acrimony, seemed to cut down the War on Poverty in its infancy. There wasn't enough money for the growing programs, and LBJ became increasingly discredited. Many of the Great Society programs were subsequently dismantled or left to quietly die on the vine. Some say the Great Society was never given a chance. The conservative conventional wisdom of the late 1970s and early 1980s held that the undertaking was inherently impossible, a waste of money that often did more harm than good.[14]

[13]See Norman J. Vig and Michael E. Kraft, eds., *Environmental Policy in the 1980s: Reagan's New Agenda* (Washington, D.C.: Congressional Quarterly Press, 1984).

[14]The leading attack on the Great Society programs is Charles Murray, *Losing Ground: American Social Policy, 1950–1980*. (New York: Basic Books, 1984).

Some specialists in that area, however, say the Great Society programs generally did succeed and markedly lowered the incidence of poverty in the United States. Conservatives have exaggerated the inefficiency and misuses that accompany any welfare program and have understated the very real accomplishments.[15]

What is Poverty?

But what is "poverty" in the United States? What's "poor" here might be defined as comfortable elsewhere. Trying to define "poverty" could be as tricky as trying to define "policy." The U.S. Department of Labor came up with a formula in 1955 that has been used ever since, although it is obviously not a complete definition. The Labor Department found that families spend about one-third of their incomes on food. The department therefore set the "poverty line" at three times an economy food budget, usually for non-farm families of four. Using this definition, the percentage of Americans below the poverty line fell from 17.3 percent in 1965, when LBJ's War on Poverty started, to 11.7 percent in 1973, according to the Census Bureau. With the economic recession and budget-tightening that started under Carter and expanded under Reagan, however, by 1983 the poverty rate was back up to 15.2 percent, the highest in eighteen years. (By 1985, it was down to 14 percent.) The black and Hispanic rates were much higher throughout the whole period.

Conservatives and defenders of the Reagan program hastened to point out that the figures did not tell the whole story, for the Labor Department definition of poverty does not include *noncash* benefits transferred to the poor by government programs—food stamps, for example. Taking this into account raised most poor families above the poverty line, according to one economist.[16] The poor, in other words, now had a certain cushion.

Further, before we conclude that the War on Poverty was either a success or a failure, we must take a look at the poverty rate in longer perspective. In 1950, some 30 percent of the U.S. population was classified as below the poverty line.[17] Since then, the rate has dropped almost steadily, with one of the fastest decreases occurring between 1960 and 1965, *before* the War on Poverty programs were enacted. What explains this? The U.S. economy expanded during this decade and a half, especially during the early 1960s. Jobs were plentiful. It's hard to tell if the further drop in the poverty rate from 1965 to 1973 was the result of government programs or of an economy fueled by Vietnam war spending. The biggest government program of all was—and still is—military spending.

[15]See Sar A. Levitan, *Programs in Aid of the Poor*, 5th ed. (Baltimore, Md.: Johns Hopkins University Press, 1985).

[16]Martin C. Anderson, *Welfare: The Political Economy of Welfare Reform in the United States* (Stanford, Cal.: Hoover Institution Press, 1978).

[17]Dye, in *Understanding Public Policy*, p. 107, has constructed an excellent chart from Census Bureau figures showing the poverty rate.

By the same token, when the poverty rate began to go up again in the mid-1970s, the cutback in antipoverty spending was only partly to blame; also responsible were the recessions caused by oil prices and high interest rates. Antipoverty programs should receive neither all of the praise in good times nor all of the blame in bad times. The biggest factor in the poverty rate is the unemployment rate; when unemployment jumps up, antipoverty programs can't do much to offset it.[18]

The Feminization of Poverty

One of the most interesting and disturbing trends of recent decades is the "feminization of poverty," reflecting the fact that there are more households headed by females and that they are more likely to fall under the poverty line. By 1982, some 42 percent of all female-headed households were classified as poor, comprising almost one-third of all poor Americans, and both figures were growing. Single women with dependent children formed the biggest bloc of poor people in the United States, over 11 million.[19]

What had happened to produce this situation? For one thing, the divorce rate rose, and divorce automatically makes many poor. Consider a household in which both husband and wife work for the minimum wage. Together, they bring home some $14,000 a year—not much, but above the poverty line. They still might be entitled to food stamps and reduced-price school lunches. But if they get divorced, the wife, who is usually given custody of the kids, is making only about $7,000 a year and may have trouble holding down the job and watching after her children. Her chances of working her way out of poverty are slim.

Further, the illegitimacy rate rose, meaning that more young women with no job skills found themselves heads of households—and poor. Conservatives argued that increased welfare programs, by enabling single mothers to exist—in many cases without working—contributed to the growth of both welfare costs and sexual immorality. Liberals countered that the breakup of the family, deplorable as it may be, was under way long before the growth in welfare; it was the expression of a long-term shift in values and sexual morals unrelated to government programs. Legislative efforts to combat "immorality" are notably unsuccessful.

What can be done about the feminization of poverty? Certain small proposals have been offered to ameliorate, if not solve, the problem. For one thing, a widespread, low-cost network of day-care centers would enable single mothers to work. These would have to be government-subsidized. Second, changes in welfare regulations to let the working poor keep some of their

[18]One political scientist argues that the great success of governmental intervention in the 1960s and 1970s was the absorption of a 50 percent increase in the U.S. work force as the baby-boom children came of age. See John E. Schwarz, *America's Hidden Success: A Reassessment of Twenty Years of Public Policy* (New York: Norton, 1983).

[19]See Ruth Sidel, *Women and Children Last: The Plight of Poor Women in Affluent America* (New York: Viking Books, 1986).

benefits while bringing home a small paycheck would help the problem of welfare mothers having to choose between a job and welfare when the job may actually pay less than welfare. In many cases, there is a disincentive to getting a job, because welfare benefits are then automatically canceled. A blending of the two for a transitional period might encourage people to find work. Whatever the proposals, no administration in Washington can afford to ignore the problems of single mothers, for this issue is one of the factors contributing to the "gender gap" between men and women, with the women several percentage points more liberal than men.

The Costs of Welfare

In the year 1960, 20¢ of every federal, state, and local government dollar was a "transfer payment," meaning it went to the poor, blind, disabled, and elderly. By the year 1980, 32¢ of every government dollar went for such payments, according to Yale economist Laurence J. Kotlikoff. Programs that started small in the 1960s ballooned into major expenditures by the 1980s.

Food Stamps. Begun as a modest trial program under Kennedy in 1961, the Food Stamp program was made nationwide under Johnson in 1964. From a few million dollars a year, it rose in the 1980s to around $13 billion a year until the Reagan administration cut the program (along with the number of eligible recipients) to around $11 billion a year. Some 9 percent of all U.S. households benefited, getting an average of $990 a year in 1982, or $19 a week. One did not dine royally on food stamps; cost per meal per person was figured at 46¢. Thirty-one percent of families headed by women received food stamps.

The Carter administration simplified the program in 1977 by eliminating the provision that recipients *buy* the stamps at a discount with their own money.[20] This had meant that the absolutely destitute, people with no money at all, could get no food stamps. Congress changed the law to eliminate the cash payment, and the number of recipients expanded. Ronald Reagan, citing an apocryphal story of a young man who used food stamps to buy vodka, tightened eligibility requirements in an effort to eliminate fraud and misuse. The trouble was that some genuinely poor families were also bumped from the program, and hunger in America reappeared. Callous remarks by a White House official that he saw no proof of hunger flew in the face of widespread reports of a big increase in the number of people eating at soup kitchens.

What should be done? The Food Stamp program has been expensive, but outright fraud and waste have not been major factors. Stories of students, who have generally not been eligible, buying steak and lobster echoed out of all proportion. There are poor people in America. Should they be helped? Outright cash grants, considered for a time by Carter as a replacement for food stamps,

---

[20]For a critical view of the efforts and mistakes of the Carter Administration's efforts at welfare reform see Laurence E. Lynn, Jr., and David deF. Whitman, *The President as Policymaker: Jimmy Carter and Welfare Reform* (Philadelphia: Temple University Press, 1981).

could easily be used for nonessentials, such as liquor. Direct delivery of surplus commodities, as was done on a small scale in the 1950s and episodically in the 1980s to get rid of government cheese stocks (the result of price supports for dairy farmers), was clumsy and spotty. One alternative to food stamps might be to borrow a tactic applied in many countries: subsidizing basic foodstuffs, such as bread and milk. However, subsidizing food basics, because it would benefit the nonpoor as well, would not necessarily cost less than food stamps. The Food Stamp program will probably continue with little change, for there is no clear, acceptable alternative.[21]

Aid to Families with Dependent Children (AFDC). Originally set up by the 1935 Social Security Act, Aid to Dependent Children (ADC, as it was then known) provided federal matching funds for state programs. For years, most states had either no ADC programs or only small programs. Starting in the 1960s, though, participation grew steadily, until costs just about matched the $13 billion spent each year on food stamps. The program was renamed AFDC in 1967, when Congress mandated work training for all adult recipients and gave dollar incentives. Day-care centers were to be provided. In practice, most of this aid went to single mothers for whom child care was unavailable. State efforts to make sure no man was around the house—if one was, the aid would be stopped—led to early-morning snooping. Conservatives pointed to AFDC as underwriting immorality and "welfare dependency"; it was the favorite target of those who liked to speak of the "welfare mess." Because recipients were heavily nonwhite, the issue became connected with the struggle for racial equality. Attacks against "welfare mothers" were sometimes veiled racism.

What can be done? Undoubtedly, some welfare dependency—that is, getting stuck on welfare with no incentive to get off—was created. AFDC may also have encouraged a casual attitude toward bringing fatherless children into the world. But can we make it illegal for poor people to have babies? Should there be mandatory sterilization or abortion? Once a child is born, can we let it starve or freeze? Stopping or greatly curtailing AFDC would provoke such an uproar that it might cost elected officials reelection. It seems that whereas everyone wishes to limit the growth of AFDC, few responsible people want to end it.

Medicare and Medicaid. Dwarfing both food stamps and AFDC are the federally supported medical assistance programs. The Medicare and Medicaid programs, both enacted in 1965, serve two different purposes. Medicare is for elderly people; Medicaid is for poor people. Both grew so rapidly that even supporters admitted that benefits had to be limited and eligibility requirements tightened. By the late 1980s the two programs cost more than $100 billion a year.

At least two factors induced exponential growth in medical assistance: greater numbers of people becoming eligible and soaring medical costs. Medi-

---

[21]For a brief overview of food stamps, see Barbara A. Claffey and Thomas A. Stucker, "The Food Stamp Program," in *Food Policy and Far Programs,* ed. Don F. Hadwiger and Ross B. Talbot (New York: Academy of Political Science, 1982).

care is especially expensive, for it is an "entitlement" program, meaning that people are automatically eligible on reaching age 65; they do not need to demonstrate any financial need. Middle-class and even rich people receive Medicare. The proportion of older people in American society is increasing steadily, and the elderly are the biggest consumers of medical care. Strictly speaking, Medicare is not a "welfare" program but a form of insurance; Medicaid is welfare. In the public mind, however, the two tend to get mixed up.

Hospitals and doctors, once they are assured of payment, have no incentive to economize. When in doubt, they put the patient in the hospital—often at $1,000 a day—and order batteries of expensive tests with the latest multimillion-dollar machines. Some hospitals expanded into medical palaces, and some physicians got rich from Medicare and Medicaid. (Ironically, the powerful American Medical Association had for years lobbied against such "socialized medicine.") By the 1980s, medical costs consumed one-tenth of the U.S. gross national product, in part as a result of Medicare and Medicaid, which paid nearly half the nation's medical bills.

Washington tried various ways of tightening up.[22] Recipients were required to contribute more of the total payment to hold down overuse. Hospitals and doctors were monitored on costs and on how long they kept patients hospitalized. Hospices—nursing homes for the terminally ill—were made allowable under Medicare, as such care is cheaper than hospital care. Competitive bidding was begun in some states, and patients were assigned only to low-bid hospitals. Fees for each type of disorder were established, and overruns were not reimbursed. Every time the government tightens medical assistance, however, patients, doctors, and hospitals complain bitterly, and they form a powerful lobby. Some hospitals turn away poor patients.

Hooked on Welfare

As with the weather, everybody complains about the "welfare mess" but no one has succeeded in cleaning it up. Critics speak of "welfare dependency" in referring to successive generations of one family that are either unable or unwilling to get jobs. But in a larger sense, the United States as a whole has become welfare-dependent, for it is impossible to repeal the programs.

In the first place, much of what is conventionally called "welfare" really isn't; that is, it is not designed specifically to aid the poor. Most "welfare" in America is for the middle class. Social Security, Medicare, college loans, and unemployment compensation go mostly to middle-class people. These are "entitlements," programs for which one is automatically eligible. By 1980, entitlements for the middle class cost the government four times as much as welfare programs that were based on need.[23] But it is very difficult to cut an

[22]See Joseph A. Califano, Jr., *America's Health Care Revolution: Who Lives? Who Dies? Who Pays?* (New York: Random House, 1986).
[23]Robert B. Reich, "Whatever Happened to the Welfare Ideal?" *New York Times Book Review*, 1 January 1984, p. 17.

entitlement program. When President Reagan announced his intention to tighten up some aspects of the Social Security program, many older people screamed in rage that he was cutting Social Security. The White House and Congress quickly backed off from anything that looked remotely like cutting Social Security. To gain a more personal understanding, the student reader might consider how he or she would feel about cuts in federally guaranteed student loans. "Why, that's not welfare," some say. "That's investment in the country's future!" Thus we can begin to approach a definition of "welfare program": government funds spent to help *other* people.

A program once in place, be it welfare or entitlement, takes on a life of its own. It develops a constituency of recipients, bureaucrats, and private administrators, people with voices and votes. They organize lobbies and threaten electoral punishment of officials who oppose their program. Even conservatives recognize this; the best they can do is keep the programs from expanding much more. When voters say they want to clean up the welfare mess, they usually mean cutting someone else's benefits. Since a large part of the U.S. population benefits from one or another welfare or entitlement program, it is hard to muster sufficient congressional votes to trim or end any or all of them. We are stuck with welfare.

But in comparative perspective, how extensive is the U.S. welfare state? Not very. Most countries of West Europe have more extensive programs, and of course pay higher taxes for their benefits. As was mentioned in Chapter 6, over half of Sweden's income goes to the government for its "cradle-to-grave" welfare system. Few Americans would like to go that far. Welfare programs seem to go hand in hand with being an advanced, industrialized country. Efforts to move the clock backward simply divert us from trying to make our welfare measures work better.

Conclusion: How Big Should Government Be?

We have but touched briefly on a few of the more prominent areas of public policy. We could add education, defense, criminal justice, civil rights, urban policy, and much more. But we would keep coming back to one question: Should government intervention in these areas expand? Just how big do we want government to get?

The American answer is to keep government small and to suspect and criticize expansion of governmental power. But we also recognize that we need government intervention in the economy, energy planning, environmental protection, and so on. We have trouble making up our minds how much government we want.[24] Americans want various forms of government intervention, but scarcely is the ink on new laws dry before we begin to criticize

[24]Samuel P. Huntington identifies fear of governmental power as a major component of the "American creed" and an important factor in periodic political upheavals. See his *American Politics: The Promise of Disharmony* (Cambridge, Mass.: Belknap Press, 1981).

governmental bungling. The Europeans generally do not suffer from this kind of split personality; they mostly accept that government has a major role to play and try to live with this fact.

This reluctance to expand government's role may redound to America's long-term advantage. Government programs tend to expand, bureaucracy is inherently inefficient, and ending an established program is all but impossible. Government programs become so sprawling and complex that officials don't even *know* what is in operation, much less how to control it. As political scientist Ira Sharkansky put it, "All modern states are welfare states, and all welfare states are incoherent."[25] Accordingly, it is probably wise to act with caution in expanding government's power.

SUGGESTED READINGS

CHAMPAGNE, ANTHONY, AND EDWARD J. HARPHAM, EDS. *The Attack on the Welfare State.* Prospect Heights, Ill.: Waveland Press, 1984. Collection of articles detailing the Reagan administration's efforts to role back welfare programs.

DANZIGER, SHELDON, AND DANIEL WEINBERG, EDS. *Fighting Poverty: What Works and What Doesn't.* Cambridge, Mass.: Harvard University Press, 1986. Sophisticated but readable essays that cut through many partisan myths.

DAVIS, KAREN, AND DIANE ROWLAND. *Medicare Policy: New Directions for Health and Long-Term Care.* Baltimore, Md.: Johns Hopkins University Press, 1985. Suggestions on how to trim costs but still provide wider health care coverage.

FERGUSON, THOMAS, AND JOEL ROGERS, EDS. *The Political Economy: Readings in the Politics and Economics of American Public Policy.* Armonk, N.Y.: M. E. Sharpe, 1984. Excellent selection of articles on how politics and economics interlock.

FREEMAN, ROGER A. *The Wayward Welfare State.* Stanford, Cal.: Hoover Institution Press, 1983. A conservative examines and criticizes the trend toward greater welfare measures.

HARRINGTON, MICHAEL. *The New American Poverty.* New York: Holt, Rinehart and Winston, 1984. Worried look at the increase in poverty under Reagan, by the man who helped bring the poverty issue to political attention in the 1950s.

HARRISS, C. LOWELL, ED. *Control of Federal Spending.* New York: Academy of Political Science, 1985. Suggestions from many experts on how to limit growth of federal programs.

HEIDENHEIMER, ARNOLD J., HUGH HECLO, AND CAROLYN TEICH ADAMS. *Comparative Public Policy: The Politics of Social Choice in Europe and America,* 2d ed. New York: St. Martin's, 1983. Excellent comparative perspective on several categories of public policy.

LASH, JONATHAN, ET AL. *A Season of Spoils: The Story of the Reagan Administration's Attack on the Environment.* New York: Pantheon, 1984. A scathing but solid indictment of the Reagan administration's abandonment of ecological concerns.

MEAD, LAWRENCE M. *Beyond Entitlement: The Social Obligations of Citizenship.* New York: Free Press, 1986. Argues for welfare support but only in return for self-improvement on the part of recipients.

MILLS, GREGORY B., AND JOHN L. PALMER. *The Deficit Dilemma: Budget Policy in the Reagan Era.* Baltimore, Md.: Urban Institute Press, 1983. Worried look at the swelling of the federal deficit and proposals to reduce it.

MOYNIHAN, DANIEL PATRICK. *Family and Nation.* San Diego, Cal.: Harcourt Brace Jovanovich, 1986. A U.S. senator and expert on family policy urges more support for poor children.

NORTON, HUGH S. *The Quest for Economic Stability: Roosevelt to Reagan.* Columbia, S.C.: University of South Carolina Press, 1985. Insightful review of the U.S. government's economic policy with emphasis on unemployment and crises.

PETERS, B. GUY. *American Public Policy: Promise and Performance,* 2d ed. Chatham, N.J.: Chatham House, 1986. Thoughtful introductory roundup.

RODGERS, HARRELL R., JR. *Poor Women, Poor Families: The Economic Plight of America's Female-Headed Households.* Armonk, N.Y.: M. E. Sharpe, 1986. Good analysis and detailing of the rapidly growing "feminization of poverty."

[25]Ira Sharkansky, *Wither the State? Politics and Public Enterprise in Three Countries* (Chatham, N.J.: Chatham House, 1979), p. 7.

chapter 18

Violence
and Revolution

Many political science texts talk about systems and stability; some even depict political systems as well-oiled machines that never break down. Pick up a newspaper, on the other hand, and you will find it filled with stories of violence and revolution. Some years ago, political scientists began criticizing the seeming status-quo orientation of much of their discipline and began to direct their attention to breakdown and upheaval.[1] The systems approach, it was argued, is incomplete if it cannot account for the violent and often bloody changes that are wracking the world.

Sometimes scholars overlooked the tension and violence in their own backyards. With the black riots of 1965–68, academics suddenly rediscovered violence in America.[2] From viewing violence as abnormal, many came to suggest, along with black militant H. Rap Brown that "violence is as American as cherry pie."

SYSTEM BREAKDOWN

Political systems can and do break down.[3] Indeed most countries in the world today have suffered or are suffering system breakdown. Such systems are marked by major riots, revolutionary movements, military coups, and authoritarian governments of varying degrees of harshness. Dictatorships are rarely the work of small bands of conspirators alone; they are the result of system collapse that permits small but well-organized groups—usually the military—to take over. This is why it does little good to denounce a cruel military regime. It is true enough that some regimes commit acts of great evil; military regimes in Argentina, Chile, and Guatemala killed thousands on the slightest suspicion of leftism. But how is it that these military regimes came to power? Why does system breakdown recur repeatedly in such countries? These are the deeper questions that must be asked if we are to begin to understand these horror stories.

Underlying breakdown is the erosion of legitimacy. Legitimacy is the feeling among citizens that the regime's rule is rightful, that it should be generally obeyed. Where legitimacy is high, governments need few policemen; where it is low, they need many. In England, for example, people are mostly law-abiding; police are few in number and most carry no firearms. In Northern Ireland, on the other hand, terrorists routinely kill with bombs and bullets, for a large minority of the population sees the government as illegitimate. Here the police are armed and British troops patrol with automatic weapons and armored cars. The civil war in Northern Ireland has cost more than 2500 lives.

[1]One of the first and best efforts to integrate systems theory with revolution is that of Chalmers Johnson, *Revolutionary Change* (Boston: Little, Brown, 1966).

[2]President Johnson appointed a commission to study the riots, and its reports contributed to further scholarly inquiry. See *Report of the National Advisory Commission on Civil Disorders* (New York: Bantam Books, 1968); and Hugh Davis Graham and Ted Robert Gurr, eds., *Violence in America: Historical and Comparative Perspectives* (New York: New American Library, 1969).

[3]For a magisterial study of system breakdown, see Juan J. Linz and Alfred Stepan, eds., *The Breakdown of Democratic Regimes* (Baltimore, Md.: Johns Hopkins University Press, 1978).

One prominent reason for an erosion of legitimacy is the regime's loss of effectiveness in running the country. Uncontrollable inflation, blatant corruption, massive unemployment, or defeat in a war demonstrate that the government is ineffective. War is especially important in this regard. A long, costly war, particularly one that is being lost, saps public confidence. Russia would probably never have had a revolution if it had not entered World War I in 1914. The poor performance of its army and economic collapse made the tsarist regime look ridiculous. Likewise, communism would probably not have triumphed in China had not the Japanese invaded in 1937, and destroyed the credibility of the Nationalist regime. As Karl Marx put it, "War is the midwife of revolution."

Happily, though, regime ineptitude in war can favor democracy at times. Portugal's authoritarian regime, bogged down in guerrilla wars in Africa, was overthrown by the military in 1974, which then stepped aside for an elected democratic government. That same year, the blustering military dictators of Greece, facing a war with Turkey over Cyprus, handed power back to a civilian government which reinstituted a democracy. The Argentine military was so humiliated by the British in the Falklands that it let an elected, civilian government take over in 1983.

The United States has not been immune to this phenomenon. As the Vietnam war—the longest in U.S. history—seemed to drag on with mounting casualties, economic drain, and no progress, the home front was shaken by riots and protests. Respect for and trust in government declined in public opinion polls. Although the United States never came close to system breakdown, the episode illustrates that even a well-established democracy can lose effectiveness and legitimacy. The moral might be: Don't go to war unless you absolutely have to, and then be sure to win and win quickly. Ignoring this lesson in Lebanon forced President Reagan into a major policy reversal in 1984.

Violence as Symptom

Violence—riots, mass strikes, terrorist bombings, and political assasinations—by itself does not indicate that revolution is nigh. Indeed, the most common response to serious domestic unrest is not revolution at all but military takeover. Violence can instead be seen as symptomatic of the erosion of the government's effectiveness and legitimacy. Perhaps nothing major will come of the unrest; perhaps new leadership will calm and encourage the nation and begin to deal with the problems that caused the unrest, as Franklin D. Roosevelt did in the 1930s. But if the government is clumsy, if it tries to simply crush and silence discontent, it can make things worse. In 1932, the "Bonus Army" of World War I veterans seeking early payment of veterans' benefits to tide them through the mass unemployment of the Depression was dispersed by Army troops under Gen. Douglas MacArthur. Public revulsion at the veterans' rough treatment helped turn the country decisively against President Herbert Hoover in that fall's election.

Domestic violence is both deplorable and informative. It tells that not all is going well, that there are certain groups that, out of desperation or conviction, are willing to break the law in order to bring change. A government's first impulse when faced with domestic unrest is to crush it and blame a handful of "radicals and troublemakers." To be sure, there may well be instigators deliberately trying to provoke incidents, but the fact that people are willing to get involved should telegraph a message to the authorities that something is wrong. At the Democratic convention in 1968, Chicago police went wild in attacking those who had come to protest the Vietnam war—as well as many who just happened to be in the wrong place at the wrong time. The convention ignored the protesters and nominated President Johnson's vice-president, Hubert Humphrey, who lost, largely because of his equivocal position on the war. The riot showed that the Democratic party had drifted out of touch with important elements of its constituency that only four years earlier had voted for Johnson because he said he'd keep the country out of war. The Democrats should have been listening to instead of ignoring the protesters.

As much as we may deplore violence, we have to admit that in some cases it serves its purpose. The United States as a whole and Congress in particular paid little attention to the plight of inner-city blacks until a series of riots ripped U.S. cities in the late 1960s. The death and destruction were terrible, but there seemed to be no other way to get the media's, the public's and the government's attention. The rioting in this case "worked," that is, it brought a major—if not very successful—effort to improve America's decaying cities.

When Poles protested against rising food prices in 1970, police guns cut down workers in Gdansk. Threatened with major riots, one corrupt leader resigned and was replaced by another. Far from crushing Polish workers, the Gdansk massacre provided a site for a worker-made memorial—three giant steel crosses, connoting martyrdom—and became the rallying point of the Solidarity union, which shook the regime ten years later. Mass discontent can't really be crushed; it keeps resurfacing. People get angry and have long memories. In the 1980s, government legitimacy in Poland is close to zero; the regime rules by means of the army and ZOMO police thugs, a condition that cannot last forever.

Likewise, the white minority government of South Africa announces with pride the capture or killing of black guerrillas. The South African security forces are indeed proficient, but shouldn't the fact that thousands of young black South Africans are willing to take up arms against the whites-only regime tell the Pretoria government something? The ruling National party has been telling its supporters for decades that blacks (73 percent of the country's population) will simply keep their place (on 13 percent of the land) and that any white who thinks overwise is infirm of purpose.[4] The South African government has engaged in no dialogue with blacks; it expects them merely to obey. The growing violence in

[4]For a good overview of the South African problem, see Study Commission on U.S. Policy Toward Southern Africa, *South Africa: Time Running Out* (Berkeley, Cal.: University of California Press, 1981).

South Africa is in part a message—that the government would be well advised to start listening, for a change.

Types of Violence

Not all violence is the same. Various thinkers have categorized violence in several ways. One of the best categorizations is that of political scientist Fred R. von der Mehden, who sees five general types of violence.[5]

Primordial.   This type of violence grows out of conflicts among the basic communities—ethnic, national, or religious—into which people are born. Sikh riots in India, the multi-group conflict in Lebanon, and the tribal conflicts in some African nations are examples of primordial violence. It is not necessarily confined to the developing areas of the world, though, for such antagonisms appear in Quebec, the Basque country of Spain, and Northern Ireland, where there is something akin to a tribal feud between Protestants and Catholics.

Separatist.   Separatist violence, which is sometimes an outgrowth of primordial conflict, aims at independence for the group in question. The Ibos tried to break away from Nigeria with their new state of Biafra in the late 1960s, but they were defeated in a long and costly war. The Bengalis, on the other hand, did succeed in breaking away from Pakistan with their new state of Bangladesh in 1971. The Eritreans have fought a long war with Ethiopia to set up a separate Eritrea along the Red Sea coast and still have not been completely crushed. In Europe, the Basques, Bretons, and Corsicans have given rise to separatist movements which are, given Europe's well-established borders, politically hopeless.

Revolutionary.   This is violence aimed at overthrowing or replacing an existing regime. The Sandinistas' ouster of Somoza in Nicaragua in 1979, the fall of the Shah of Iran that same year, and the independence of the former Portuguese colonies of Angola and Mozambique in 1975 are examples of successful revolutionary violence. Central America and Southern Africa are scenes of continuing revolutionary violence. Von der Mehden includes under this category "counter-revolutionary" violence, the efforts of more conservative groups to counteract revolutionary attempts—for instance, the efforts of Salvadoran rightists. The crushing of liberalizing movements in Hungary, Czechoslovakia, and Poland would also come under this heading, with the ironic twist that here the Communists have become the counter-revolutionary, conservative force. The distinctive form of terror of the 1980s, the car-bomb, would probably come under the rubric of revolutionary violence as well.

---

[5]This discussion draws on Fred R. von der Mehden, *Comparative Political Violence* (Englewood Cliffs, N.J.: Prentice-Hall, 1973), Chapter 1.

Coups. Coups are usually counterrevolutionary in intent, aimed at heading off a feared revolutionary takeover. Coups are almost always military, although the military usually has connections with and support from key civilian groups, as in the Brazilian coup of 1964. Most coups don't involve much violence, at least initially. Army tanks surround the presidential palace, forcing the president's resignation and usually exile, and a general takes over as president. Some coups are virtually bloodless. When the military still senses leftist opposition, though, it sometimes goes insane with legalized murder. The Chilean military killed tens of thousands following the 1973 coup. Some 9000 Argentines "disappeared" following the military takeover of 1976. The military rulers of little Guatemala murdered some forty thousand of their fellow citizens in the 1970s and 1980s on suspicion of opposing the regime. In Latin America, the counterrevolutionary terror that follows some coups is far bloodier than anything the revolutionaries have done. Once a country has had one coup, chances are it will have another. Some countries get stuck in "praetorianism"—named after the Praetorian Guard in ancient Rome—and take decades to return to civilian rule.[6] In part, coups occur because the conventional institutions of government—parties, parliaments, and executives—are terribly weak, leaving the military with the choice of either taking over or facing growing chaos.

Issues. Some violence doesn't fit into any of the above categories. Violence oriented to particular issues is a catchall category and generally less deadly than the other kinds. The protests against the Vietnam war, the student strikes at American and French universities in the late 1960s, the sometimes violent protest at nuclear power plant or missile sites, and the anger that grows around some economic problems are examples of issue-oriented violence. In 1983, amidst worsening unemployment and rapidly rising prices, lower-class Brazilians invaded and looted supermarkets. French farmers stopped and burned trucks of Spanish produce, which they perceived as undercutting their livelihood. In 1976, black students in South Africa's Soweto protested against having to learn Afrikaans in school; police shot down several hundred of them. There may be a fine line between issue-oriented violence and revolutionary violence, for if the issue is serious enough and the police repression brutal enough, protests over an issue can turn into a revolutionary tide.

All these categories—and others one might think of—are apt to be arbitrary.[7] Some situations fit more than one category. Some start in one category and escalate into another. No country, even a highly developed one, is totally immune to some kind of violence, however.

---

[6]For a thorough discussion of praetorianism, see Eric A. Nordlinger, *Soldiers in Politics: Military Coups and Governments* (Englewood Cliffs, N.J.: Prentice-Hall, 1977).

[7]Some writers include a category called "anomic violence," representing spontaneous and unorganized rampages, such as the looting of shops during a power blackout or frustrations vented by slum dwellers against police.

Change as a Cause of Violence

Many writers have found the underlying cause of domestic unrest in the changes a given society may be going through. Purely traditional societies with long-established patterns of authority and simple but workable economies are relatively untroubled by violence. People live as their ancestors lived and do not expect much. Likewise, modern, advanced societies with rational types of authority and productive economies have relatively minor types of violence. It is at the in-between stage, when modernization is stirring and upsetting traditional societies, that violence is most likely.[8] The modernizing societies have left one world, that of traditional stability, but have not yet arrived at the new world of modern stability. Everything is changing in such societies—the economy, religious attitudes, lifestyle, and the political system—leaving people worried, confused, and ripe for violent actions.

Economic change can be the most unsettling. The curious thing about economic change is that improvement can be as dangerous as impoverishment. The great French social scientist, Alexis de Tocqueville, observed in the last century that "though the reign of Louis XVI was the most prosperous period of the monarchy, this very prosperity hastened the outbreak of the Revolution" of 1789.[9] Why should this be? There are several reasons. When people are permanently poor and beaten down, they have no hope for the future; they are miserable but quiet. When things improve, they start imagining a better future; their aspirations are awakened. No longer content with their lot, they want improvement fast, faster than even a growing economy can deliver. Worse, during times of prosperity, some people get richer faster than others, arousing jealousy. Certain groups feel bypassed by the economic changes and turn especially bitter; the Marxists call this "class antagonisms." Revolutionary feeling, however, typically does not arise among the poor, but among what Crane Brinton called the "not unprosperous people who feel restraint, cramp, annoyance" at a government that impedes their right to even faster progress.[10]

Rising Expectations. One way of looking at what economic growth does to a society is to represent it graphically. In Figure 18-1, the solid line represents actual economic change in a modernizing society—generally upward. The broken line represents people's *expectations*. In a still-traditional society—at the graph's left—both actual performance and expectations are low. As growth takes hold, however, expectations start rising faster than actual improvement. Then may come a situation that produces a downturn in the economy—bad harvests, a drop in the price of the leading export commodity, or too much foreign indebtedness—and expectations are frustrated. A big gap suddenly opens between what

---

[8]Samuel P. Huntington, *Political Order in Changing Societies* (New Haven, Conn.: Yale University Press, 1968), especially pp. 32–71.

[9]Alexis de Tocqueville, *The Old Regime and the French Revolution* (Garden City, N.Y.: Doubleday Anchor, 1955), p. 169.

[10]Crane Brinton, *The Anatomy of Revolution*, rev. ed. (New York: Vintage Books, 1965), p. 250.

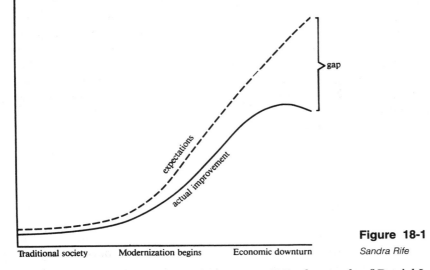

Figure 18-1

Sandra Rife

people want and what they can get.[11] In the words of Daniel Lerner, the "want:get ratio" becomes unhinged, producing a "revolution of rising frustrations."[12]

This is an extremely delicate time in the life of a nation. Rebellion and revolution can break out. The underlying problem, as Ted Robert Gurr has emphasized, is not poverty itself but "relative deprivation."[13] The very poor seldom revolt; they're too busy feeding their families. But once people have a full belly they start looking around and notice that some people are living much better than they. This sense of relative deprivation may spur them to anger, violence, and occasionally revolution. Gurr's findings, it is interesting to note, are consonant with those of de Tocqueville and Brinton: revolutions come when things are generally getting better, not when they're getting worse.

Other economic change can spur unrest. Anthropologist Eric R. Wolf has argued that the shift from simple subsistence farming to cash crops dependent on markets, landlords, and bankers impoverishes many peasants and turns them from quietude to revolution. It was precisely the economic modernization of agriculture in Mexico, Russia, China, Vietnam, Algeria, and Cuba that paved the way for successful peasant-based revolutions in those countries, according to Wolf.[14]

[11]This figure was inspired by F. LaMond Tullis, *Politics and Social Change in Third World Countries* (New York: John Wiley, 1973), Chap. 12.

[12]Daniel Lerner, "Toward a Communication Theory of Modernization," in *Communications and Political Development* ed. by Lucian Pye (Princeton, N.J.: Princeton University Press, 1963), pp. 330–33.

[13]Ted Robert Gurr, *Why Men Rebel* (Princeton, N.J.: Princeton University Press, 1970).

[14]Eric R. Wolf, *Peasant Wars of the Twentieth Century* (New York: Harper & Row, 1969). Another work that stresses the peasant as the basis for revolution is James C. Scott, *The Moral Economy of the Peasant: Rebellion and Subsistence in Southeast Asia* (New Haven, Conn.: Yale University Press, 1976).

Economic change is, to be sure, not the only pressure on a modernizing society. The political system may be out of date as well, based on inherited position with no opportunity for mass participation. As the economy improves, educational levels rise. People become more aware of abstract ideas such as "freedom" and "democracy." Especially among intellectuals, the educated elite, there is growing fury at the despotism that rules the land. The peasant may hate the system for squeezing him economically, but the urban intellectuals will hate it for suppressing rights and freedoms. It is the confluence of these two forces, argues Huntington—the "numbers" of the peasants and the "brains" of the intellectuals—that makes revolutions.[15]

REVOLUTIONS

Frustration is one thing; revolution is something else. People may be unhappy over one thing or another—peasants over crop prices, intellectuals over lack of freedom, business people over corruption, and so on. But if there is no organization to focus their discontents, probably not much will happen. Unrest and discontent by themselves will not bring down a regime; for that to happen, organization is absolutely essential. In a study of Brazilian political attitudes, Peter McDonough and Antonio Lopez Pina found "a substantial amount of unchanneled dissatisfaction with the authoritarian regime," but it was "free-floating" resentment not especially directed against the military-run government. They suggest that "in the absence of organizational alternatives, resistance is most likely to take the form of apathy and indifference."[16]

The previous factors we have considered may point to violence—rioting and strikes—but without organization they will not produce a revolution. Who provides the organization? For this we turn to the role of intellectuals.

Intellectuals and Revolution. Intellectuals are nearly everywhere discontent with the existing state of affairs, because they are highly educated and acquainted with a wide variety of ideas, some of them utopian. Preachers, teachers, lawyers, journalists, and others who deal with ideas often have a professional stake in criticizing the system. If everything were fine, there wouldn't be much to talk or write about. Intellectuals although often among the better-off, are seldom wealthy. They may resent people who are richer but not as smart—businesspeople and government officials.

Such factors predispose some intellectuals—but by no means all or even a majority—to develop what James Billington called a "revolutionary faith" that the current system can be replaced with something much better.[17] According to

[15]Huntington, *Political Order in Changing Societies*, p. 241.

[16]Peter McDonough and Antonio Lopez Pina, "Authoritarian Brazil and Democratic Spain: Toward a Theory of Political Legitimacy" (paper presented at the Latin American Studies Association, Pittsburgh, 1979), pp. 57–58.

[17]James H. Billington, *Fire in the Minds of Men: Origins of the Revolutionary Faith* (New York: Basic Books, 1980).

Billington, revolution begins, first and foremost, with this "fire in the minds of men." Common folk, ordinary workers and peasants, are seldom interested in the intellectuals' abstract ideologies (see Chapter 6); they want improved material conditions. It is the intellectuals' idealistic convictions, however, that provide revolutionary movements with the cement that holds them together, the goals they aim for, and a leadership stratum.

It is an interesting fact that most twentieth-century revolutionary movements have been founded and led by educated people. Lenin, son of a provincial education official, was a brilliant and highly educated man. Mao Zedong helped found the Chinese Communist party while he was a library assistant at the Beijing National University. Fidel Castro and most of his original guerrilla fighters were law-school graduates. One of them, however—the famous Che Guevara, who was killed in 1967 while trying to foment revolution in Bolivia— was a medical doctor. The leader of Peru's Shining Path guerrillas was a university professor. The leaders of Iran's revolution against the Shah were either religious or academically trained intellectuals.

Revolutionary Political Warfare

Many people speak of "guerrilla warfare," but this is a misnomer—and a redundancy, for *guerrilla* is simply Spanish for "little war." It is not the use of ambush and punji stakes that should interest us, but the accompanying political action. The two, when combined, equal revolutionary political warfare, which Bernard Fall described as the struggle "to establish a competitive system of control over the population." Fall, an expert on Vietnam who died when he stepped on a land mine there in 1967, emphasized *administration* as the crux of revolutionary warfare. "When a country is being subverted it is not being outfought; it is being outadministered. Subversion is literally administration with a minus sign in front."[18]

In studies Fall conducted, both under the French in North Vietnam during the early 1950s and under the Americans in South Vietnam during the early 1960s, he discovered that the Communists were collecting taxes throughout most of the country under the very noses of the regimes they were overthrowing. The occupying power, whether French or American, deceives itself through its ability to drive through a village in an armored convoy; this does not indicate administrative control, which may be in the hands of the insurgents. The emphasis on military hardware is a big mistake, argued Fall, for it detracts from the human element.

The Vietnamese insurgents were able to outadminister the regime for several reasons. In the first place, they were able to closely identify with the

---

[18]Bernard B. Fall, "The Theory and Practice of Insurgency and Counterinsurgency," in *Last Reflections on a War* (Garden City, N.Y.: Doubleday, 1967), p. 220. The article first appeared in the *Naval War College Review,* April 1965, and was a transcription of a talk Fall gave at the Naval War College on 10 December 1964.

population, something the French and Americans could never do. Indeed, the fact that the anti-Communist side in both Vietnam wars was connected with white foreigners gave the kiss of death to the effort. There was no political package the French or Americans might assemble that could be sold to the locals. Even the Saigon rulers had trouble identifying their own countrymen. The Diem and subsequent Saigon governments were run by Central and North Vietnamese Catholics who were at a considerable psychological distance from the largely Buddhist South Vietnamese. The Saigon officials were urban dwellers who disdained assignments in the provinces and working with the peasants. This was precisely the Communists' strong point.

Terror, to be sure, plays a role in revolutionary political warfare. The Viet Cong murdered many Saigon officials and government-appointed village headmen. The villagers were not uniformly horrified at such terror, however, because it was selective and targeted at people who were outsiders anyway. To many peasants, the Viet Cong executions seemed like extra-legal punishment for collaborators. When the Americans made whole villages disappear, that was terror. There's nothing selective about napalm.

While the insurgent is patiently building a network to supplant the regime, the occupier or government is impatiently trying to substitute firepower for legitimacy. The killing of civilians produces more sympathizers and recruits for the guerrillas. The government's overreliance on firepower erodes its tenuous moral claims to leadership of the nation. Fall urged that:

> . . . what America should want to prove in Vietnam is that the Free World is "better," *not* that it can kill people more efficiently. If we would induce 100,000 Viet Cong to surrender to our side because our offers of social reform are better than those of the other side's, *that* would be victory. Hence, even a total military or technological defeat of the Viet Cong is going to be a partial defeat of our own purposes—a defeat of ourselves, by ourselves, as it were.[19]

Some critics wonder if the American people and leadership ever understood what we were up against in Vietnam. We fought a military war while our opponents fought a political war, and in the end the political mattered more than the military. Said one American officer as he surveyed the smoking ruins of a village, "Unfortunately, we had to destroy the village in order to save it." Some who are familiar with Vietnam believe the United States has been getting into a similar situation in Central America.[20]

Stages of Revolution

In a little book published in 1938 that became a classic, Harvard historian Crane Brinton developed a theory that all revolutions pass through

---

[19]Fall, "This isn't Munich, It's Spain," in *Last Reflections on a War*, p. 234. The original appeared in *Ramparts*, December 1965.
[20]Marvin E. Gettleman, et al., eds., *El Salvador: Central America in the New Cold War* (New York: Grove Press, 1981).

similar stages, rather like a human body passing through the stages of an illness.[21] In the English revolution of the 1640s, the American Revolution of 1776, the French Revolution of 1789, and the Russian Revolution of 1917, Brinton found the following rough uniformities:

The Old Regime Decays. Administration breaks down and taxes rise. People no longer believe in the government; in fact, the government doesn't believe in itself. The intellectuals transfer their allegiance from the regime to a proposed idealized system. All this is happening while the economy is generally on the upgrade, but this provokes discontent and jealousy.

The First Stage of Revolution. Committees, networks, cells, or conspiracies form, dedicated to overthrowing the old regime. People refuse to pay taxes. A political impasse arises that cannot be solved because the lines are too deeply drawn. When the government calls out troops, the move backfires, because the troops desert and the people are further enraged. The initial seizure of power is easy, for the old regime has just about put itself out of business. Popular exultation breaks out.

At First, The Moderates Take Over. People who opposed the old regime but were still connected with it by dint of background or training assume command. They initiate moderate, middle-of-the-road reforms. These changes are not enough for the extremists among the revolutionaries; they accuse the moderates of being cowardly and of trying to compromise with the forces of the old regime. The moderates are "nice guys" and are not ruthless enough to crush the radicals.

The Extremists Take Over. More ruthless and better organized than the moderates, knowing exactly what they want, the extremists oust the moderates and drive the revolution to a frenzied high point. Everything old is thrown out. People are required to be "good" according to the canons of the new, idealistic society the extremists try to instigate. "Bad" people are punished in a reign of terror. Even revolutionary comrades who are deemed to have strayed from the true path are executed: "the revolution devours its children." The entire society appears to go mad in what Brinton likened to a high fever during an illness.

A "Thermidor" Ends The Reign of Terror. Eventually the society can take no more. People come to a breaking point at which they long to settle down, get the economy working again, and enjoy some personal security and pleasure. They've had enough of revolution. Even the extremists get tired of it. Then comes a "Thermidor"—so named after the French revolutionary month during which the extremist, Robespierre, was himself guillotined—which Brinton described as a convalescence after a fever. Often a dictator, who ends up

---

[21]Brinton, *The Anatomy of Revolution.*

resembling the tyrants of the old regime, takes over to restore order, and most people don't mind.

Iran as a Case Study

Although written two generations ago, Brinton's *Anatomy of Revolution* can be applied to our day. The Iranian revolution unrolled as if its participants had read Brinton's script.[22] The Iranian economy boomed, especially following the quadrupling of oil prices in 1973–74, but economic growth was uneven. Some people became very rich very fast, provoking jealousy. Corruption and inflation soared. Most educated Iranians came to oppose the shah's regime; students especially hated the shah for his repression of freedoms. Networks of conspirators formed, rallying around the figure of exiled Ayatollah Khomeini and using mosques as their meeting places. By 1978 there was extensive rioting, and the use of troops to quell the rioting simply enraged more Iranians. Troops began to desert. Always disdainful of democracy and mass participation in politics, the shah had relied on his dread SAVAK secret police, but even they could no longer contain the revolution. In January 1979, the shah left and Khomeini returned to Iran.

Before he left, the shah named a moderate revolutionary, Bakhtiar, to head the government. But the very fact of being chosen by the shah ruined Bakhtiar, and the newly returned Ayatollah, who instantly became the de facto power in Iran, replaced him with Bazargan, another moderate, but one never connected with the shah. Bazargan's government didn't count for much, though, because real power resided with Khomeini's Revolutionary Council. In November 1979, radical Islamic students, angered over the shah's admission into the United States, seized the U.S. Embassy and began the famous "hostage crisis" that lasted over a year. Bazargan, realizing he was powerless, resigned.

The Iranian Moslem extremists, totally devoted to Khomeini, took over and a bloodbath ensued. Firing squads worked overtime to eliminate suspected "bad" people, including fellow revolutionaries who had deviated. Tens of thousands of young Iranians, promised instant admission to heaven, threw their lives away in repelling the Iraqi invaders. Strict Islamic standards of morality were enforced—no alcohol or drugs, veils for women, and suppression of non-Islamic religions. As of this writing, only one thing is lacking: the Thermidor, the period of calming down after the revolutionary excesses. If Brinton is approximately right, however, we can expect such a period, probably after the elderly Khomeini dies. No revolution lasts forever; all must establish some kind of normalcy sooner or later. One probable sign of an Iranian Thermidor would be the reestablishment of diplomatic relations with the United States.

---

[22]For a short review of the Iranian revolution, see Richard W. Cottam, "Revolutionary Iran," *Current History*, January 1980. For a longer study that includes the U.S. role, see Barry Rubin, *Paved with Good Intentions: The American Experience and Iran* (New York: Penguin, 1981).

IRAN ERUPTS: Pro-Khomeini demonstrators burn an American flag in Tehran. The Iranian Moslem-fundamentalist revolutionaries called the United States the "great satan."
UPI/Bettmann Newsphotos

AFTER THE REVOLUTION

The big problem with revolutions is not that they change things so much, but, ironically, that they end up changing things so little. Revolutions show a persistent tendency to overthrow one form of tyranny only to replace it with another. In little more than a decade, the French kings had been replaced by Napoleon, who crowned himself emperor and supervised a police state far more thorough than anything the kings had had at their disposal. The partial despotism of the tsars was replaced by the perfect despotism of Stalin. Life was freer and economic growth faster at the turn of the century under the inefficient tsarist system than it has been at any time in Russia since. Fidel Castro thew out the crooked Batista regime, and Cuban freedom and economic growth declined abruptly.

What good are revolutions? One is tempted to despair with Simon Bolivar, the liberator of South America, who said, "He who aids a revolution plows the sea." In general, revolutions end badly.

But what about the United States? Don't we call our 1776–81 struggle with Britain the Revolutionary War? One way to handle this question is to say that it wasn't really a revolution, for it was not an effort to remake American society. Indeed, some of its greatest leaders were wealthy and prominent figures in colonial society. They wanted simply to get rid of British rule, not overturn society as a whole. The American struggle was more a war of independence than a revolution. Extremists never seized control, and there was no reign of terror. Some 100,000 Tories, colonials who remained pro-British, simply got up and left, many to the lands the Crown gave them in New Brunswick and Nova Scotia in Canada.

The late, great Hannah Arendt, on the other hand, thought the American struggle was indeed a revolution, perhaps the only complete revolution that has ever been carried out, for it alone ended with a new foundation of liberty instead of the tyranny of other revolutions.[23] According to Arendt, the fortunate thing for the American revolutionists is that they did not have to wrestle with the difficult "Social Question" that obsessed the French revolutionists. America was prosperous and wealth was distributed rather equally. The American struggle didn't become sidetracked by the poverty problem, so it could focus on establishing a just and durable constitution with balanced powers and political freedom. It was the genius—or, in part, luck—of the American Revolution that it was a purely *political* and not a social matter. America needed no guillotine, for there was no artistocratic class to behead. It needed no demagogues of the Robespierre stripe because there was no rabble to arouse. The French Revolution, deeply involved in these social matters, became a bloody mess and ended in a dictatorship. In Arendt's terms, it wasn't a really successful revolution because it didn't end with the constituting of liberty the way the American Revolution did.

America was lucky; most of the other countries of the world aren't. Faced with the terrible problems of poverty, revolutionists in the Third World tend to be drawn to Marxist prescriptions and try to remake their societies. The result is usually bloodshed, tyranny, and, in the end, little improvement.

A Revolutionary World

One of the greatest questions of our day is how the United States should react to the many revolutions around the globe. This concerns all young American people personally, for resumption of the draft is likely in the next few years. America's military commitments have been increasing while the number of eighteen-year-olds has been declining. In 1983, with relatively few American troops sent to Lebanon, Grenada, and Honduras, the Pentagon was already worried that our forces were stretched too thin.

Can the United States understand revolutions? We sometimes like to call ourselves the first revolutionary country, but, as considered above, ours was a special, limited kind of revolution, one that did not attempt to restructure society. We behold radical revolutions with great distaste, even horror. Former Senator J. William Fulbright argued that America is basically a conservative

---

[23]Hannah Arendt, *On Revolution* (New York: Viking Press, 1963), especially Chapter 4. "Foundation I: Constitutio Libertatis."

EL SALVADOR refugees live on the sidewalks. They fled their native town after a rebel attack left some 200 dead.

UPI/Bettmann Newsphotos

country and cannot really understand the world's revolutions today.[24] We don't like the extremism rampant in various countries; we prefer moderate, middle-of-the-road reformers who can build democracy and carry out important changes at the same time. In Latin America, for example, we like Christian Democrats such as Eduardo Frei of Chile and Jose Napoleon Duarte of El Salvador. But under the extreme political and economic pressures of Latin America, these moderates usually lose, Frei was followed by the radical Socialist Salvador Allende, who was killed in the rightist military coup of Augusto Pinchoet, who seized control of Chile with an iron hand.[25] Napoleon Duarte was displaced by extreme rightists who argued that they could prevent revolution by using even greater force and more ruthless tactics. In 1984, Duarte was elected again, with U.S. support, but still faced a hostile military.

In point of fact, Chile and El Salvador today would be in vastly better shape if somehow the rule and programs of Frei and Napoleon Duarte, respectively, could have been vigorously pursued. But how can reformist programs work when faced with the extremist forces of both left and right? For the leftists in Chile and El Salvador, the moderate reforms were mere palliatives that hardly touched the underlying problems; only revolution could do that. The leftists attempted their revolutions, but that only provoked rightist extremists to take over and murder suspected leftists by the tens of thousands. The leftists would actually have been much better off if they had stayed with the Christian Democrats and worked for gradual, not revolutionary change. But how do you tell that to a revolutionary?

It would seem that Edmund Burke (see Chapter 6) was right: Evolution is better than revolution. But in the Third World, this is usually not the choice. The middle gets squeezed out, leaving only right-wing dictatorship or left-wing

---

[24]J. William Fulbright, *The Arrogance of Power* (New York: Vintage Books, 1966), especially Chapter 3, "America and Revolution."

[25]See Arturo Valenzuela, *The Breakdown of Democratic Regimes: Chile* (Baltimore, Md.: Johns Hopkins University Press, 1978).

revolution. "We ought to aim at the first," said President Kennedy, referring to moderate, democratic regimes, "but we really can't renounce the second until we are sure that we can avoid the third."[26] In other words, distasteful as it may be, we might have to stick with friendly dictatorships rather than run the risk of promoting pro-Soviet takeovers.

But this is difficult for a democratic America to do. We are appalled at the bloody excesses of some of these dictatorships and seek a middle-of-the-road "good guy" to set the country on the path to reform and progress. Most Americans welcomed the fall of the Somoza regime in Nicaragua in 1979, especially after TV cameras recorded the cold-blooded murder of an American newsperson by a member of Somoza's national guard. But, proclaiming Marxist goals, the triumphant Sandinistas soon pushed out moderate elements, controlled the press and opposition parties, harshly treated the Miskito Indians (many of whom fled the country), built a large army with Soviet weapons, and aided their fellow revolutionaries in El Salvador. Washington turned disappointed and angry at the Managua regime. We wanted a moderate, democratic revolution; the Sandinistas wanted a radical, socialist revolution.

What can we do? What should we do? Intervene or keep out? If we intervene, are we willing to run the risk of getting bogged down in another Vietnam? If we stay out, are we willing to witness the rise of radical, pro-Soviet regimes, some in our own backyard?[27] Can America lead and consolidate a moderate revolution? We did so in West Germany and Japan as part of our military occupation after the war. Economically, politically, and socially, these countries, under U.S. guidance, attained remarkable success. But the context was different; they had been beaten in a gigantic war and had surrendered, at least temporarily, their sovereignty. The Japanese postwar constitution was drafted by U.S. experts on the staff of General Douglas MacArthur; to this day it is known as the "MacArthur constitution." Could we do the same in other countries, take them over and reform them along democratic lines? As diplomat and historian George Kennan noted long ago, "The ruling of distant peoples is not our dish."[28] Americans, despite what some Marxists say, really don't make good imperialists.

Do we have the *sang froid* (cold blood) to step back and watch these revolutions run their probable course, peaking in extremism and then calming down to some kind of stability? During their extremist phase, the revolutionary regimes are highly anti-American and a test of our patience. In time, they may become anti-Soviet and pro-American, as Egypt did in the 1970s. The Soviets, after enormous expense, have established few loyal client states in the Third World. Perhaps we shouldn't be so concerned about revolution. In 1910

---

[26]Recounted in Arthur Schlesinger, Jr., *A Thousand Days* (Boston: Houghton Mifflin, 1965), p. 769.

[27]For an excellent compilation of the difficulties facing U.S. decision makers, see Martin Diskin, ed., *Trouble in Our Backyard: Central America and the United States in the Eighties* (New York, Pantheon, 1983).

[28]George F. Kennan, *American Diplomacy, 1900–1950* (New York: Mentor, 1951), p. 22.

revolution broke out in Mexico and greatly alarmed the United States. President Wilson sent U.S. troops into Vera Cruz and northern Mexico. Americans feared chaos and revolution would sweep northward, backed by nonhemispheric powers, very much as Americans fear the spread of Marxist revolution in Central America today. But the Mexican revolution calmed and stabilized, and now Mexico and the United States are good friends. Should we intervene against revolutions or let them run their course? The answer to this question will help decide the question of war or peace for your generation.

SUGGESTED READINGS

ANDRIOLE, STEPHEN J., AND GERALD W. HOPPLE. *Revolution and Political Instability: Applied Research Methods.* New York: St. Martin's, 1984. Comparison of theories of revolution and attempts at quantifying revolutionary behavior.

DJILAS, MILOVAN. *Memoir of a Revolutionary.* New York: Harcourt Brace Jovanovich, 1973. Recollections of how a Yugoslav revolutionary—who was once Tito's right-hand man but turned against socialism—became a Communist.

EISENSTADT, S. N. *Revolution and the Transformation of Societies: A Comparative Study of Civilizations.* New York: Free Press, 1978. An advanced sociological study of how revolutions transform societies. Not for beginners.

FAGEN, RICHARD R., AND OLGA PELLICER, EDS. *The Future of Central America: Policy Choices for the U.S. and Mexico.* Stanford, Cal.: Stanford University Press, 1983. A highly critical review of U.S. policy as unable to handle revolutionary change in the Caribbean.

GOLDSTONE, JACK A., ED. *Revolutions: Theoretical, Comparative, and Historical Studies.* San Diego, Cal.: Harcourt Brace Jovanovich, 1986. Good selection of readings on theories and case studies.

GURR, TED ROBERT. *Why Men Rebel.* Princeton, N.J.: Princeton University Press, 1970. Theory that "relative deprivation" underlies revolutionary impulse.

HOBSBAWM, E. J. *Revolutionaries.* New York: New American Library, 1973. A Marxist interpretation of revolution in our time, with emphasis on class analysis.

HUNTINGTON, SAMUEL P. *Political Order in Changing Societies.* New Haven, Conn.: Yale University Press, 1968. Impressive theory of how change in society gives rise to revolution when political institutions can no longer handle growing mass participation.

KEDDIE, NIKKI R. *Roots of Revolution: An Interpretive History of Modern Iran.* New Haven, Conn.: Yale University Press, 1981. Excellent study of the weaknesses of the shah's regime.

KREJCI, JAROSLAV. *Great Revolutions Compared: The Search for a Theory.* New York: St. Martin's, 1984. Interesting theory, similar to Brinton's, that revolutions go through distinct phases.

LAFEBER, WALTER. *Inevitable Revolutions: The United States in Central America.* New York: Norton, 1983. An excellent historical overview that urges the United States to keep out of the region.

LEIDEN, CARL, AND KARL M. SCHMIDT. *The Politics of Violence: Revolution in the Modern World.* Englewood Cliffs, N.J.: Prentice-Hall, 1968. A more recent updating of Brinton's classic.

LINZ, JUAN J., AND ALFRED STEPAN, EDS. *The Breakdown of Democratic Regimes.* Baltimore, Md.: Johns Hopkins University Press, 1978. Reviews numerous breakdowns and finds that leftist attempts at takeover provoke rightist military coups.

MERKL, PETER H., ED. *Political Violence and Terror: Motifs and Motivations.* Berkeley, Cal.: University of California Press, 1986. Collection of sophisticated and probing articles on different approaches to violence and the kinds of people drawn to violence.

MOORE, BARRINGTON, JR. *Social Origins of Dictatorship and Democracy: Lord and Peasant in the Making of the Modern World.* Boston: Beacon Press, 1966. Complex study of how traditional agricultural relations between lord and peasant must dissolve before society can progress.

NORDLINGER, ERIC A. *Soldiers in Politics: Military Coups and Governments.* Englewood Cliffs, N.J.: Prentice-Hall, 1977. Good synthesis of recent material on the most common types of governments in the Third World.

VON DER MEHDEN, FRED R. *Comparative Political Violence.* Englewood Cliffs, N.J.: Prentice-Hall, 1973. Overview and compilation of findings on violence that grew out of the U.S. concern with the subject during the late 1960s.

chapter 19

International Relations

POLITICS WITHOUT SOVEREIGNTY

International politics is quite a bit different from the domestic politics we have been studying. Domestic politics generally occurs *within* a sovereign entity—what we call a state or nation—whereas international politics occurs *among* such entities. Sovereignty, as we considered in Chapter 1, means being boss on your own turf, the last legal word within a country. The concept grew up in the sixteenth century, when absolutist monarchs were strengthening their positions and sought legal justification for it.[1] Sovereignty is the restraining force within a country. Criminals, rebels, and breakaway elements are, in theory, controlled or crushed by the sovereign, who now, of course, is no longer a king but the national government. Sovereignty also means that foreign powers have no business intruding into your country's affairs; their reach—again in theory—stops at your borders.

So much for theory. In practice, nothing is so clear-cut. Just because a nation is legally sovereign does not necessarily mean it really controls its own turf. Witness poor Lebanon in the early 1980s: its territory occupied by three outside forces (Syria, Israel, and the Palestine Liberation Organization), its weak government propped up by friendly "peace-keeping" forces (the United States, France, and Italy), unable to stop the violence among its several politico-religious private armies. At the same time, there was much more peace and order among the sovereign states of Europe who formed the Common Market. They had agreed to settle their economic differences by negotiating and politicking at the Common Market headquarters in Brussels.

Further, the idea that sovereignty precludes outside intervention doesn't hold up. Small, poor countries are routinely dominated and influenced by large, rich countries. Afghanistan could scarcely be said to be sovereign under Soviet occupation, nor could the small countries of Central America under the watchful eye of the United States. Some Canadians claimed U.S. economic and cultural penetration was so great that they had lost some of their sovereignty.

Still, the term sovereignty has some utility. Where established, national sovereignty does indeed bring internal peace, and most countries can claim to have done this. By and large, countries still do what they want. When Britain and France sold the Soviets parts for their gas line, there was nothing the United States could do to stop its allies, although President Reagan had come out strongly against the sale. That was sovereignty in action.

Within a sovereign entity there is—or at least there is supposed to be—law. If you have a grievance against someone, you "don't take the law into your own hands. Take him to court." In international relations, nearly the opposite applies: Taking the law into your own hands—by the threat or use of military force—is quite normal. Often there is no other recourse.

This important difference between domestic and international politics sometimes exasperates skilled practitioners of one when they enter into the realm of the other. President Johnson was a master of domestic politics;

---

[1] Jean Bodin is credited with developing the concept, Thomas Hobbes with amplifying it in the next century.

whatever he wanted from Congress he got. But he couldn't make skinny little Ho Chi Minh back down, for Ho was boss on *his* own turf. What worked domestically for Johnson—deals, threats, persuasion—flopped internationally. Some have suggested that it was Nixon's use of the "dirty tricks" of international politics in domestic politics that brought about the Watergate scandal and his downfall. Nixon was indeed a clever statesman; he simultaneously improved ties with the Soviet Union and China. But his deviousness and penchant for secrecy served him ill in dealing with a delicate domestic problem. International politics is not just domestic politics on a grander scale. Without a world sovereignty to establish rules and authority, international politics is wilder and more complex.

Politics as Power

Lacking the sovereignty that prevails in most domestic situations, international relations depend a lot on power. The late, great Hans Morgenthau held that power is the basic element of international politics and that idealists ignore it at their peril.[2] Without sufficient power, a country cannot survive, let alone prevail, in a tumultuous world. One should bear in mind that power is not the same as force. Force is the specific application of military might; power is a country's more general ability to get its way. Power includes military, economic, political, and psychological factors.[3] Power is tricky to calculate. Whole departments of the CIA (and presumably its Soviet counterpart) spend millions trying to figure out how much power their adversaries have. Some elements of power are tangible or calculable. These include:

Geography. Size, terrain, climate, and natural boundaries make some countries easier to defend than others. Insular Britain hasn't been successfully invaded since 1066. Poland, on a plain between Germany and Russia, has been conquered repeatedly. Israel, a sliver of a country, felt compelled to retain the West Bank and Golan Heights for defensive reasons. To a considerable extent, in the lives of nations, geography is destiny.

Natural Resources. Food, minerals, and petroleum are important power factors. West Europe and Japan are dependent on Middle East petroleum. As U.S. oil reserves dwindled, America also looked overseas. The Soviet Union has oil and natural gas but is chronically short of food, a major weakness. In the technological age, certain "strategic minerals" assumed major importance, raising interest in Southern Africa.

Population. Quantity and quality both count here. Bigger is not necessarily better. A large, impoverished, poorly educated population may not be a

---

[2]Morgenthau, in fact, defined *all* politics as a "struggle for power." See *Politics among Nations,* 6th ed. (New York: Knopf, 1985), p. 31.

[3]See John G. Stoessinger, *The Might of Nations,* 8th ed. (New York: Random House, 1986).

source of strength, as the Arabs discovered in fighting Israel. All things being equal, of course, a bigger population to draw soldiers and workers from means increased national strength.

Economy.   An industrialized country is generally much stronger than an agricultural country. The former can produce its own weapons and has a more highly trained population to use them. A more highly developed economy can sustain a war effort longer. Apart from war, an industrialized economy has more to trade and commands more respect than a backward economy. Japan did with trade what it could not do with military might.

Government.   A government firmly in control is a much tougher opponent than one that isn't. A strong government can improve its economy and population and perfect its national integration. A weak government is a natural target for invaders: hence Japan in China in the 1930s, Syria in Lebanon in the 1970s, and Libya in Chad in the 1980s.

The foregoing factors in determining power can be looked up, and some can even be measured in numbers. But they may not be the most important factors. The following may be harder to calculate:

Military Capability.   A nation can have all of the foregoing and fail to translate them into armed power. France and Britain, recoiling from the losses of World War I, neglected to build their strength against Hitler. Japan, an industrial giant, is a military dwarf, for its American-drafted constitution forbids it to have an army, a point many Japanese wish to change. Military capability involves more than the number and training of troops and the quantity and quality of weapons. The really crucial factors are leadership and morale. Intelligent, energetic officers can make an army. High morale may enable an army to triumph over a larger foe. Napoleon said morale factors are three times as important as physical factors. But how do you know when an army has good leadership and morale? You don't, not until you've seen it in war. The lightly armed Viet Cong and North Vietnamese ultimately beat the Saigon government and the Americans because of leadership and morale factors.

Psychological Sources of Power.   The biggest "if" in the equation is the psychology of the nation. Is it unified, sure of itself and its cause, willing to sacrifice? Here is where the biggest mistakes are made. Lyndon Johnson marched America into Vietnam thinking we would easily win. But the Communists knew what they wanted: a unified Vietnam without foreigners under some kind of socialism. Our side wasn't nearly so sure, and because of this the war was lost on the home front, both in Saigon and in Washington. In 1980, Iraq, surveying the seeming chaos of the Iranian revolution, thought Iranian territory would be easy pickings. But the Iranians fought like maniacs, sacrificing thousands in suicide attacks that pushed the Iraqis back onto their own territory. In 1982, Argentina, suffering from disunity and a brutal military government itself, thought the Falklands would be easy to take from an economically weakened Britain. But it was the British who proved psychologically strong and the Argentines weak.

Some elements of power can be calculated, but the most important elements—the psychological—can't be. This is what makes international politics so tricky and so fascinating. Shrewd political leaders can use their nation's power to both preserve their country and keep the peace. Stupid or arrogant leaders, on the other hand, can fail to understand that their power has limits and that the game is highly unpredictable. They can both ruin their country and plunge the world into war.

WHY WAR?

Much has been written on why there is war. Most thinkers agree that war has many causes, not just one. Very broadly, though, theories on the cause of war are divided into two general camps, the micro and the macro—the little, closeup picture that focuses on individuals, as opposed to the big, panoramic picture that focuses on whole nations and their interactions.[4]

Micro Theories

Micro theories are rooted largely in biology and psychology. They might attempt to explain war as the result of genetic human aggressiveness. Millions of years of evolution have made people fighters—to obtain food, defend their families, and guard their territory. In this, humans are no different from many animals.[5] Most anthropologists angrily refute such biological determinism, arguing that primitive peoples exhibit a wide variety of behavior—some are aggressive and some aren't—that can be explained only by culture. Writers with a psychological orientation explore the personalities of leaders, what made them this way, and how they obtained their hold over the masses, with an ability to bring them to war.[6]

Biological and psychological theories offer some insights but fall far short of explaining wars. If man is naturally aggressive, why aren't nations at war all the time? How is it that countries can fight a long series of wars—the Russian-Turkish struggle around the Black Sea or the Arab-Israeli wars—under different leaders who surely must have been psychologically distinct? Biological and psychological approaches may offer insights into some of the *underlying* causes of war but not the immediate causes. There is a certain human

---

[4]The terms "micro" and "macro" are drawn from the lucid discussions of James E. Dougherty and Robert L. Pfaltzgraff, Jr., *Contending Theories of International Relations: A Comprehensive Survey,* 2d ed. (New York: Harper & Row, 1981).

[5]Konrad Lorenz, *On Aggression* (New York: Bantam Books, 1967).

[6]John G. Stoessinger has adopted a mostly psychological viewpoint in his readable *Why Nations Go to War,* 5th ed. (New York: St. Martin's, 1988).

aggressiveness, but under what circumstances does it come out? For this we turn to macro theories.

Macro Theories

Macro theories are rooted largely in history and political science. They concentrate chiefly on the power and ambitions of states. States, not individuals, are the key actors. Where they can, states expand, as in the Germans' medieval push to the east, the Americans' "manifest destiny," the growth of the British empire, and the Soviets' takeover of East Europe and Afghanistan. Only countervailing power may stop the drive to expand. One country, fearing the growth of a neighbor, will strengthen its defenses or form alliances to offset the neighbor's power. Much international behavior can be explained by the aphorisms *"Si vis pacem para bellum"* ("If you want peace, prepare for war") and "The enemy of my enemy is my friend." Political leaders have an almost automatic feel for national interest and power and move to enhance them.[7] Does the pursuit of power lead to war or peace? Again, there are two broad theories:

Balance of Power. The oldest and most commonly held theory is that peace results when several states, improving their national power and forming alliances, balance one another. Would-be expansionists are blocked. According to balance-of-power theorists, the great periods of relative peace—between the Peace of Westphalia in 1648 and the wars that grew out of the French Revolution (1792–1814), and again from 1815 to the start of World War I in 1914—have been times when the European powers balanced each other. When the balances broke down, there was war.

Hierarchy of Power. Sophisticated analysts have called the balance-of-power theory into question. In the first place, because calculations of power are so problematic, it is impossible to know when power balances. The periods of peace, some writers note, were when power was out of balance, when states were ranked hierarchically in terms of power. Then every nation knew where it stood. It is in times of transition, when the power hierarchy is blurred, that countries are tempted to go to war. After a big war with definitive outcome, there is peace, because then relative power is clearly known.[8] If this theory is correct, then trying to achieve an accurate balance of power is precisely the wrong thing to do; it will lead to war, because the participating states will think they have a good chance of victory.

---

[7]Morgenthau claimed that when we understand a nation's power and national interests, we in effect "look over the shoulder" of political leaders as they write their dispatches. *Politics Among Nations*, p. 5.

[8]A. F. K. Organski developed this in his *World Politics* (New York: Knopf, 1958). More recently, Geoffrey Blainey has rendered it in highly readable form in *The Causes of War* (New York: Free Press, 1973).

PRESIDENT REAGAN, no lover of Communism, found he could get along well with China's Deng Xiaoping, as in this 1984 visit. Mutual interest rather than ideology moved the United States and China closer.
Bill Fitz-Patrick, The White House

Misperception

Weaving micro and macro approaches together, some thinkers have focused on "image" or "perception" as the key to war.[9] Both psychological and power approaches have something to contribute, but they are incomplete. It's not the real situation (which is hard to know) but what leaders perceive it to be that makes them decide for war or peace. They often misperceive, seeing hostility and development of superior weaponry in another country which sees itself as acting defensively and as just trying to catch up in weaponry. John F. Kennedy portrayed the Soviets as enjoying a "missile gap" over us; he greatly increased U.S. missile-manufacturing efforts. It turned out that the Soviets were actually behind us, and they perceived the American effort as a threat that they had to match. President Reagan saw Soviet strength as greater than ours and

[9]Robert Jervis, *Perception and Misperception in International Politics* (Princeton, N.J.: Princeton University Press, 1976).

extremely dangerous; he sped up development of new missiles to offset it. The Soviets saw this as an aggressive move and countered it with new weapons of their own. Both sides are trapped in their own insecurities. As Henry Kissinger brilliantly put it, "Absolute security for one power means absolute insecurity for all others."[10]

In misperception or image theory, the psychological and real worlds bounce against each other in the minds of political leaders. They think they are acting defensively, but their picture of the situation may be distorted. In our time, it is interesting to note, no country ever calls its actions anything but defensive. The Americans in Vietnam saw themselves as defending the free world; the Soviets in Afghanistan saw themselves as defending socialism. In its own eyes, a nation is never aggressive. A country, under the guidance of its leaders, its ideology, and its mass media, may work itself into such a state of fear that even its most aggressive moves are rationalized as defensive.[11] Even Hitler and the Germans in World War II saw themselves as defending Germany against hostile powers.

Keeping Peace

Whatever its causes, what can be done to prevent or at least limit war? Many proposals have been advanced; none has really worked.[12]

World Government. The real culprit, many thinkers claim, is the old doctrine of sovereignty. The solution is to have states give up at least some of their sovereignty—the ability to decide to go to war—to an international confederation that would prevent war much as an individual country keeps the peace within its borders. But that's exactly the rub: What country would give up its sovereignty? Would the United States place its future in the hands of 160-odd members of the UN General Assembly who might vote to have it pull out of West Europe and Central America? No way. Would the Soviets heed a United Nations call to withdraw from Afghanistan? They didn't. Without the teeth of sovereignty, the United Nations or any organization like it becomes a debating society, perhaps useful as a place for diplomatic contact, but little more.

Collective Security. The United Nations' predecessor, the League of Nations, tried to implement an idea that had been around for some time, collective security. Members of the League (which did not include the United States) pledged to join immediately in economic and military action against any

---

[10]Henry Kissinger, *The Necessity for Choice: Prospects of American Foreign Policy* (New York: Harper & Row, 1961), p. 148.

[11]For a social psychologist's review of the kind of thinking that leads up to war, see Ralph K. White, *Nobody Wanted War: Misperception in Vietnam and Other Wars* (Garden City, N.Y.: Doubleday, 1968).

[12]This section draws on the excellent discussion in David Ziegler, *War, Peace and International Politics,* 4th ed. (Boston: Little, Brown, 1987), Chapters 8–11.

UNITED NATIONS General Assembly meets in New York. Its 160-odd
members each have one vote.
United Nations

aggressor state. If Japan, for example, invaded China, every other power would
break trade relations and send forces to defend China. Aggressors, faced with
having the rest of the world against them, would not practice aggression. It was
a great idea on paper, but it didn't work in practice. When Japan took
Manchuria from China in 1931, the League merely sent a commission to study
the situation, Japan claimed the Chinese started it (a lie), and the other powers
saw no point in getting involved in a distant conflict where none of their interests
were involved. Aggression went unpunished because the League had no
mechanism to make the other countries respond. The same happened when
Italy invaded Ethiopia in 1935. Japan, Italy, and Germany withdrew from the
League to practice aggression on a larger scale, and the League collapsed with
World War II.

Functionalism. Another idea related to world organizations is to get
countries cooperating first in specialized or "functional" areas so that they will
see that they can accomplish more by cooperation than by conflict. Gradually
they will work up to a stable peace as a result of being increasingly able to trust
each other. Functional cooperation will produce a "spillover" effect. Dozens of
United Nations related agencies now promote international cooperation in
disease control, food production, weather forecasting, civil aviation, and nuclear
energy. Even hostile countries are sometimes able to sit down to solve a mutual

problem in these and other specialized areas. But there is no spillover; they remain hostile. Sometimes the functional organization becomes a scene of conflict, as when the Third World bloc expelled Israel and South Africa from the United Nations Educational, Scientific, and Cultural Organization (UNESCO) and the United States quit UNESCO over alleged Soviet dominance. The functionalist approach has brought some help in world problems but has not touched the biggest problem, war.

Third-Party Assistance.   One way to settle a dispute is to have a third party not involved in the conflict shuttle between the contending parties to try to find a middle ground. The third party may simply carry messages back and forth, as the United Nations' Ralph Bunche did between Arabs and Israelis in 1949. Or the third party may provide suggestions, as President Carter did with Begin and Sadat at Camp David in 1978. Third parties can help calm a tense situation, but the contenders have to *want* to find a solution. If not, third-party assistance is futile.

Diplomacy.   The oldest approach to preserving peace is through diplomatic contact, with envoys sent from one head of state to another. A good diplomat knows all of the foregoing power factors and the interests of the countries involved and has some suggestions for reaching a compromise that leaves both parties at least partly satisfied. This is crucial: there must be a willingness to compromise. This is often very difficult, because countries define their vital, nonnegotiable interests grandly and are unwilling to cut them down to compromisable size. If successful, diplomats draw up treaties—contracts between countries—which must be ratified and, one hopes, supported in practice. If one country feels a treaty harms it, there is nothing to stop it from opting out of the bargain. Countries enter into and observe treaties because it suits them. Some observers say the United States and Soviet Union, both relative newcomers to the world of great-power politics, are unskilled at diplomacy, too unwilling to compromise. There is, however, one factor that may eventually frighten them into some compromises.

NUCLEAR HOLOCAUST

There is a possibility that humanity will come to an end in our lifetimes, with the earth inherited by "a republic of insects and grass."[13] Both nuclear superpowers have enough warheads to blow each other up several times and put enough soot into the atmosphere to create a "nuclear winter." A small tactical nuclear weapon fired by one superpower in Europe would likely produce a bigger nuclear reaction from the other superpower. Soon they would be trying to knock out

[13]The phrase is Jonathan's Schell's from his chilling *The Fate of the Earth* (New York: Avon, 1982).

each other's missile silos. Then they would go for cities. The process is called *escalation,* the mutual hitting back that could make any Soviet–United States conflict a total one. American leaders say our decisions to use nuclear weapons are under tight control, that there would be no automatic escalation.[14] But once Americans were bombed, would our leaders remain cool and rational? Would Soviet leaders?

Some strategic thinkers say the "balance of terror" is stable because both sides are afraid of setting off even one bomb. They point out that the United States and the Soviet Union have existed in mutual tension for over a third of a century with no war between them. This is called *deterrence,* the mutual fear of national destruction that restrains both superpowers. The warheads are not there to be used but to deter the other side from using *its* warheads.

But is deterrence stable? A number of things could go wrong. First, there is the danger of accidental war, a computer or radar "glitch," perhaps. The U.S. warning system has gone on alert several times because of mistakes. Second, there is the possibility that a technological breakthrough could leave one side feeling that it has an edge and should strike first. Or it might make the other side so insecure that it feels *it* must strike first, before the new techology can be put in place. Third, there is the climate of fear and suspicion that clouds the perceptions of leaders on both sides. Each side is convinced the other is "out to get 'em." A situation of mutual misperceptions could lead both superpowers to reach for their nukes. Although deterrence has been stable up to now, it is sobering to remember that there has never been a weapon system in history that hasn't eventually been used.

The Technology of the Holocaust

The field of nuclear strategy uses some specialized vocabulary. It behooves students and lay persons alike to learn some of these words.

Countervalue. Countervalue weapons are nuclear weapons aimed at population or industrial centers—"city-busting" weapons. Weapons for this task don't need to be as accurate as weapons for the next category, "counterforce." Submarine-launched missiles are not yet as accurate as land-based missiles and so are believed to be countervalue. Terrifying as it sounds, when both sides adopt countervalue strategies they hold each other's cities as mutual hostages, and nuclear deterrence is more stable because such destructive capability is less likely to ever be used.

Counterforce. Counterforce weapons are nuclear weapons aimed at other nuclear weapons—for example, to knock out enemy missiles in their hardened silos. To do this requires great accuracy, and no one knows how

---

[14]See Richard Smoke, *War: Controlling Escalation* (Cambridge, Mass.: Harvard University Press, 1977).

accurate these missiles will be in actual flight over the Arctic. Both sides continually try to improve missile accuracy. It is estimated that two incoming missiles are required for fair assurance of knocking out one missile in its silo. Because counterforce weapons are aimed only at military targets, they are probably more likely to be used.

First Strike. This is hitting the enemy first with strategic nuclear weapons. Almost axiomatically, this would be a counterforce strike, for if you hit your enemy's cities, you would leave your enemy's missiles intact to hit *you*. Whereas both the United States and Soviet Union have foresworn a first strike, it might be tempting if one side felt it could knock out practically all the other side's missiles in one quick blow, leaving it nearly defenseless. This, however, is believed to be technologically impossible, at least for the time being.

First Use. First use is hitting an attacking enemy with relatively small tactical nuclear weapons ("tac nukes"). The United States says it would be willing to use nuclear weapons against a Soviet invasion of West Europe. The Soviets say *any* use of nuclear weapons, even small ones, would be crossing a threshold and would lead to rapid escalation. They say first use would really be the same as first strike; we disagree. It is impossible to tell exactly what would happen after the first tac nuke goes off.

Second Strike. To make a second strike, one must have enough strategic missiles left after a first strike to be able to hit back. Presumably, much second-strike capability would be countervalue, aimed at the enemy's cities. Some, of course, would be counterforce, committed to knocking out the enemy's remaining missiles so as to spare one's own cities. Each side's dream is to have perfect second-strike capability and thus deter the other side's first strike. Short of that, both sides strive for "credible second-strike capability." This hinges on the next term, "survivability."

Survivability. This is the ability of one's missiles to withstand a nuclear strike. This is the crux of nuclear deterrence, for with sufficient survivability, one has credible second-strike capability and with it the power to deter a first strike. Survivability can be gained in several ways, any of which can become obsolete. Under President Kennedy, the United States went to hardened silos, but now Soviet accuracy is probably sufficient to bust them. Now we think in terms of mobile launchers whose location at a given hour is hard to determine. These might include the small cruise missiles or the proposed "Midgetman." So far, the most survivable missiles are those aboard submarines. The United States has about half its strategic nuclear force so deployed, giving it excellent survivability. (The Soviets have only about a quarter of theirs on submarines, and they are not at sea as long as ours.) President Reagan aimed at greatly improved survivability with his proposed Strategic Defense Initiative (popularly dubbed "Star Wars"), a space-based shield that would shoot down incoming Soviet missiles. If it really worked, however, the extremely expensive system would leave the Soviets largely defenseless—we could hit them but they couldn't hit us. This could destabilize mutual deterrence with unforeseeable consequences. One nation's survivability is another's threat.

MIRVs. Multiple Independently Targetable Reentry Vehicles are missiles with several warheads on them that split apart in flight and go to separate, predetermined targets. The United States MIRVed first, but the Soviets soon followed. In the 1960s, it was thought that MIRVing, because it delivers more warheads with fewer missiles, was an impressive deterrent. In the 1980s, however, strategic thinkers fear that MIRVed missiles in silos present tempting first-strike targets. With perhaps two missiles, a first-striker could knock out a dozen enemy warheads in the ground. This was one of the criticisms of the ten-warhead MX: a lot of eggs in one vulnerable basket. Many now suggest a smaller, mobile, single-warhead Midgetman that could be dispersed around the country in sufficient quantity to make an effective first strike impossible.

Finite Deterrence. This is the view or strategy that it takes only a relatively small number of nuclear weapons, say one to two thousand, to deter a first strike. This was an early view of nuclear thinkers and is still French policy. With perhaps a few hundred warheads, we can "tear off an arm," says Paris. Most nuclear thinkers rejected finite deterrence, however, and reasoned as follows: If you settle for a finite number, say a thousand warheads, your opponent will produce two or three times that many, enough to knock out most of your missiles with plenty left over to threaten your cities. Accordingly, both sides felt compelled to add to their arsenals until now each has some ten thousand strategic warheads. More recently, with enough warheads to destroy each other several times over, strategic planners have begun to realize that adding more bombs really gives no advantage; there would be nothing left to destroy.

Underlying many arms-control proposals is a form of finite deterrence; namely, that some figure lower than that of current arsenals is ample for both sides to defend themselves and preserve stability. Hawks, however, continue to see strength in ever-increasing numbers of warheads. In 1974 Henry Kissinger, then secretary of state, was pursuing an arms-control agreement with the Soviets that met with great opposition from senatorial hawks. The exasperated Kissinger exclaimed, "What in the name of God is strategic superiority? What is the significance of it, politically, militarily, operationally, at these levels of numbers? What do you do with it?"[15] If there is to be an eventual agreement, both sides will have to say enough is enough.

---

[15]Henry Kissinger, *Years of Upheaval* (Boston: Little, Brown, 1982), p. 1175.

In Praise of Uncertainty

What would happen in a nuclear war is all guesswork. No one knows, not even the very bright people who make a living at nuclear strategy. And this is good. It's what has preserved the precarious peace so far. If one superpower knew with absolute certainty that it could beat the other with little or no damage to itself, it would be awfully tempted to strike. But if only a few enemy missiles survived, decision-makers would have to reckon with the destruction of many of their cities. For example, even if the Soviets knocked out all land-based U.S. missiles, the survival of just one Trident nuclear sub, with its twenty-four MIRVed missiles, would be enough to destroy a large part of the Soviet Union's population and industry. Accordingly, even if the generals and scientists assured their respective top leaders that they could get "almost all" of their opponent's missiles, what leader would take the chance?

Uncertainty also restrains leaders at lower levels of violence. The Soviets have more conventional forces in East Europe than the United States has in West Europe. But the Americans have several thousand tactical nuclear warheads in West Europe and say they would use them. The Soviets say that if the Americans were to go nuclear, so would they. Would either side do it? Are they bluffing? Who wants to take on the risk of finding out? It is interesting to note that the Soviets and Americans have not tangled with each other directly and are extremely reluctant to do so. The closest we ever came to direct fighting was during the Cuban missile crisis of 1962, and then the Soviets backed down. We cannot be sure, however, that they would back down again, and they have sworn—with the anger of someone who's been humiliated—that next time it is the Americans who will back down.

The really frightening point in superpower relations would come when one side concluded that it was *rational* to launch a nuclear strike. Could that ever happen? In the right combination of circumstances, it could—if one side were to think it had a substantial technological lead but might lose it in the future, if there were a local crisis in which it was being forced to back down, if it were to think it could knock out the enemy's command-and-control network, or if it were to think it would have enough missiles left over to deter a retaliatory second strike from the wounded foe.

The chances of this happening, though, are slim, for leaders on both sides know they are not completely rational. Suppose the United States had most of its land-based missiles knocked out in a Soviet first strike that spared America's cities and most of its population. Rationally, an American president would pause and think, "I have only a few missiles left. Should I hit their cities? If I do, they'll hit ours. I guess the best I can do is to do nothing." But would an American president be rational if American soil were blasted by Soviet nuclear bombs and if even a relatively few Americans were killed? For the sake of deterrence, it's actually better for a U.S. president to appear slightly mad, willing to lose American cities just to hit back. President Nixon recognized the advantage in appearing somewhat irrational to the Soviets so as to deter whatever they might have in mind.

Preventing the Holocaust

Soviet and American diplomats have negotiated on arms control for decades with little success. Both sides fear giving up too much, and both see the other side as ahead. The Americans are adamant about being able to *verify* any arms-control agreement, but the Soviets are equally adamant against permitting any on-site inspections. Both sides would have to rely on "national-technical means of verification," a euphemism for electronic eavesdropping and spy satellites. These record a great deal, but they cannot record everything, for example, the storage of small cruise-type missiles or the number of warheads on a launcher. When one side is unable to securely verify what the other side is up to, there is reluctance to enter into an agreement that may leave the other side stronger.

Despite these formidable obstacles, which grow out of the climate of mutual mistrust, there has been limited and halting progress toward controlling nuclear arms. In 1963, alarmed by worldwide radioactive fallout from nuclear testing in the atmosphere, the United States and the Soviet Union agreed to conduct all such tests underground. At the same time, worried about the slowness of communications during the October 1962 Cuban missile crisis, the two sides agreed to maintain a "hotline" between Washington and Moscow to be used in crises.

In the early 1970s, President Nixon attempted a far-reaching *détente* (relaxation of tensions) with the Soviets, carried out by his national security assistant, Henry Kissinger. This included the Strategic Arms Limitation Talks (SALT). The first agreement, the modest SALT I, reached in 1972, limited the number of antiballistic missiles (ABMs) each country could install. The fear was that a really effective ABM system could embolden one side to try something, and that a mutual effort to implant ABMs could destabilize deterrence. Both sides took this limited step because neither was sure ABMs would ever work properly anyway; using a missile to shoot down an incoming missile is a tricky business.

SALT II started then amidst hopes for a major step, one that would set a numerical ceiling on each side's missiles. Details were worked out under Presidents Nixon, Ford, and Carter. But by then the American climate of opinion had changed. Nixon had been paralyzed by the Watergate scandal and then ousted. South Vietnam went down to defeat under Ford. Finally, the Soviets occupied Afghanistan at the end of 1979 and an angry Carter withdrew SALT II from consideration in the Senate, which wouldn't have ratified it anyway. Curiously, although SALT II was never ratified, both sides agreed to abide by it until President Reagan ordered its limits exceeded in 1987.

Could the arms-control process get moving again? Reagan took a hard line and appointed like-minded people who severely mistrusted the Soviets. Still, presidents change. Reagan's gigantic defense budget provoked criticism even from Republicans. The American public, alarmed by bellicose rhetoric from Reagan appointees, showed a new interest in arms control: peace marches and protests appeared. President Kennedy started his term as a hawk, but, sobered by events, turned conciliatory. Another American president could make the same transition, for no matter how anti-Communist, no president wants to blow up the world.

SUGGESTED READINGS

ARON, RAYMOND. *Peace and War: A Theory of International Relations.* New York: Praeger, 1968. A masterful *tour d'horizon* and critique of international-relations theory.

BLAINEY, GEOFFREY. *The Causes of War.* New York: Free Press, 1973. Written like a detective story, this small volume shoots down many theories of war and comes up with its own.

BRZEZINSKI, ZBIGNIEW. *Game Plan: A Geostrategic Framework for the Conduct of the U.S.-Soviet Contest.* Boston: Atlantic Monthly Press, 1986. A noted political scientist and Carter adviser urges a firm policy of U.S. military containment of Soviet expansionist attempts.

CRAIG, GORDON A., AND ALEXANDER L. GEORGE. *Force and Statecraft: Diplomatic Problems of Our Time.* New York: Oxford University Press, 1983. A superb collection of essays by two Stanford professors on how we can use the past to maintain a tolerable international stability.

DOUGHERTY, JAMES E., AND ROBERT L. PFALTZGRAFF, JR. *Contending Theories of International Relations: A Comprehensive Survey,* 2d ed. New York: Harper & Row, 1981. Complete, balanced, indispensable.

DYSON, FREEMAN. *Weapons and Hope.* New York: Harper & Row, 1984. A physicist who is also concerned with the human element in war has written perhaps the best single work on our current predicament. Must reading.

FREEDMAN, LAWRENCE. *The Evolution of Nuclear Strategy.* New York: St. Martin's, 1983. Excellent review of how thinking on nuclear war has changed over the decades.

GILPIN, ROBERT. *War and Change in World Politics.* New York: Cambridge University Press, 1981. A sophisticated and theoretical balance-of-power approach to international relations.

HARVARD NUCLEAR STUDY GROUP. *Living with Nuclear Weapons.* New York: Bantam Books, 1983. A superb introduction to the complexities of the nuclear dilemma without hysteria by a group of top academic specialists.

HOWARD, MICHAEL. *The Causes of Wars and Other Essays.* Cambridge, Mass.: Harvard University Press, 1983. A noted Oxford don argues that war's causes haven't changed much, even in the nuclear age.

KAHN, HERMAN. *Thinking About the Unthinkable in the 1980s.* New York: Simon and Schuster, 1984. An updating of Kahn's scary 1960 classic, *On Thermonuclear War.*

KEGLEY, CHARLES W., JR., AND EUGENE WITTKOPF, EDS. *The Nuclear Reader: Strategy, Weapons, War.* New York: St. Martin's 1985. Wide-ranging views of nuclear dangers, mostly critical of the Reagan program.

KENNAN, GEORGE F. *Nuclear Delusion: Soviet-American Relations in the Atomic Age.* New York: Pantheon, 1982. The scholar-diplomat who urged "containment" of Soviet power now worries about nuclear war.

LEBOW, RICHARD NED. *Between Peace and War: The Nature of International Crisis.* Baltimore, Md.: Johns Hopkins University Press, 1981. Impressive study of how crises arise and how they may or may not lead to war.

McNAMARA, ROBERT. *Blundering into Disaster: Surviving the First Century of the Nuclear Age.* New York: Pantheon, 1986. Former defense secretary warns that nuclear weapons are good for nothing but deterrence.

VASQUEZ, JOHN A., ED. *Classics of International Relations.* Englewood Cliffs, N.J.: Prentice-Hall, 1986. Fine selection of major statements from the ancient to the modern.

Index